This is a book about the continuing influence of Hume's ideas on moral and political philosophy. In part it is a critical exegesis of Hume's most impressive and challenging doctrines in Book III of the *Treatise of Human Nature* on such topics as morals, motivation, justice and social institutions.

However, the main thrust of the argument is to throw into relief the importance of that discussion for contemporary philosophy. While the author subjects most contemporary defenses of Humean doctrines to intense criticism, he also seeks to discover what versions of Hume's theories might still be defensible and viable.

CAMBRIDGE STUDIES IN PHILOSOPHY

Morals, Motivation and Convention

CAMBRIDGE STUDIES IN PHILOSOPHY

General editor SYDNEY SHOEMAKER

Advisory editors J.E.J. ALTHAM, SIMON BLACKBURN,
GILBERT HARMAN, MARTIN HOLLIS, FRANK JACKSON,
JONATHAN LEAR, WILLIAM G. LYCAN, JOHN PERRY,
BARRY STROUD

RECENT TITLES

Morals, Motivation and Convention

HUME'S INFLUENTIAL DOCTRINES

Francis Snare

University of Sydney

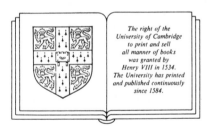

The right of the
University of Cambridge
to print and sell
all manner of books
was granted by
Henry VIII in 1534.
The University has printed
and published continuously
since 1584.

Cambridge University Press

Cambridge

New York   Port Chester   Melbourne   Sydney

Published by the Press Syndicate of the University of Cambridge
The Pitt Building, Trumpington Street, Cambridge CB2 1RP
40 West 20th Street, New York, NY 10011, USA
10 Stamford Road, Oakleigh, Melbourne 3166, Australia

© Cambridge University Press 1991

First published 1991

Printed in the United States of America

Library of Congress Cataloging-in-Publication Data
Snare, Francis.

Morals, motivation and convention : Hume's influential doctrines
/ Francis Snare.

p.   cm. – (Cambridge studies in philosophy)
Includes bibliographical references and index.
ISBN 0-521-39261-6

1. Hume, David, 1711–1776. I. Title. II. Series.
B1498.S62   1991
170′.92 – dc20   90-38743
                                                                         CIP

British Library Cataloguing in Publication Data
Snare, Francis.

Morals, motivation and convention : Hume's influential
doctrines. – (Cambridge studies in philosophy).

1. Politics. Theories of Hume, David, 1711–1776
I. Title
320.5092

ISBN 0-521-39261-6 hardback

Verum haec nobis in maiores certamina ex honesto maneant.

– Tacitus, Ann. iii. 55

Contents

Acknowledgements

The present discussion arose out of a series of lectures presented in 1987 as a departmental philosophy seminar for staff and advanced students at the University of Sydney. The idea was modest, to give a straight-forward exposition of Hume's moral and political philosophy as an approach to contemporary philosophical discussions of many of the same basic issues. While I thought such an exposition would be useful for fourth year undergraduates and even postgraduates, I suspected my fellow staff members would find it a bit simple and obvious. In the event, their comments and objections indicated to me that my account was controversial if not provocative, that what had seemed hardly to need saying in fact required some elaboration.

Consequently I am indebted to the critical remarks of my colleagues David Armstrong, John Bacon, Keith Campbell, Stephen Gaukroger, Adrian Heathcote, Michael McDermott, Peter Menzies, Lloyd Reinhardt and David Stove. I have particular debts to David Armstrong, who provided detailed critical comments on a draft of Part I as well as much useful advice about exposition, and to John Bacon, who made technical comments on certain logical matters. I would also like to thank the students in my seminars on Hume in 1987 and 1989.

Philip Pettit contributed useful advice and encouraging support in my submitting to publishers. I also greatly benefitted from the expertise and patience of two departmental typists: Valerie Jorgensen who completed the entire first draft, and Helen Brown who then typed my various revisions affecting about every page. I would like to thank Anthea Bankoff, the departmental secretary, for her helpful organisation and encouragement throughout.

Francis Snare

NOTE

Francis Snare died after completing the manuscript but before seeing page proofs of this book. He had, however, prepared entries for the index. John Bacon, Anthea Bankoff, Stephen Gaukroger, Michael McDermott, Huw Price and I have done the little that Francis was unable to finish. The work stands as a memorial to a good man, a good colleague and a good philosopher.

David Armstrong
University of Sydney
September 1990

Introduction

Certain doctrines are to be found in an important and influential text: David Hume's *Treatise of Human Nature,* Book III, especially Parts i and ii (along with the supporting passage in II, iii, 3 and some passages from his *Enquiry concerning the Principles of Morals*).[1] These provide the *loci classici* of a number of apparently interrelated theses and arguments in moral philosophy, philosophical psychology, social and political philosophy which have become a part of the intellectual baggage of no small number of contemporary philosophers. With only a bit of exaggeration I will call such philosophers and such doctrines 'Humean'. Such philosophers need not be Humean in other respects, e.g. in epistemology or general philosophy of mind. Nor do all explicitly recognise their Humean tendencies even in the areas in question.

This is not so much an essay on Hume as on Humeans. It is about certain doctrines and arguments from Book III which are still of contemporary influence and importance. This essay enters into a dialogue with these Humean traditions. In some cases contemporary Humeans have re-shaped and re-argued the basic Humean positions so extensively that their positions are clearly not Hume's even if Humean. They are in the spirit of Hume. Many might be regarded as continuing or perfecting the basic Humean ideas or altering them in ways more satisfactory but somehow still in the spirit of the basic enterprise. Thus in some cases it will be more appropriate to discuss these contemporary refinements (e.g. the

1 *A Treatise of Human Nature,* first published in 1739 and 1740. Unprefixed page numbers in the text and notes are to the Oxford University Press edition edited by L.A. Selby-Bigge and revised by P.H. Nidditch. *An Enquiry concerning the Principles of Morals,* published in 1751 [hereafter *Enquiry*], is generally regarded as intended as a more popular work thus omitting much of philosophical interest. Page references are to the Oxford University Press edition of Hume's *Enquiries* edited by L.A. Selby-Bigge and revised by P.H. Nidditch.

1

work of contemporary philosophers such as D. Davidson, B. Williams, or D. Lewis) rather than the original, insufficient or outdated argument of Hume's Book III. And precisely because this essay is in the end addressed to contemporary Humeans it is not my purpose to take up everything discussed in Book III. Certain of Hume's doctrines and arguments are not of much interest or influence today. And rightly so. Contemporary Humeans are the first to disown them. Rather, I will concentrate on those strands of Hume's discussion which, in one form or another, continue to influence and be of interest. And what are they?

In Part i of Book III Hume presents, and argues for, what to philosophers today seems a meta-ethical view. Hume's Section 1 of Part i raises the question whether 'moral distinctions' are 'derived from reason'. Hume responds with a firm 'No' and provides various arguments thereto. By far his most influential argument relies on certain theses in philosophical psychology (and action theory) for which the groundwork was laid in II, iii, 3: Reason alone can never have an influence on the actions or passions; There is no combat between 'reason' and 'passion'; No action or passion is 'contrary to reason' or 'unreasonable'; 'Reason is and ought only to be the slave of the passions'. Whatever exactly these claims mean they are Humean to the core. While Section 1 of Part i makes a negative claim (it tells us what morality is *not*), Section 2 defends the complementary positive thesis (it tells us then what *is* the nature of making moral distinctions). In some way it is a matter of feeling or 'sentiment' or 'agreeable feeling'. To contemporary philosophers this readily suggests a meta-ethics with a large dose of subjectivism. Following Mackie (1980) we call Hume's meta-ethics, whatever it is exactly, Hume's 'sentimentalism'.

By contrast to the apparent meta-ethics in Part i, Parts ii and iii seem to develop a moral theory or at least a theory of morality (as a psychological and social phenomenon). Still, to some extent the discussion here harks back to and directly develops the 'sentimentalism' of Part i. Unlike some twentieth century meta-ethicists Hume is not content to speak vaguely of 'sentiments', 'pro-attitudes' or 'emotings'. Hume clearly sees that the sentiments of which he speaks in his account of the making of moral distinctions are not just any and every sentiment, passion, feeling or attitude but are sentiments of some special sort (472). Then, roughly speaking, Hume gives a reductive account of the peculiarly moral sen-

2

timent in terms of self-interest, 'sympathy' and other more basic notions of his philosophy psychology. The moral sentiment is of a peculiar kind but it is not *sui generis*. It can be explained in terms of prior psychological mechanisms.

However a couple of features of Hume's moral theory in Parts ii and iii are less easy to explain in connection to the meta-ethical theses in Part i which have been so influential. Also they have not been taken over by contemporary 'Humeans'. First, Hume seems to presuppose a rather extreme version of virtue morality. Hume thinks moral evaluation of *motives* (and virtue talk) is logically basic and prior to moral evaluation of *acts* (what others would regard as obligation or right action talk). Hume's examples all centre on praise and blame, responsibility and innocence, merit and demerit. This is clearly so even when Hume is speaking of 'virtuous' *acts*. This is in contrast to many moral theories (such as utilitarianism or the deontological theory of W.D. Ross) which begin with questions about what features of acts are good reasons for choosing those acts. Only secondarily do they go on to the important class of judgments we make when making assessments of virtue and vice, blame and innocence, etc. However for Hume, our moral 'distinctions' are not only virtue-oriented, but indeed virtue-*based*. In this regard Hume's moral theory is somewhat distinctive and contentious in a way he hardly recognised.

A second distinctive feature of Hume's moral theory is the fundamental distinction he makes between two classes of virtues: natural (Part iii) and artificial, such as justice (Part ii). Hume's assumption that moral judgments are morally virtue-based assessments applies plausibly in the cases of virtues he classes as 'natural virtues' for there is always a natural, independently specifiable *motive* which Hume can use to specify the corresponding virtue. However the obligations of justice seem, at first glance, the most obvious counter-example to view that our ordinary moral sentiments are virtue-based. These seem to be obligation-based. Hence one reason for Hume's comparatively elaborate treatment of justice in Part ii. He has special problems with justice.

The two above features of Hume's moral theory are somewhat idiosyncratic and not really influential. By contrast, Hume's account of the artificial virtue of justice in Part ii has been particularly influential in recent moral and political philosophy. Most influential is his naturalistic starting point, 'the circumstances of human nature'. Hume's account of the human condition is taken up by philosophers such as H.L.A. Hart (1961), John Rawls (1971), J.L. Mackie (1977, ch. 5) and many others. Of further contemporary interest is Hume's seemingly no-nonsense, naturalistic account of justice (and systems of conventions in general). Hume requires no mysterious, autonomous, non-natural properties. No super-empirical faculty of intuition. No queer entities. Nor again is his account merely the result of a don's armchair investigations into ordinary language or ordinary concepts. Hume thinks that the notion of justice and the obligations of justice, the notion we have, is to be accounted for naturalistically in terms of, among other things, the operation of social conventions. Finally, he gives a (tantalisingly fleeting) naturalistic account of convention.

Contemporary philosophy can find Hume's attempted account of convention of interest in itself quite apart from the use to which Hume puts it within his larger account of our ideas of justice. A general theory of convention promises to be of interest, perhaps even crucial, in a number of areas outside moral philosophy, e.g. philosophy of the social sciences, philosophy of language. For example it seems important in any real explanation of how 'institutional facts' differ from 'brute facts'. If not moralists, then at least social scientists and anthropologists may well require the notion of social norms or social rules to describe societies and institutions (and not only to describe the particular institutions of property, contract and law upon which Hume concentrates). Naturalistic accounts often come to a dead stop when confronted with the social. Hume provides a naturalistic account of such social facts in terms of his notion of a convention. If that in turn can be given a plausible naturalistic account, the job is done. Here Hume's approach, if not his exact attempt, continues to be of interest.

Contemporary philosophy owes much to Book III of Hume's *Treatise*. From it come many 'Humean' doctrines of great contemporary interest. However, the individual philosophers I call 'Humean' really tend to pick and choose from the doctrines. It is more accurate to say they tend to be Humeans in one respect (meta-ethics, philosophical psychology, theory of justice, theory of convention) but not always in others. For example Rawls and others develop Hume's account of the circumstances of justice in Part ii without any commitment to Hume's sentimentalism in Part i. Conversely, those philosophers who concentrate on what Hume says

4

about 'is' and 'ought' in Part i are generally uninterested (even embarrassed) about what Hume says on the virtues or justice. Contemporary Humeans may preserve something like individual Humean doctrines from Book III, but they do not take over the continuity. They take parts of the structure, like re-usable parts from a wrecked automobile, but not the structure, not even a stripped down structure. It is worth asking whether there is a *continuity* in Hume's discussion which is of contemporary interest. Is there more re-usable here than just a lot of individual parts? I will argue that there is.

While I am mainly concerned with the elaboration of Humean doctrines in a way that is of contemporary interest, I am also concerned to be accurate in the understanding and interpretation of Hume. I do claim that these doctrines and issues are in Hume, although mixed in with, and confused with, much else of less interest. In any case my interpretation of Hume is not idiosyncratic but broadly sympathetic with the clear exposition by J.L. Mackie in *Hume's Moral Theory* (1980), the detailed work of Jonathan Harrison in *Hume's Moral Epistemology* (1976) and *Hume's Theory of Justice* (1981), and David Miller's careful handling of Hume's theory in historical context in *Hume's Political Thought* (1981).

For those solely interested in Hume studies and the interpretation of Hume I do, however, have some things to offer. I will be concerned with the question of how Part i relates to Parts ii and iii in Book III, with the question of how deeply embedded Hume's political conservativism is in his philosophical argument, and, finally, with exactly why Hume thinks he has such a special problem about the virtue of justice and the 'regard to justice'. However in another respect mere students of history may be somewhat disconcerted. I attribute to Hume several long-running, systematic ambiguities throughout Book III, certain conceptual confusions which fall in together with such unexpected precision that the effect is one of door-slamming farce. A comedy of philosophical errors. Thus the student of history who merely wants to re-create the intellectual feel, the texture of the past will find my discussion somewhat destroys the ability to do so. To think exactly like Hume did requires being subject to many of the same conceptual illusions. Insofar as this essay exposes these ambiguities and illusions, it renders the reader less able to look at things as Hume did. We may, in a certain respect, understand Hume less. While we may have an un-

5

derstanding of *how* different theses could be confused, we will find it much more difficult to work up the state of mind which *sees* them as one. I make no apologies for this result.

My main concern, then, in discussing Book III is critical and contemporary rather than exegetical. But I should admit to another motivation as well. The examination of some of the Humean arguments is of a certain clinical interest. Book III and the more contemporary elaborations of such doctrines provide rather nice case studies of some of the pathologies of philosophical argumentation. The study of conceptual confusions in influential thought is a worthwhile study in itself. I doubt whether the usual introductory courses in formal or informal logic (or any list of 'informal fallacies') really prepare one for the pitfalls of philosophy. For one thing, many of the more seductive confusions are more or less once-off, not easily categorised under some general heading. For another, great confusions often involve systematic intertwinings of different confusions (no one of which would be very deceiving). I suspect the best way to gain expertise in avoiding conceptual confusions is by examining particular, commonly seductive instances of conceptual confusion, i.e., by case studies. One of the classic case studies of conceptual confusion in the history of philosophy is the Butler-Broad refutation of armchair psychological egoism. There are several parallels here with the present study. Many Humeans in meta-ethics and philosophical psychology tend to be smug in much the same way armchair psychological egoists tend to be. Just as these latter can never be quite so smug once subjected to Butler's attack, so likewise it is the purpose of this book to make it difficult for Humeans to be too smug.

However the use of the influential Humean doctrines as case studies is only a part of the purpose of this study. The main aim is a bit more constructive. One naturally wonders, having swept aside the vulgar confusions, self-incapsulating dogmas, and conceptual illusions, whether something can be made of the basic Humean claims and approach. This essay tries to point the directions in which the various Humean projects might go to avoid the main pitfalls.

Because this book is mainly addressed to Humeans, it will say little to those (very few) who cannot feel even a bit of the seductive pull of Hume's views (especially his meta-ethics) in the first place. It is criticism from within, not from without. Here a confession is

6

in order. I admit to being a Humean myself, once a smug Humean. Thus the 'vulgar fallacies' and 'conceptual confusions' discussed are usually the views I held five minutes ago – in intellectual time. I am a loyal Humean with the doubtful habit of raising questions like 'Just what is our argument for that?' and 'What would we say against someone who didn't already concede that . . . ?' So it is quite natural to begin the investigation with Hume himself, who hardly shirked these questions. This essay is the work of a self-critical Humean.

Unless it's the work of a 'mole'.

Part I

The argument for sentimentalism

1

A systematic ambiguity

Certain of Hume's arguments at the beginning of Book III have remained influential, although often altered, in contemporary philosophy. The immediately following chapters will examine these arguments, one especially, in some detail. But the question of this chapter is a simple one: What is at issue in these arguments? That is, what is Hume's basic thesis in his discussion of 'moral subjects'? Actually we are raising two questions at once. The slightly more boring question is the historical one: 'What did Hume think he was showing in Part i of Book III?' The more interesting question for contemporary Humeans is: 'What do his best arguments there, or charitable reconstructions of them, actually succeed in showing?' Of course the latter question bears on the former. Those with any respect for Hume's genius think that what his arguments actually do prove is some (if not conclusive) evidence as to what he thought he was proving. Among other things this chapter will briefly examine three kinds of evidence that bear on the former, the historical, question of what Hume himself thought he was proving:

i.   How Hume describes the thesis for which he argues.
ii. The philosophical positions (e.g. of Clarke, Wollaston) which Hume opposes and which he means to rule out by his thesis.

and again:

iii. What the arguments he gives could plausibly be taken to prove.

HUME'S DESCRIPTION OF THE ISSUE

The place to begin is with Hume's own description of the conclusion he wished to prove. The thesis is about the making of 'moral distinctions' which is perhaps something like the holding or making of a moral judgment or else what it is we hold when we hold a

11

moral judgment. Hume's thesis is composed of two complementary claims. The negative part of the thesis (III,i,1) makes a claim about what the making of moral distinctions *is not:*

1. Moral distinctions are 'not deriv'd from reason'.

The positive part of the thesis (III,i,2) adds to the above negative claim an account of what it then *is* a matter of:

2. Moral distinctions are in some way a matter of 'sentiment' ('agreeable impressions', 'moral sense').

Hume also expresses what he intends to prove in the technical language of the epistemology and philosophy of mind already developed in Books I and II. Hume asks:

Whether 'tis by means of our ideas or impressions we distinguish betwixt vice and virtue, and pronounce an action blameable or praise-worthy? (456)

Hume's peculiar philosophy of mind and knowledge sets up this dichotomous question. Hume's proposed answer is, negatively, that it *isn't* by means of ideas and so, positively, it is by impressions. This way of expressing what he intends to prove requires us to know a little about Hume's general epistemology.[1]

Hume, rather non-standardly, uses 'perception' to cover any content or operation of the mind. (Hence Hume concedes nothing when he says that the distinguishing of moral good or evil is a 'perception' (456).) Perceptions are of two main sorts: 'impressions' and 'ideas' (1). The latter, ideas, seems to cover rather indiscriminately, the having of concepts, the entertaining of propositions, the having of beliefs (or 'judgment').[2] The former, impressions, include 'original' sensations (e.g. of pleasure, heat, thirst) as well as the secondary 'impressions of reflexion' (e.g. passions, desires, emotions) (7–8). These impressions of reflexion can be either reflections of an original impression or, more likely, reflections on ideas as well. The story is something like what we see in figure 1 (1, 7–8, 275–6). So when Hume asks whether the making of moral distinctions is a matter of 'ideas' or a matter of 'impressions' he is asking whether it is to be classified under the right side of this chart or somewhere or other on the left side.

Here the relevance of Hume's discussion in Books I and II is little

1 Cf. Harrison (1976), introduction and ch. 3 for a detailed discussion.
2 Cf. Harrison (1976), ch. 3.

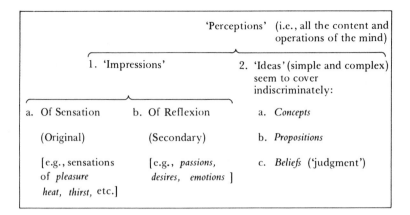

Figure 1

more than terminological. Whenever Hume happens to state the basic thesis of Book III in the technical terms of the earlier books, we need to know a little about what he classifies under those terms. But this does not require Hume's thesis about moral distinctions to depend upon, or be based upon, the famous epistemological doctrines of I and II. Hume perhaps thought there was such a dependence. His own description of the *Treatise* on the original title page calls it 'an attempt to introduce the experimental method of reasoning into moral subjects'.[3] But in fact the connection between Book III and the earlier books is not as strong as it first seems when we start to look at the arguments Hume gives. As we shall see, most of his arguments, especially the most interesting, require nothing of the basic doctrines of the earlier books or, at most, nothing more than something like, broadly speaking, an empiricist or naturalistic outlook. (A quite important exception is discussed by D. Miller, 1981, chs. 1 and 2, especially p. 41.) This lack of any strong dependence on the earlier books (with exceptions to be duly noted) is actually a virtue of these arguments – from the point of view of the contemporary Humean. It has allowed the doctrines in Book III and the arguments for them to be taken up again and again in

3 Of course Hume uses 'moral subjects' broadly to cover, as Stroud (1977, p. 2) puts it, all subjects which 'deal with human thought, actions, feelings, perceptions, passions and language'. Thus it covers the subject matter of Book II as much as Book III.

different forms without any commitment to Hume's own peculiar epistemology and philosophy of mind. The well-known breakdowns of the latter need not impair the performance of the former. Book III is something of a 're-usable part' in philosophy. It has been plugged into many other total systems other than Hume's and perhaps even functions better there.

META-ETHICAL VERSIONS OF
THE NEGATIVE THESIS

What might Hume mean when he says that moral distinctions are 'not derived from reason'? Following Mackie (1980, pp. 51ff.), we certainly want to distinguish at least the three following negative theses.[4] The claims get progressively more modest, each succeeding one ruling out rather less:

N1. Moral judgments are not 'beliefs' (narrow sense) at all.
N2. Moral judgments are not *inferred* (deductively or inductively or whatever) 'beliefs' (narrow sense).
N3. Moral judgments are not *deductively inferred* 'beliefs' (narrow sense).

Claim (N1) is the most sweeping and thus the most interesting. It rules out a moral judgment's being anything 'cognitive' at all. (N2) is a little less sweeping. (N2) only insists that moral judgments are not rationally derived (by deduction, induction or any other reputable mode of inference) from other true beliefs. However (N2) does not close the door entirely on moral knowledge. Our distinctions between virtue and vice might be of a relatively direct sort of apprehension, not requiring anything in the way of explicit reasoning or inference for such beliefs to be reached. An analogy might be to ordinary perception or to some of our, relatively direct, knowledge of our own mental states.[5] Claim (N3) is the most modest. It does not deny the possibility of moral knowledge. Nor does it rule out such knowledge being inferable from other true beliefs. It merely rules out moral judgments being reached in a way 'analogous to that which establishes mathematical conclusions' (as Mackie puts it). (N3) merely rules out rationalist *a priori* metaethics. It rules out Samuel Clarke, for example.

4 Cf. also Harrison (1976), pp. 110–25.
5 Cf. also Harrison (1976), p. 2.

Claim (N1) is close to an assertion of non-cognitivism. At least it is if not understood too literally in a psychological or epistemological fashion. Of course (N1) isn't merely saying that we poor humans are no good at discovering the moral facts as though the fault were in us or our cognitive faculties. (Nor are (N2) and (N3) merely alleging massive human failure in inference and deduction when it comes to moral facts.) It's rather that there's nothing of that sort to be discovered. Thus non-cognitivism is less misleadingly expressed in terms of propositions or statements, or the use of moral language, or facts and fact-stating. For example:

N1'. There are no moral 'propositions' (in the narrow sense),

or:

N1". The function of sentences containing moral words is not to enable us to 'make statements' (narrow sense),

etc.

Thus Harrison (1976, pp. 117–20) speaks of the possibility of attributing a 'non-propositional' theory to Hume in this regard.

All of these characterisations are a bit strained by the standards of ordinary usage. These ways of expressing non-cognitivism all employ unusually *narrow* senses of 'belief', 'proposition', 'statement', etc. Thus, necessarily, a 'belief' (in the narrow sense) is something capable of being true or false. Given that the term 'cognitive' just means 'capable of being true or false', the phrase 'cognitive belief' can only be a pointlessly redundant expression when 'belief' is taken in this narrow sense. There is no other kind of 'belief'. Likewise, in the narrow sense of 'proposition' required for (N1), the phrase 'cognitive proposition' would be pointlessly redundant. By definition a proposition is something with a truth value.

This reliance on narrow notions of 'belief', 'proposition', 'statement', etc. has several disadvantages. One is that it's a bit misleading because ordinary language is rather looser with these terms. We ordinarily speak of 'moral beliefs' as a way of speaking of moral opinions and judgments (whatever sorts of things these may be). Another disadvantage is that these narrow usages tend to obscure the fact that moral judgments (whatever they are) bear logical relations to other judgments (especially other moral judgments). If we perversely refuse to speak of moral propositions we shall probably still have to talk about something like the 'content' of a moral judgment which can enter into logical relations with the 'content' of other moral judgments. But perhaps the greatest objection to expressing non-cognitivism (and for that matter the other negative theses) in this unusually narrow terminology is that it obscures the fact that non-cognitivism in the end has to make some reference to the notion of truth. The narrow terminology nicely obscures the necessity of talking explicitly about 'true' and 'false' and tends to make non-cognitivism look more like a psychological or epistemological issue rather than a metaphysical (or at least semantic) one. It is better for the non-cognitivist to put his cards on the table in that regard.

However, non-cognitivism can just as easily be restated employing the wider senses of 'belief' or 'proposition' (under which such things are not automatically cognitive):

N1*. Moral beliefs (broad sense) are not simply *cognitive* beliefs (i.e., capable of being true or false),

or:

N1**. Moral propositions (broad sense) are not in their entirety simply cognitive propositions,

etc.

This ploy of course only transfers the pressure from 'belief' and 'proposition' to 'cognitive' and thus, ultimately, to 'true' and 'false.' But it has the virtue of making clear just where the weight should be borne. Of course, even 'true' has a broad, manner-of-speaking, sense. There is no linguistic impropriety in saying 'That's quite true' to someone's moral judgment if only as a way of indicating agreement. At this point the buck stops. The non-cognitivist (or anyone merely trying to understand what it is) must insist there is a narrow, 'robust' sense of 'true' and 'false' and that the proper notion of 'cognitive' is 'capable of being *robustly* true or *robustly* false'. I do not require the non-cognitivist to have a worked out, explicit theory of this robust notion of truth (any more than I shout 'Define your terms!' whenever a philosopher uses 'cause' or 'exists' or 'believes'). Nor indeed must all non-cognitivists have the same theory. But any non-cognitivist is committed to there being this robust sense, whatever the proper account of it may be. And of course finding a proper account is not peculiarly his problem. It is an important problem for all philosophy. Certainly his opponent, the cognitivist, is just as committed to there being some such robust notion. He wants to say something more interesting than that there is no linguistic impropriety in calling moral judgments 'true' in a broad, manner-of-speaking sense. The cognitivist wants to insist they can be true in some robust or interesting sense. The debate between the cognitivist and the non-cognitivist presupposes this. The only ones who will resist the view that there is some such appropriately robust sense of 'true' are those, rather less fashionable now than several decades ago, who 'solved' philosophical issues by pretending not to see them.

There is certainly textual evidence to support the view that Hume's negative thesis is some proto-version of non-cognitivism rather than one of the more modest theses (N2) or (N3). A reasonable interpretation of Hume's system (cf. figure 1 above) is that all *cognitive* beliefs (what Hume calls 'judgment') get classified on the 'Ideas' side. Thus when Hume asks whether it's by means of our ideas or by our impressions that we distinguish between vice and virtue he is really asking whether moral judgments are a matter of (cognitive) belief or whether it's a matter not of (cognitive) belief but of something which has more to do with some of the mental phenomena that get classified on the 'Impression' side (e.g. passion, desire, emotion).

Suppose non-cognitivism, (N1*), is Hume's negative thesis. What then is his total view, the 'sentimentalism' which adds a positive thesis to the negative one? It would seem to be something like:

S1. Negatively, (N1*) moral judgments are not cognitive judgments; but positively, moral judgments are, or essentially involve, the having of certain special sentiments on the part of the judger toward the object judged.

Emotivism would be a leading example of (S1), i.e., the theory that making a moral judgment is not *stating* (narrow sense) that one has a certain kind of sentiment toward the object but is rather the *expression* of that special sentiment. Again, another version of (S1) might suppose assenting to a moral judgment is *not believing* (narrow sense) that one has a certain sentiment but is rather the very *having* of the appropriate sentiment. 'Morality . . . is more properly felt than judg'd of' says Hume (470, cf. 471).[6]

DIRECT MORAL KNOWLEDGE

The second interpretation, (N2), of Hume's negative thesis supposes 'derived from reason' to mean 'inferred'. This essentially turns it into an epistemological thesis. To say that our moral distinctions are not derived from reason is meant to rule out the possibility of inferred (either deductively or inductively) knowledge, but not the possibility of non-inferential, relatively direct, moral knowledge. Unlike the first interpretation, (N2) would put all inferential knowledge under 'Ideas' but find a place for non-inferential knowledge somewhere or other under 'Impressions'. Hume's 'reason' is restricted to inference. But some knowledge we can have fairly directly without employing much if any reasoning. Moral knowledge is then claimed to be of that sort. It is knowledge but not '*derived from reason*'.

However, this negative thesis (N2) is compatible with two quite different interpretations of the positive thesis. It depends on where exactly under 'Impressions' in figure 1 it is supposed Hume would locate the supposed non-inferential moral knowledge. Suppose we locate it under 'Impressions of Sensation'. Then we might consider whether what Hume holds is a moral sense theory:

S2a. Negatively, (N2) moral knowledge is not inferred; but positively, it is a matter of direct perception by a special moral sensing faculty.

This interpretation would turn Hume's sentiments into something more like sensings rather than passions or emotions. Hume would better have said that morality is neither felt nor judged of; it's just seen right off. (S2a) makes Hume a cognitivist *par excellence*. Moral judgments are knowledge, but directly perceived knowledge analogous to our perceptual knowledge of physical objects in typical circumstances. There is almost nothing to support interpretation (S2a) except perhaps Hume's unfortunately ambiguous phrase

6 Possibly some versions of non-cognitivism would not qualify as variants of (S1) as I have described it. For example many versions of prescriptivism (the view that moral judgments are something like imperatives) might not. Even so, many of Hume's arguments can be, and have been, appropriately adapted for the defence of these versions of non-cognitivism as well.

'moral sense'.[7] And much to be said against it. Hume's own arguments, so far from suggesting (S2a), seem to rule it out.

The more likely interpretation of the positive thesis building on (N2) would put moral non-inferential knowledge under 'Impressions of Reflexion'. It would make it less like knowledge of colours, sounds and pin pricks and much more like knowledge of our own affective mental states. Thus we have:

S2b. Negatively, (N2) moral knowledge is not inferred, but positively, it consists of direct apprehension of one's own sentiments (i.e., passions, emotions) toward the object judged.

Along with (S2b) goes the claim that moral language and moral belief always involve an indexical reference. If I say or think that *a* is virtuous, I am, according to this view, saying or thinking that *I* have a certain special psychological reaction to *a,* which reaction is known directly rather than inferentially. Unlike (S1) this is a cognitivist view, but like (S1) it is a radically subjectivist view. Moral judgments turn out to be cognitive under (S2b) because they make factual claims about one's own mental state. They are thus true or false. But (S2b) makes moral dispute a radically subjective matter (cf. ch. 6, pp. 154–5, below). If you and I 'disagree', as we would ordinarily say, about the virtue or vice of a given action, neither of us need be mistaken or saying anything false for each of us is only describing his own psychological reactions (his sentiments) to the action. Our two claims are not in contradiction and might both be true although the two sentiments in question may be in some sort of opposition or conflict.

NON-DEMONSTRABLE (BUT PERHAPS INFERABLE) MORAL KNOWLEDGE

The most modest of the interpretations of the negative thesis is (N3). It seems clear that Hume was concerned to show (N3) at the very least. The only question is whether he wished to make any of the stronger negative claims as well. With clear reference to Samuel Clarke, Hume wants to oppose the view that

. . . there are eternal fitnesses and unfitnesses of things, which are the same to every rational being that considers them; that the immutable measures

7 Cf. Harrison (1976), pp. 115–17.

of right and wrong impose an obligation, . . . that morality . . . is discern'd merely by ideas, and by their juxta-position and comparison. (456–7)

This passage suggests that Hume wants to exclude, among many others, a Clarke-like view that holds all of:[8]

i.   The fact that action a is right in circumstances c is just the fact that a is F-related to c where F is Clarke's special 'fittingness' relation (i.e., it is the fact that aFc).
ii. The F-relation is objective, and so the proposition that aFc is cognitive.
iii. If it is true that aFc, it is necessarily true.
iv. If it is true that aFc, that fact (and its necessity) is knowable *a priori*.

That Hume, as the passage indicates, wants to rule out some rationalist cognitivist views like the above is some evidence that at the very least he held (N3).

However if we base our interpretation of Hume's negative thesis on evidence about the sorts of views he intended to exclude, the same passage presents us with some difficulties. Hume also characterises the view he wishes to oppose as the view that:

v.   'virtue is nothing but a conformity to reason' (456).

Nothing like (v) is entailed in the rationalist cognitivist theory of (i) through (iv). My Clarke in (i) through (iv) holds only that an act's moral properties are a matter of its objective relationship to its circumstances and that whether or not the appropriate relationship holds is in principle knowable by an exercise of *a priori* reason. But to allege that a moral fact of the form aFc is knowable by reason is not to say that a reference to 'reason' must come essentially *within* the characterisation of that fact (in the description of a's property of being F-related to c). We need not attribute the view that virtue is conformity to reason to someone who says only that moral facts (including any truths about what virtue is or is not) are *knowable* by reason. That still leaves open the nature of what is known.

If Hume's negative thesis was meant to oppose a view like (v) rather than something like the Clarkean conjunction of (i) through (iv), we must suppose Hume's negative thesis to be something radically different from any of the three interpretations, (N1*), (N2), (N3), that we have given it so far. Thus we shall eventually have to discuss a fourth interpretation as well:

8 Clarke [1706]. Cf. selections in Selby-Bigge, ed. (1897), or Raphael, ed. (1969).

N4. While virtue exists, it does not consist in conformity to reason but in something else.

But setting aside this further interpretation for the moment, let us return to the question of whether Hume's negative thesis is intended to exclude all cognitivist views or only some (e.g. Clarke's).

ADDITIONAL COGNITIVIST VERSIONS OF SENTIMENTALISM

We might suppose that Hume did not hold (N1*), that he was instead a cognitivist, with a negative thesis weaker than (N1*), non-cognitivism, but at least as strong as (N3). More particularly we might suppose his view to be that moral judgments, while indeed cognitive, are not quite about what they seem on the surface to be about: They are not so much about the agents or actions they seem to be about as about *someone or other's* sentiments in reaction to them. Thus we have:

S3. Positively, moral judgments are cognitive judgments of a particular sort about special sentimental reactions of *some special person or persons* to acts or agents. Negatively, they are not any other cognitive judgment about those acts or agents (especially ones about their intrinsic properties or relations to non-psychological circumstances).

Of course this is just a schema. A particular interpretation of a cognitivist Hume results from specifying just what precisely the claim about the sentiment is, whose sentiment it is, etc. Thus all of the following have been suggested as interpretations of a cognitivist Hume:[9]

S3a. A moral judgment 'about' an action (person) is a cognitive one about the judger's *actual* special sentimental reaction to the action (person) judged.

This differs from (S2b) in not requiring the additional epistemological claim that our knowledge of such matters is non-inferential. (S3a) leaves it open whether knowledge of such psychological facts is direct or inferential (as long as it is not a matter of demonstration). Hence we may regard (S3a) as a slightly broader version of the notoriously subjectivist (S2b).

Another version of (S3) makes it a matter of the *disposition* the

9 Mackie (1980), pp. 66–7, 73.

21

object has to evoke the special sentiment in the judger. (Knowledge of this is less likely to be direct).

S3b. A moral judgment 'about' an action (person) is a cognitive one about the *disposition* it has to evoke a special sentiment in the judger.

Another version is *hypothetical* or *ideal*. It alludes to the dispositions that *would* be evoked in the judger *were* he in certain hypothetical or ideal circumstances:

S3c. A moral judgment 'about' an action (person) is a cognitive one about the disposition it *would* have to evoke a special sentiment in the judger *were* the judger in circumstances *C,*

where the judger's circumstances *C* get variously interpreted under different further interpretations as the judger's:

i.   Being clear and rational about all the relevant factual background,
ii. Compensating for the action's distance in time and space,

or:

iii. Taking some '*steady* and *general* point of view'.

(S3a), (S3b) and (S3c) make moral judgments all self-descriptions by the judger. Another interpretation, suggested by Mackie, is that the judgments are not about the sentiments of the judger but about the sentiments of mankind. Thus we can get three further versions, (S3d), (S3e) and (S3f), by substituting 'mankind' for 'judger' in (S3a), (S3b) and (S3c) respectively.

However, these three further versions (which speak of the sentiments of mankind) have certainly passed an important threshold. They all would make morality a rather more 'objective' matter. Indeed they make it look like it is just a matter of anthropological inquiry. By contrast the former three (which speak of the judger's sentiments) still have a kind of subjectivity which puts them closer to (S1) in that respect. We can illustrate it in this way. Suppose you and I 'disagree', as we would ordinarily say, over a moral matter. You claim a person's act is vicious. I claim it is virtuous. Under any of versions (S3a) through (S3c) it is in principle possible that neither of us is making a mistaken claim. Indeed it could be that each of us is saying something *true,* you about your (actual, dispositional, or ideal) reaction, I about my (corresponding kind of) reaction. By contrast, versions (S3d) through (S3f) have a kind

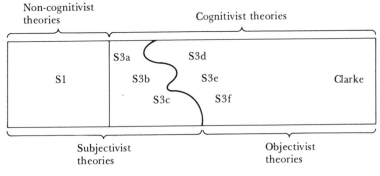

Figure 2

of objectivity even though they too are about psychological matters. If you and I disagree about an act's virtue, then (at least in the clear cut cases) one of us is just wrong. One of us fails to understand what is the actual, dispositional or ideal general human response. In these cases both of us can't be right.

This difference between the 'subjective' and the 'objective' versions of (S3) may not seem important to those who would remind us that Hume no doubt thought that *in fact* humans don't differ too fundamentally in the kinds of reactions they have to things. But as we shall see it makes a difference when we consider, in Chapter 2, a certain argument Hume gives for his sentimentalism. What the argument actually seems to support is some highly subjectivist meta-ethics. The most plausible view is that it's some non-cognitivist theory such as (S1) and if we insist instead that Hume is some kind of cognitivist, he will at the very least have to be a highly subjectivist one. In particular, (S3d) through (S3f) are not subjectivist enough to be what Hume's argument attempts to prove. And we have real doubts even about (S3a) through (S3c). Our picture is something like figure 2.

But for now we might settle for some textual support. Hume's own characterisation of his negative thesis is that moral distinctions are not 'derived from reason'. However in the relevant passages and throughout the *Treatise* he uses 'reason' in a broad sense to cover *both:*

i.   'comparisons of ideas'

and

ii. 'inferring of matters of fact'

23

where he thinks the former is what goes on in *a priori* reasoning and the latter in the case of *a posteriori* reasoning (463).[10]

If we accept this, Hume's negative thesis could not have been *just* (N3). He also must have denied that making moral distinction is a matter of 'inferring matters of fact'. But in that case a good many of our proposed versions of (S3) must be eliminated. Certainly our knowledge of (actual, dispositional and hypothetical) *human* reactions is a matter of inferring matters of fact. For that matter, even one's knowledge of one's own dispositions (not to mention one's dispositions in hypothetical circumstances) would seem to be a matter of drawing conclusions from observations. Thus it would seem (S3b) through (S3f) get eliminated for they would make morality a matter of inferring matters of fact. Even (S3a) has its problems. Only that knowledge of one's own actual, occurrent sentiments which is perceived directly, not inferred, would not be excluded. In effect we are back to (S2b) again. And even to settle for (S2b) requires putting a great deal of pressure on Hume's word 'inferring'. However if we think Hume was really saying it isn't a matter of *any* kind of empirical knowledge, then we are left with (S1). The choice really seems to be between (S2b) and (S1).

Of course I don't suppose Hume made all the distinctions that contemporary Humeans do and which the above discussion involves. We must not suppose Hume would have cared to distinguish between (S1) on the one hand and (S2b) or (S3a) or the other. So hereafter when I speak of Hume's sentimentalism, or just (S), I will be a bit ambiguous too. Mainly, I will intend the non-cognitivist version (S1) but I will not close the door entirely on the extreme subjectivist cognitivist versions in (S2b) or (S3a). I am suggesting that Hume was a non-cognitivist, or if not a non-cognitivist, then such an extremely subjectivist cognitivist that he might as well have been a non-cognitivist. That is Hume's sentimentalism.

THE FOURTH INTERPRETATION: VIRTUE MORALITY

But on occasion (e.g. 458–62) Hume seems to be arguing for a thesis which isn't any version of sentimentalism or indeed a meta-ethical thesis at all. Instead he seems to be defending a particular

10 Cf. also 124, 458, and *Enquiry*, 287. But also see 466.

moral viewpoint and opposing competing moral viewpoints. He is discussing no longer what is, or isn't, involved in making a moral judgment but rather what is, or isn't, involved in an agent's (or an agent's act's) being virtuous. This must dismay the contemporary Humean. In a previous section I noted that, in his discussion of rationalists such as Clarke, Hume sometimes seems to be doing no more than opposing a certain account of virtue and virtuous acts and proposing his own account of virtue instead. Hume is concerned to oppose the view 'that virtue is nothing but a conformity to reason' (456). Thus quite another version of the negative thesis is, suggested by Hume's words:

[A]ctions do not derive their merit from a conformity to reason, nor their blame from a contrariety to it. (458)

It is very easy not to notice that this can represent a new version of the negative thesis for there is a nice ambiguity in Hume's use of the word 'derive' so that the above can seem to be nothing but a restating of one of the earlier versions of the negative thesis. One could read the above sentence to mean only that moral judgments (beliefs, propositions) *cannot be* based on, or *justified* in terms of, reasoning of some certain sorts (or of any sort). This would take us back to the earlier versions (N1*), (N2) and (N3). On the other hand the above sentence can also be read to say that an act's being virtuous is never a matter of its *having resulted from* the agent's correct reasoning and correct beliefs (nor is an act's vice ever just a matter of its having resulted from a mistake of fact or error of reason). Before, we were speaking of propositions and their justification, but now we are speaking of acts and their motivational background. Before, about propositions concerning virtuous acts, now, about the virtuous acts themselves.

Thus sometimes Hume's negative thesis seems to be:

N4. The vice (virtue) of an act never consists [in entirety? even in part?] in the act's resulting, in some suitable manner, from the agent's cognitive error (correct reasoning).

The supplementary positive thesis then tells us what virtue and vice do consist in. It's a matter of something like sentiments, viz. the agent's motives (or perhaps the motives that typically produce such acts):

25

'Tis evident, that when we praise actions, we regard only the motives that produce them, and consider the actions as signs or indications of certain principles in the mind and temper. The external performance has no merit. We must look within to find the moral quality. (477)

Here Hume does not mean, as he does elsewhere, 'within *ourselves*'; he means 'within the *person we are praising*'. Thus the supplementary positive thesis is no longer sentimentalism but a kind of virtue morality, a view which allows there really are virtuous and vicious acts:

V. Negatively, (N4), but positively, virtue (vice) always consists [in part? in entirety?] in the motive which did [or commonly does?] produce the act.

Hume's mode of argument is significantly different when he is addressing virtue morality (V), from what it is when he is addressing some version of sentimentalism, (S). In arguing for (V) Hume appeals to conventional common sense moral intuitions. Hume claims in defence of (V) that we don't count mistakes of fact criminal (459–60) but that the agent's motives are relevant to blame, excuse, and praise. This mode of argument seems to have swept all the meta-ethical questions into the background. That Hume is momentarily abandoning meta-ethical questions can be illustrated in two ways. First, it does seem that some societies have rejected our conventional moral wisdom that vice never consists just in intellectual error. Some ancient Greeks, for example, seem to have regarded Oedipus as morally polluted by an act that was, notoriously, just based on a mistake of fact. (I reject here the move that says they *could not* have believed that.) Now the meta-ethical issue is not '*Who* is right here, the Greek view or (V)?' That is a substantive moral or value issue. The meta-ethical issue is rather '*Can* either be wrong or right about an issue such as that?' The subjectivist allows that it needn't be the case that either is mistaken. The noncognitivist is even more extreme, insisting that neither side is saying anything capable of being true or false. Hume, in discussing (V), has pushed these fundamental questions into the background. He is no longer asking 'What is the game all about?' He has actually joined one side. And furthermore – this is the second point – he has joined a side that even the most extreme rationalist objectivist cognitivist, such as Clarke, could join as well. That is, the acceptance of (V) is quite consistent with the rejection of the subjectivism of (S), indeed with quite extreme ways of rejecting (S). It's worth making this point in some detail.

Let us take up as our example the Clarke-like view (p. 20 above). However that is a view, not about virtue or virtuous acts, but about rightness and right acts. As before, the judgment that act *a* is right is just the statement that act *a* bears the objective relation F to its circumstances *c*. Any claim of this form, aFc, is not only cognitive but, where true, necessarily true and knowable *a priori*. However this says nothing of virtue (or what is praiseworthy, blameworthy, culpable, innocent, guilty, responsible, to be excused, etc.). A Clarke-like view might suppose that to be a matter of further, *second-order* moral judgments which perhaps involve claims about a further relation F', not the same as F, which is a four-place, not a two-place, relation. F' relates an act, *a*, its external circumstances, *c*, the agent, *p*, and the agent's *mens rea* or state of mind in so acting, *s*. We speak of second-order moral judgments here to leave again the possibility that the *mens rea*, *s*, might in some cases involve the agent's beliefs about first-order moral matters (i.e., matters of the form aFc). Thus at the first-order level the agent's act would be *right* or *wrong* depending on its fittingness F to its objective circumstances. But the agent's *virtue* or *vice* in doing the act would be a separate, second-order matter involving the agent's state of mind and perhaps motives. A judgment at this second-order level would have, not the form $F(a,c)$, but the Form $F'(a,c,p,s)$. The difference between F-relation judgments and F'-relation judgments would roughly correspond to the difference between morally evaluating actions when we are trying to decide what to do (rightness judgments) and the moral assessments we make of a person's having done or doing a particular act (virtue judgments). Of course I do not claim this view accurately reflects the historical Clarke. (It owes rather more to W.D. Ross.) Instead it is a spectre we conjure up to haunt the Humean.

Now if we take Hume's virtue morality thesis, (V), to be not a claim about all kinds of moral judgments but just the class of (second-order) virtue judgments, then (V) is a claim perfectly consistent with (although not required by) the Clarke-like view. There is no reason why *s* in true judgments of the form $F'(a,c,p,s)$ might not always be a matter of *p*'s motives (and never just, or even at all, a matter of his beliefs or their correctness). What makes our Clarke-like view an arch-rationalist one is *not* a matter of the sort

27

of thing it requires '*s*' to refer to in true judgments of this form, rather it is rationalist because it thinks F'-relation judgments are sometimes (robustly) *true* and, even worse, *necessarily true*. What's more, the Clarkean thinks such facts are knowable *a priori*. The point at issue here is not whether this Clarke-like view is plausible. (Its rationalism strikes me as very implausible.) The point is that what is at issue in the virtue morality thesis, (V), does not bear on the meta-ethical issue. It does nothing to support sentimentalism, (S), for even an extreme objectivist opponent of (S), such as the Clarke-like view, could in consistency embrace (V). ('I can be a virtue moralist too, if I like', says our Clarke.) Conversely, I do not see that a supporter of sentimentalism particularly has to accept virtue morality. (Does not sentimentalism have to provide just as much an account of those who held the ancient Greek view as of those who hold (V)?) Naturally we begin to wonder why Hume discusses (V) at all.

VIRTUE-BASED MORALITY

It gets worse before it gets better. Hume seems to have held something even stronger than (V), something which admittedly would exclude the particular Clarke-like view of our example but also at the same time take it further away from our common sense moral intuitions. Hume seems to have wanted to apply the claim in (V) not merely to judgments of virtue and vice but even to judgments of right and wrong. Indeed, unlike our Clarkean, he does not recognise a *distinct* (first-order) class of rightness judgments. All of Hume's actual examples are of judgments of virtue and vice. While Hume does discuss judgments of actions, it is judgments of *virtuous* and *vicious* action. And, as Hume clearly states, 'all virtuous actions derive their merit only from virtuous motives, and are consider'd merely as signs of those motives' (478). Insofar as Hume does concede there are moral judgments of right and wrong action, they seem to be the logically secondary ones, i.e., they presuppose judgments about virtuous motives. 'Actions are at first only consider'd as signs of motives' (479). If there is a notion of right action here (distinct from virtuous action) it seems to be something like 'an action such as would typically be done by someone with a certain virtuous motive'. This inverts the scheme of the Clarke-like view. Instead of rightness judgments being primary (or at least independent) and virtue judgments being secondary, it's precisely the other way around. Virtue judgments seem to be basic in Hume and rightness judgments, insofar as they are distinct from these, are logically secondary, requiring the notion of virtuous motive in their explanation. Thus we may say Hume holds something stronger than a virtue morality (V), Hume holds a virtue-*based* morality:[11]

Vb. (V) is the correct account for all virtue judgments but, furthermore, virtue judgments are the logically basic kind of moral judgments. (i.e., there is no important kind of moral judgment not based in the end on a virtue judgment).

Hume does not argue for (Vb) so much as assume it. He might have supposed it would be conceded by common sense moral thinking. I think this is not so.

Hume is fond of giving what I call his 'animals and inanimate objects arguments' (466–8; *Enquiry,* 293). Hume likes to point out that we ordinarily don't blame animals and inanimate objects for doing *exactly* (or so Hume claims) what we would find blameworthy in humans (examples: ingratitude, incest, parricide). In the context of that argument, Hume rejects the reply that the reason we don't blame animals is that they don't understand the wrongness of what they are doing. To Hume this reply just seems circular (467). How can an act's property of being vicious depend on the agent's *already* seeing its property of being vicious (as if this were some prior, independently existing property the act already had)? Hume seems to be *assuming* here that the only sort of judgment the agent could be making in 'understanding the wrongness' is a judgment of virtue or vice. But a more plausible view, one closer to common sense morality, is that in such a case judgments as to an agent's vice involve judgments about his *mens rea* in doing the act and that for this *mens rea* condition to be met the agent must have at least a capacity for understanding appropriate *first-order* judgments of right and wrong action. Furthermore, whatever judgments of right action may be, they do not in turn *invariably* depend on virtue judgments. A judgment in a choice situation needn't be a virtue judgment or a vice judgment, or anything with a *mens rea* condition. It could just be the thought 'This is wrong because it would harm others'. Very few of us are complete moral narcissists, concerned

---

11 It has been suggested to me that the source of (Vb) is to be found in Shaftesbury and Hutcheson.

only with the fine figure of virtue we cut in front of the moral mirror.[12] It's not impossible just to think 'This suffering of others is morally undesirable' and that apart from raising further questions of anyone's responsibility, innocence, virtue or vice. Not every moral judgment comes out in the form of a virtue/vice judgment or is dependent on such. Hence (Vb) is not an uncontroversial claim of our common sense morality.

Even the more modest claim (V) is not as obviously in accordance with common sense as it might first appear. Hume's argument for (V) really seems to rest on the deliverances of common sense morality such as that 'a mistake of *fact* be not criminal' (460). But even defended on those terms the claim in (V) is not a commonplace of conventional moral thought, at least not without much qualification. Two examples: First, we do sometimes seem to count defects in forming beliefs (e.g. negligence or recklessness in forming conclusions) as possibly culpable where one had the capacity to reason and where the consequences of the belief are particularly harmful to others.[13] In the case of negligence no particular motive need be present. It could simply be a matter of failing to take sufficient care in reasoning when one could have done so. It's what one didn't do. Secondly, we might refer the recent discussion of 'moral luck' in the literature.[14] Here the suggestion is that virtue and vice is in some important respect not purely a matter of the motives and intentions of the agent judged. Natural circumstances play a role. At any rate it is wrong to exaggerate the role of motives and intentions.

In any case Hume's virtue-based morality (Vb) is logically independent of his sentimentalism (S). It does not entail (S) nor does (S) entail (Vb). These two theses concern quite different issues. While sentimentalism is about the sentiment allegedly expressed by one who judges some agent (or act) to be virtuous, virtue-based morality is the claim that, in the end, acts are (actually!) virtuous or vicious because of the motives of agents. What then is the role of virtue-based morality in Hume's discussion? Of course, one possibility is that Hume might have never intended to put forward

12 For further references and discussion on virtue-based morality see Louden (1984).
13 An interesting discussion in regard to a particular moral and legal issue is in Curley (1976). In regard to negligence cf. Fitzgerald, ed. (1966), secs. 88–9, 95–9; Hart (1968), ch. 6; White (1985), ch. 7.
14 B. Williams (1976) and T. Nagel (1979).

sentimentalism but only a thesis of virtue-based morality. In that case we must see the *Treatise*, Book III, as a defence of a particular kind of substantive moral theory and it would be a mistake to read any contemporary meta-ethical views, such as sentimentalism, into it. If this interpretation of Hume were correct, I think it would make for a very much diminished Hume. He would not be the Hume of the first two books asking deep questions, but merely a Hume who puts forward a particular, in some ways idiosyncratic, moral theory, mostly on the basis of appeals to the conventional moral wisdom of our culture. And, as we have seen, even by the standards of that methodology, he isn't terribly convincing. Nor would this be at all the Hume who has influenced so many contemporary Humeans.

But there is another account of the respective roles (Vb) and (S) play in Hume thinking. We can cease looking for some possible relationship Hume might have imagined between them. Nor do we deny Hume held both of them. Instead, there was for Hume no issue of how to relate the two, because he just didn't distinguish them. In his best and most influential arguments Hume mainly has his eye on (S). In his worst and best forgotten arguments he seems somewhat more firmly fixed on (Vb). But he doesn't realise he has blinked. Hume systematically confuses his sentimentalism with his virtue-based morality.

THE SYSTEMATIC AMBIGUITY

Both sentimentalism and virtue morality (as well as the even stronger claim of a totally virtue-based morality) consist of a negative thesis and a further positive claim as well. In both, the negative thesis alludes to 'reason' or the 'understanding' while the positive addition speaks of 'sentiments' or else 'motives', i.e., a 'passion' of some sort. But while there is a reference to reason and to certain passions in both (S) and (V) these notions play a quite different role in each case. The use of 'reason' in the virtue morality thesis (V), is to raise the question of the relevance of an agent's beliefs and reasonings to the moral question of what virtues or vices he displays in acting. By contrast, 'reason' is employed in sentimentalism, (S), to raise the meta-ethical question of whether it is possible to demonstrate, or justify, or give cognitive status to, any moral proposition. In regard to a proposition of the form 'Agent *p*'s act *a* has

31

virtue v', (S) is addressing, among other things, the issue of whether this whole proposition can be rationally justified while (V) is addressing the quite different issue of whether the virtue of p's act could consist in, or perhaps depend upon, p's beliefs and reasonings in doing a.

The reference to a passion undergoes an analogous shift in employment in (S) and (V). The sentiment alluded to by (S) is in the judger (the person making the moral distinction), not in the judged (even though the judger's sentiment is typically directed toward, as Hume thinks, a passion in the judged). Suppose I judge you, or your act, to have a certain virtue. The sentiment (S) talks about is mine, even when it is a sentiment toward your passion. Hume seems to have his eye firmly fixed on (S) when he says:

... when you pronounce any action or character to be vicious, you mean nothing, but that from the constitution of your nature you have a feeling or sentiment of blame from the contemplation of it. (469, cf. Enquiry 289)

However the passion alluded to by (V) lies in the judged. Your having a certain virtue is said to consist in your motive.

In addition Hume's initial formulation of his thesis facilitates the confusion. The claim that 'moral distinctions' are 'not derived from reason' but are instead a matter of 'feeling' nicely obscures the difference between (S) and (V) so that both Hume and the reader are unlikely to distinguish them and likely to think there is really only one issue under discussion. Thus Hume begins Book III (on 457–8) discussing an argument which bears strongly on (S). By pp. 459–60 the discussion has clearly shifted to (V). And the intermediate paragraph (458, bottom) is a paradigm of confusions and ambiguities. It seems to be a discussion of both at once.

In fairness to Hume, there is another possible interpretation. Whether or not Hume sometimes confused sentimentalism and virtue morality, perhaps in his best moments he distinguished them and saw the relationship as follows: (S) does not entail (V). But when we do additional empirical investigation into the sorts of things the special moral sentiment in (S) is directed toward, we discover that in fact it is always toward motivations in the object of the judgment. Thus our moral judgments always turn out to have the form that (V) suggests. (V) would then not be a moral claim about what things really are virtuous but a descriptive claim about what things in other persons evoke the moral sentiment in the ordinary judger.

This is the most charitable interpretation of Hume. But if, as I have suggested, (V), and certainly (Vb), don't actually *describe* the form of all our moral thoughts (not to mention those of other cultures), then those descriptive theses must be abandoned. Fortunately this can be done without doing any damage to (S). If (V) and (Vb) are put forward as further descriptive theses and if they turn out to be discredited, that in no way reflects on (S). This is indeed another reason why it is important to distinguish (S) and (V). Sentimentalism must not suffer from too close association with the virtue morality thesis.

I have been working toward the conclusion that sentimentalism, (S), is the basic thesis in Hume and his starting point. On that view moral judgments are not just cognitive judgments about their objects (i.e., acts or agents) but, rather, express (or perhaps state) the *judger's* sentiments toward those objects. Hume's also holding the virtue morality thesis, (V), is either a confusion on his part or just a dispensable subsidiary claim. It is the quite different claim that the (actual!) virtue of agents and their acts is never just (or perhaps at all) a matter of agents' correct reasonings and beliefs but also always involves (or even consists in) agents' motives for so acting. I have given three reasons why (S) rather than (V) is the serious issue to be considered:

i. (S) fits best with Hume's description of the thesis, for example, with how he uses 'reason' in the rest of the *Treatise*.

ii. (S) is by far the more basic and interesting philosophical issue. Thus it is more in keeping with the level of discussion in Hume's first two books and is intrinsically more interesting to the contemporary Humean.

iii. Even on its own level, (V) is a rather dubious thesis put forward with rather little discussion as though it were just obvious and universal. It isn't. [Also, Chapter 7 below discusses further, quite conclusive, reasons for rejecting that special version of (V) I have called (Vb)].

To these we will soon be able to add a fourth:

iv. The best arguments that Hume gives, indeed the ones which have rightly retained their influence in various forms, would, if they work, show (S) or something on the philosophical level of (S). The best arguments have nothing to do (except by confusion) with (V).

What are those arguments?

33

2

The influence argument

Hume's arguments for sentimentalism are, for the most part, arguments for the large negative component of that thesis, viz. something close to non-cognitivism. Hume no doubt thought that the difficult part was to prove that moral distinctions are '*not* derived from reason'. After that, the defence of the further thesis that moral distinctions *are* a matter of sentiment might be just a matter of putting forward the only remaining plausible hypothesis, a matter of inference to the best explanation. Three discussions to be found in Hume's discussion (III,i,1) have been enormously influential in contemporary thinking about non-cognitivism. The third in order of Hume's presentation (469–70) is an observation about 'is' and 'ought'. In my view it is really a non-argument. Either Hume's discussion should not be taken as an independent argument at all or it should be discarded as a very bad argument indeed. This has not kept the relevant passage from being very influential just on its own. The second in Hume's order (463–69), the empiricist argument, depends on an application of Hume's specific epistemology developed in Book I of the *Treatise*. While Hume's specific epistemology may no longer be tenable, the general epistemological approach remains influential. Thus the same kind of argument for non-cognitivism can be given over and over again starting from new empiricist theories almost as soon as an old one has been scrapped. The first argument in Hume's presentation (457–58), the influence argument, relies on what seems to be an everyday observation that one's moral judgments have some capacity to influence one's feelings and behavior. This is contrasted with the alleged implausibility of supposing a mere cognitive judgment could ever do this all by itself. This argument also has the advantage, in contrast to the epistemological argument, of providing some support to what Hume's positive thesis adds to his negative thesis, viz. that there is some involvement of the passions in what it is to make a moral judgment. It is the influence argument that will occupy our main discussion. This is for reasons to be given shortly.

It is fair to say that, in one way or another, the empiricist argument and the influence argument still represent the two main ways in which non-cognitivism is defended.[1] One does not find a plausible contemporary argument which does not at least find its inspiration in one or the other of them. Hume is the ultimate source of whatever good arguments there are for non-cognitivism.

THE DOGMATIC HUMEAN

That is, when arguments are given. Some Humeans have little awareness of the need to argue, much less of Hume's arguments. What they do accept, sometimes more implicitly than explicitly, are Hume's conclusions, at any rate doctrines we can reasonably claim go back to Hume:

1. Non-cognitivism: No moral judgment is, in its entirety, a cognitive one as well [Or: No moral proposition is also a cognitive one].
2. No 'ought' from 'is' thesis: No moral conclusion ever follows deductively from cognitive premises alone.

The 'dogmatic Humean' in regard to (1) and (2) holds them in such a way that they are dogmas rather than anything that might require real arguments or ever be subject to reasonable criticism. Of these, some would not in fact know what to say if asked for an argument for (1) or (2). I include here first year philosophy students who, at the mere presentation of these theses, are quite convinced they are true and this before any arguments one way or the other are considered. Also I would include here some of my academic colleagues whose beliefs were molded in introductory philosophy courses and who quite firmly believe (1) and (2) but whose faith in the truth of them is greater by far than their memory of what the arguments, if any, are. But unlike these, another sort of dogmatic Humean does give arguments, but arguments of a patently question-begging sort. These dogmatists argue, but in a self-incapsulated world of belief so that, even in the process of arguing for (1) and (2), they simply assume the truth of these propositions at crucial points. The

1 Cf. Urmson (1968), ch. 2.

dogmatist is unable, even for the sake of argument, to imagine his dogmas not true.

The study of dogmatic Humeans is, of course, not a matter of logic and argument so much as a study of the pathology of argument. The interest here is rather more clinical than logical. Our approach is not a matter of coming up with better counter-arguments but rather of diagnosis and therapy. Diagnosis can begin with this practical test for dogmatism in regard to the Humean theses. Present an alleged counter-example to either of the two theses, for example, a case where, contrary to (2), some moral 'ought' allegedly follows deductively from a cognitive 'is'. One might suppose it important here to come up with a very convincing counter-example. But this actually isn't that important where the purpose is not refutation but diagnosis. The following crude, and not really convincing, alleged counter-example will do. Let's take c to be any uncontroversial cognitive proposition and let m be some equally uncontroversially moral, or evaluative, proposition. Consider then this argument:

i. not-c

ii. c or m

iii. m

The argument form, a case of the disjunctive syllogism, is deductively valid. Surely there is a strong case for thinking (i) is cognitive given it is the denial of the cognitive proposition c. Furthermore, m is some paradigm case of a moral judgment. So if (ii) turns out to be cognitive as well, we have a clear counter-example to the 'is'–'ought' thesis of (2).

The point is not to consider what we, ultimately, think about this particular example. The point is to observe the Humean's response to alleged counter-examples. What makes him dogmatic is not *what* he holds but in *how* he defends it. So what are the indicators of dogmatism? An initial indicator of dogmatism is the failure to look at the specific alleged counter-example. A typical dogmatist gives any alleged counter-example only a cursory glance, if that, and then proceeds with the litany he would have given in any case – *whatever* the specific counter-example had been. Of course it is in these further, all-purpose litanies, that we find more conclusive indicators of dogmatism.

Sometimes this involves arguing in a very small circle indeed.

For example there is the litanous response: 'Well, if a moral "ought" judgment really does follow from the premisses in your example, that only *shows* that at least one of the premisses, contrary to first appearances, really *isn't* cognitive (i.e., an "is" judgment).' Thus, it is said in regard to the above example, since premiss (i) is pretty clearly cognitive, this only shows that the other premiss, (ii) – admittedly the somewhat suspect, hybrid proposition *c or m* – just *can't* be cognitive. And this 'can't' is affirmed with amazing self-assurance. It would be quite different, and much more modest, to fend off the counter-example by looking more closely at the second premiss in order to provide some specific, independent grounds for thinking it isn't factual. This might involve appeals to what we would want to say about other similar hybrid propositions – perhaps for quite different philosophical reasons. Again, it would be more modest and not at all dogmatic, just to say it really isn't clear *yet* whether *c or m* is or is not cognitive. Indeed that might in the end have to wait on the prior issue of whether cognitivism or non-cognitivism is true (for if cognitivism is true, then (ii) is surely cognitive). So perhaps the cognitive status of (ii) is a 'spoils for the victor' matter. The non-dogmatic defender of the 'is'–'ought' thesis could then say that the suggested counter-example is not a clear, but a very controversial, case. But he doesn't insist, as the dogmatist does, that clearly premiss (ii) *can't* be cognitive. We must wait and see. It is the dogmatist who, without even a second glance at the particular case, asserts that the offending premiss *can't* be cognitive. But exactly why, we might ask, *can't* it be cognitive – apart, that is, from a fanatical application of the 'is'–'ought' thesis, the very thesis at issue? An uncomprehending stare at this point is an indicator of 'tiny circle' dogmatism.

More likely, however, the litanous response involves a somewhat larger circle. For example the response sometimes involves these two steps:

Step A: If the conclusion of the alleged counter-example really is moral, then at least one of the premisses *must* be moral, because:
The conclusion of any deductively valid argument is always *already contained* in the premisses.

Step B: But since, as per step A, one of the premisses at least is moral, it then *cannot* be cognitive as well.

Thus, it will be said in regard to our disjunctive syllogism example that, first of all, premiss (ii) must be evaluative (given that premiss

37

(i) is a poor candidate in that regard) and, second, that because (ii) is evaluative it cannot be cognitive as well. Step A is dubious on its own. In what sense must the conclusion of a valid argument be 'contained' somewhere in the premisses? If all that this means is that the premisses do after all *entail* the conclusion then this is granted – indeed insisted upon – by the proposer of the counter-example. But that is not yet to say that one of the premisses has to be a moral proposition. If that is so, it is not obviously so. But for the sake of argument let's grant step A and suppose that at least one of the premisses is a moral proposition. That admission has not yet conceded that such a premiss isn't cognitive. Why not both? Of course step B insists it *can't* be cognitive if it is moral, but step B is nothing but a bald assertion of non-cognitivism, that other thesis of Humean dogmatism. Of course there is nothing dogmatic about defending one controversial thesis, (2) the 'is'–'ought' thesis, in terms of another, just as controversial thesis, viz. (1) non-cognitivism, as long as one then goes on to give some further independent argument for the latter. Indeed I think the 'is'–'ought' thesis is best defended as a consequence of non-cognitivism.[2] What is dogmatic is not to notice one is defending one controversial thesis in terms of another which, if anything, is more controversial. Even worse is to proceed then with a defence of non-cognitivism which, at the crucial point, just assumes the 'is'–'ought' thesis thus bringing us round full circle. The defence of (2) assumes (1) and the defence of (1) assumes (2), but there is no entertaining of the position which doubts both at once. That is just beyond the imagination of the truly dogmatic Humean.

IS AND OUGHT

Hume's short discussion of 'is' and 'ought' (469–70) has provoked as much discussion as either the empiricist argument or the influence argument. Clearly he held an 'is'–'ought' thesis something like (2) (although possibly narrower in scope). Even so there is no inter-

2 G.E. Moore's 'open question argument', even if it worked, would not be an argument for non-cognitivism. It also does not entail the 'is'–'ought' thesis. Cf. Snare (1977) for further discussion of the logical relations among these three theses. A good place to begin on the logical issues in the 'is'–'ought' claim is in Prior (1960) and Jackson (1974). Essential for the discussion of 'open question argument' is the discussion of the naturalistic fallacy in Moore (1903), preface and ch. 1, secs. 1–17, and Frankena (1939).

esting argument here. Hume himself calls it an 'observation' rather than an argument and may have only been raising an issue rather than settling it. That is, the point might only have been that the transition from 'is' judgments to 'ought' judgments typically needs some further explanation. However, rather more strongly, he also says that it seems "inconceivable" that an 'ought' judgment could ever be deduced from 'is' judgments. That would be a rather stronger thesis, much more like (2). However if this is what Hume held, what is his argument? One possibility, suggested by the placing of this discussion after his other arguments, is that he regarded (2), the 'is'–'ought' thesis, as a consequence of (1), non-cognitivism, for which he had already given the influence and the empiricist arguments.[3] Perhaps his observation then was merely that this further consequence of his non-cognitivism shows that many authors of works on morality have made illegitimate transitions from 'is' to 'ought'. This claim, of course, could be no better than the two arguments already given for non-cognitivism. There would be no new argument here.

Another possibility is that Hume thought he was giving a new and distinct argument in this passage. If so, it would be a particularly question-begging argument and would make Hume himself the first of the dogmatic Humeans. Thus Hume seems to argue that a new 'ought' relation (or affirmation) cannot be deduced from others 'entirely different from it' (i.e., 'is' ones). But is it so clear that 'new' relations or affirmations cannot be deduced from 'old'? Of course one can build into the very meaning of 'new' that it is not deducible from the other sort. But then to assume moral affirmations are 'new' in this sense is just to beg the issue of (2). Even if we adopt some less tendentious understanding of 'new' whereby it begs no issues to call moral affirmations 'new', it still begs the issue to suppose it just obvious that new propositions never get derived from old. Also, it begs the issue to assume that 'ought' judgments are 'entirely different' from 'is' judgments. One requires here more of an ability to imagine the cognitivist's viewpoint. If, as the cognitivist thinks, 'ought' judgments are a very special kind of 'is' judgment, this 'entirely different' is quite misleading. The transition from a non-moral 'is' to a moral 'is' would not then seem quite so inconceivable. We can perhaps detect in Hume's own dis-

3 For why one might think that see Snare (1977).

cussion of 'is' and 'ought' a few of the symptoms of dogmatism. Of course Hume might, or might not, be right to say that 'ought' claims are 'new' and 'entirely different from' 'is' claims and that it is 'inconceivable' that the former be a deduction from the latter. But his saying so is not a further argument. It's a part of the very issue at question. For argument we must look to Hume's empiricist argument or else his influence argument.

THE EMPIRICIST ARGUMENT

What I call Hume's empiricist argument (463–9; cf. *Enquiry* 287–9) builds directly on the theory of knowledge developed in Book I of the *Treatise*. Human understanding, according to Hume, is either a matter of comparing ideas, or of inferring matters of fact. Moral 'knowledge', if it were a matter of comparing ideas, would be 'susceptible of certainty and demonstration'. Hume's own, somewhat idiosyncratic, view is that the comparison would have to involve one or more of his four relations. Hume argues that, since making moral distinctions is not just a matter of comparing ideas to find these four relations, there is no such thing as moral knowledge by demonstration (463–4).

So if our making moral distinctions is to be knowledge at all, on Hume's view, it must be a matter of inferring matters of fact. But at this point Hume challenges us to find any empirical basis that can completely account for our moral distinctions:

Take any action allow'd to be vicious: Wilful murder, for instance. Examine it in all lights, and see if you can find that matter of fact, or real existence, which you call *vice*. In which-ever way you take it, you find only certain passions, motives, volitions and thoughts. There is no other matter of fact in the case. The vice entirely escapes you, as long as you consider the object. (468)

And elsewhere he says:

. . . anatomise all these circumstances, and examine, by your reason alone, in what consists the demerit or blame . . . , point it out: determine the time of its existence; describe its essence or nature; explain the sense or faculty to which it discovers itself. (*Enquiry,* 287)

Hume concludes that if our making moral distinctions is neither a matter of demonstration nor of empirical observation, then it isn't a matter of the understanding at all but the work of something else (the passions perhaps?).

Hume's influence on contemporary Humean arguments for non-cognitivism is not so much a matter of the details of his particular empiricist epistemology as of his general empiricist approach. For contemporary Humeans the approach begins less as an account of knowledge and more as an account of what it is for a belief (or a proposition or a judgment or a use of language) to be cognitive. The classical empiricist account is that there are two ways of its being cognitive: Either it is analytically true (or false) or else it must be such that sense experience, observation (or something of that order) bears on its truth or falsity in some appropriate manner. A.J. Ayer's *Language, Truth and Logic* (1936) is of course the classic example of this approach in contemporary philosophy. Such empiricists do not have a primary interest in moral philosophy. Their first interest is in developing a general empiricist philosophy. But typically, at a certain point (ch. 6 in Ayer's case) they notice that moral judgments do not seem to pass the cognitivity test. None of the interesting and substantive moral judgments seem to be analytically true (or false). Nor, it is claimed, do these seem to have any empirical basis when we 'examine in all lights' or 'anatomise' the circumstances. The defence of empiricism then proceeds by deciding that moral judgments need to go into the 'non-cognitive' bin even though their indicative linguistic form might first have suggested otherwise.

Of course the Ayer-Hume tests for cognitivity are much too crude. The problem is that a lot more than just moral distinctions get thrown out by their tests. If more light or even a microscope will not get us closer to revealing that matter of fact which is the vice, neither will those things help in revealing what is the fact which is a law of nature, or a causal connection, or a dispositional property, or an institutional fact. Watching more carefully the salt dissolving does not reveal the solubility. A close-up of the billiard balls in contact does not reveal the causation. We can miss the table by examining too much the wood. Nor will we observe the parliament, the law, or the football match.[4] If moral distinctions get thrown out, they will at least be in rather good company. And this

4 Cf. Kovesi (1967) who pushes these points about as far as they will go.

may well suggest that the problem here is not in morality but in an inadequate empiricist philosophy.

Of course not all empiricism is this crude. It is considered an important and difficult problem to come up with a defensible empiricist account of, say, causation. Perhaps we need to posit certain theoretical entities. Perhaps certain kinds of facts 'supervene' on other kinds of facts. And so forth. But all such complications make the empiricists' test for cognitivity less and less decisive in the case of moral judgments. (Might they not be about certain supervenient facts, for example?) The point is that the use of empiricist criteria for cognitivity makes for a somewhat inconclusive argument for non-cognitivism. The less sophisticated versions of empiricism exclude moral judgments, but they exclude very much else as well, too much to be plausible theories of cognitivity. However, while the more sophisticated versions of empiricism may succeed in giving empiricists accounts of what the others exclude, they do it at a certain cost, viz. creating a lot of loopholes (supervenience, theoretical entities, etc.) which just might be used to find some equally empirical basis for ethics.[5] At best the sophisticated empiricist can proceed by way of a challenge to cognitivists to give respectable empiricist basis for moral distinctions. A challenge unmet might be all the argument there is here, but not an unreservedly convincing one since it has in the past seemed quite difficult to give empiricist accounts of a great many things, not just moral distinctions.

MORAL ELIMINATIVISM

Another contemporary approach is not epistemological or even conceptual but metaphysical. It's based on a scientific naturalism rather than empiricism. It claims that the best naturalistic account we have of what there is involves no reference to moral facts or properties. We have no need of that hypothesis. Of course there are psychological and social phenomena such as moral beliefs, moral emotions, moral social norms, but these can be best explained without recourse to moral facts or properties. Indeed these explanations only require notions we already need for other purposes of scientific explanation.

Philosophers who seem to take this approach are Mackie and

5 Cf. Brink (1984) and Werner (1983).

perhaps Harman.[6] This approach is not conceptual nor an account of the meaning of moral discourse. It allows that our use of moral language could be based on a metaphysical error, the mistaken belief that there are such facts. Hence versions of this approach are sometimes called an 'error theory' of morality or a 'projection theory' of morality, where the 'projection' is a mechanism alleged to explain why we should make this mistake. Again, this approach is not a matter of pure philosophical theory and *a priori* reasoning – nor even of philosophical argument assisted with everyday observation – as Hume's empiricist argument seems to be. Instead this approach rests in large part on actual developments in the various contemporary sciences such as psychology, biology, anthropology, sociology. It is very much less concerned with philosophical armchair questions such as 'What is the meaning of moral discourse?' and rather more with asking 'What, on the basis of the best available science, do we have reason to believe exists?'

I shall not be discussing further in this book the empiricist or the eliminativist arguments for non-cognitivism (or something similar).[7] There are two reasons for this. First, both take us away from moral philosophy and back to quite general and fundamental issues in epistemology or philosophy of science. Thus, the empiricist argument naturally takes us back to general questions about the validity of any form of empiricism. Likewise, any discussion of moral eliminativism takes us back quite quickly to issues about inference to the 'best' explanation and to questions about how an explanation that 'eliminates' differs from one than merely 'reduces' or one that only gives origins. These issues are better discussed elsewhere.

---

6 Cf. Harman (1977), chs. 1, 2; Mackie (1977), ch 1; Mackie (1980), pp. 51–2, 71–5; Snare (1984); Gauthier (1986), pp. 56–9.

7 It might reasonably be supposed that moral eliminativism is not non-cognitivism because it holds, for example, that propositions of the form '*a* is wrong' *are false*. Indeed it claims there is no such property as wrongness for the act *a* to have. However for purposes of my discussion in Part II eliminativism is close enough to non-cognitivism for that discussion to apply to eliminativism as well as to non-cognitivism. What is crucial for this to be so is that the eliminativist also holds that propositions of the form '*a* is permissible' be just as false as '*a* is wrong' or '*a* is right', there being no property of permissibility any more than there is one of wrongness. In short, the sense in which the eliminativist thinks certain moral judgments (e.g. '*a* is wrong') are false can never allow him to derive the truth of other moral judgments (e.g. '*a* is permissible') from the claims of falsehood. Cf. Chapter 6 below.

The second reason relates to the purpose of this book. Neither empiricism nor eliminativism can claim to provide a *conclusive* argument for non-cognitivism (or something similar), not one that would justify the smugness of many contemporary Humeans. We have seen how the empiricist approach is something of a two-edged sword. Likewise moral eliminativism, while in my view very much more plausible, is still somewhat inconclusive. Philosophical eliminativism of any kind is always a tricky business. It involves proving a negative, that contemporary science has no place at all for certain alleged facts or properties, that they are not even facts reducible to other facts or facts that supervene on other facts. One expects something a bit more messy: that the best available naturalistic account of the world will neither clearly reduce nor clearly eliminate 'moral facts' but only relegate them to some indeterminate status in between (thus providing entree for endless philosophical chatter). Hence the claim that moral facts and properties are *clearly* eliminable is one that bears a heavy burden of proof.

Contemporary Humeans tend to be rather smug, smugger, I think, than either the empiricist argument or the eliminativist arguments would ever warrant. Smug Humeans don't wait around biting their nails to see how the latest version of empiricism will fare or whether the most recent version of science will support a case for moral eliminativism. This smugness often reveals itself in a certain *double standard* we find even within the empiricist and eliminativist arguments. When, for example, a proposed empiricist view does not account for moral judgments, that is just assumed to be a problem for morality, not for the criterion. But if that same criterion cannot account for our talk about dispositions, or causal connections, or laws of nature, that is assumed to be a problem for the empiricist criterion. ('Please let us tinker a bit more.') What could be the ground for the smug assumption that moral distinctions are already in trouble somehow? Perhaps it rests on some other argument, perhaps the argument Hume gives us first before all?

THE INFLUENCE ARGUMENT

What I call 'Hume's Influence Argument'[8] is the first in his order of presentation (457–8). It deserves special attention for several

8 Some of the points in the remainder of this chapter were first made in Snare

reasons. First, it depends not at all on Hume's epistemology and really, despite first appearance, not on his distinctive philosophy of mind. Hence it remains available to a very wide range of philosophers including those who are not empiricists. Second, this argument, in comparison to the others, does more to explain what Hume's positive thesis adds to his negative thesis, i.e., the claim that sentiment or passion comes into the making of moral distinctions. Third, the argument claims to be much more conclusive than the others. Thus the empiricist argument consists in nothing more than the repeated *failure,* after a finite number of attempts, to see, literally, the moral distinctions in actions or persons. Nor can such an argument be any less controversial than the particular sort of empiricism on which it is currently based. By contrast, the influence argument claims to demonstrate its conclusion and on the basis of premises of a somewhat wider appeal than empiricism. Fourth, something similar to the considerations raised in this argument seems to get involved in almost any contemporary defence of versions of non-cognitivism, at least in those like Stevenson or Hare, but unlike Ayer, who give arguments not based on some more basic and general epistemology. Finally, the premises of this argument, in various forms, are frequently held and defended by contemporary philosophers (whom we also call 'Humean') quite apart from any conscious use of them in this particular argument. They are views typical of a 'Humean' philosophical psychology. These premises are of interest in themselves.

Here is how Hume states his argument (457–8, cf. *Enquiry* 171–3):

1. Reason alone can never have an influence on the actions and affections (passions) [Or: Reason has no influence, is utterly impotent, is perfectly inert].
2. The moral distinctions we make [morals, morality] have an influence on the actions and affections [excite passions, produce or prevent actions].

3. The moral distinctions we make [morals, morality] cannot be derived

(1975). The author is grateful to the editor of *Mind* for permission to use that material here.

Discussion of the influence argument can be found in Broad (1930), ch. 4; Laird (1932); Kydd (1946); Foot (1963); Kemp (1964), ch. 4; Broiles (1969); Harrison (1976), ch. 1; Mackie (1977), pp. 40–41; Stroud (1977) ch. 8; Mackie (1980), pp. 52–5. Blackburn (1984, pp. 187–8) presents the argument more broadly in terms of explanation rather than (causal) influence.

from reason alone [i.e., it is false that morality is discovered only by a deduction of reason; the rules of morality are not conclusions of our reason].

The argument is not epistemological but depends on a philosophical psychology. It concerns what sorts of things do and don't, can or can't, excite or prevent actions and passions. Consequently in the *second premiss* we must suppose that what does any influencing here is something on the order of one's moral judgments, moral opinions, moral beliefs. It is one's holding them, believing them, assenting to them (rather than their simply being true, if that is possible) which does the influencing. No Humean need object to my use of the term 'belief' in this regard for I employ the broad sense of 'belief' here. This leaves it quite open whether a 'moral belief' is the sort of thing which can be true or false.

In regard to that same premiss we might note that Hume is not entirely clear as to how strong or weak a premiss he intends. He might, variously, be saying about the moral beliefs we have that

2a. They must have an influence,
2b. They always have an influence,
2c. They sometimes have an influence,

or perhaps only:

2d. They have a capacity to influence (whether or not it ever gets actualised),

where these versions are listed in order of rapidly decreasing strength. His wording in his main statement of the argument (457) suggests something as moderate as (2b) or (2c); however in slightly different context (465) he seems to hold something as strong as (2a), actually using the word 'necessary' and the phrase 'must... have its influence'. For the Humean today the choice must be determined in part by what version makes for a valid argument and in part by how easy it is to show the premiss true.

One thing that will make the second premiss, in any version, easier to defend, is that well-put phrase 'have *an* influence' (457). Clearly one's moral beliefs often do not have sufficient motivational force to result in the action one believes called-for. Moral weakness of the will is a much discussed case. But it can be plausibly maintained in cases of weakness of the will that one's moral belief still had *some* motivational force even if not sufficient force. Hence we

46

think of moral weakness as involving a *conflict* of motivations. The influence of one's moral beliefs might easily provide only one motivational 'vector' where the final action is the result of a great many other vectors as well.

The *first premiss* poses rather more difficulties of interpretation. In regard to that premiss it is important to see that Hume has to mean, not merely that reason the faculty or capacity (or even reasoning the activity) is motivationally inert, he must say that everything produced by reason (alone) is also motivationally inert. Otherwise the conclusion, (3), simply does not follow. Even if the faculty reason is motivationally inert (perhaps just because it is of the wrong category), if what reason produces could influence action, then morals might influence and yet be reason-produced. Thus Hume must hold that everything produced by reason (alone) is motivationally inert. And indeed he does say that '[a]n active principle can never be founded on an inactive' (457). We might put Hume's view thus: Beliefs which are *solely* reason-based are inert. One latent function of the 'alone' in Hume's first premiss is to suggest that beliefs (broad sense) produced *only* by reason (i.e., only by comparing ideas and/or inferring matter of fact) have to be utterly impotent. A way of putting Hume's claim which doesn't refer to the terms of his particular epistemology or his notion of reason is just to speak of 'cognitive beliefs' rather than 'beliefs which are *solely* reason-based'.

However the 'alone' in the first premiss has a further, rather more important, function as well. 'Alone' means 'just by itself without teaming up with a quite separate passion, desire, need, or such'. Thus Hume says:

> . . . reason, in a strict and philosophical sense, can have an influence on our conduct only after two ways: Either when it excites a passion by informing us of the existence of something which is a proper object of it; or when it discovers the connection of causes and effects, so as to afford us means of exerting any passion. (459)

So Hume's claim in premiss (1) is best read as the claim that *solely* reason-based beliefs (i.e., cognitive beliefs) cannot *alone* have (even some) influence on the actions as passions.

However this has implications for how we must read the second premiss. It must also be qualified with precisely the same 'alone'. Otherwise the argument is not really valid. Once it is admitted that cognitive beliefs can be at least part of an influence on action, it does not set moral beliefs apart to say that they get into an influencing story too. Instead what (2) must claim is distinctive about moral judgments is that they manage this influencing *alone* – something a cognitive judgment could never manage by itself. Thus Hume's second premiss must be understood as: Morals *alone* have an influence. However this 'alone' must be read in exactly the same sense as in the first premiss. It does not mean 'utterly alone'. Your moral belief may well be impotent if you suffer a cerebral haemorrhage in that split second or, more typically, if it doesn't connect up properly with other appropriate beliefs. What the 'alone' here means is not 'completely on its own' but rather more the idea that you can add as much as you like as long as it isn't a further passion or desire or such. No matter how much you add to a cognitive belief, e.g. endless other cognitive beliefs, if you don't add a passion it will remain inert. However in the case of moral beliefs, while you may need to add more to get the influencing (e.g. some further cognitive beliefs, standard background conditions, etc.) a further, separate passion or desire is not required. In this respect moral beliefs differ fundamentally from cognitive beliefs.

How then do we interpret the *conclusion,* (3)? There is one way of trying to interpret the conclusion that would make Hume a cognitivist, but a rather odd one. Hume's claim that our moral beliefs cannot be derived from reason might be taken as the claim that moral beliefs are indeed cognitive beliefs, but never *true* cognitive beliefs. Hume does speak of reason as 'the discovery of truth or falsehood' (458). And of course 'discovery' is a success word. So perhaps the intended conclusion was that moral beliefs are never *true* cognitive beliefs, leaving open the odd possibility that the moral judgments which motivate us are indeed cognitive, but invariably false cognitive judgments. However all of Hume's (or anyone's) arguments for the first premiss in the argument show, if anything, that *any* cognitive belief, true or false, is alone inert. This then supports the wider conclusion in (3) that no moral judgment is ever a cognitive belief (not even a *false* cognitive belief). That is, it supports non-cognitivism. At any rate we shall call the conclusion (N) from now on.

Apart from what Hume may have actually thought, it is hard to turn the influence argument into anything other than an argument for something close to non-cognitivism. This argument seems actually to exclude the various cognitivist versions of sentimentalism discussed in Chapter 1. For example one's cognitive beliefs about common human reactions or even one's beliefs about one's own dispositional or hypothetical sentimental reactions would not seem *alone* capable of influencing. Must we not add some interest or desire before such beliefs become influential? The usual arguments given in defence of premiss (1) would seem to make no exceptions here. It is not even clear that a *belief* about one's own occurrent desires can *alone* influence (as opposed to the desire it is *about,* which may influence). Admittedly Hume's own epistemology does not always allow us to distinguish too clearly between a present desire and a present cognitive belief about that desire. But suppose the belief about a present desire is mistaken? Is not self-deception of this sort possible? In which case it is odd, on Humean grounds, to suppose the mistaken belief about a desire could be an influence without help from some further desire (and of course the desire it is *about* doesn't exist). Again the usual arguments for the first premiss of the influence argument give no reason for excepting these cases of cognitive beliefs about passions from the general rule that cognitive beliefs are inert.

We perhaps can't be too precise about what Hume thought he was proving, but if the influence argument proves anything at all, it is something very close to non-cognitivism, or at the very least a highly subjectivist version of cognitivism. That Hume's most interesting argument proves something close to non-cognitivism if it proves anything at all is now the result which we could only foreshadow at the end of Chapter 1.

OBSERVING INSTANCES OF INFLUENCING

Hume's usual way of stating the influence argument suggests he wants a rather strong first premiss. He uses the phrase 'can never' and metaphors such as 'impotent' and 'inert'. This suggests a claim of some sort of necessity. By contrast the second premiss is more usually presented as merely the claim that morals do (rather than must) have an influence. He speaks of this premiss as being 'confirm'd by common experience' (457). This suggests an argument of this form with a rather strong first premiss and a weaker second premiss:

Argument A:
1. □ [All C-beliefs are non-I's]
2. All M-beliefs are I's
___
N. No M-belief is also a C-belief

where '□' is the necessity operator operating on the entire bracketed proposition following it, 'C-beliefs' and 'M-beliefs' mean cognitive and moral beliefs respectively, and where being an 'I' means being an 'alone influencer' in the special sense of 'alone' discussed previously. This argument is clearly valid. But viewing it may lead us to ask why we need the necessity operator '□' in front of the first premiss. After all, the following is just as valid:

Argument A':
1. All C-beliefs are non-I's
2. All M-beliefs are I's
___
N. No M-belief is also a C-belief

Now the question I want to raise here is really epistemological. I want to ask Humeans how they are going to argue for each of the two premisses. One sort of argument is, at least in part, conceptual. Thus the usual way to argue for premiss (1), these days at least, is to appeal to the concepts of 'folk psychology', i.e., notions like 'belief' and 'desire'. Such an argument would seem to be able to show, for example, not merely that all C-beliefs are non-I's, but indeed that this *must* be so. The 'must' here need not be a matter of logical or philosophical necessity. It might merely be that the truth of premiss (1) is required by the concepts central to the best empirical theory in the area, i.e., folk psychology. Thus we could challenge the truth of (1) only by challenging folk psychology and the adequacy of its notions (thus becoming 'psychological eliminativists'). At any rate a (partly) conceptual argument for the first premiss would make the '□' operator in argument (A) appropriate. An alternative way of arguing for a premiss is simply by everyday observation of cases where these are used as data to confirm or disconfirm the premiss in question. Hume sometimes suggests that is what is going on in regard to the second premiss. But what I am considering in regard to argument (A') is the possibility of defending *both* premisses in that observational, confirming-instance manner.

50

But there is a rather deep problem with supporting the premises just with observed cases. Such arguments are in great danger of begging the issue. We can see this by considering a simple parody of argument (A'):

1. No sort of fish interests me
2. Trout do interest me

---

3. Trout are not fish

One might call this way of proceeding 'sentimental zoology'. I determine my zoological classifications on the basis of my reactions. The argument is valid. Its problem is that it is question-begging. If, contrary to the conclusion, trout are fish, then my interest in trout actually serves as a counter-example to (1). There is no way I can tell, just from observing instances, that *no* sort of fish interests me until I settle the classificatory issue we find in the conclusion. Nor is the problem just the falsehood of the first premiss. If we substitute 'whale' for 'trout' in the parody we get a valid argument with true premisses and conclusion but an argument just as question-begging. The argument has nothing at all to do with why whales are not fish. And of course we know what a Samuel Clarke will say about (A'). Given that M-beliefs are influencers, we cannot know that this very fact does not provide a counter-instance to the first premiss until we settle the prior classificatory issue of whether M-beliefs are instances of C-beliefs. On Clarke's view they are. (The Humean must exercise his imagination a bit here.)

Of course this is not a mistake Hume makes. Indeed it vindicates Hume's employing argument (A) rather than (A'). The stronger first premiss does not make the argument any more valid but it does suggest the grounds for the first premiss are to some extent conceptual. Hume might have thought the second premiss could be grounded just on the observed powers of moral judgments, but the case for the first premiss has to be slightly more *a priori*.

HUME'S NIGHTMARE

There is still a worry about the conclusion, (N), of argument (A). Is it really non-cognitivism? This wouldn't be much of a worry if (N) is, at least, something close to non-cognitivism

51

such as a highly subjectivist, just-over-the-border, cognitivism. But it is a worry if (N) should turn out to be consistent with even extremely objectivist rationalist versions of cognitivism. Certainly if Samuel Clarke, or his ilk, can embrace (N), then something has gone wrong. For a start, here is a slight problem to keep the Humean tossing at night before falling to sleep. The conclusion, (N) of argument (A) is a contingent claim; there is no necessity operator, '$\square$', in front of it. Nor can the conclusion be made any stronger where the second premiss just proceeds by observation of a lot of cases. But that doesn't seem as strong a conclusion as the Humean would like. It says only that no actual M-belief is also a C-belief. But this might indicate no more than a rather depressing human failing. Even a claim of empirical necessity in this regard might indicate no more than a lawlike human incapacity. It doesn't actually rule out Clarkean moral truths. At most it says we aren't lucky enough ever to believe them. What we do believe in the moral area isn't cognitive. But that doesn't show there isn't such. Admittedly a conclusion about human incapacity is depressing enough. But a non-cognitivist really would want to argue for its being a necessary truth that our moral beliefs are never just cognitive beliefs. (This is then a reason for making the second premiss a matter of necessity as well.)

But this small matter is not enough to keep a Humean from sleep at last. However there is a slightly more nagging difficulty. Under the right sort of linguistic-verbal-conceptual conditions the conclusion of (A) might be acceptable even to that arch-objectivist Samuel Clarke. Nor will it help much in this regard to put a '$\square$' in front of the conclusion. Note, as a preliminary, that the validity of (A) in no way depends on 'belief' in the total expression 'M-belief' having the same meaning as the 'belief?' in 'C-belief'. Its meaning could be context-dependent (just as 'mate' occurs both in 'check mate' and in 'flat mate'). This prompts a nightmare. Hume dreams – what most Humeans can barely imagine – a world where there are Clarkean 'fittingness' facts, facts of the form 'aFc'. In this nightmare world we even find people forming (true and false) C-beliefs about such moral matters of fact. But the frightening twist is a semantic one. Hume discovers that what we *call* 'moral beliefs' consist of two things:

i. C-beliefs about some moral matter of fact (some Clarkean *aFc*-fact), *and*

ii. Having some appropriate motivation, passion, affection (say, in regard to the fact that *aFc*).

Thus a cognitive belief about some moral *aFc*-fact is not called a 'moral *belief*' unless accompanied by an appropriate interest in such matters. This bit of linguistic usage might even be explained by the empirical fact that humans just are overwhelmingly interested in *aFc* facts so that there is never a need for a special term to mark out the quite non-existent case where (i) is present but (ii) is not.

In this dream Clarke embraces argument (A) *but without conceding a thing*. Clarke decides that, after all, premiss (1) is true. C-beliefs (even when about moral *aFc*-type facts) do not alone influence. Premiss (2) is true and indeed analytic but in that sort of way we disparagingly call 'merely semantic'. We just don't call it a 'moral belief' unless the appropriate interest is there as well. The conclusion is then true, but uninteresting. It only marks the peculiarity of our linguistic usage that 'belief' when it occurs after the word 'moral' gets a somewhat more fortified meaning than otherwise. It is only the superficial grammatical form of (N) which misleads us into thinking something more important is being said. 'We are all "non-cognitivists" now', says Clarke.

How disturbing is this dream? Of course it is only philosophical paranoia to imagine one's words will always desert to the enemy. Nevertheless is it worth making a stock distinction here. 'Belief' in ordinary usage is ambiguous. It can mean the proposition or content believed (i.e., *p*) or it can mean the psychological state of mind a person might have to such a proposition (one's belief that *p*). As before, I take 'proposition' in as broad a sense as I do 'belief'. 'That torture for fun is wicked' is an example of a proposition whether or not it is the sort of thing which can be true or false. Now there might be just a shred of plausibility in the linguistic claim that the total phrase 'moral belief' (or, more commonly, 'moral opinion' or 'attitude' or 'view') marks the presence of an additional motivational or emotional element on the part of the 'believer'. However this suggestion is very much less plausible in regard to 'moral proposition' for we tend to think what makes a proposition moral (just as what makes it mathematical or geological) is a matter of its content rather than, in addition, how that content is commonly received. We can make lists of moral propositions (e.g. 'Torture is wrong') without saying anything about anyone's state of mind. However lists of believings ('Clarke's believing torture is wrong') do use the notion 'believe' or some equally tendentious notion.

A WIDE-EYED REWORKING

So I suggest that what the Humean wants for the conclusion, in (N), is not merely that no 'moral belief' is a cognitive belief, but that *what* is thereby believed, i.e., the proposition, is also not cognitive. Hence argument (A) might best be read as:

Argument A*
1. $\Box$(x)[Cx $\supset$ ~($\exists$y)Ixy]
2. (x)[Mx $\supset$ ($\exists$y)Ixy]

N. ~($\exists$x)[Mx & Cx]

where:

'x'   ranges over propositions
'y'   ranges over persons (or perhaps possible persons?)
'C': 'is cognitive'
'M': 'is moral'
'Ixy': 'there are occasions when y's believing x '*would* "alone" influence y to appropriate actions or affections'.[9]

Basically the first premiss says it is necessarily the case that any proposition correctly classifiable as cognitive will not be an alone influencer. The second premiss says that any proposition correctly classifiable as 'moral' is an 'alone influencer'. Consequently there is no proposition which is both a moral one and a cognitive one. Taking '($\exists$y)Ixy' to mean 'x is an alone influencer', i.e., as 'Ax', we may simplify argument (A*) thus:

9 The 'would' in the explanation of 'Ixy' marks some claim of empirical connection. Thus 'Ixy' will not be true simply because, as it happens, *y* fails to believe *x*. It should, in any case, be noted that there are a wide range of other plausible interpretations of 'Ixy' available, some of which may be more plausible than my off-handed suggestion. While this may be important, when it comes to the defence of the truth of the two premisses, the exact choice is not important when considering the questions of validity and form of the influence argument.

1. $\Box(x)[Cx \supset {\sim}Ax]$
2. $(x)[Mx \supset Ax]$

N. ${\sim}(x)[Mx \,\&\, Cx]$

Having recast the argument in terms of propositions rather than instances of believings, we may start to feel there is rather less point to adding the '$\Box$' operator in front of any of the premisses. It does not seem as if much would be lost if it were deleted. Claims about propositions are typically of a conceptual sort. Now in one respect nothing is lost. The conclusion in (A*), in contrast to (A), is about propositions, not just about instances of believings of propositions. We do not expect the propositions of other possible worlds to be any different or have different logical and conceptual properties than they do in the actual world. In most of our dreams the conclusion of (A*), even without the necessity operator, will be what we want non-cognitivism to be.

But in another respect, there still is some point to marking an important *epistemological* difference between the two premisses, i.e., between the way the two premisses get defended. We are still supposing with Hume that the first premiss is to be considered some sort of conceptual truth (with or without the '$\Box$') supported at least in part by conceptual arguments and considerations. By contrast, the second premiss, whatever kind of claim it may be, is to be supported by observing instances, just the observed powers of moral judgments.

But there is a deep problem in defending the second premiss in this way (rather than as something for which conceptual arguments must be given). The problem is not just the usual difficulty of how we can go from observance of particular cases to generalisations. The problem is rather worse than that. It really concerns the observed cases rather than our induction to the unobserved cases. What actually do we observe? As Harrison points out, we may indeed have empirical grounds for supposing morality moves us to action *in some way or other,* but do we have empirical grounds for supposing that morality, unlike reason, *alone* influences us. Are we sure that no further desire or passion was required such as a desire to be moral?[10] There may be ways to answer this question, but it is not clear that more

---

10 Harrison (1976), p. 11.

55

careful observation is a way. One wouldn't expect that anatomising the circumstances and examining them in all lights would do a great deal here. It seems to be more a matter of how we ought to describe what we do observe rather than observing more closely. For this reason it is not surprising that contemporary Humeans tend to go for a second premiss which makes some claim to conceptual necessity.

TWO STRONG PREMISSES

We might then consider the best form of the argument to be one where the second premiss makes just as much a claim of conceptual necessity as does the first. Thus we have:

Argument B:
1. $\Box(x)[Cx \supset \sim Ax]$
2. $\Box(x)[Mx \supset Ax]$

N. $\Box \sim(\exists x) [Mx \& Cx]$

The first premiss says that necessarily all cognitive propositions are not 'alone influencers'. The second, by contrast, says that necessarily all moral propositions are 'alone influencers'. Thus no proposition can be both a moral one and cognitive as well.

We now think of premiss (2) as a 'conceptual truth', but not in a sense that automatically requires it to be a logical truth or even something not empirical. It could be something required by the concepts of 'common sense psychology', a theory that might be claimed to be a better explanation of the area than any competitor. In which case, the truth of premiss (2) might be something knowable by an *a priori* examination of the common sense concepts we already have. In the literature, premiss (2) is a leading instance of what is known as 'internalism' in meta-ethics.[11] 'Externalism', by

11 Falk (1947–8); Frankena (1958); Nagel (1970), ch. 2; Richards (1971), chs. 5, 13.
   Actually internalism is in a certain respect more specific, and thus more controversial, than the second premiss of either argument (B) or (D). Properly, internalism alleges the necessary connection is with a motivation *to act* (thus deleting the 'or the passions' loophole in Hume's formulation). For our purposes it is convenient to use 'internalism' in the wider sense (closer to Hume). The disadvantage of the narrower view is that it has a great many problems about many kinds of moral judgments, e.g. historical moral judgments, judgments about things on which one can have no effect, or just observations like 'There

contrast, is the view that the connection between moral belief and motivation is not a matter of this sort of conceptual necessity although such connections may exist as a matter of contingent fact or even as a matter of empirical necessity given human nature.[12] But the externalist denies it is necessary in virtue of the concepts involved.

It is sometimes supposed that accepting internalism commits one straightaway to non-cognitivism or at least a fairly subjectivist meta-ethics of some sort. The above arguments suggest this is not the case. It seems to take the first premiss as well to get the non-cognitivism of the conclusion. Plato might be a good example here. Plato denied the conclusion. He thought some propositions about the form of the Good were true (and that the truth of ordinary moral propositions must derive from this). But he also accepted a form of internalism very like premiss (2). Facts about the Good were such that, necessarily, to know them is to be attracted. Indeed the Platonic claim that to know the Good is to do it is much stronger (and rather less plausible) than Hume's mere claim that there has to be *an* influence. Of course Plato is consistent in holding both the denial of (N) and the affirmation of (2) by denying (1). Presumably he would have thought our C-beliefs about the Good provide a central counter-example to Hume's claim that C-beliefs in no case are 'alone-influencers'.

are very likely some (I don't know which) unjust judges'. Perhaps the influence argument should not concern all moral judgments but only first person present tense 'ought' or 'should' judgments. This would be sceptical enough for all practical purposes. The conclusions of the argument would tend to be that a moral judgment can be cognitive only if not related to action. They are either not practical or not cognitive.

However the wider version (closer to Hume) has a very serious difficulty in regard to its defence. Cf. note 17 below.

12 In fact internalism makes the stronger claim (2'): $\Box(x)[Mx \supset (y)Ixy]$ rather than the present claim (2): $\Box(x)[Mx \supset (\exists y)Ixy]$. The former says of any given moral proposition that *anyone* who believes it would in the right circumstances undergo some influence. The latter merely requires that for each such moral proposition there be *someone* of that sort. The usual arguments for internalism are really arguments for (2'), not just (2). Likewise externalism is better understood as the denial of (2') rather than just of (2). However, it simplifies my expositions in several respects to use the weaker (2) rather than the more usual (2'). Analogous remarks apply to the (2**) I examine in argument (D). It is similarly weaker than what we expect internalism to be.

57

But is a premiss as strong as internalism really necessary as the second premiss of the influence argument? We might try something like the following version of the argument with a terribly weak second premiss:

Argument C:
1. Cognitive propositions are such that they *can't* 'alone influence'.
2. Moral propositions, by contrast, are such that, while they don't have to, they at least *might* 'alone influence'.

N. Moral propositions are not cognitive propositions

This second premiss looks much weaker than internalism. It doesn't say that one's moral beliefs *must* be an influence in the right circumstances. It only says that a moral belief *can* influence in the right circumstances whether or not it actually goes on to be any influence at all in those circumstances. A moral belief might have done some influencing (without adding a further desire or passion) which is not to say a moral belief even in its best of circumstances *has to* (which is what internalism requires). They might influence, but needn't. But is an argument with that sort of second premiss going to be valid? Well, that depends very much on how we interpret this new version of the second premiss. The English sentence we used above for premiss (2) is nicely ambiguous. Logical symbolism is much better at disambiguating than any number of English sentences. What won't work is anything like:

1. $\Box(x)[Cx \supset {\sim}Ax]$
2. ${\sim}\Box(x)[Mx \supset {\sim}Ax]$

N. ${\sim}(\exists x)[Mx \ \& \ Cx]$

The first premiss takes a certain claim about all cognitive propositions (that they are not 'alone influencers') and asserts that claim is a *necessary* truth. The second premiss considers an analogous claim this time in regard to moral propositions and then asserts it is not a necessary truth. It is *possible* that someone believe a moral proposition and be somewhat influenced by it without there being some further desire involved in this influencing.

This argument has the advantage that the possibility claim in the second premiss is much easier to defend than the necessity claim of internalism. It has one disadvantage however. It isn't valid.[13] I propose that what we want instead is something subtly but importantly different from the above:

Argument C:
1.* $(x)[Cx \supset \Box \sim Ax]$
2.* $(x)[Mx \supset \sim\Box \sim Ax]$

N. $\sim(\exists x)[Mx \,\&\, Cx]$

The premisses of this argument make claims of *de re* necessity rather than as before *de dicto* necessity.[14] The first premiss alludes to a certain property's (i.e., not being an 'alone influencer') being an essential property of C-beliefs while the second premiss alludes to that same property's being an accidental property of M-beliefs. Talk of essential properties, while controversial in many areas, is somewhat less problematic when what we are talking about is propositions. For example, 'being believed by Hume' is an accidental property of the proposition that $2 + 2 = 4$, but 'being mathematical' is surely one of its essential properties. We can better catch the meaning of the *de re* necessity premisses in (C) if we allow ourselves the conceit of speaking in terms of possible worlds. For example, let us compare the *de dicto* necessity first premiss of both (A) and (B):

1. $\Box(x)[Cx \supset \sim Ax]$

with the *de re* necessity first premiss of argument (C):

1*. $(x)[Cx \supset \Box \sim Ax]$

The former, (1), says that in each possible world the propositions which in *that* world are cognitive will all fail to be 'alone influencers' in *that* world. The latter, (1*), says that if a proposition is cognitive, then in this or any other possible world IT (that same proposition) will continue to fail to be an 'alone influencer'. Actually it is the *de re* necessity claim (1*), rather than the *de dicto* necessity claim (1), which sounds like what the Humean would want to say. Even so,

---

13 It's just as invalid as: 'It is necessarily the case that all mathematical truths are not falsehoods, but it is not necessarily the case that all propositions believed by Hume are not falsehoods, therefore no proposition believed by Hume is also a mathematical truth'.
14 Cf. Plantinga's (1974, chs. 1, 2) discussion of *de re* and *de dicto* necessity claims. Cf. also Hughes & Cresswell (1972), pp. 183ff.

they are quite close. If proposition (1) is true, proposition (1*) would be false only if (rather oddly) the propositions which are cognitive in one world sometimes fail to be cognitive in another. (Is there perhaps a world where the Pythagorean theorem is not a cognitive proposition and where even, unlike this world, it alone influences me when I believe it?)[15]

The new second premiss, (2*), seems to capture the weaker sort of second premiss we had in mind. It only says: Take any moral proposition. There is a possible world where someone believes that proposition and is 'alone influenced' by it. That is, moral propositions (logically) can 'alone influence' when believed, even if they needn't. Thus (2*) does not even say that a moral proposition ever has actually done this, only that in each case its doing so is a logical possibility.

Thus this version, (C), of the influence argument has two advantages which centre on the second premiss. First, the second premiss is a claim very much weaker than internalism. Morals can, but needn't, be an influence. Thus there is less to defend as regards the second premiss. Second, this version of the argument, while weaker than internalism, still seems not all that susceptible to the Harrison objection which was a serious problem for the second premiss of argument (A). The second premiss of (C), i.e., (2*), says only that moral beliefs have a certain logical capacity to influence, not that they actually do or have been observed to. Presumably the argument for (2*) is going to be on logical or conceptual grounds rather than on the basis of any observations of actual cases.

We can put forward argument (C) as a partial vindication of Hume's making his second premiss weaker than his first. Hume was right in not (usually) putting anything so strong as internalism as the second premiss. Something as weak as (2*) would do. However Hume was perhaps wrong if he thought the second premiss could, without objection, be based on the everyday observation that moral beliefs 'alone influence' us. For, as Harrison points out, it is far from obvious that this is what we do observe. The argument is really rather more *a priori* than Hume suggests. Neither premiss is just a matter of everyday observation of instances.

---

15 If we accept the Barcan principle, $\Box(x)B \supset (x)\Box B$ and the plausible (as I have just argued) $(x)[Cx \supset \Box Cx]$, then (1) entails (1*). Also in modal system S5, (1*) would entail (1). Altogether we have rather good reason to consider (1) and (1*) equivalent. I owe clarification of this point to John Bacon.

Hume prefers a strong claim in the first premiss and a possibly weaker one in the second. If we are not afraid to leave Hume behind, we might consider doing it just the reverse way (e.g. Foot, 1963, p. 78). We make the second premiss some strong version of internalism and then see how much we can weaken the first premiss and still have a valid argument. Thus we have:

Argument D:

1**. $(x)[Cx \supset \sim\square Ax]$

2**. $(x)[Mx \supset \square Ax]$

N. $\sim(\exists x)[Mx \& Cx]$

The first premiss, (1**), is now much weaker. It does not say believing a cognitive proposition always has to leave everyone cold – in Hume's special way. It only says that for each cognitive proposition that is a logical possibility. This, of course, is much too weak for Hume. (Rather surprisingly some of the most recent Humean discussion seems to centre on the defense of a thesis no stronger than this.)[16] By contrast, the second premiss, (2**), is a particularly strong and interesting version of internalism. It might be contrasted with the brand of internalism found in the second premiss of argument (B):

2. $\square(x)[Mx \supset Ax]$

---

16 Thus Lewis (1988) gives an important argument against the anti-Humean view that 'some beliefs are . . . necessarily conjoined with corresponding desires' (pp. 323–4), and *a fortiori* against the more specific view that some beliefs just are desires (e.g. desires about the good). Lewis takes the views he opposes to be committed to the view that where there is such a necessary connection, the degree of credence in the belief will equal the degree of desire (cf. pp. 326–7).

Consequently the 'Humean' view Lewis defends in opposing the above is in fact weaker than even (1**), for (1**) would also rule out necessary connections between beliefs and desires even where the degrees are disparate. With *only* the very weak 'Humean' claim Lewis' argument proves as the first premiss (in an influence argument), the corresponding second premiss would have to be a particularly strong version of internalism, viz. that accepting a moral judgment is not only necessarily related to some corresponding motivation, but that the degree of acceptance of the moral judgment must *equal* the degree of the corresponding motivation. Possibly Plato held such a view, but it strikes me as a particularly implausible version of internalism. This does not provide a convincing version of the influence argument (although it might provide an *ad hominem* against some views such as Plato's).

A steady diet of proposition (2) might lead to *Hume's second nightmare*. Hume dreams that as a matter of linguistic-verbal-conceptual fact we don't call a proposition a moral proposition unless, in addition to whatever other conditions there may be, we have a special interest in its subject matter. Consequently, 'being moral' is an accidental property of propositions. The propositions which are moral ones in this world may not be the moral ones in some other possible world. Perhaps in another possible world 'Torture is wrong' is not a moral proposition because no one gets influenced at all in the right way when he believes it. Perhaps the Pythagorean theorem is a moral proposition in that world. (Well, this is a dream.) Thus, rather trivially, in any possible world all the propositions which *there* meet the qualifications for being 'moral' will also be interesting or influencing in *that* possible world (but perhaps not in others). Indeed that is all (2) requires. As it happens, Hume dreams, Clarke's special *aFc*-facts are of special interest to us in the actual world. Such beliefs do influence us. There is no necessity in this, of course. In other possible worlds such beliefs leave everyone completely cold. But the fact that we warm to them in this world allows Clarke's *aFc* propositions to satisfy the final condition for being 'moral' propositions (in this world). Thus Clarke's *aFc* propositions turn out to be, not only cognitive propositions, but moral ones as well in this world (which is where it counts). 'We are all internalists now', says Clarke.

However no such bad dreams come from a diet of (2**). It seems more like what an internalist wants internalism to be. It says: Take a moral proposition. In this, or any possible world, it will continue to be an 'alone influencer'. The necessity attaches, not to *moral* propositions but to the *content* of the propositions which are moral. Such propositions have the property of being an 'alone influencer' essentially not accidentally. That is, they have it *qua* their propositional content and not *qua* their description as 'moral'. Thus, what the internalist wants to say is, not merely that 'moral' beliefs (or propositions) must be this kind of an influencer, but that each such belief (proposition) has this property in virtue of what it is about, its content. A belief or proposition which is moral is influential not under the description 'moral' but in virtue of what it is, i.e., its content.

Analogous remarks apply when we consider how a non-cognitivist really wants to express his non-cognitivism. The non-cognitivist wants to say, not that what gets a proposition properly classified as 'moral' is some accidental feature beyond its propositional content, he wants to say that the content of any proposition which is moral is always itself something more than cognitive. It is its propositional content, and not its description as 'moral', which keeps it from being cognitive at the same time. More particularly, it isn't just that we don't *call* any proposition 'moral' unless as a mere matter of fact it also tends to influence us in the right way. The Humean who keeps this in mind can hope to have fewer sleepless nights.

CONCLUSIONS

The defensible versions of the influence argument turn out, rather surprisingly, to be rather more *a priori* than Hume suggests. Both premisses involve subtle notions of conceptual necessity and possibility. Neither is a matter of everyday observation as argument (A) suggests.

Of the other three versions which don't appeal to such observation, argument (B) is the most ambitious for a Humean to try to defend for it involves two strong premisses. Its first premiss is committed to a Humean theory of motivation. Its second premiss, a kind of internalism, is just as controversial. By contrast, argument (C) looks easier to defend. Its first premiss is still committed to a Humean theory of motivation but something very much weaker than internalism takes over in the second premiss.

On the other hand, in either argument (B) or (D) the Humean has the task of defending the strong thesis of internalism in the second premiss. These days it is rather more difficult for a Humean to be smug about internalism. I hope, in fact, I have contributed to the Humean's doubts by showing how easy it is to confuse internalism with those rather trivial, close-counterfeits of internalism which occur in 'Hume's two nightmares' and which are in fact of some consolation to his enemies. The versions of internalism which Hume needs for the influence argument to work are far from trivial and involve some subtle modal claims. But in addition to this, other, more substantial, objections to the plausibility of internalism have been raised in the literature.[17] I will not repeat these

17 Cf. Richards (1971), chs. 5, 13.
When pressed the Humean might try to extricate himself by using the loop-

here. I do not say that internalism has been demonstrated to be false. I only make the modest claim that it is very difficult these days to be smug about internalism or confidently to base a case for non-cognitivism on such a controversial premiss. I leave the further discussion of internalism to the philosophical literature since the point of this book is the pursuit of smug Humeans.

Humeans tend to have fewer doubts about the strong version of the first premiss, the one involving some Humean theory of motivation and action, than about the strong version of the second, some version of internalism. Thus, argument (C) would seem to have a clear advantage over the others. Besides being the argument closest to Hume's text (once we reject (A)), it has the clear advantage that it doesn't require anything as strong as internalism in the second premiss so that just about all the burden shifts to the first premiss. Humeans who are confident about Hume's theory of motivation will consider this, after all, the best way to proceed. In fact this all seems to vindicate Hume's exposition of the argument with emphasis on a strong first premiss. The theory of motivation and action in that premiss bears the weight (and we don't bother with anything as strong as internalism in the other premiss).

And what could be very controversial about that first premiss?

holes provided by Hume's 'and affections' in the second premiss. Thus, if there isn't, after all, any kind of influence on the actions, in a given case, it might still be claimed there is some influence on the passions. This way out looks very suspect. Typically, moral beliefs do go along not with just any old passions, feelings, emotions, etc., but specifically with *moral* ones. Motivations to feel are rather different in this respect from motivations to act. The latter can be specified in terms of the actions they tend to produce while the latter typically are specified in terms of a tendency to feel *moral* feelings. A stock point in recent philosophical psychology is that the analysis of moral emotions typically involves the attribution of moral beliefs to the agent. Cf. Bedford (1956–7). Thus the Humean trying to utilise the loophole provided by the 'and affections' clause must be able to specify the passion or affection in a way that makes no question-begging reference to the agent's moral beliefs (for whether the latter are passions rather than cognitive beliefs is the very issue at question in the influence argument). Certainly we must view with suspicion the Humean who defends the second premiss in a particularly difficult case by saying such things as 'Well, the agent's belief that torture is wrong admittedly didn't have any influence at all on his tendency to act but it still tends to produce in him *the attitude* that torture is wrong'. Dogmatic Humeans, especially, are good at being always able to find that sort of 'affection' as a vindication of Hume's second premiss.

3

Some bad reasons for believing the first premiss

Those who say philosophy is the search for truth overlook that other pursuit of philosophy, the search for nonsense. They miss a good part of the fun. The investigation of really magnificent confusions or of irresistibly compelling conceptual illusions usually has it all over plodding along after wherever the argument leads. Chapters 4 and 5 risk that kind of dullness. They pursue some good reasons for not believing Hume's first premiss. But the present chapter considers the bad, but seductive, reasons so many have had for accepting that premiss. This is important. It is usually not enough to give good arguments against a prevailing prejudice. One must also explain why so many have found it compelling.

Something close to Hume's first premiss (strong version) is held, or just assumed, by a great many contemporary philosophers.[1] We can find something like it, for example, in D. Davidson's classic article 'Actions, Reasons and Causes' (1963). (This and other contemporary versions are discussed in Chapter 4.) Davidson presents as relatively unproblematic what I will call his 'pro-attitude account' of what it is for an agent to have done something for a reason (or to have a reason for doing it). Where an agent 'does something for a reason' (or 'has a reason for doing something'):

1. He has some sort of pro-attitude toward actions of that kind,

and

2. He believes that his action is of that kind,

where 'pro-attitude' covers not only:

a. Desires, wantings, urges, promptings,

but also:

1 Cf., for example, Brandt (1979), ch. 3, particularly p. 83.

b. Moral views, aesthetic principles, economic prejudices, social conventions, public and private goals and values.

In Chapter 4 I discuss how this jargon word 'pro-attitude' covers a multitude of ambiguities and how many of the things in (b) are importantly different from most of the things in (a). However for the present it is enough to be a bit suspicious of such an open-ended notion covering such a mixed bag of things. One suspects it will be rather too easy to defend a thesis involving 'pro-attitudes' just because one should be able to manufacture a 'pro-attitude' for almost any counter-example which is proposed. A term like 'pro-attitude' can expand or contract as the occasion, or the counter-example, requires.

In addition to the above pro-attitude thesis, Davidson has a further thesis, viz. that explanations of the above sort are *causal*. His essay and much of his subsequent work are concerned with the difficulties which arise in regard to this further thesis, his 'causal thesis'. By contrast, his 'pro-attitude account', just by itself, is treated as relatively unproblematic. Perhaps he just thinks it common sense (or 'folk psychology').

Davidson's pro-attitude account of (motivating) reasons for action seems to entail everything Hume's first premiss says about action and indeed a bit more as well. Davidson's account entails that in an explanation of action we need both (1) pro-attitudes and (2) cognitive beliefs. Thus it follows that just cognitive beliefs alone are insufficient, which is pretty close to Hume's first premiss (as regards action). But the pro-attitude account seems to be saying a bit more as well. It does not merely say that beliefs alone are insufficient to explain action, it says that a pro-attitude is required as well. But even this further bit sounds like Hume when he says that reason is the 'slave of the passions' (reading 'pro-attitudes' for 'passions'). But we can say more than this. We have seen that the way we must read Hume's influence argument to make it both valid and initially plausible requires a special sense of 'alone' in both premisses. 'Alone' does not mean 'utterly alone' but only 'without the help of a distinct, separate desire'. Thus Hume's first premiss, properly read, comes close to requiring what the pro-attitude account does, a distinct additional passion. Indeed, at the beginning of Chapter 4 I discuss one reason for thinking Davidson's account makes for a rather better first premiss in an influence argument than Hume's own formulation.

So something like Hume's first premiss is often held in contemporary philosophy as something just obvious, self-evident, or perhaps an implicit axiom of 'folk psychology'. Of course another possibility is that it is only certain vulgar conceptual confusions which lead people to think it obvious (in much the same way as first year philosophy students who have not read Butler think psychological egoism is armchair-obvious). A preliminary, at any rate, must be to sweep away all the confusions. Here are some.

EXCESSIVE PRESSURE ON 'ALONE'

Normal claims of the form '*a* caused *b*' assume normal circumstances, standard background conditions, or some such thing. For example we are often happy to say things like: 'The spark caused the explosion'. Of course it is possible to put great pressure on the poor word 'alone' so that it comes to mean 'utterly alone', i.e., 'even apart from all the normal background conditions'. With such a stretched usage then even in cases where we would ordinarily say 'The spark caused the explosion' we will not be able to say 'The spark *alone* caused the explosion'. Indeed it now becomes most unlikely that anything ever *alone* causes anything else. And that, of course, provides a rather cheap way of defending Hume's first premiss, should it ever get into too much difficulty. Just as sparks never do it *utterly alone,* so a mere belief has no chance of being a cause apart from the standard conditions where the person is not drugged, not asleep, not suffering a cerebral haemorrhage before the belief has a chance to do anything, etc. The cost of ensuring the truth of premiss (1) in this cheap manner is that it also almost certainly ensures the falsehood of the second premiss (even under its weakest interpretation). When we say that our moral judgments do, or even can, have an influence on our actions, we are assuming standard background conditions. A moral belief is no more able than a cognitive belief to have an influence on a person asleep, drugged, or suffering a cerebral haemorrhage. Even under the best of circumstances a moral judgment can't do its influencing utterly alone.

I suppose one way to avoid the above difficulty is to understand 'alone' such that it excludes none of the standard background conditions. But now we must avoid letting the pendulum swing back too far in that direction. The standard background conditions might well include certain long-standing, quite wired-in passions or pro-attitudes. Thus, if 'alone' means 'without any help except such assistance as the standard background conditions provide', even on Hume-Davidson grounds, a belief might well be an influence 'alone'. The solution, of course, is to understand 'alone' in the influence argument to exclude nothing more than distinct, additional passions (or pro-attitudes) but to allow everything else. Thus 'alone' does not exclude normal background conditions *except* any passions (pro-attitudes) in those conditions. Nor does it exclude any number of additional factors (such as cognitive beliefs) as long as they do not involve distinct, additional passions (pro-attitudes). This is the meaning required for the influence argument to be plausible at all. But it also means that premiss (1) cannot be defended by stretching the meaning of 'alone' out to 'utterly alone' just because that makes premiss (1) so much easier to defend.

A VULGAR MODAL FALLACY

It is a common fallacy, facilitated by ordinary language, to slide from 'need not' to 'cannot', i.e., to suppose the former just entails the latter, or worse, just not to distinguish them at all. The claim that cognitive beliefs *need not* influence makes for a weak premiss (1) such as we find in argument (D) of Chapter 2. The claim that they *cannot* influence is more like the strong claim we find in the first premisses of arguments (B) and (C). It is the claim we are now considering. Naturally a strong premiss is more convenient when one is trying to draw conclusions from it, but a weaker premiss is nicer when one has to defend it.

The fallacy consists in going from something of the form '$\sim\Box$ p' to something of the form '$\Box \sim p$'. Here is a clear counter-example. Suppose a struck match caused an explosion. While this is a fact, it is only a contingent fact. It is not a necessary truth that the match caused the explosion. Even if not empirically, then at least *logically*, it *need not* have caused the explosion. However it does not follow from the fact that it need not have caused the explosion that it *could not* have caused the explosion. Indeed by our original hypothesis it was the cause. Likewise it is fallacious to suppose that because a cognitive belief in any particular case need not have been an influence it could not have been an influence. Who could confuse 'need not' with 'cannot'?

Two examples: First, Rachel Kydd defending Hume's first premiss has us consider any cognitive judgment and says, 'it is always possible to make this judgment and remain quite unaffected by it' (1946, p. 70). This is true. Even if my learning the building is about to collapse did influence me, it need not have in the sense that there is a logically possible world where I greet this news with indifference. But all that this says is that no (cognitive) judgment need have been an influence. By contrast Hume's first premiss is about how, in a certain manner, no cognitive judgment can be an influence. A second example: In an allusion to Hume's argument G.E.M. Anscombe says 'And no amount of truth as to what *is* the case could possibly have a logical claim to have influence on your actions' (1958, p. 31). This sentence suffers from an excess of modalities (perhaps the redundance is to provide emphasis). One way to read it is as 'no amount of truth . . . ha[s] a logical claim to have influence'. This could mean that it is never of logical necessity that a cognitive belief be an influence, i.e., the 'need not' claim. It is this interpretation which gives the sentence the aura of the obvious and the uncontroversial. But perhaps it should read: 'No amount of truth . . . could . . . have an influence'. That is the 'cannot' claim. Anscombe, indeed, does go on to say, 'It is not judgment as such that sets us in motion; but our judgment on how to get or do something we *want*'. This would seem to be the stronger claim that belief alone (without a want) *cannot* move us to act. Of course it is this stronger and more controversial thesis which is required in Hume's version of the argument.

The confusion perpetrated becomes almost irresistible if one combines the modal fallacy with excessive pressure on 'alone'. Here the argument is from 'While it did it, it *need not* have' to 'Therefore, it *cannot* have done it *alone*'. Here something like principle of sufficient reason gets used as well. The argument goes like this: Let us suppose that *a* did cause *b* but that, as we would expect, this is a *contingent* truth, that is:

i. *a* caused *b* in actual world W

but

ii. There is another possible world, W', (with *a*) where it is false that *a* caused *b*.

We also accept a certain principle of sufficient reason which entails:

iii. There must be some difference between W and W′ which explains, or is the reason why, *a* caused *b* in W but not in W′.

Consequently, from (i), (ii), (iii):

iv. It was not 'alone' that *a* caused *b* even in world W for it also required the presence (or absence) of some feature in W which was absent (or present) in W′.

But precisely this whole argument is repeatable for any possible world, not just W, in which *a* contingently causes *b*. Thus in any possible world where *a* contingently causes *b*, it is not the case that *a* did it 'alone'. Hence:

v. It is impossible that *a* 'alone' causes *b* as a matter of contingent fact.

We need an exterminator before this proliferates further. First, we should probably reject the principle of sufficient reason behind (iii), for reasons I will not discuss here. Second, even if we accept (iii) we must certainly resist the move from it to (iv). The relevant difference in the two possible worlds might be in their causal laws, world W having a law, L, connecting *a*'s with *b*'s while W′ lacks L. But L is not another cause along with *a*. Nor was *a* causally insufficient by itself. Finally, if this were a good argument it would prove too much. Being perfectly general, it would apply to the ability of moral judgments to influence us 'alone'. Even the weak version of premiss (2) would have been refuted.

THE MOTIVATION ONE CAN ALWAYS FIND

Suppose we were on the point of producing a clear counter-example to the Humean. That is, we had a case of a cognitive belief which did succeed in influencing, motivating, affecting action. There's still one way for the Humean to snatch victory from defeat. If a belief by itself did do some influencing, there is still something a bit conative-looking in all this, viz. the influencing done by this belief. To be a counter-example at all to premiss (1), there must be the belief's influencing, motivating to action, affecting, moving to action. And why not call this a 'pro-attitude' as well (since we slap this label about with few reservations as it is)? So the pro-attitude was there after all! Humeans need worry no further about

70

premiss (1); even the *imaginary* counter-examples conform to the Hume-Davidson model. Even the counter-examples – aren't.[2]

Now this is as bad as arguing that no cause ever brought about an effect *by itself* because there always had to be one further thing present, viz. the causal connection between it and the effect. But the causal connection is not itself another cause, not itself one of the relata it relates. Sparks sometimes cause explosions and, whatever other causes may have had to be present, a free sprinkling of essence of causation is not among those further causes.

It is this bogus ploy of turning counter-examples into further confirming instances (of finding the pro-attitude or the passion in the very influencing relation) which may account for that 'but-how-could-it-be-false' feeling we have about Hume's first premiss. But we will not allow Humeans to find their pro-attitudes in the very influencing (or moving or motivating) relation. What they must show is that there must always be a *further* passion or pro-attitude present distinct from the influencing relation that relates it, as distinct, indeed, as the cognitive belief is distinct from that relation. If the Humean says it takes more than a belief to move us, that it takes a passion, we will not allow him to find that passion precisely in our being moved by the belief.

HUME'S ARGUMENT FOR THE FIRST PREMISS

Humeans will no doubt deny that they are guilty of the silly mistakes discussed in the last few pages. We will accept their word and keep them to it. Certainly Hume's defence of the first premiss is not simply a matter of these mistakes. Hume tries to prove his strong first premiss by appeal to a prior claim I will label 'proposition (P)'. This proposition is an unusually powerful and fruitful one, if Hume is to be believed. Hume expresses this proposition in several different ways (458):

2 Nagel (1970, ch. 5) and others (e.g., Platts, 1980, p. 74) accuse the Humean of some such trivialising move. The present point broadly overlaps with the one Nagel makes about turning mere motivational direction into a desire. Hume's notion of 'influencing' is clearly causal, so the present objection can be put in a slightly different way as the charge that it is a mistake to turn the causing into another cause. Such general trivialising moves need to be sharply distinguished from the trivialising defenses of what I call the 'provocative Humean theory of motivation'. Cf. Chapter 5.

i. No action, passion or volition can be either (a) true or (b) false.

ii. No action, passion or volition can be either (a) conformable to reason or (b) contrary to reason.

iii. No action, passion or volition can be either (a) reasonable or (b) unreasonable.

We need to distinguish a number of quite different interpretations of what Hume's claim is here. The first, which is really Hume's official version, goes back to the discussion in II, iii, 3. There Hume points out that a passion (and presumably an action or volition) 'contains not any representative quality, which renders it a copy of any other existence, or modification' (415). Hume says passions, volitions and actions are 'original facts and realities, compleat in themselves, and implying no reference to other passions, volitions, and actions. 'Tis impossible, therefore, they can be pronounced either true or false' (458). Passions (and actions and volitions) are not simply representations of, or statements of, any state of affairs. Thus, we may say, Hume's official interpretation of (P) is:

P1. No action, passion, volition is, in its entirely, the sort of thing to be either (a) true or (b) false.

except that they may be 'false' in two (manner-of-speaking) senses (416):

a. When 'founded on the supposition of the existence of objects, which really do not exist'.

and,

b. When 'we choose means insufficient for the design'd end and deceive ourselves in our judgment of causes and effects'.

In short, Hume denies that any action or passion *as a whole* is a proposition even if sometimes an action or a passion *involves* a judgment. Actions and passions are not propositions. Of course, as Clarke might point out, there can still be propositions *about* actions and passions. Thus Clarke's view so far seems perfectly consistent with (P1). Clarke's view is that moral propositions about actions and passions are true or false (i.e., propositions of form '*aFc*' are true or false). That is consistent with the claim in (P1) that actions and passions are not themselves true or false (i.e., what '*a*' refers to in '*aFc*' is not something true or false).

While this is the official interpretation, sometimes Hume's wording suggests another. He wants to oppose all the usual talk in philosophy about a 'combat of passion and reason' (413). Hume says it is impossible that a passion 'can be oppos'd by . . . truth and reason' (415). Thus we may also have:

P2. No action, passion, volition can be either (a) motivated by cognitive beliefs alone or (b) motivationally opposed by cognitive beliefs alone.

Thus (a) and (b) above give us another sense of 'conformable to reason' and 'contrary to reason' respectively. The problem with (P2) is not that it does not entail Hume's first premiss. It does that admirably. It *is* that same premiss. Hence (P2) gives us no new reason for believing premiss (1) of the influence argument, although the confusion of (P2) with the other interpretations of proposition (P) may create the illusion that it does.

Hume sometimes expressed (P) as the view that no action, passion, or volition can be either (a) reasonable or (b) unreasonable. In that regard we cannot omit quoting one of Hume's more notorious passages (416):

'Tis not contrary to reason to prefer the destruction of the whole world to the scratching of my finger. 'Tis not contrary to reason for me to chuse my total ruin, to prevent the least uneasiness of an *Indian* or person wholly unknown to me. 'Tis as little contrary to reason to prefer my own acknowledg'd lesser good to my greater, and have a more ardent affection for the former than the latter.

Hume denies that such preferences (unless based on false C-judgments) are in themselves 'unreasonable'.

Now in ordinary English 'reasonable' and 'unreasonable' are often used to evaluate actions and feelings. Sometimes the term is used to make a kind of moral criticism, to suggest that one is not looking at things from a social point of view. Sometimes the term is used in a way that is normative but not particularly moral. To say 'x is unreasonable' is to say, perhaps along with other things, that x is wrong, or is a mistake, or exhibits a mistake in practical reasoning. Now one way it is tempting to interpret (P), whether or not Hume ever intended it, is:

P3. No proposition of the form 'x is reasonable' or of the form 'x is unreasonable' (where 'x' refers to an action, passion, volition and where 'reasonable' and 'unreasonable' have moral or normative force) is capable of being true or false.

(P3) is not to be confused with (P1). The latter says actions, etc., cannot be true or false. The former says certain propositions about actions cannot be true or false. Of course the problem with (P3) is that it begs the issue in a manner even worse than (P2) does. (P3) just *is* the conclusion of the influence argument. That is, it already is (N), non-cognitivism, or at least its application to the central case of normatively reasonable and unreasonable action. (P3) is a large part of the non-cognitivism Hume wants for the conclusion of the influence argument. Consequently to use it to ground (the relatively less controversial) first premiss, (1), of that argument can only beg the question. (P3) must be rejected as firmly as (P2) as a usable interpretation of proposition (P).

However Hume's famous "Tis not contrary to reason' passage and the ordinary normative use of 'reasonable' and 'unreasonable' readily suggest two further interpretations of (P). Rather oddly, both of these are themselves normative propositions (rather than being about normative propositions), although that is sometimes disputed in the first case:

P4. Every action (passion, volition) is permissible (i.e., nothing is wrong).

Even choosing the destruction of the world, or one's own ruin, isn't wrong. Some will perhaps think that (P4) is in fact no different from (P3), that non-cognitivism is, or entails, the universal permission in (P4). However, I argue in Chapter 6 that (P4) is a normative claim. After all it is the denial of the clearly normative view that sometimes some things are wrong. It is one side of a very large moral issue. Thus the normative claim of (P4) is not to be confused with the non-cognitivism of (P3). The latter makes a claim about the status of moral judgments but is not itself a moral judgment. But, as I will argue, (P4) is itself a moral judgment.

Indeed, if Hume could show that (P4) is *true,* which is what he must do to use it to support premiss (1), then he would have produced a clear counter-example to (N), the non-cognitivism he wants to prove as conclusion of the influence argument. For (N) says that all moral judgments, including the moral judgment in (P4) above, are neither true nor false. On the other hand if (P4) is merely a moral judgment Hume assents to (perhaps thereby expressing a sentiment or a lack of a sentiment) but not anything which is true or false, then (P4) becomes a rather unsuitable basis for arguing for premiss (1) and, ultimately, the conclusion (N).

Hume wants to show non-cognitivism is true. Thus he doesn't want to base his argument for (N) on a non-cognitive proposition such as (P4). In short, (P4) neither follows from (N), non-cognitivism, nor can it be part of the argument for (N). At best it is a totally unrelated attitude or sentiment that one might (with great difficulty, I think) sustain.

There is yet another way to interpret Hume's famous 'not contrary to reason' passage. This gives us an interpretation which is quite clearly and uncontroversially normative. It becomes the thesis that passions are indeed good reasons for acting, indeed they are ultimately the only good reasons. Thus we get:

P5. Humean Theory of Justifying Reasons: Desires (preferences, sentiments) are the only good (i.e., rationally justifying) grounds for acting (choosing, preferring).

This is the view that actions are indeed reasonable or unreasonable. They are to be rationally justified in terms of the agent's passions and *only* in terms of his passions. However ultimately passions (desires) are not themselves reasonable or unreasonable (rationally justified or unjustified). You just have them. Well, actually Hume qualifies this. Even a passion may be criticised as unreasonable or unjustified when based on a mistaken judgment about existence or causal connections (416). But if the destruction of the world is what you really want (i.e., if it is based on no mistaken beliefs), then it does provide a rationally justifying reason for acting. (P5) is a normative theory (although perhaps not a moral theory). It allows there is such a thing as rational justification of action and sets the terms of such justification in terms of the agent's desires and nothing else. It is a theory of justifying reasons held by many Humeans and we have reason to discuss it further in Chapters 4 and 5. Whether Hume actually entertained (P5) is perhaps not clear. There is the famous passage where he says that reason not only is the slave of the passions but 'ought' to be as well (415). There is also the nicely ambiguous passage in the *Enquiry* (293) which we will take up in this regard in Chapter 4. I am going to count (P5) as a 'Humean' doctrine just because it so inevitably gets entangled in the issues I want to discuss.

The theory of justification of action in (P5) is clearly and blatantly normative. Non-cognitivism gives us no more reason to assent to this normative view than to any other. While a non-cognitivist might express a favourable sentiment toward deciding what to do on the basis of (P5), nothing in non-cognitivism says one must, or must not, do so. In any case there is a certain dilemma involved in trying to use (P5), or any normative claim, to prove premiss (1) and, thus, conclusion (N). If one insists (P5) is *true,* then that automatically provides a clear counter-example to the conclusion (N). We have a normative claim that is cognitive and indeed true. Nor does it do any good to insist that non-cognitivism only claims no *moral* propositions are cognitive and that (P5) is normative but not moral. The influence argument, if it works at all, can be easily generalised to show any normative claim is non-cognitive. On the other hand, if one says (P5) is not the sort of thing to be true or false, then it is hardly the sort of thing to use to show the truth of non-cognitivism. And of course the non-cognitivist wants to say it is *true* that moral judgments are neither true nor false.

We can now summarise our conclusions on which interpretation of (P) is going to be of use to ground the first premiss of Hume's influence argument. (P2) just *is* Hume's premiss (1) so its use is question-begging. (P3) just is the conclusion, (N), or at least is a large part of (N). Its use would be even more question-begging. (P4) and, more obviously, (P5) are normative claims. As such, they are hardly what a non-cognitivist wants in order to prove non-cognitivism is *true.* This leaves (P1) as the only respectable version of (P). (P1) also seems to be true. From now on, unless otherwise indicated, we will take (P) to be the same as (P1).

THE 'DIRECT ARGUMENT' FROM (P) TO (N)

Proposition (P), whatever exactly it is supposed to mean, is nothing short of miraculous. As we have seen, Hume thinks it proves non-cognitivism, (N), 'indirectly' by proving the first premiss of the influence argument which, along with the second, proves the conclusion (N). But Hume thinks (P) is also capable of dispensing with all the 'middle men', i.e., premisses (1) and (2) of the influence argument, and proving quite 'directly' the same conclusion. If we had known this earlier it might have saved us all that complicated discussion about *de re* and *de dicto* versions of premisses (1) and (2) of the influence argument. We could have got the conclusion quite directly with just (P) alone. (And will it also cure warts, one wonders?)

Why does Hume think (P) proves his conclusion 'directly'? This is one of the several points where the systematic ambiguity discussed in Chapter 1 bears on an understanding of Hume. Hume is ambiguous, indeed confused, as to what the conclusion of this direct argument is supposed to be:

For it [i.e., (P)] proves *directly* that actions do not derive their merit from a conformity to reason, nor their blame from a contrariety to it. (458)

What follows the 'that' is subtly ambiguous. Hume does not notice it could mean either of two different things. However we must insist on distinguishing:

i. A version of non-cognitivism: Any claim of the form 'action *a* has merit' or 'action *a* is blameworthy' is not a claim that can be derived from reason alone (i.e., is neither true nor false).

ii. A thesis of virtue morality: Actions do indeed have merit, but the merit never simply consists in ('does not derive from') agents' correct reasoning; likewise, some acts really are blameworthy but that's never just a matter of agents' cognitive error.

Just a blink and the question of whether the wonderful proposition (P) proves (N), non-cognitivism, has become instead the question of whether it proves (V), virtue morality. We suddenly seem involved in substantive moral issues about which just a second ago it was claimed reason cannot determine either truth or falsehood.

But let's keep our eye fixed firmly on the issue. Does (P) prove *non-cognitivism* 'directly'? (P1), the only respectable version of (P), says that actions, passion, and such do not represent, are not literally true or false (except in the two senses Hume allows). (N) says that certain set of propositions (i.e., the moral ones), *about* actions, passions, etc., are neither true nor false. Surely the truth of (P1) is consistent with the falsehood of (N). For example, Samuel Clarke can agree that actions and passions themselves are not true or false (except in Hume's two senses) but still insist that propositions *about* actions and passions, including moral ones, can be true or false. (N) simply will not follow from (P1). Possibly the Humean is just assuming his sentimentalism, (S), at this point. According to some versions of (S), moral judgments just are passions. In which case, given (P1), they will be neither true nor false. But this is only arguing in circles. We might remember that the Humean's argu-

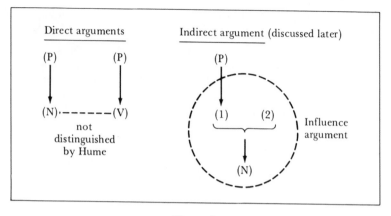

Figure 3

ment for (S) rests precisely on whatever argument there is for its negative component, i.e., (N). And (N) is what the direct argument now tries to prove with just (P1). This is the sort of circle worthy of only the most dogmatic Humean. There is no direct argument from (P) to (N).

THE 'DIRECT ARGUMENT' FROM (P) TO (V)

This argument is of pathological interest. The confusion of this direct argument with the preceding one explains why Hume would have thought there was some sort of 'direct' argument available as well as the more 'indirect' one employing the influence argument.[3] But the confusion consists in thinking that an argument for virtue morality is the same thing as an argument for non-cognitivism, that in proving (V) he is proving (N). Even this second direct argument (from (P) to (V)) has at least a couple of versions depending on which particular interpretation of that all-purpose proposition (P) is employed. For example, if we take the official interpretation, (P1), we get:

3 The claim that (P) proves (V) is what Harrison (1976, ch. 2) calls 'Hume's second argument'. It is distinct from the influence argument ('Hume's first argument') because its conclusion is (V) rather than (N). This 'second argument' runs from 458 (where it is entangled with the influence argument) to the top of 463.

P1. No action, passion, etc., as a whole represents, i.e., is true or false.

[A. Assumption: There are some actual cases of acts, etc. which are virtuous and others which are vicious.]

V1. The virtue (vice) found in any actual act, etc., does not consist in its being literally true (false).

Hence Wollaston's moral theory (or something close to it) is just wrong.[4] If there are actual cases of virtue then that virtue cannot consist in a property of acts which it is quite impossible for them to have.

Sometimes the argument from (P) to (V) takes the second interpretation of (P):

P2. No action, passion, etc. is either (a) alone motivated by C-beliefs nor (b) motivationally opposed by C-beliefs alone.

[Assumption A as before]

V2. The virtue found in any actual act, etc., does not derive from its being motivated solely by C-beliefs nor does an act's vice ever consist in its being motivationally opposed by C-beliefs on their own.

As before the argument is that the virtue and vice in actual cases cannot consist in a property which is metaphysically impossible. Of course this depends on the controversial claim in philosophical psychology, (P2), which as we have noted just *is* premiss (1) of the influence argument. We have not yet in our discussion encountered anything like a good argument for this claim although we have encountered a few bad ones.

Hume actually wants to argue for something additional to (V2). He also wants to claim:

V2′. The virtue (vice) in actions, passions, etc., does not consist in either its *being caused* (even with appropriate assistance) by true (false) beliefs nor in its *causing* true (false) beliefs.

Hume admits that no form of (P) can be used to argue for (V2′). Hume cannot argue, parallel to the previous cases: Being virtuous cannot consist in having this causal connection to beliefs because then virtue would be impossible. Hume explicitly admits that *these* kinds of casual connections between actions, etc., and 'reason' are not impossible (459). So Hume is forced to give special arguments for (V2′)

---

4 Wollaston [1724], cf. selections in Selby-Bigge, ed. (1897) or in Raphael, ed. (1969).

which he conceives as completing the case against Wollaston (459–61).[5] At such points in Hume's discussion he is clearly appealing to the structure of our conventionally held moral beliefs. The discussion is very far from anything bearing on non-cognitivism.

The overall verdict on the 'direct argument' has to be this. Hume thinks he has a direct argument from the amazing proposition (P) to (N), non-cognitivism, only because he systematically confuses (N) with (V), virtue morality. In giving arguments directly from (P) to (V) he really thinks that is directly proving (N).[6] This confusion about the conclusion to be shown is compounded by the fact that there are several importantly different versions of the amazing premiss (P). But after all that, there is in fact no *direct* argument at all from (P) to (N). Let us hope the *indirect* argument from (P) to (N) fares better.

THE 'INDIRECT ARGUMENT' FROM (P) TO (N)

This brings us back to the influence argument and the question of how to argue for the very strong claim in the first premiss of that argument. Hume's indirect argument meets that challenge by attempting to use the all-purpose proposition (P) to make a case for premiss (1) of the influence argument (cf. figure 3 above). Premiss (1), along with the relatively less controversial second premiss, make for the influence argument for non-cognitivism (cf. 'The influence argument' section of Chapter 2). To do this (P1) is really the only version of (P), of those we discussed, which is available. The others, (P2) through (P5), either beg the issue in some way or else, being normative, are not the kind of material on which a non-cognitivist would want to build.

Does (P1) then support Hume's premiss (1)? It seems to me the idea of such an argument would go something like this:

P1.   A passion is just something you have (an 'original existence'). It is not, in its entirety, a belief or a representation of what is the case. Conversely, a belief is not a passion.

Premiss (1): A belief alone cannot be an influence on the actions or preferences.

5 Here Hume rests a lot on his a-mistake-of-fact-be-not-criminal argument (460) which I questioned briefly in Chapter 1.
6 Harrison (1976, pp. 24–5) accuses Hume of an *ignoratio elenchi* in this regard.

This does not follow if it is consistent to suppose the amazing (P1) and yet deny (1). Let us then suppose (1) is false, that is there is a possible case where a certain belief alone influences. Of course it is very difficult to get Humeans to imagine just this. Some will say, 'But if the belief really did influence one, then there was something extra after all, i.e., the "influencing" '. So a *further* 'passion' was there after all and the belief didn't really do it *alone*. But this is just the mistake of supposing the influencing relation is itself among the influences it relates (see an earlier section of this chapter, 'The motivation one can always find'). So we ask the Humean to try again to imagine that a belief alone influences us. But once the Humean succeeds in imagining this, he is likely to say that anything that really did succeed in influencing us by itself must, for that very reason, be *counted as* a passion. But that means he is being asked to imagine a belief which is also a passion. And that is to imagine the amazing (P1) false. So this Humean can imagine premiss (1) of the influence argument false only by imagining the amazing (P1) false. But the Humean really thinks (P1) is true, so he must in consistency hold Hume's (1) as well.

This seems to me to be a bad argument. It would also be a bad argument on Hume's own grounds. He would not have agreed that a thing is to be classified as a 'passion' just because it bears the alone-influencing relation to some act or passion in the agent. That would allow things to get classified as 'passions', not for what they are, but because of their causal relationships to other things. But as figure 1 in Chapter 1 makes clear, Hume thought of passions as something before the mind, as a species of impressions and ultimately a species of perceptions. They don't get classified as such for their further casual powers. However some contemporary Humeans reject Hume on just this point (cf. Smith, 1987, pp. 45–50). They would replace Hume's 'phenomenological conception' of passion with a more dispositional account.

But if we do suppose that being an alone-influencer (or having a disposition to alone-influence) is enough to make anything a 'passion', we then start to question the plausibility of (P1). Admittedly, this supposition supports the view that (P1) entails (1), but at the cost of undermining proposition (P1). If, in the imagined case, a belief really did (or can) influence by itself, why not say it is both a belief and a passion – contrary to (P1)? It is a belief in virtue of its representative qualities, a passion in virtue of what it tends to cause or influence. Such a belief is indeed true or false (i.e., representative), while its being an influence (i.e., a passion) as well is not itself anything representative or capable of being true or false but a causal relation that the belief bears to other things. In short, we have a dilemma here: Insofar as, like Hume, we think of what makes something a passion as *not* a matter of the causal influencing relations it bears but something more 'internal', it becomes less obvious that (P1) does entail (1). But insofar as, unlike Hume, we ensure (P1) entails (1) by making a thing's causal influencing relations a sufficient condition for its being a passion, we thereby construct a sense of 'passion' under which (P1) starts to look very dubious. Only by shifting about the notion of a 'passion' as suits the occasion can one make it appear there is a sound argument from (P1) to Hume's premiss (1).[7]

CONCLUSION

The first premiss of Hume's influence argument may seem more plausible than it should to those subject to the vulgar fallacies and conceptual confusions discussed in the first half of this chapter. Hume argued for this premiss on quite different grounds, but grounds which I think are also bad. It is important to sweep all these confusions and bad arguments aside and not confuse them with whatever good arguments there are for this thesis.

I would suggest there is a more reputable way of arguing for premiss (1) of the influence argument. One might see it as a deeply embedded axiom of 'folk psychology' or as something required by its core concepts. If premiss (1) is something we are committed to by the acceptance common sense psychology, then premiss (1) rises or falls with the empirical adequacy of that theory. This is not at all Hume's way of arguing. His is rather more a matter of peering at and comparing all the immediately available contents of the mind.

---

7 Harrison (1976, pp. 21–2) thinks Hume goes wrong in a different way.
  For an important contemporary defence of something close to (P1) see Lewis (1988) and J. Collins (1988). However the refutation of the 'desire as belief' thesis, as they call it, still falls short of showing anything as strong as Hume's 'cannot influence' first premiss (although the latter entails the falsehood of the 'desire as belief' thesis). Cf. note 16 to Chapter 2 above.

But the suggested alternative approach is one that contemporary philosophers congenial to Hume's claim will find much more plausible.

Can Hume's first premiss be defended as a truth required by the concepts and implicit theory of common sense psychology?

4

The Humean theory of motivating reasons

There could well be two theories about reasons for acting and preferring in Hume. One is a theory of motivating reasons. The other is a theory of justifying reasons.[1] While they might be related in some way, they are not to be just confused outright. The former is a descriptive thesis about what further has to be involved beyond a belief if an agent is to have a *motivating reason* for acting (or preferring) where a motivating reason is one sort of thing that can sometimes help to explain an agent's acting (or preferring). The latter thesis is a normative thesis about what has to be involved if there is to exist a *good reason* for an agent to act (or prefer) in certain ways (whether or not the agent is aware of this or motivated by it) where a good reason is something that can justify an agent's acting (or preferring) in certain ways. In both cases, however, it is something like a passion, desire, want, pro-attitude, etc., which is said to be this further thing which has always to be involved.

In contemporary philosophy we can find both a Humean theory of motivating reasons and a Humean theory of justifying reasons, whether or not we can find both of these in Hume. The former clearly can be found in premiss (1) of the influence argument. However it is not quite so obvious that we can attribute the Humean theory of justifying reasons to Hume, although he may have lapsed into it in unguarded, rhetorical moments. Furthermore, not only is the justificatory thesis independent of the influence argument, it actually fits rather oddly alongside the conclusion of that argument and, thus, with Hume's sentimentalism. Hence it is particularly important to distinguish these two Humean theses.

---

1 For a particularly clear discussion of this and related distinctions see the introduction in Raz, ed. (1978).

At first glance Hume's premiss (1) seems very much weaker than the contemporary Humean theories of motivating reasons, for example Davidson's (1963) theory discussed in Chapter 3 above. Hume's premiss (1) only says that a belief can't do it alone while contemporary Humean views actually specify what else is required, e.g. 'pro-attitudes' of the right sort appropriately teamed with the belief. However something rather like this further requirement is already implicit in Hume's premiss in that unassuming word 'alone' which, I have argued, has to mean 'without any help from a further, distinct passion'. In Hume there will be no influencing at all without a passion for the belief to serve, just as in Davidson a belief will not be an agent's (motivating) reason for acting unless it is a belief that an act has a property toward which the agent also has a pro-attitude. Thus Hume's view is like the contemporary view in what is required beyond a mere belief. It is not particularly important, I think, that Hume calls this further requirement a 'passion' or 'affection' while Davidson speaks of 'pro-attitudes' and other Humeans speak of 'wants' or 'desires' (Smith, 1987) and others, perhaps, of 'elements of an agent's subjective motivational set' (Williams, 1980).[2]

There is one respect, however, in which the contemporary versions are significantly different from Hume's formulation. The contemporary theory no longer pretends to apply to all action (or preference) but only to those cases where an agent's reasons play a motivational role. It is, unlike Hume's, a theory of motivating *reasons*. I think this restriction is absolutely necessary for the plausibility of the thesis. We can see this by considering a fairly fatal objection to Hume's thesis as it stands. The problem is this. If one is thinking in terms of just any kind of influencing, one wonders why a belief couldn't, without any help from a desire, just cause

---

2 Contemporary Humean views are typically less restricted than Hume's version which supposes that desires (passions) are phenomenological states (at any rate a species of 'impressions'). Smith (1987, pp. 45–50), for example, gives a dispositional account. I disagree with Smith's assumption that the main difficulties anti-Humeans have with Hume's theory of motivation derive from their foisting a phenomenological conception of desire (p. 49) upon the theory. The difficulties I raise for various versions of the Humean theory in Chapters 4 and 5 are of a more general nature (except for the occasional throw-away *ad hominen* to Hume).

an action in some crude, straightforward manner. For example, as a result of hypnosis (or conditioning, or brain damage) I might be put into such a state that whenever the belief that 2 + 2 = 4 pops into my head I just raise my hand unthinkingly (unless I catch myself in time). In general terms, it's hard to put any *a priori* limits on what might be the cause of what. (Hume himself says, '[T]o consider the matter *a priori,* any thing may produce any thing' (247).) Of course some things are not of the right category to be causes of certain other things. But a belief is something psychological, so that's at least of the kind of category we might expect.

It won't help the Humean here to insist that the belief in this case didn't do it *alone* because all sorts of background conditions and intermediate causal steps were also required. We need to remember that Hume's first premiss does not take 'alone' to mean 'utterly solo'; it allows any kind of further assistance as long as it isn't a passion. Nor does it help the Humean to insist the desire was there after all; it was the being influenced to raise one's hand. That is merely the trivial 'motivation one can always find' which we discussed in Chapter 3, i.e., just the causing. In desperation the Humean might insist that what is caused in such cases is not really an 'action', thus putting a lot of weight here on the allegedly ordinary notion of an action. Unless caused in the right manner (by a belief and a desire) it won't be an action. (Presumably this means abandoning the claim that a belief cannot alone cause an affection for a parallel move is not at all plausible with 'affection'.) However this defence fails to understand the particular counter-examples and also distorts the ordinary notion of action. In the example the hand did not go up as a kind of uncontrollable reflex. Rather it was more like absent-minded doodling or inadvertently knocking the cup over with one's elbow. These could have been avoided with proper concentration and control and, thus, are actions of mine when they do occur. Not all action has to be motivated action or action done for reasons. A great deal isn't.

The right thing to say about the case in question is that, while my belief may have caused me to raise my hand, that belief was no part of the *reason why* I did it. I didn't raise my hand *because* 2 + 2 = 4. It was not even a part of a *motivating* reason I had for raising my hand which might explain why I did so. In fact in this case there was no motivating reason that I had. What this shows is that the Humean thesis is best understood, not as the claim that no belief can alone cause (in whatever manner) an action or passion, but as the claim that no belief will be the special sort of cause or explanation we commonly call a 'motivating reason' unless a further appropriate passion gets involved in the right way. Not all explanation of actions is in terms of the agent's 'motivating reasons', but where it is, more than beliefs must be involved. A motivating reason requires something like a passion in the agent as well. Thus Davidson, and contemporary Humeans generally, are right carefully to restrict Hume's thesis to explanations in terms of an agent's motivating reasons. This is a particularly crucial restriction, however. For one thing, in employing the notion of 'motivating reasons' (or 'reasons for action' or 'reasons for wanting') to exclude the clear counter-examples to Hume's cruder thesis, the contemporary version entangles itself quite securely in the core notions of 'folk psychology'. The consequences of this will become clearer later in this chapter.

However we might note two more immediate consequences of this move. First, it makes the contemporary formulation of the Humean thesis more general, in a certain respect, than Hume's could be. Contemporary versions can be formulated in terms of what, beyond agent's beliefs, are required in any *explanation* of an agent's act (or preference) where the explanation is in terms of the agent's motivating reasons. This formulation can leave it open as a further issue whether in such cases the explanation is a causal one. By contrast, Hume's talk of 'influence' must surely commit him to a causal connection in such cases. Contemporary Humeans are divided over the question of whether explanation in terms of motivating reasons is causal or not.[3] The advantage of a Humean thesis of motivation posed in terms of explanation is that, unlike Hume's formulation, its tenability does not depend on the quite separate issue of whether such explanation is causal.

There is another implication of the contemporary formulation in terms of motivating reasons. We use an agent's motivating reasons to explain not only some of his actions but also some of his desires, wants, preferences. I not only *do* things because . . . , or in order to . . . , but I also *want* things because . . . , or in order to . . . , where what fills the blanks is some reference to motivating reasons for doing or wanting. One can have reasons for wanting just as one

3 Compare Davidson (1963) with Smith (1987).

87

can have reasons for doing. Naturally, not all wants and preferences are to be explained in terms of an agent's motivating reasons for wanting or preferring. Some desires (the ones Nagel calls 'unmotivated') you just have. They have explanations, causes and origins, but the explanation is not in terms of any reasons for wanting. But other desires are to be explained in terms of reasons the agent has (what Nagel calls 'motivated desires').[4] Consequently the best contemporary version doesn't have to be quite so restricted as the Davidson version. It can speak of explaining certain desires as well as certain actions in terms of the agent's motivating reasons. However it will still be more restricted than Hume's version in that it will not concern all passions but only 'motivated' passions.

One moral to be drawn from the case where my belief just causes me to raise my hand is that Hume's thesis must be restricted to cases of motivated action. But there is another moral to be drawn. Obviously the thesis must put some minimal conditions on the further passion (or pro-attitude) which is required. It will be no vindication of Hume's thesis that one in fact can attribute to the agent some desire or other in the circumstances. It would in fact be remarkable not to be able to find a rather large list of desires attributable to the agent at any instant of time. That I believe the Pythagorean theorem and also would like to read a book on opera does not explain why I raise my hand. Hence any reputable Humean theory must give an account of how particular beliefs team up with particular desires appropriate to them to make for a motivating reason capable of doing some explaining of action or preference. Hume (459) and Davidson (1963) do this. A rather careful formulation of the very weakest thing a Humean can say in this regard is given by Smith (1987, p. 36):

Agent A at t has a motivating reason to ϕ only if there is some ψ such that, at t, A desires to ϕ and believes that were he to ϕ he would ψ.

Of course a worked out Humean position would aspire to necessary and sufficient conditions or perhaps even a kind of motivational calculus.[5] But the more modest necessary condition above is all that need concern us. The way the belief teams up with a desire in motivating reason explanations is in part a matter of the objects of the belief and the objects of the desire. The above is one typical

4 Nagel (1970), pp. 29–30.
5 Brandt (1979, ch. 3) is a striking example.

Humean expression of how exactly this is supposed to be. But another point is made clear by that formulation as well. Time of existence is important too. The desire and appropriately teamed belief must exist concurrently and, indeed, be present at the same times as the motivating reason is said to be present.

In summary, I take the best contemporary versions of Hume's theory of motivation to have the following features: It is a theory cast in terms of (i) *explanation* (causal or otherwise) of (ii) *motivated* actions, as well as of (iii) *motivated* preferences, i.e., explanation in terms of the agent's motivated reasons for acting or preferring. Furthermore, what such explanations require further, beyond (cognitive) beliefs, is something rather conative, i.e., (iv) a *desire* (or pro-attitude, passion, etc.) whether this be understood in a phenomenological or in a dispositional way. Further, (v) the *object* of the desire must be appropriate to the object of the belief. Finally, the desire and the belief must exist (vi) *concurrently* and, indeed, be present at the time of the motivating reason they are, at the very least, the conditions for.

JUSTIFYING REASONS

The Humean theory of justifying reasons bears some superficial isomorphy to the Humean theory of motivating reasons. The former insists that a course of action (or a preference) is justified for an agent only if somewhere within the justifying argument there is mention of an appropriate desire (want, pro-attitude, etc.) the agent now has. But indeed the theory of justifying reasons says more. It insists that the agent's desires so mentioned are justifying reasons and that only agent's desires can provide justifying reasons. Thus the normative proposition (P5) discussed in Chapter 3 foreshadowed this kind of theory. In its most common form the Humean normative theory claims that the only good reasons for acting (preferring) rests on an argument with a form something like Aristotle's practical syllogism with the ultimate premiss mentioning (or just being) a desire the agent has while the other premisses connect the action to be justified with the object of that desire in some appropriate way, e.g. by means-ends connections, or perhaps just by identifying instances of acting which have the feature desired. Hume probably comes closest to such a thesis in the following passage from the *Enquiry* (293):

89

Ask a man *why he uses exercise;* he will answer, *because he desires to keep his health.* If you then enquire, *why he desires health,* he will readily reply, *because sickness is painful.* If you push your enquiries farther, and desire a reason *why he hates pain,* it is impossible he can ever give any. This is an ultimate end, and is never referred to any other object... beyond this it is an absurdity to ask for a reason. It is impossible there can be a progress *in infinitum;* and that one thing can always be a reason why another is desired. Something must be desirable on its own account, and because of its immediate accord or agreement with human sentiment and affection.

This passage is nicely ambiguous. It could, of course, just be the Humean theory of motivating reasons all over again, i.e., the claim that you are not going to be subject to even a little motivational influence in cases where you accept a justification unless this justification rests in the end on a desire (possibly in the first premiss of that argument) you just have. Hume must mean at least this. But the passage seems to suggest another thesis as well, i.e., the normative thesis that all good justification must end ultimately in your having a desire (perhaps mentioned in an ultimate premiss). The former claim says you won't actually have any motivation otherwise. The latter says you won't be doing the right thing (or have a good reason for acting) otherwise. A view approaching the Humean theory of justifying reasons is perhaps to be found in Foot who says (1958–9, pp. 126–7): 'In general, anyone is given a reason for acting when he is shown the way to something he wants.' (Here it is justifying reasons which are meant). But a quite uncompromising statement can be found in Gauthier (1986, p. 37), who claims 'only a consideration entering into one's present preferences can provide, rational support for choice'.[6]

A more subtle, or perhaps more evasive, version of the normative thesis of justifying reasons is to be found in Williams (1980). Williams does not speak in terms of 'desires' or 'wants' but in terms of what is apparently more general, 'subjective motivational set' (not much of an improvement over 'pro–attitude', I should think). Furthermore Williams does not say that elements of this set have to actually *be* the ultimate justifying reasons. He goes for what

6 Cf. Norman (1971, ch. 1) and Bond (1983, introduction) for discussions of such views. See also the exchange between Woods (1972) and Foot (1972b).
   Foot's version is more moderate in that it allows that interests and future desires not based on present desires may provide justifying reasons. This is less an outrage to common sense than Gauthier's version which, I think, is more consistent or, at least, less *ad hoc.*

seems to be a weaker thesis, i.e., that some such element is always (something like) a necessary *condition of* anything's being an ultimate justifying reason. (One wonders whether there is anything besides uneasy caution behind this variation.) Williams' claim is not just the trivial claim that something from your 'subjective motivational set' is required for you to be *motivated*. It seems to be the very much less trivial claim that some such thing is always an (ultimate) condition of anything's really being a good reason for acting (cf. Williams, 1980, p. 102). The more usual versions of the Humean theory of justifying reasons always make some desire (or something 'conative') identical to the ultimate justifying reason. Williams' rather hedged version makes some such thing always an ultimate condition of anything's being a justifying reason. Nothing could be a justifying reason for you unless some appropriate element were present in your 'SMS'.

The Humean theory of justifying reasons is logically distinct from the Humean theory of motivating reasons. But in actual practice Humean defenders of the former, the normative, thesis very often retreat to the latter, the motivational, thesis when pressed. This is analogous to the way other famous normative theories sometimes appeal to the analogous corresponding motivational theory when really pressed. Thus the ultimate defence of ethical egoism (or hedonism) may just be that, anyway, one really can't be motivated in any other way, i.e., psychological egoism (or hedonism) is true. Or the idea might be that, given that we just are so constituted as psychological egoism (or hedonism) says, there can be nothing further to a theory of justification than showing that such reasons are, as a matter of psychological fact, the only things we take to be justifying and which, consequently, move us to action. Likewise, when really pressed for a justification of the Humean theory of justifying reasons, a very common defence is just to say that only such justifications are capable of moving us, i.e., what the Humean theory of motivating reasons says. Thus it seems to me that Williams' claim (that the only reasons which are good ones rest on something in one's 'subjective motivational set') rests in the end solely on the claim that any other sort of alleged justifying reason just couldn't motivate one (1980, pp. 106–7). Consequently, to undermine the motivational theory does a great deal to undermine the special plausibility of the corresponding normative thesis. If we really can be motivated by justifications other than of the sort the

Humean theory of justifying reasons favours, then it is no longer so obvious that only the Humean-approved sorts of justifying reasons have sole claim to the title 'good reasons'. The Humean theory of justifying reasons then becomes only one normative view among many (and one which we would expect a non-cognitivist to say is no more true or false than any of its competitors).

Humeans tend to give their theory of motivating reasons two, not entirely compatible, employments. The first, of course, is as premiss (1) in the influence argument for non-cognitivism. The second use is to bolster somehow the case for (P5) the Humean theory of justifying reasons. It would really be quite remarkable, indeed almost paradoxical, if precisely the same motivational thesis could do both of these at once. In the rest of this chapter and in the next I will be mainly concerned with the theory of motivating reasons. And while the occasional glance at the theory of justifying reasons will sometimes be in order, I will be mainly concerned with whether any version of the motivational theory can successfully serve as a first premiss in the influence argument.

THE CONCEPTS OF COMMON
SENSE PSYCHOLOGY

The result of an earlier section, that Hume's premiss (1) is only plausible when stated as a thesis about motivating reasons, has important consequences. It means the thesis is to be stated in terms of the concepts of common sense psychology. Notably, it uses the notion of an agent's reasons for acting (preferring) where that can be a part of a psychological explanation of his actions and choices. Hence it is very far from accidental that my examination of the Humean theory of motivating reasons will proceed by appealing to certain cases described in common sense psychological terms. What I shall be asking is whether common sense psychology really does rule out what the Humean theory rules out. Thus I am taking that theory to be a conceptual claim (as Chapter 2 insisted), i.e., one true in virtue of the concepts of common sense psychology.

In taking this approach I avoid two extremes. Many philosophers in the English-speaking tradition (such as Butler or Prichard) would probably take the results of any such conceptual investigation to reveal philosophical truths totally beyond refutation by any possible scientific inquiry or investigation. That puts it rather too strongly,

I think. It is possible (but not what we have reason to expect) that science might develop in such a way as to lead us to be justified in altering radically or even abandoning the core concepts of common sense psychology in favour of a theory whose concepts have no analogues at all in common sense psychology. Thus, while my investigation is *a priori,* I don't take this to reveal claims that must be true no matter what. I take the slightly more modest view that the claims which hold in virtue of the concepts of a common sense psychology are as good as that framework, which indeed seems the only real framework of explanation we have for quite a sizable area of phenomena.

The other extreme is held by those who would dismiss the results of any such *a priori* investigation as mere 'folk psychology', their disparaging term for common sense psychology.[7] Here a few kind words for common sense psychology are in order against its detractors. The conceptual framework of common sense psychology is the one employed, not only in sciences and studies such as economics, (sensible) anthropology and sociology, or decision theory and game theory, it is what is employed by its sophisticated practitioners in business, international negotiations, politics, not to mention poker. Common sense psychology has a rather high degree of success in these hard-headed, practical areas, certainly in comparison with the alternatives. For the alternative here is not a different psychological theory, but something not employing such concepts at all. In fact no actual alternative is at present available. What there is instead is a matter of promises and faith. Nor should the detractors of common sense psychology forget that the power of this, or any, conceptual framework needs to be judged in terms of its use by its most sophisticated practitioners, not by those tributes paid to its power by mimics, charlatans or the simple. Hence the talk of 'folk' is out of place. The power of the notion of a 'black hole' is to be judged by how certain scientists, not Walt Disney, use it. Likewise the power of common sense psychology is not a matter of the common folk beliefs posed in terms of common sense psychological notions (which we often discover to be false) but is a matter of the framework inevitably used in the more sophisticated practical sciences or in the understanding required in sophisticated

---

7 See references to works by P. Feyerabend and R. Rorty under the heading 'The Disappearance View' in Armstrong (1983), pp. 52–5. Cf. also Churchland (1985) and Stich (1983).

negotiations. Would we ever contemplate sending a *practising* psychological eliminativist to the conference table?

There is nothing anti-naturalist or even anti-physicalist in the position I take here. Let us suppose that science eventually does produce a complete physicalist or naturalist theory which can plausibly claim to be a complete account of reality. Where would this leave claims made (as a result of a *a priori* inquiry) about common sense psychological notions (e.g. claims that Hume's theory of motivation is, or is not, in conflict with common sense psychology)? A lot depends here on whether it is fairer to say that what happens to common sense psychology is a reduction or an elimination (which are perhaps really on opposite ends of a spectrum with a great deal in between). If what the ultimate physicalist theory results in is a reduction of common sense psychological notions, we should really take this as a vindication of common sense psychological notions. Claims made involving those notions could sometimes be true (just like claims about tables or universities) even if they do not refer to what is metaphysically basic. Hence a physicalism or naturalism which merely gives a reduction of common sense psychological notions is no threat at all to the discussion which follows.

However a physicalism or naturalism which results in psychological eliminativism is rather different. The first point to be made about this logical possibility is that at present we have rather a lot of reason to think it unlikely that any such successful theory will eliminate rather than reduce. Not only would the alternative have to do a better overall job of explaining the phenomena and be more useful (than, say, game theory) to sophisticated practitioners (as in negotiation or card playing) but it would also have to explain why common sense psychological notions should be so pervasive and should have seemed so successful (and give this explanation in terms which are not themselves psychological).

The second point in regard to psychological eliminativism is rather more important. Let us suppose a naturalist or physicalist elimination succeeds. In that case, 'beliefs', 'desires', 'agent's motivating reasons' all go the way of 'phlogiston' and 'vital spirits'. That will undermine completely my examination and criticism of the Humean theory of motivating reasons. But it will undermine the need to criticise the Humean theory. That theory is itself posed in 'folk psychological' notions and indeed relies fairly heavily on such notions to avoid quick counter-example. In that event an eliminativist would be in no position at all to defend Hume's influence argument as an argument for non-cognitivism nor could he think there is something even a bit right about the theory of motivation in its first premiss. The very issue it raises gets eliminated.

An analogy might be useful here, viz. the Butler-Broad attack on psychological egoism (and psychological hedonism). The 'refutation' is merely a matter of showing, by *a priori* conceptual analysis, that there is nothing in common sense psychological notions to limit the objects of desire to the objects to which the egoists or hedonists limit it. These latter theories rule out as conceptually possible what common sense psychological notions do not rule out. I suppose a contemporary psychological egoist or hedonist might attempt to reply by appeal to some comprehensive physicalist, or naturalist, account of reality (always yet to be produced, of course) as some sort of reply. But if the comprehensive account affords a reduction of common sense notions, it equally gives a reduction of all common sense motivations including the non-egoistic, non-hedonistic ones (unless the egoist's case rests only on the *hope* that there will be a selective reduction of the one but not the other). On the other hand, if the comprehensive physicalist account eliminates 'folk psychology', it will also eliminate the egoistic and hedonistic motivations along with all the other ones of common sense psychology. No doubt eliminativism, like psychological egoism and psychological hedonism, tends to have special appeal to those who think of themselves as hard-headed. It is not always noticed that one cannot be hard-headed in all ways at once. Psychological eliminativism is a two-edged sword. It cuts equally against the defenders, as against the common sense detractors, of psychological egoism, psychological hedonism, or the Humean theory of motivating reasons.

THE METHOD OF EXAMINING HUME'S THEORY

I propose to examine the Humean theory of motivating reasons by describing particular cases of actions done for reasons. This description will be in common sense psychological terms. I shall argue that there is nothing conceptually impossible about the cases as I describe them. That is, they are not ruled out just by the common sense psychological notions involved in their characterisation. Furthermore, I will claim that everyday observations (laden, no doubt, with the theory and concepts of common sense psychology) seem to show that such cases as these actually do occur. They are not only possible cases, but to go on appearances, actually somewhat common cases. The point is then to confront the Humean theory of motivating reasons with these commonplace cases.

There are two points to confronting the Humean theory with these common sense cases. One is that it will allow us to distinguish four versions of the Humean thesis depending on the way the Humean reacts to these cases, what he thinks must be said about such cases. I will distinguish a 'provocative version', and three other, rather more innocuous, versions of the Humean thesis. Another point to discussing these common sense cases is that some of them may provide counter-examples to some versions of the Humean theory. I will want to ask 'How can this version of the Humean theory of motivation reasons account for cases like this? Can it allow them?' If the version rules out cases which common sense psychology allows, and even commonly observes, then I shall conclude the particular version of the Humean theory is not only not supported by, but is in fact in conflict with, the most successful theory in the area, common sense psychology. This would be as much a 'refutation' of that version of the Humean theory as Butler's 'refutation' of psychological egoism.

It is important to see that in describing these particular cases I am not offering a philosophical or scientific theory at all. (It is more like 'data' than 'theory'.) *I give no explanation or account of these cases.* I merely say that common sense psychology allows them as conceptual possibilities (and even seems to observe many actual cases). In discussing these cases I scrupulously try to remain neutral on the philosophical issues that are at issue in the influence argument. Thus I assume neither non-cognitivism (the conclusion of the influence argument) nor cognitivism. I assume neither internalism (i.e., the strong version of the second premiss of the influence argument) nor externalism in regard to moral motivation. In describing these cases I am not putting forward a philosophical theory.

96

THREE CASES OF JUSTIFYING REASONS

While the eventual point is to discuss three cases of motivating reasons which explain acting, I shall begin in a rather indirect way by discussing, not motivating reasons, but allegedly justifying reasons. This is a matter of distinguishing, not motivations persons might have, but merely normative arguments. The following are the beginnings of three distinct normative arguments:

Practical Argument 1 (first part)

i.   I now desire [to do] ψ
ii. My doing φ now is the only way to get [do] ψ

   · [further subsidiary premisses, if needed]
   ·

---

iii. I have some (justifying) reason to φ

Practical Argument 2 (first part)

i.   I promised [to do] ψ
ii. My doing φ now is the only way to get [do] ψ

   · [further subsidiary premisses, if needed]
   ·

---

iii. I have some (justifying) reason to do φ

Practical Argument 3 (first part)

i.   Person B (perhaps related to me in a certain way) has need N
ii. My doing φ now is the only way to satisfy B's need N

   · [further subsidiary premisses, if needed]
   ·

---

iii. I have some (justifying) reason to do φ

In all cases I conceive the first premiss to be providing the reason to which the conclusion alludes.[8] The other premisses connect the

---

8 Some, following Aristotle, take the proper conclusion of a practical argument just to be the action (i.e., φ) or, more moderately, take the premisses of a practical argument to provide reasons for *doing* the action (cf. Edgley, 1969 and essay I in Raz, ed., 1978). I think such views are mistaken for reasons put nicely by Raz (1978), Introduction, pp. 5–6) and, in more detail, by Aune (1977, ch. 3). Likewise I reject the parallel characterisation of theoretical arguments as providing reasons for *believing* a proposition rather than the more standard view that they provide reasons for the truth of the proposition. Where the reasons for *believing* a proposition are not just pragmatic or moral, as in Pascal's wager, I think they will,

reason given applying it to the particular case. I use a crude means-end premiss (ii) to accomplish this, but that is not the only way this might be done. The 'further subsidiary premisses' in each case never involve further reasons, but ensure that the reason provided in (i) does not get defeated or cancelled somewhere along the way.[9] For example, a further premiss in PA 2 might say that one has not been released from the promise in the meantime by the promisee. Another might say that what was promised is not of a certain sort (e.g. immoral or illegal). Otherwise, it is commonly supposed, the promise might provide not even some reason. Again, in PA 1 it might be important that the desire is not itself based on a false belief or in some way pathological. I leave the reader to fill in what details seem plausible here. The subsidiary premisses, including (ii) in each case, may be altered in whatever way seems plausible as long as it remains clear that it is premiss (i) in each case which is providing the reason for acting.

Contrary to first appearances I am not actually saying any of these practical arguments are good ones or that any of the first premisses do really provide justifying reasons. I am only making the conceptual point that they are normative arguments and distinct normative arguments. It is enough for my purposes that you can understand and distinguish them. Even if you think a particular practical argument is a bad one (i.e., does not even begin to provide a justifying reason), you must understand it to think it is bad. Furthermore, even if a non-cognitivist thinks that all such arguments can never give grounds for thinking their respective conclusions are *true,* he must still give some account of what such practical judgments mean, how each is different in meaning from all the others, how to believe one is different from believing all the others, and what "believing" amounts to in such cases. In short, I only require that you understand and be able to distinguish these three practical arguments, not necessarily that you agree with any of them even when most generously conceived.

In saying this I remain quite neutral on the issue between cog-

at least, presuppose there can be independent reasoning toward the *truth* of the proposition.

But, in any case, I do not rule out these Aristotelian approaches in my discussion. If one thinks the premisses are reasons for doing ϕ, surely one will also be committed to the proposition in (iii) that one has some (justifying) reason to do ϕ.

9 For further discussion of kinds of defeating or cancelling conditions see Raz (1975).

nitivists and non-cognitivists. The cognitivist might well think that in some cases like the above the normative claim which is the conclusion will actually be true and indeed rationally warranted by the (cognitive, we assume) premisses of the practical argument. By contrast the non-cognitivist will have to insist that the conclusions are in no case the sort of thing to be true or false and that, furthermore, the claim that the first premiss, in each case, gives a 'good reason' for doing φ must itself also be non-cognitive. Hence, on this view, the claim that any one of these practical arguments is a good (or bad) argument must itself be neither true nor false but just another normative claim. (No clear-headed non-cognitivist will regard the Humean theory of justifying reasons as either true or false.) But in any case, both cognitivist and non-cognitivist will understand the three practical arguments I am discussing even if they have different philosophical accounts of them.

PA1 differs from PA2 and PA3 in an interesting respect. PA1 gives a *desire of the agent* as the justifying reason, while PA2 and PA3 do not. I assume that the 'subsidiary premisses' in each case (premisses (ii) and after) do not mention further desires, pro-attitudes, passions, etc., or, if they do, not in such a way as to provide a reason but only to connect the reason in the first premiss to the particular action in the conclusion. Hence Hume's theory of *justifying* reasons, (P5), has the consequence that, while practical argument 1 is a good argument, the other two practical arguments are bad, i.e., actually give no justifying reason at all as they stand. Perhaps they would be good arguments with the addition of another premiss giving an agent's desire as a reason, but as they stand they are bad. I think even the more evasive view of Bernard Williams must have something like this consequence. His view does not require that the element from the 'subjective motivational set' literally be the reason, but that it be a condition of the reason's being a reason. Hence in practical arguments 2 and 3 the consideration given in premiss (i) will not provide any sort of reason at all unless some appropriate 'subjective motivational set' element is present in the agent. Thus something further is required, something not already sufficiently covered by the 'subsidiary premisses'. For these latter are only a matter of connecting the reason with the particular case. Rather, the mental element is actually a condition of its being a justifying reason at all. It would be best to be open about this and put in this extra 'subjective motivational set' condition explicitly as another major (rather than subsidiary) premiss. In which case, Williams is saying that PA2 and PA3 as they stand are bad arguments. (If their first premisses are not examples of the 'external reasons' Williams rejects, one despairs of finding a case.)

The three practical arguments are incomplete if they are ever to be practical. In not every case that a person believes he has some reason does he think he has sufficient reason. Nor does the latter quite come to thinking one should, all things considered, do φ. We might then complete each of the three practical arguments thus:

Practical Arguments 1, 2, or 3 (final part)
iii. I have some (justifying) reason to do φ

· [further premisses]

·

---

iv. I should (all things considered) do φ

Here the further premisses might well involve other normative claims. Thus a person might consider the justifying reasons provided by other practical arguments both for doing and not doing φ in order to reach the final judgment in (iv). However in other cases it might just be a matter of thinking the reason provided is particularly strong in justificatory weight and that no other reasons bear on the issue.

THREE CASES OF MOTIVATION

I shall now describe three different persons who happen to 'believe' (broad sense) three different normative judgments respectively:

First specification
P1 'accepts' practical argument 1
P2 'accepts' practical argument 2
P3 'accepts' practical argument 3

where 'accepting' such a practical argument means three things. First, it means believing (broad sense) all the premisses (or at least tacitly holding them). In the case of the 'first part' of each argument, these premisses would seem to be all cognitive. In any case the first premiss (the reason-providing one) will be cognitive. Second, accepting the practical argument means in each case 'believing' (broad sense) the conclusion (iv), i.e., believing of oneself 'I should, all things considered, do φ '. Cognitivists and non-cognitivists differ on whether these are 'beliefs' in the narrow sense. That is, they differ as to whether such beliefs (broad sense) can be true or false. But they do not disagree that there is such a thing as believing such things in the broad sense. Third, accepting the practical argument in each case means thinking the conclusion of the 'first part', i.e., (iii), is normatively justified by the premisses of that part. That is, it is to think that the consideration in (i) is some justifying reason for one's doing φ. This is a normative claim. But it is more than the normative claim that one should do φ. It involves the further normative claim that such and such is a justifying reason for doing it. Again, cognitivists and non-cognitivists differ as to whether what a person thinks here can be true or false, but they do not disagree that there are such thoughts. This is worth remembering. Non-cognitivism has not only the (comparatively easy) task of giving some positive account of what it is to believe one should do φ. It also has the very much harder task of explaining what one is thinking when one thinks that some factual consideration is a justifying reason for doing φ. Of course the more sophisticated non-cognitivists (beginning with Stevenson and Hare) see just this further problem and do try to give some account of just this.

We now add a further specification to the cases we want to discuss:

Second specification
P1's accepting argument 1 motivates P1 a bit to doing φ
P2's accepting argument 2 motivates P2 a bit to doing φ
P3's accepting argument 3 motivates P3 a bit to doing φ

It is a philosophical controversy whether accepting a practical argument (especially its conclusion) *must* motivate or merely *can* motivate one. The internalist claims that one's accepting such a practical argument *must* motivate one (at least a bit, even if not sufficiently). So he thinks what I have described in my 'second specification' will inevitably occur in cases meeting the 'first specification'. By contrast, the externalist denies the necessary connection here, but he still allows that accepting a normative argument can be a part of the motivational story on certain occasions. It is controversial whether this acceptance can motivate 'alone' (in the sense of Hume's second premiss). Some externalists will insist it needs an additional desire for there to be motivation, e.g. a desire to be moral, or a desire to be rational, a desire to do what one, all things considered, should do. Hence I omit 'alone' after the 'motivates' in the above specification. I simply leave it open whether, when it does it, it does it with or without help from some such additional desire or pro-attitude. All that the 'second specification' claims is that accepting a practical argument on occasion is a part of the motivational story. I simply choose to discuss three cases where that happens, not caring to take any stand on whether it must happen or whether it requires outside help when it does happen.

Hence in the description of these common sense cases I remain scrupulously neutral on the internalism/externalism issue just as I remain neutral on the non-cognitivism/cognitivism issue. Furthermore, just as non-cognitivism has no particular bias for practical argument 1 over practical arguments 2 and 3, so internalism does not rule out the accepting of arguments 2 or 3 as possible motivations. On the contrary, internalism insists that to accept such practical arguments is of necessity to have a bit of motivation to do φ. Internalism (like non-cognitivism in this regard) gives no special brief to the Humean theory of justifying reasons. According to this Humean theory, practical arguments 2 and 3 are just rotten justifications. But non-cognitivism must work no less as hard to explain the phenomenon of persons' accepting either of these two arguments. Likewise internalism also insists that those who do accept such arguments as PA2 or PA3 are necessarily motivated a bit by their acceptance.

It is worth noting that a reference to something conative (or passionate, or motivational or pro-attitudinal) occurs one more time in our specification so far of P1's case than in our specification of P2's or P3's case. In all three cases there is the 'being motivated a bit' by the acceptance of a practical argument. In cases 2 or 3 these might sometimes get described as 'the desire to do one's duty' or 'the desire to keep one's promises' or 'the desire to see to the needs of certain others'. But case 1, while also having the 'being motivated a bit' by the practical argument, also has a reference to a desire of the agent *within* the very argument P1 accepts. In the other cases the motivation present is not actually alluded to within the argument but is a matter of being somehow moved a bit by that argument.

Now we can add the final specifications of the three particular cases to be discussed. Of course having a bit of motivation to do φ does not always eventuate in one's actually doing φ. It's not even clear to me that thinking you really should all things considered do something has to eventuate in an actual decision to do φ. But even where there is a decision and where also one is not prevented in other ways (e.g. physically), various defects in the person can render the motivation insufficient, e.g. forgetfulness, laziness, competing motivations, weakness of will, etc. Even so, common sense holds that sometimes all goes well and person P does go on to do φ and the explanation involves, conspicuously, P's motivation to do φ in virtue of his having accepted a certain practical argument. I just choose to discuss three cases where all does go right and where what happens is:

Third specification
P1 does φ because of his having accepted argument 1
P2 does φ because of his having accepted argument 2
P3 does φ because of his having accepted argument 3

Here we explain the actions of P1, P2, P3 in terms of their motivating reasons, which were here sufficient in the circumstances. Furthermore the motivating reasons involve the acceptance of certain justifying reasons. They were believed to be justifying (whether they are or not). Whether or not all explanations in terms of motivating reasons are like these in involving acceptance of justifying reasons (i.e., the having of normative beliefs) is not important. (We may attribute motivating reasons to some animals and to ourselves on occasions where nothing like the acceptance of a normative argument can be supposed.) But this is at least a central and important sort of motivating reason. One wonders whether without such cases we would speak of motivating *reasons* at all. Certainly, common sense allows and seems to observe these central cases.

FOUR VERSIONS OF THE HUMEAN THEORY OF MOTIVATING REASONS

We now have three particular cases to discuss: *Case 1,* the case of person P1 as specified by the three specifications on P1, and similarly a *case 2* and a *case 3* involving persons P2 and P3 respectively. Case 1 is particularly useful because, using it as an example, we can disambiguate four very different versions of the Humean theory of motivating reasons. The way to do it is to ask any holder of the

Humean theory just *where* in case 1 we are to find the beliefs and (especially) the coordinated passion (or pro-attitude). Different Humeans answer this question differently and thus hold significantly different theories. It is possible that in other motivational cases than the above Humeans would all agree on where to locate the pro-attitude. But the fact that they differ on these (not unimportant) cases, proves a difference. Thus we are able to distinguish different versions of the Humean theory without having to know exactly what the further details of those versions may be, for we distinguish them according to their consequences, i.e., according to what they say about particular cases.

The four versions of the Humean thesis I will call the 'provocative version', the 'question-begging version', the 'vacuous version' and the 'defeating version' for reasons I will make clear. In the *provocative version* the search for the further required pro-attitude goes on *within* each of the practical arguments in the three cases. The provocative version says that unless there is some appropriate desire, pro-attitude, passion of the agent mentioned in the ultimate premiss of the practical argument (or perhaps mentioned in a proposition stating a condition for the first premiss to be a reason), then the acceptance of that practical argument cannot possibly be a part of the motivational explanation of why the agent did φ. Hence, while the provocative version allows that case 1 is possible, cases 2 and 3 as I have described them are ruled out. Precisely the practical arguments which the Humean theory of *justifying* reasons counts as good arguments, the provocative Humean theory of *motivating* reasons counts as capable of motivating – and no others.

The *question-begging version* of the Humean theory of motivating reasons identifies the required further passion or pro-attitude with P's 'accepting' certain normative judgments, e.g. accepting the judgment in the conclusion (iv) 'I should do φ' or perhaps in accepting the judgment in the 'first part' of the practical argument that the fact stated by premiss (i) provides a 'good reason' for doing φ. This version mentions no limits on what can occur *within* the practical arguments that motivate. Thus, unlike the provocative version, the question-begging version does not rule out cases 2 and 3 as motivational possibilities. Indeed cases 2 and 3 differ from case 1 only in regard to the kind of fact which gets mentioned in the first premiss of the practical arguments. The question-begging version is uninterested in the fact that in case 1 the first premiss of the practical argument alludes to a psychological state of the agent rather than to some other sort of fact, e.g. a promise made, or the need of another. That is not where the passion gets located in this version. Hence no obvious limits are put on what sort of justifying reasons, when accepted, can motivate. This version allows that practical justifications which the Humean theory of justifying reasons rejects (such as PA 2 and PA 3) may, nevertheless, be capable of motivating those benighted individuals who accept them.

The question-begging version of the Humean theory may well be true. In my view it is the most plausible version. The problem is that our knowing its truth waits on our knowing the truth of something like sentimentalism or emotivism. And that, the Humean may have innocently forgotten, is just the object of the whole enterprise. Of course if we had some good *independent* reason for believing Hume's sentimentalism, then we would already be in a position to know that accepting a normative judgment or a practical argument just *is* (or involves) a passion or pro-attitude. But if the main case for sentimentalism rests on first showing non-cognitivism, and if we intend to use the influence argument to add anything to the case for non-cognitivism, we cannot then defend the first premiss of that argument (the Humean motivation theory) by just assuming sentimentalism at the crucial point. Here the 'dogmatic Humean' will probably not understand what all the fuss is about, for halfway through his circular reasoning he has already forgotten what has to be proved and happily assumes it when that's what is required to bail out the Humean theory of motivating reasons. (In the diagnosis of 'Humean dogmatism' the shamelessness with which this circle is perpetrated must be some sort of indicator.)

The *vacuous version* of the Humean theory of motivating reasons must be true. This version does not locate the pro-attitude within the practical argument accepted. Nor does it locate the pro-attitude in the 'accepting' of that practical argument and its normative conclusion (hence it does not have to assume that such 'accepting' is a pro-attitude rather than a cognitive belief). Rather it locates the pro-attitude in the *being moved* by that acceptance (whatever that acceptance may be). In short this version of the Humean theory looks around and immediately alights on the 'motivation one can always find' (Chapter 3 above) and turns this into a philosophy of action. The vacuous version is not false, but, as previously noted, it is utterly useless as a first premiss in the influence argument for this way of insuring the truth of the first premiss thereby insures the falsehood of the second premiss.

The *defeating version* of the Humean theory of motivating reasons tries to secure its truth in a way no Humean really wants. It supposes (exactly opposite to the question-begging version) that 'accepting' a practical argument and its 'I should' conclusion is a cognitive believing. It assumes cognitivism. But it then insists, as per the Humean theory of motivating reasons, that such a cognitive belief is incapable of motivating without a further desire or pro-attitude. So it takes the view that a further desire was required in all three of our cases, viz. something like the desire to be rational, or the desire to do one's duty, etc. That's where the extra pro-attitude gets located in this version. Consequently, this version ensures that the second premiss of the influence argument, even in its weakest form, will be false. A moral belief, being also cognitive, cannot alone motivationally explain an agent's action except in the presence of a further, distinct desire to do what is right. Furthermore, this view presupposes the falsehood of the conclusion of the influence argument, i.e., it presupposes non-cognitivism is false. With friends who support the Humean theory of motivation in this manner, Humeans will need no enemies.

SUMMARY

The question-begging version may be true, but our knowing it to be true waits on our first knowing something close to sentimentalism to be true. The vacuous version is surely true but is of no use in the influence argument. And, while the defeating version may be true, the Humean can only hope it isn't. That leaves the provocative version. We should now be a bit more suspicious of the provocative version. Its seeming plausibility may only be due to its confusion with the question-begging version, or worse, with the defeating version, one of which must have some claim to real plausibility. Or it may be due to its confusion with the vacuous version which has rather too much claim. It is not uncommon in philosophy that the confusion of a patent falsehood with a commonplace or even a vacuous truth produces the illusion of a provocatively profound truth. The provocative version of Hume's theory does seem to be in conflict with common sense in a way the other versions are not. For the other versions allow, what the provocative version rules out, viz. motivational cases like 2 and 3. Thus, the provocative version imposes limits on what is conceptually possible which the concepts of common sense psychology do not seem to impose.

Can the provocative version defend itself in the face of these common sense counter-examples?

5

The provocative
Humean theory of motivation

What Hume's influence argument requires as its first premiss is
not just any version of Hume's theory of motivation but the
'provocative' version. However the preceding chapter alleged
that the provocative version, conceived as a proposition conceptually true in virtue of the fundamental concepts of common
sense psychology, in fact misunderstands that conceptual framework. The provocative version rules out motivational cases
such as the cases 2 and 3 of the preceding chapter while common
concepts of common sense psychology do not rule out these, very
far from peripheral, cases. No good Humean, however,
is really ever convinced by these alleged counter-examples.
For a start, two ploys are commonly employed by Humeans in regard to cases 2 and 3.

THE REDESCRIPTION PLOY

One defence of the provocative version of Hume's theory is the
simple redescription ploy. It consists in replacing common sense
cases like 2 and 3 with superficially similar motivational cases
which, then, the provocative version can handle. That version cannot handle 2 and 3 as they stand, for what individuates the provocative version from the other versions is precisely a matter of
what is, or is not, to be found within the practical arguments
'accepted', as we would ordinarily say, in these cases. What the
redescription ploy accomplishes is, not a proof of the provocative
version, but a defence against putative counter-examples. It does
this by offering an explanation of how it could have seemed that
common sense psychology did allow cases 2 and 3. The explanation
is just that we have confused cases like 2 and 3 with other similar-
looking ones which common sense does allow although it does not

allow 2 and 3. Furthermore, the ones which common sense does allow are not only not counter-examples, but indeed instances of the provocative Humean theory in action. Thus, taking the practical argument in case 2, the Humean writes in a further premiss, (i*), to get:

Practical Argument 2*

i*. I *desire* to keep my promises
i. I promised [to do] ψ
ii. My doing φ now is the only way to do [get] ψ
.
.
.
_____

iii. I have some (justifying) reason to φ
.
.
.
_____

iv. I should (all things considered) do φ

Similarly, the Humean adds a further premiss to argument 3 to get:

Practical Argument 3*

i*. I *like* helping other persons (perhaps related to me in certain ways) who are in need of that help
i. Person B (related in that way to me) has need N
ii. My doing φ now is the only way to satisfy B's need N
.
.
.
_____

iii. I have some (justifying) reason to φ
.
.
.
_____

iv. I should (all things considered) do φ

The starred premiss which has been added in each case may seem too crude to some, much too upfront. A more sophisticated (or evasive) version of (i*), in each case, might merely attribute some 'subjective motivational state' to the agent which, were it not present, would according to the practical argument prevent the next premiss, (i), from being *any* sort of justifying reason in itself. But such variations are unimportant. What is important is that the extra motivational premiss be seen as providing a ground for there being a justifying reason at all rather than merely providing a way of

109

connecting the reason there already is to particular actions and circumstances. The Humean can now specify possible motivational cases, parallel to cases 2 and 3, such as:

Case 2*
P2* 'accepts' practical argument 2*
P2*'s 'accepting' argument 2* motivated P2* a bit to doing φ
P2* does φ because of his having accepted argument 2*

Case 3*
P3* 'accepts' practical argument 3*
P3*'s 'accepting' argument 3* motivated P3* a bit to doing φ
P3* does φ because of his having accepted argument 3*

Motivational cases 2 and 3 are the original counter-example cases. The above motivational cases, 2* and 3*, are their, respective, Humean redescriptions. The redescription ploy consists in asserting that the redescribed cases, 2* and 3*, are the real (common sense) cases of doing φ in order to keep a promise (or in order to help another in need). By contrast, the counter-example cases, 2 and 3, are impossible, just as the provocative version of Hume's theory says. In really 'dogmatic' Humeans, the ploy is not so much a matter of conscious redescription as just the inability to *see* 2 and 3, when thrown up, as anything different from 2* and 3*. The dogmatic Humean imagines even his opponents, when they cite 2 or 3, are, like any good Humean, really thinking 2* or 3*. He just fails to distinguish them.

But the counter-example cases are to be distinguished from their Humean redescriptions. The practical argument in PA2 (or PA3) is not the same as the practical argument in PA2* (or PA3*). Hence 'accepting' the former is a different psychological state from 'accepting' the latter. And hence the motivation in cases 2 or 3 is not to be confused with the motivation in cases 2* or 3*. There are a couple of ways in which we might try to bring out this difference in psychological state between the original cases and the redescribed cases. The *first difference* comes out in cases where the agent has reason to believe that in the future the desire he has now (to keep promises or to help those in need) will cease. In the redescribed cases this present desire, which will cease, is located precisely in the justifying reason of the practical argument which he accepts. Thus in the redescribed cases the agent's thought (now) is that when in the future the desire ceases, so will all justifying reason conditional on it. Even *now*, while he has the desire, he thinks that. By contrast, in the original cases, the agent's thought is that it is the promise, or the need, which provides the justifying reason. The justifying reason is not conditional upon the presence of these desires. Something like such a desire is indeed present in these *motivational* cases. But it is not to be found *within* the practical argument accepted but in the capacity the acceptance of the argument has to motivate. Thus the agent's thought is that, should this being motivated by the acceptance of the argument cease in the future, the justifying reason would not (as he sees it now) cease although the being motivated would. He predicts weakness, indeed collapse, of will. His thought bears some analogy to what we ordinarily think in regard to theoretical, rather than moral, reasoning. When I think evidence *e* rationally supports conclusion *c,* I think that the former will continue to be good reason to believe that conclusion even when, in the future as I predict, because of brain damage or brainwashing, I shall lose the capacity to reason from *e* to *c.* If I fail to be moved by a good argument in the future, the failing is in me, not the argument.

The *second difference* comes out in cases where the agent thinks that in the future the relevant desire will not cease but will be somewhat diminished. The strength of the desire will vary from the present. Presumably, in the redescribed cases the thought will be that as the desire lessens (or increases) so does the justifying reason. The thought is 'If I like promise keeping less in the future, I will *then* have somewhat less justifying reason'. However in the original counter-example cases the agent's view, given the practical argument he accepts, is that he will have just as much justification even if not always sufficient motivation. Indeed, not only can he think this about his own future, he can think this about his own present. He may regret that his present motivation is insufficient for the justifying reason he now believes he has. He recognises weakness of the will in himself.

It is natural to think these differences in thought between the original cases and the redescribed cases might come out at certain points in actual tendencies in actions and feelings. For example, if I am really of the view that it is the promise (or the need) which provides the reason and not my motivation, and if I believe that in the future my motivation will cease or decline, I might (now) have some tendency to:

111

a. Take steps now to forestall my impending motivational drain. Or if I am unable to staunch its drain, I might:

b. Take steps now that will compel my future self to do what will be keeping promises (even if not for the right reasons). And if that too isn't possible, I might:

c. Hope that in the future I will, even if only by coincidence or accident, be doing what I have promised.

Not only do I (now) think these (present) actions and feelings rational, I might consequently (now) be somewhat motivated to act and feel in these ways. This is a difference from the motivations in the Humean redescriptions.

However, no sooner do I mention these distinguishing tendencies than the Humean has an immediate reply: another round of redescription. Wielding his pen freely the Humean simply alters 2* and 3* by adding the desires to do (a) and (b) above as well as the desire behind the hope in (c) to the Humean premiss (i*) of the practical argument the agent accepts. I suppose this makes for slightly different motivational cases, a 2** and a 3**. These, and not the crude first attempts 2* and 3*, are the answer to the putative counter-examples 2 and 3. On the re-redescribed version the first premiss of the practical argument mentions as a justifying reason not only the agent's present desire to, say, keep promises, but also a desire that the desire continue unabated, a desire to force himself to keep promises should the interest flag in the future, even a present desire that it all happen by chance should the other precautions fail. Everything we thought might be distinguishing is now just added and packed into that re-redescribed first premiss.

Although the target has moved a bit, we might try to think of some new differences, i.e., some subtle motivational differences between the original cases, 2 and 3, and the re-redescribed cases 2** and 3**. But even as we ponder this, we notice the Humean wielding his pen somewhat menacingly. Surely we are playing a game we cannot win. When, after some thought, we do produce some motivational differences, the Humean needs only a stroke of the pen to add the results of our hard work to a suitably re-re-redescribed case, a 2***, or a 2****, or whatever. The pen, it seems, is quicker than the counter-example. This is the clear advantage of the redescription ploy. It saves a lot of thinking.

Three things need to be said about the redescription ploy. First, the ploy doesn't really handle differences in the way the agents *look*

112

at their own futures. In the counter-example cases, 2 and 3, the agent who hopes he will continue to act in certain ways even should he lose his present motivation is thinking *now* that if he does so he will be doing what he will even then have reason (but not motivation) to do. By contrast, the agents in the redescribed cases are hoping (or taking steps to ensure) that they will do what they *even now* grant will then be irrational for them to do. Of course desiring (or taking steps to ensure) irrational action in the future is not necessarily itself irrational. As Parfit shows, there can be reasons (now) to cause oneself to act irrationally (Parfit, 1984, pp. 12–13). The point is only that the agents in the redescribed cases look at their hopes and precautions for the future in an importantly different way from the way the agents in the original cases do. The former think they have reason to ensure their future irrationality, the latter, their future rationality.

The second point to be made is that the Humean's repeated redescriptions result in an agent's attributing to himself (as per the first premiss of this practical argument) a rather large mixed bag of just brute desires with no clear principle of unity or explanation. The principle of selection is that whatever is needed to mimic the counter-example cases goes into the bag and for no really good independent reason. A great many everyday desires don't take along with them all this extra baggage of further desires about the situation when one loses the initial desire. So this requires an explanation. Of course in the original motivational cases, these further motives have a unifying explanation in terms of the agent's being moved (now) by his accepting that he will still have justifying reasons (not based on his desires) even in the future. That's rather simple.

But third, we should not be impressed merely by the Humean's facility with a pen. What allows the redescription ploy to seem so plausible is that there is ready at hand always a candidate for the desire the Humean wants to put into the first premiss of the agent's practical argument. Even the descriptions in the counter-example cases, like 2 or 3, allow that something motivational is present in those cases. Naturally that is so because they are *motivational* cases. For example, in case 2 there is P2's being motivated a bit by his acceptance of a certain practical argument. It would be natural to call this motivation something like 'a desire to keep one's promises'. But in case 2, unlike 2*, reference to this motivation does not occur *within* the practical argument (PA2) accepted. Rather, it consists precisely in the fact that P2's acceptance of that argument *does motivate* him a bit. The redescription ploy consists in taking the 'desire to keep promises', for example, and writing it into the description of the premises of the argument the agent is said to accept. But there is still a real issue here even after the demonstration of facility with a pen. The issue remains as to whether a reference to a desire (or motivation, or passion, etc.) always has to be written into the story about justification which the agent accepts for that accepting ever to be motivating or whether, alternatively, in some cases the content which is accepted and motivates has no such reference. 'But doesn't a desire have to be found within the justificatory story in order to explain how the agent could ever be motivated by accepting that justification?' the Humean objects. 'How can a motivational something come from a motivational nothing?' But that objection, at least, indicates the use of a somewhat different ploy.

THE MOTIVATIONAL SOURCE PLOY

The second ploy depends on the assertion that one couldn't (say, in the three motivational cases of Chapter 4) be motivated (say, to do φ) by the acceptance of a justificatory argument unless *within* that argument there were a reference to a motivational state (say, the desire for ψ) as a justificatory reason (or condition of such a reason). The thinking here is that there must be a motivation 'for the agent to deliberate *from*' if he is 'to reach this new motivation' (cf. Williams, 1980, p. 109). That is what explains why case 1 is a possible motivational case while cases 2 and 3 (as opposed to 2* and 3*) are not. In case 1 the motivation to do φ comes ultimately from the motivation toward ψ. But in cases 2 and 3 it remains a mystery where the moving power to do φ could come from. The persuasive pull of this ploy (what Williams calls the 'great force in Hume's basic point') can be broken by observing that if there really were this motivational mystery about cases 2 and 3, there would also seem to be some similar mystery about case 1. If it really were impossible for cases 2 and 3 to get off the ground, case 1 might be subject to much the same difficulty. We can begin to see this by observing that the motivation to do φ which eventuates in case 1 is to be distinguished from the desire for [to get] ψ mentioned in the first premiss of practical argument 1, the one accepted by the agent in that case. There are three, possibly four, respects in which these are to be distinguished. First, the motivations are, at the very least, conceptually distinct insofar as they have different objects. The one has *doing* ϕ as its object, the other has ψ as its object. Motivations, just as with beliefs, are distinguished *by their objects*.

But, second, the two motivations differ not only in object but *in kind*. In the case we choose to specify as case 1, *doing* ϕ is desired only as a means but not for itself, while ψ is not also desired as a means (although that could be another case) but just for itself. Here we rely on one of the indispensible distinctions of common sense psychology, the distinction between desiring something as an end and desiring something as a means (where the mere distinction does not prohibit something being desired in both ways). Brandt (1979, pp. 30–1) points out rather nicely the power of common sense psychology in this regard in terms of the difficulties involved in attempts to ignore the distinction by speaking indiscriminately in terms of wants. The difficulties arise here not only for cases where we would be inclined to attribute the acceptance of practical arguments to agents, but also even in the more primitive cases where that might be inappropriate. There is, for example, the difficulty of explaining why a rat running a maze ('in order to get food' as we might ordinarily say) doesn't slow down, or even stop, as the number of 'wanted experiences' behind ('desired as a means' as we usually say) increases more and more as the rat approaches the food (the 'desired end' as we otherwise might say). Common sense psychology seems to get it right that typically (if not inevitably) the desires for the means get discarded right along with the use of those means or with the use of alternative means to the same end.

One might try to account for this difference by allowing the possibility of conditional desires, i.e., desires of the sort that when one is in circumstance x, one then desires (simply, and not conditionally) to be in y, but when in y, one desires to be in z, etc., until perhaps this chain ends with a state wherein one desires to be in no further state. While there are conditional desires (e.g., 'grass is greener' desires), desires of this form do not explain what it is to desire something merely as a means. As Brandt notes (1979, p. 31, n.2), 'This theory, however, cannot explain why, when a rat has, prior to being placed on the runway, been put in a familiar goal-box and found it empty, he shows little or no interest in

115

running the maze. It is evident that what he thinks is in the goal-box is highly relevant to what he does.' In short, the distinction between desiring something as a means and just desiring it for itself is one which common sense psychology treats as a distinction of enough fundamental importance in explanation of behavior as to be regarded as a difference in kind. Thus the desire to do φ and the desire for ψ in case 1 differ not merely in object but also in fundamental explanatory kind.

There is a third respect in which these two desires are to be distinguished. The desire to do φ can differ from the desire for ψ *in strength*. Rather typically the desire for the former can be weaker than the desire for the latter. If we think that people can differ (and even one person can change over time) in how prudent or rational they are, we may well be thinking that while both may accept the same practical arguments for their respective actions, the less rational or prudent person is somewhat less motivated to pursue the required means as per that argument. But if the desire to do φ can differ in strength from the desire for ψ, that is yet another reason to distinguish the two desires.

Finally, and fourth, we might consider whether there isn't another respect in which the two desires can differ. One wonders whether there aren't cases in which the desire to do φ comes into some sort of motivational conflict with the desire for ψ. The dog that can see the food through the glass barrier and knows well enough the rather long way around can be slowed down a bit, pulled back by the sight of the food. Likewise I might find it difficult to pull myself away from the shop window to go inside to complete the usual purchasing procedures. There seem to be at least some aspects of the desire for ψ which can come into motivational conflict with the desire to do φ as a means to ψ. But the fact that some sort of conflict is possible suggests that the desire for ψ for itself is not the same sort of motivation as the motivation to do φ as a means to the desired ψ. In these four ways, then, the desire for ψ mentioned in the practical argument accepted by the agent in case 1 is importantly different from that agent's motivation to do φ. The two motivations differ in object, in explanatory kind, in strength, and sometimes even in direction. This being so, there must also be a sort of motivational mystery about case 1 (if there was any about cases 2 or 3). How does the one motivation explain the other when not only are they not the same motivation but are importantly different?

But there is an additional problem. In motivational case 1 it is not even necessary that the desire for ψ be as strong as the agent imagines it to be or even that it exist. What is required is that the agent believe it to exist in that strength and accept a certain practical argument alluding to such a desire. But if self-deception about desires is possible (if one can discover that one didn't really want it after all, even given all the trouble one went to) one might well be motivated to do φ in order to satisfy a desire one mistakenly believed one had. So now we see the case where a person is motivated to do φ falsely believing (or perhaps exaggerating) his desire for ψ is going to be just as mysterious as what goes on in cases 2 or 3. It should be just as mysterious that one can be motivated by the belief that one has a desire as that one can be motivated by the belief that one promised or that another is in need. Humeans may well think that the moral to be gained from examples such as this is that the 'passion' required by the Humean theory of motivation is not to be located, in case 1, *within* the practical argument accepted, but somewhere else, e.g. in the being moved by that argument, or in what it is to 'accept' a practical argument or to 'accept' its conclusion, or in some special separate desire to be rational or do one's duty. Some such move is perhaps good sense, but it is also to leave behind quite decisively the provocative version of the Humean theory of motivation in favour of one of the other versions discussed in the preceding chapter. Locating the passion *within* the practical argument accepted when it came to cases like case 1 is precisely what distinguished the provocative version of Hume's theory from the others. And it is precisely for this reason that all these other versions have no grounds to allege some special motivational mystery about cases like 2 and 3. These other versions do not, by the terms of their theses, put any limits on what kinds of practical arguments might motivate upon acceptance. For these other views the Humean 'passion' comes in *during or after* the acceptance of a practical argument but not within that argument. In short, all the other versions of Hume's theory have no special difficulty about the conceptual possibility of cases like 2 and 3. For these versions the 'source' of the motivation to do φ is ultimately in *that* 'during or after' passion. By contrast, the provocative version is unique in

117

excluding the conceptual possibility of cases like 2 and 3. It is on particularly shaky ground if it insists cases 2 and 3 are impossible for the particular reason that they lack a motivational source from a motivation mentioned within the practical argument accepted. On that sort of ground even cases like case 1 start to look like a motivational mystery.

THE ANALOGY TO BUTLER'S REFUTATION

Psychological hedonism and psychological egoism are theories of motivation that restrict, to different degrees, the range of possible motivations rather more than common sense psychology does. While psychological egoism can perhaps pride itself in not being so narrow, or philistine, as psychological hedonism, it still rules out as possible motivations what common sense psychology does not. This is much the point of what might be called the 'refutation' of psychological egoism in the tradition of Butler and Broad.[1] The refutation may be broken down into two steps. The first makes a conceptual point, viz. that the concepts of common sense psychology put rather fewer limits on what can be the object of a desire in comparison with what *conceptual* psychological egoism does. The common sense concept of a desire allows desires to take 'other-regarding' objects. Indeed a wide range of non-egoistic desire (where this is a matter of the kind of object desired) is conceptually possible. This is the refutation of *conceptual* psychological egoism. The second step of the 'refutation' then confronts a more modest version of psychological egoism. Even if conceptual psychological egoism is false, psychological egoism might be true as a *contingent* empirical fact: The second stage consists merely in reminding us that we seem to observe a certain number of everyday cases of desires with non-egoistic objects and that we have no real evidence to suppose that we are systematically deceived or suffering from mass hallucinations in all this (although we sometimes detect mistakes about particular instances). Such everyday observations make it reasonable to believe psychological egoism has clear counter-instances. Of course, as with any *contingent* claim, it is still logically possible that if the right evidence showed up in the future we would in those circumstances find it reasonable to accept psychological

1 Butler [1726], especially ch. 11; Broad (1930); Broad (1949–50).

egoism as the best motivational theory.[2] (This would not be to reject common sense psychological concepts but it would be to reject currently common beliefs expressed in those notions.) But mere logical possibilities of such evidence do not in fact constitute evidence for egoism. The actual, everyday evidence to the contrary is in no way diminished by the mere logical possibility of that evidence being overturned by further possible evidence. The sensible defender of psychological egoism has to produce that evidence in fact.

Psychological egoists not up to the challenge to produce the further, overturning evidence can try a few armchair ploys. The first is a re-description ploy. Given enough ink, the egoist can find ways of systematically re-describing any everyday example of a desire for an other-regarding object (e.g. a mother's concern for her offspring) in some similar-looking, but egoistic, way (e.g. the mother's concern for self-enhancement through child nurture). But every desire is what it is and not another. The two desires are not to be simply confused. Indeed the former is as conceptually possible as the latter. The second ploy the egoist uses is a 'source' ploy. Only like can come from like. 'How could *I* be motivated unless the object of the desire were *me* or *my welfare*?' This ploy, notoriously, confuses the subject of the motivation (*who* has the desire) with the object of the motivation (*what* is desired) or else assumes the object (thing desired) must be like, or suitably related to, the subject (person desiring it). But in common sense psychology no such conceptual limits are put on the possible objects of desire.

Butler's refutation of psychological egoism bears a strong analogy to what we might call the 'refutation' of the provocative version of Hume's theory of motivating reasons. Admittedly the defender of the provocative version who has absorbed the Butler-Broad discussion will reject and feel superior to the psychological egoist. The latter, he will admit, construes much too narrowly the possible objects of desire. The Humean agrees that we can have desires for non-egoistic objects. (In turn the psychological egoist feels a step ahead of the psychological hedonist who has a much too narrow conception of self-interest or welfare, construing it in terms of bodily pleasures and the avoidance of pain sensations.) My view is that all three, the psychological hedonist (P.H.), the psychological

2 For example, Slote (1964).

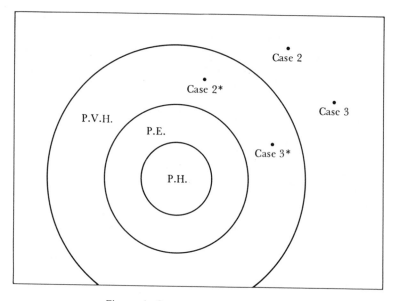

Figure 4. Common sense psychology

egoist (P.E.), and the provocative version of Hume (P.V.H.), construe common sense psychology and what we seem to observe every day much too narrowly. No doubt there is an increase in sophistication as we proceed along this sequence of views, but all are philistine views of human nature to varying degrees. The picture as I see it is something like figure 4. Each point on the area represents a different kind of motivation or desire, as distinguished by their objects. A given theory of human motivation is represented by a circle. The theory allows the motivations represented by all the points within the circle but rules out those outside the circle. Thus, psychological egoism (P.E.) allows all the motivational cases psychological hedonism (P.H.) does, and more besides; the provocative Humean theory (P.V.H.) allows all that psychological egoism does and some more. Finally, I allege, common sense psychology allows those and a lot more besides (such as cases 2 and 3).

The first step of the 'refutation' of the provocative version of the Humean theory consists in making the conceptual point that common sense psychology puts relatively few limits on what might be a practical argument which, when accepted, might motivate. In particular, it does not rule out motivational cases 2 and 3. It reminds us that practical arguments other than those allowed by that normative theory we have called the Humean theory of *justifying* reasons can be accepted and motivate. Even if Humean ones should be the only good arguments, they are very far from being the only motivating ones. The second step of the 'refutation' consists in reminding ourselves that we seem to observe a lot of everyday cases of 'non-Humean' motivations. People just do count a number of things besides their own desires as justifying reasons why they should act and such views (however rational or irrational) sometimes figure in the explanations of their actions. Furthermore, there is no evidence at present to suggest we are systematically deceived or suffering mass hallucinations in all this (although we sometimes detect mistakes about particular cases). Such everyday observations make it reasonable to believe the provocative Humean theory has clear counter-instances. Of course it is still logically possible that the right evidence will turn up which will show this theory is true after all, contrary to initial appearances. But to gesture at a logical possibility is not to produce the empirical goods. Both Santa Claus and unicorns have logical possibility going for them. The sensible defender of the provocative theory has to produce the evidence that will show how appearances have systematically deceived us.

Humeans not up to the challenge to produce actual evidence may well try two armchair ploys on us. The one is the redescription ploy which attempts to turn our attention from the difficult cases for provocative theory to others which fit the theory better. Our response to this must be 'But everything is what it is and not another thing'. Butler would be proud. The other ploy relies on insisting that one just couldn't be motivated by a practical argument that didn't bring a motivation into the justifying reason. Our response to this must be that it is no more obvious that only this narrow range of practical arguments is capable of motivating than before, in regard to psychological egoisms, it was obvious that only a narrow range of objects of desire was possible. The very concept of a desire seems to put very few limits on what might be the object of a desire. Likewise, the very concept of motivating reasons for acting seems to put very few limits on what kinds of justifying reasons might, if accepted, motivate. While the argument against the provocative Humean theory is not in every detail the same as the argument against psychological egoism, it is hard to see how anyone who has seen through the psychological egoist's two ploys

121

should suddenly find the use of their exact analogues a credible defence of the provocative Humean theory of motivation. Don't we have a sense of *déjà vu?*

THE PARALLELS IN THEORETICAL REASONING

Normative notions, e.g. the notion of a 'justifying reason', have a place not merely within moral thought but in at least two other kinds of thinking as well. The notion of a justifying reason has crucial application both in theoretical reason and in prudential reasoning. In regard to the former, we talk of good (i.e., justifying) reasons for believing as much as of good reasons for doing. One may easily think of inference or deduction as a matter of norms, of what there is good reason to believe given certain other things. In regard to the latter, prudential reasoning, we are back again in the realm of reasons for acting rather than believing, but the reasons are not moral reasons but reasons of another sort. Because we find justifying reasons in areas other than morality, it is almost always illuminating (although somewhat cruel to Humeans) to ask whether any Humean thesis about justifying reasons in regard to morality could just as well apply to justification in theoretical reason or in prudential reasoning. Again it will usually be illuminating to ask of any Humean motivational thesis whether it applies not only to moral motivation but to theoretical and prudential motivations as well.

There are theoretical motivations. It is wrong to suppose one can only be motivated to act (and perhaps also to feel). One can also be moved to believe. One can have reasons for believing what one does just as one can have reasons for doing what one did. Among the things that can move us to believe further, new things are the justificatory arguments we accept. Hence it can happen that the explanation of my believing (cognitive) proposition q is just that I accept the following argument as sound:

Theoretical Argument 1

i. p

ii. If p, then q

iii. q

'Accepting' theoretical argument 1 means I believe the two (cognitive) premisses are true and I also accept (whether implicitly or

122

explicitly) that *modus ponens* is a good form of inference. (Perhaps I also have to put these three beliefs together at some point.) While it is perhaps not inevitable, in the particular case I wish to discuss this 'acceptance' of argument 1 moves me a bit to believe something else as well, viz. proposition *q*. Indeed that is what explains, or is an important part of the explanation of, my believing *q*. It is my reason for believing *q*.

In short, we can be moved to believe things by other beliefs that we have. Indeed, at face value, it would seem that sometimes beliefs are 'alone' capable of motivating other beliefs (i.e., without requiring further passions at least). If this is so, it is not, strictly speaking, a counter-example to any version of the Humean theory of motivation. The latter only denies that beliefs can 'alone' motivate us to *act* or *feel*. It takes no stand on whether they can 'alone' move us to further *beliefs*. Even so, the possibility of such 'contemplative motivations' must be an embarrassment for any Humean position. To allow that beliefs can 'alone' move us in even one respect must make it seem more of a real issue whether they can 'alone' move us in regard to actions. Beliefs, it would seem, are not motivationally inert in every respect. Thus they are not utterly of the wrong category to be involved in motivation. There is then a real question why beliefs should be so inert in regard to motivations to act. Admittedly motivations to act and motivations to believe are different kinds of motivations. But the Humean must do more than make a distinction. He must show why this distinction makes a difference, indeed, as it would seem, all the difference in the world.

Alternatively, the Humean might not stop his motivational theory short of motivations to believe. He might generalise it to apply quite across the board. In that event the Humean would hold that (cognitive) beliefs 'alone' can never move us to other beliefs unless there is a passion or pro-attitude which makes this possible. But where exactly do we find this alleged 'passion' in my *modus ponens* case of motivating theoretical reasoning? What passion was involved in the case where the explanation of my believing *q* was my having reasons for believing it? As with the moral motivational cases of the previous chapter, there will be, analogously, at least four different versions of the (generalised) Humean theory of motivating reasons, depending on just where we are to look for the passion or pro-attitude in the *modus ponens* case. The vacuous version will locate the passion precisely in my being moved (when it happens) by certain of my other beliefs (e.g. that p is true, that if p then q, that *modus ponens* is valid, etc.). That of course is just 'the motivation one can always find'. A second version (corresponding to the 'defeating version' in the moral cases) will hold that the belief that I should (for *modus ponens* reasons) believe p will not by itself move me unless I have an additional, separate passion (e.g. the desire to believe what I have rational ground for believing). To see what one should believe is not to be moved at all unless one has a separate desire to be rational as well. A third version (corresponding to the 'question-begging version' in the moral cases) will hold that the normative 'beliefs' (broad sense) that *modus ponens* is a good argument and that one has justifying reason to believe q already involve some passions or pro-attitudes. Logical inference is something 'felt of'. In this third version the passion is to be found in the 'accepting' of the theoretical argument. In the second version it is not there but in some additional alleged 'desire to be rational'. In the first version it is in neither of those but in the causal capacity of such an acceptance to induce the further belief that q.

As always the fourth version is the strangest. It is the analogue of the 'provocative version'. It holds that the *modus ponens* case I have described is quite incapable of being a possible motivation to believe. Theoretical argument 1, however good or bad it may be, cannot actually move anyone to believe q. Before any theoretical argument can, upon acceptance, move one it must have a further premise, such as (i') below, added to it to make:

Theoretical Argument 1*

i'. I like *modus ponens* (i.e., I have some desire to form my beliefs in conformity with it)

i. p

ii. If p, then q

iii. q

This justificatory argument, this version alleges, and not the previous one, is the argument that can move us. What they teach us in logic classes (e.g. theoretical argument 1) cannot, strictly speaking, move us to believe anything. This provocative view may be defended by two ploys. To the obvious objection that sometimes people seem moved to believe new things on the basis of *modus ponens* arguments they accept, the reply is that in such cases the arguments they really accept are of the form of argument 1* above. That is the redescription ploy. (But do I really think that if I liked *modus ponens* less I would have that much less justifying reason to infer q in such a case?) The second ploy insists that unless there were a motivation (to believe) 'for the agent to deliberate *from*' it would be quite impossible for him to acquire this new motivation to believe q. Where else could this new motivation come from? That is the motivational source ploy.

Cases of theoretical motivations pose a dilemma for the defender of the provocative version of the Humean theory of motivation. To apply the provocative theory generally, i.e., to motivations to believe as well as to motivations to act, clearly exposes how contrary the provocative theory is to common sense psychology. On the other hand to apply the provocative theory discriminatingly, i.e., just to motivations to act, raises the obvious question of what warrants this discrimination. Why should there be this radical difference between the two kinds of cases? Furthermore, it raises the question of why the two ploys to defend the provocative theory in regard to motivations to act are not equally good at defending a provocative theory in regard to motivations to believe. If they were good before, why aren't they good now?

PRUDENTIAL REASONS

But even if the provocative version of the Humean theory applies, as we might charitably concede, to motivated action, not to motivated beliefs, it will still apply as much to prudential motivations as to moral motivations. And in fact it is particularly worthwhile to consider prudential cases in addition to the three moral cases so far considered. One reason for doing so is that, however good our objections, Humeans are not going to be convinced by moral motivational cases such as the 2 and 3 of the preceding chapter. In particular they view case 2 (where the agent is motivated by a belief that his promise was a justifying reason) with more than a little suspicion. Hume himself seemed to have some particular difficulties with the notion of a promise, sometimes suggesting that the common notion involves an absurdity (517), sometimes that the act of a promise involves a lapse into momentary self-deception (523).

But even apart from their particular suspicions about promising, many Humeans can be said to bear a prejudice against the moral in general. Naturally a Humean who also accepts the Humean theory of *justifying* reasons will think that the practical arguments 2 and 3 are just bad arguments. The major premisses of these arguments, they think, provide no justifying reasons for acting. This normative (i.e., justificatory) Humean thesis sometimes might seem to buttress the motivational theory a bit. The feeling would be something like: 'Who could in fact be motivated by so transparently bad an argument as that offered in practical arguments 2 or 3?' They suppose that no one could be so irrational as actually to believe or act on non-Humean justifying reasons. Here the Humean motivational thesis rests on the Humean justificatory thesis plus the (quite dubious) claim that people are rational in their practical reasoning, that they make no mistakes about what sorts of things are justifying reasons.

Just as often the Humean's thoughts can run in the opposite direction, buttressing the justificatory thesis with the help of the motivational thesis. When pressure is put on the Humean to defend his rather particular view of what is a justifying reason, one defence is that, in any case, no one *could* be motivated by anything but Humean-approved justifying reasons. Here the provocative version of the motivational thesis buttresses the justificatory thesis. Of course to argue both ways at once, to use each theory as the sole or main buttress of the other creates that architectural wonder in philosophy, the totally floating system of belief. We leave such devices to 'dogmatic Humeans'. But even when the argument is not so circular, it is still true that Humeans tend to be suspicious of cases 2 and 3 on two, perhaps separate, grounds. Some Humeans, at least, think the practical arguments accepted therein are *bad* arguments, normatively speaking. More to our present concern, Humeans also tend to think that, in any case, these arguments *cannot be motivating*.

But whether a Humean has one or both of these prejudices against the moral, he cannot easily contain them. These prejudices will spill out and apply to prudential cases for the same reasons as in the moral cases. The Humean theory of justifying reasons is just as critical of leading cases of prudential reasoning as it is of leading cases of moral reasoning. The provocative Humean theory of motivation denies the latter a capacity to motivate just as much as it does the former. There is no Humean doctrine about moral justification or moral motivation that does not apply just as well to prudential reasoning and prudential motivation. To many this will seem to put the matter in a different light.

Two prudential practical arguments (and the corresponding cases of motivation for such prudential reasons) are in certain respects the prudential analogues of the moral practical arguments (and moral motivations) in cases 2 and 3. For example, just as the moral person thinks his past promise to others can, in the right circumstances, provide some justifying reason now for doing what he then promised, so the prudential person can think his past formed intentions (or perhaps a decision) can, in the appropriate circumstances, provide a justifying reason now for keeping to that intention. I do not want to exaggerate the parallel here. But both do share this similarity, both involve the notion of a past act where that very act is seen as something which binds one (in the justificatory sense) where, indeed, the very idea of such acts includes that they should have that normative force in the future. Thus we might consider this prudential argument:

Practical Argument 4

i.   I formed an intention at t1 to do φ at t2 (> t1) after considering various justifying reasons for and against doing φ

iia. No further significant considerations have come to light between t1 and t2 additional to those upon which the intention was formed

iib. No normative or factual defect was involved in the reasoning leading to my forming an intention at t1

·
·   [further subsidiary premises, if needed]
·

---

iii. At t2 I have some reason to do φ

·
·   [further premises]
·

---

iv. I should (all things considered) do φ at t2

The question of whether the fact of one's having formed an intention can, in the right circumstances, provide some additional reason for acting beyond the reasons which contributed to the forming of that intention is one much discussed in the recent philosophical literature.[3] Nor has it escaped notice that in certain respects prudential argument 4 can be considered the analogue of moral argument 2.

Another analogue has been much discussed in the recent literature.[4] The moral justifying reason which the wants or needs of others might be thought to provide according to practical argument 3 is in some respect analogous to the prudential justifying reasons provided by the desires and needs one *will* have in the future but does not now possess.[5] The demands of our future selves are a bit like the demands of others upon us. Thus we might also consider:

Practical Argument 5

i. I *will* desire ψ although I do not now desire ψ
ii. My doing ϕ *now* is the only means to get ψ

· [further subsidiary premisses]

---

iii. I have some reason *now* to do ϕ

· [further premisses]

---

iv. I should (all things considered) do ϕ now

Now in setting forth practical arguments 4 and 5 I am not doing quite the same thing as arguing for the proposition that they are good arguments (although I may believe that). I do not need to take that normative stand. Instead (and as with practical arguments 1, 2, 3) I am only doing two things. First, I am saying that the normative position behind such an argument is a conceptually coherent one given the concepts of common sense

3 Cf. Raz (1975); Harman (1976); Aune (1977); Robins (1984), pp. 29–44; Bratman (1981) and (1987). Writers typically distinguish intentions from decisions from vows or resolves (in order of increasing strength). Cf. Raz (1975) or Robins (1984). I slide over these rather important distinctions in my discussion.
4 Nagel (1970), ch. 6.
5 The claims I make are very much weaker than Nagel's (1970). For example, I do not claim that what will be a justifying reason for me at some future time must somehow generalise or extend over time to be a reason for me now. That quite general thesis about reasons is controversial. My claim is more modest, viz. that the fact that I will desire something can sometimes provide a justifying reason now (and that it is not the present desire to satisfy future desires which is the sole justifying reason in such cases).

psychology. There is nothing conceptually absurd about the normative view thereby expressed. In saying this I scrupulously avoid begging the issue between the cognitivist and the non-cognitivist (now in regard to prudential judgments rather than moral judgments). I am only saying it is possible to hold a normative view such as is expressed in 4 or 5. I leave it entirely open what 'holding' such a view may amount to, whether, for example, it is a cognitive or a non-cognitive matter. Second, whatever holding such a view may amount to, it is true that there are actual cases of people who hold such normative views. If I cite my own case that is not to constitute an argument for that normative view but only to provide some evidence for the psychological claim that some people do hold such prudential views. At least it would appear so.

RESOLVE AND PROVISION

It might seem less plausible that argument 4 is sometimes accepted than that practical argument 5 is. However, that it is commonly supposed that one's past intentions can, in the right circumstances, provide justifying reasons can be seen in cases where, otherwise, the justifying reasons (whatever they may be thought to be) between two courses of action are perfectly balanced (or perhaps not determinately comparable). Two sorts of cases are possible here. In one sort of case the 'end' can be taken as quite clearly justified (on Humean grounds, if you like) but each of two alternative means has just as much to be said in its favour. For example, suppose I think I already have sufficient justifying reason to drive to the university. But on consulting the map I see that two routes are possible, one involving a left hand turn at the next corner and the other a right hand turn. I weigh the various considerations (times of travel, likely amounts of traffic, etc.) and these balance each other perfectly or else do not make for a problem which has a determinate solution. So I just form an intention (at t1) to turn left when I get to the next corner (at t2). That it is left rather than right is admittedly arbitrary or a matter of whim. However let us suppose a few seconds later (after t1 but before t2) the question occurs to me 'What do I have reason to do at the next corner?' Whether or not I do raise that question, there is such a question. Admittedly the ordinary person does not raise this question but that is because the answer is obvious and there is no point in wasting time on the obvious. If nothing has changed in the meantime, I think I have, in addition to the perfectly balanced reasons which also applied before t1, an additional justifying reason to turn left, i.e., the fact that I formed an intention to do so. That, supposing nothing further has changed, now tips the balance in favour of the left turn.

From the point of view of the Humean theory of justifying reasons I must be making a mistake in practical reasoning. If nothing else has changed then the practical problem after t1 is just the same as before. The formation of an intention (now past) cannot *now* be any sort of justifying reason. All that is relevant is all the considerations that were relevant before (times, traffic, etc.) and, as before, these considerations come out perfectly balanced. So on Humean grounds I still (after t1 but at or before t2) have no more justifying reason to turn left than right. Even if I try a second intention, a moment later it also will have no justificatory force and the old, perfectly balanced decision problem will recur. If the Humean remains true to his justificatory principles he will be stuck like Buridan's ass at the intersection unless saved by a fortunate non-rational impulse. But even if he is saved at the last moment, his official view all the way to the intersection must be that he has no more justifying reason to go one way than the other. He will have to hope for something non-rational. I do not think that we are Humeans. We do think that a past formed intention provides, now, some justifying reason for acting. If the Humean theory of justifying reasons is right, we are irrational. If so, we are very lucky to be irrational in this way.

In a second sort of case, it is not the means which are perfectly balanced but two competing ends (Bratman, 1981, p. 253):

Suppose I must choose between law school and graduate school in philosophy. I see my desiderative reasons for each option as having roughly equal weight or – as is more commonly the case – I am unable to reach a meaningful assessment of how my desiderative reasons weigh. Faced with the need to settle the matter, I form an intention to go to law school. Having formed this intention I now have a reason for opting for some means to going to law school, a reason I did not have before.

We must not allow these two sorts of cases to be caricatured. I am not supposing it is some sort of blood vow or resolution I

130

take to turn left. If the ordinary view is superstitious, it is not quite that superstitious. Indeed the ordinary view about the reason-giving force of intentions is marked by its high degree of flexibility. First, I would not ordinarily think the justifying reason provided by a mere intention is all that strong. It can be overridden by other, not particularly weighty reasons of a conflicting sort. If my passenger says he would prefer the other route, that might provide enough reason, to outweigh the reason I have to stick to my original plan. But second, the reason provided by an intention can also be just defeated or cancelled (not merely overridden, for that still grants it some weight) under circumstances such as the following: (a) I discover a serious defect in the original reasoning which led to the intention in the first place (Robins, 1984, p. 36). For example, I might have miscalculated the distances, where this makes a great difference to the choice of means. (b) New significant considerations might come to light which bear importantly on the original reasoning leading to the intention. For example I discover the left hand route involves a long detour that I hadn't reckoned on. That makes a difference. In such cases it is rational to change one's intentions. But, as Robins points out (1984, pp. 33, 35), that it is sometimes rational to change one's intentions does not show intentions never provide any justifying reason at all. While one can form intentions somewhat arbitrarily (e.g. choose left), one cannot, without a charge of irrationality, change them arbitrarily. One must, as in (a) and (b) above, have sufficient reason for changing one's mind. If one really thought one could always change one's mind, or change one's plans, without any justifying reason at all, one would lose thereby the capacity to form intentions or make plans at all. What could be the point of a strange mental exercise which one thought in no way binding on one's future self?

There are several mistaken accounts of forming intentions and of the reason-giving force of intentions which must be avoided. First, it might be supposed that at the later time, t2, I am only remembering that earlier, at t1, I went through a practical deliberation which had the conclusion that I should do ϕ even if perhaps I can't remember all the details of that reasoning now. If I think the circumstances have not changed between t1 and t2, then I might think I still have the same (all things considered) reason to φ that I calculated before. I trust my past calculations without going through them again. This would be not to count one's past intention as itself the justifying reason but only to count it as good evidence that the things which are the justifying reasons continue to come out in favour of φ. However it was precisely to avoid confusion with this sort of consideration that we chose as our examples cases where the results of the original deliberation were perfectly balanced. Here it is the intention that gets us out of a deliberative stalemate. And the reason we have later cannot be just the evidence provided by the memory of our past deliberations, for if that is accurate we will only remember that stalemate.

Second, we must not suppose that to form an intention at t1 to do φ at t2 is to do something at t1 which causes or forces one's later self to do φ at t2 (cf. Robins, 1984, pp. 22, 29).[6] That can happen, but it is a different sort of thing. That's more like jumping off the diving board or pushing off the ski slope so that thereafter there will be no turning back. But when I get to the intersection, I still *can* turn right just as easily as left. (I haven't fitted a special temporary lock to the wheel, for example.)

Third, we must not suppose that the intention at t1 changes my desires so that when I reach the intersection I have a rather strong yen for left over right. That, too, can happen, but it is a different case. That's more like addicting oneself to heroin or eating salty things to make oneself thirsty. But if I do have a desire to turn left when I get to the intersection that will be a desire to turn left, not for itself, but only for a reason. It will be, unless I am very odd, a motivated reason. And of course the reason I will have for wanting to turn left is that it's my plan, i.e., my intention is a reason. Hence my intention brings about a new motivation only in the sense that my accepting my intention as a justifying reason for acting may motivate me to so act. But it is wrong to suppose the intention consists in bringing about in some other way a yen for left turns.

Fourth, forming an intention is not doing something at t1 which

6 I find it odd that Elster (1984, p. 43) says that 'our intuitive notion of what it is to bind oneself seems to require that we temporarily deposit our will in some external structure; that we set up a causal process in the external world that after some time returns to its source and modifies our behaviour'. Generally, cf. Elster (1984, ch. 2) on 'precommitment'.

so changes the circumstances that at t2 one has a justifying reason in those new circumstances which one would not otherwise have had. This, too, can occur but it is a different thing. For example, even a poor Humean stuck indecisively between going to law school and doing graduate work in philosophy might rush out to buy a lot of expensive non-returnable law books. (We won't inquire how exactly this comes about.) *Afterwards* he has a good reason which tips the balance in favour of law school. It would be just too expensive to do the other now. But the justifying reason here is not an intention but the new situation he finds himself in. By contrast, merely forming an intention costs less and is rather more flexible. If unexpectedly new considerations come to light which strongly favour philosophy over law, the person with all those expensive law books may find he still doesn't have enough reason to change from law, or if he does, he has wasted a lot of money on law books. The person who merely formed an intention, however, managed to solve the original decision problem without any subsequent loss in flexibility.

Practical argument 4 captures a very ordinary notion about prudential justification that the Humean theory of justifying reasons does not. It seems clear enough (given that we are not Hamlets of the intersection) that we at least think our past intentions can in the right circumstances provide some justifying reasons for acting now. Furthermore, it seems clear that, whether or not we are rational in so thinking and acting, we end up a lot better off than if we didn't. The creature that can commit his own future while continuing to retain flexibility in that regard gains immeasurably in power. He becomes the animal that 'can make promises to himself' as Nietzsche put it. The ordinary notion of prudence involves this virtue of flexible resolution. By contrast, the totally irresolute cannot even plan. They lack 'will' in one basic sense of the word. Those who resent too much the rightful authority of their own immediate past intentions risk, not only the loss of any kind of control over the world, but indeed the disintegration of the person into person time-slices. We should not underestimate too much the role of the acceptance of prudential norms in holding together whatever fragile unity there is to the soul. Accepted prudential norms may hold together the person as accepted social norms hold together society.

The above observation is not a refutation of the Humean position on justifying reasons however. As Parfit (1984, pp. 12–13) has taught us, it can sometimes turn out to be rational to cause oneself to become irrational in certain respects (without that making the latter any the less irrational). Thus, a Humean about justification might think he has reason to change himself into (or be glad he already is) the kind of person who, quite irrationally, sometimes counts his past intentions as reasons for acting. The reason is that he'll do better (in Humean terms) in the long run by a policy of acting on certain non-Humean reasons. At least a Humean might think this if he supposes he had some reason to protect his own long-term interests in the future. On what grounds does a Humean think that? That takes us to the other prudential argument.

One ground for concern about one's own future is presented in practical argument 5. But the Humean theory of justifying reasons (e.g. Brandt, 1979, pp. 81–7, or Gauthier, 1986, pp. 37–8) must reject that as much as it rejects argument 4. Argument 5 does, indeed, mention desires as providing reasons and, even more propitiously, one's own desires. But the time of the desire is inappropriate (cf. Chapter 4 under 'Motivating reasons'). There are several reasons why Humeans will reject argument 5. For one thing it seems to be the thin edge of a wedge. The desire of a future self may be in some respects different from the desire of another (even specially related) person but it doesn't seem all that different, not so radically different that the one could provide a justifying reason while the other could provide none at all under any circumstances. But another reason for Humeans to reject argument 5 is that it does not have the one advantage Humeans like to praise in their justifying reasons. It does not seem to provide a 'motivational source' for action in the present. How can a desire that does not exist now move me to action now? On the other hand if that is not a condition of being a good reason, or if the motivation comes from somewhere else than *within* the justifying reason, we might well wonder why similar things cannot be said about the desires of others or even the belief that one made a promise.

This now sets the Humean theory of *justifying* reasons in rather greater relief. It not only sets it apart from ordinary moral reasoning (arguments 2 and 3), it sets it just as much apart from ordinary prudential reasoning (arguments 4 and 5). Indeed the Humean theory strikes at what is the core of our ordinary notion of prudence:

resolution and providence. Hence it strikes at those norms the acceptance of which seems to unify the person. The Humean theory rejects the rightful claims of one's past (in one's intentions and plans) and the rightful claims of, and obligations to, one's future (in one's future desires). It is perhaps no momentary lapse or literary flourish which leads Hume to say:

'Tis not contrary to reason for me to chuse my total ruin. . . . 'Tis as little contrary to reason to prefer even my own acknowledg'd lesser good to my greater, and have a more ardent affection for the former than the latter. (416)

Indeed, according to the Humean theory of justifying reasons it is positively rational to so choose, provided you really do now want that. This view is no kinder to prudent self-interest than it is to morality. It is a normative view, indeed, but one which would do as much to replace prudence as it would morality with something radically different.

TWO PRUDENTIAL MOTIVATIONS

Whether practical arguments 4 and 5 are rationally justified or not is one question. A different question is whether they can be accepted and even motivating. It is this latter question which concerns us. If we are to go by everyday observation and appearances we must say that these arguments, whether or not justified, are motivating.

There's many a slip between acceptance and action. It is far from inevitable that in every case a person accepts a practical argument he is motivated sufficiently by that acceptance to do ϕ, so that in the actual circumstances he ends up doing ϕ. Various problems and defects typically intervene. But, as with the previous motivational cases, I shall simply choose as my examples those occasional cases where all goes well and where the explanation of the agent's doing ϕ will significantly involve his accepting a certain practical argument. Thus I choose the hits, rather than the near misses, to discuss:

Motivational Case 4
P4 'accepts' practical argument 4
P4's accepting argument 4 motivates P4 a bit to doing ϕ
P4 does ϕ because of his having accepted argument 4

Motivational Case 5
P5 'accepts' practical argument 5
P5's accepting argument 5 motivates P5 a bit to doing φ
P5 does φ because of his having accepted argument 5

We would ordinarily suppose that persons sometimes act out of prudential reasons such as those in arguments 4 or 5, just as we would ordinarily suppose persons sometimes act out of moral reasons such as those in arguments 2 or 3. The provocative version of the Humean theory of motivating reasons (quite unlike the other versions of the Humean theory) denies that motivational cases 4 or 5 can occur any more than cases 2 or 3 can. It is not that the defenders of the provocative version have extra evidence the rest of us do not have yet or that they have a defensible, empirically based scientific theory which overturns the evidence of first appearances. Instead they have two armchair ploys. Besides the usual 'motivational source ploy' there is, as we have now come to expect, the 'redescription' ploy. It is admitted that there is something we ordinarily describe as acting out of prudential reasons, but that what is really going on has to be represented in a different way. The practical arguments which are being 'accepted' in such cases are not, say, 4 or 5, but rather:

Practical Argument 4*
i*. I have a *desire* at t2 (now) to keep my (appropriately unaltered) intentions formed earlier at t1
i. I formed an intention at t1 to do φ at t2 after considering various justifying reasons for and against doing φ
iia. No further significant considerations have come to light between t1 and t2 additional to those upon which the intention to do φ at t2 was formed
iib. No normative or factual defect was involved in the reasoning leading
. to my forming my intention at t1 to do φ at t2
.
.
. [further subsidiary premises, if needed]
iii. At t2 (now) I have some reason to do φ
.
. [further premises]
.
iv. I should (all things considered) do φ at t2

and also:

i*. At t1 (now) I *desire* somewhat to provide for the desires I will have at t2

i. At t2 I will desire ψ although I do not now desire ψ

ii. My doing ϕ at t1 is the only means to get ψ at t2

.
.
. [further subsidiary premisses]
.

---

iii. At t1 (now) I have some reason to do ϕ
.
. [further premisses]
.

---

iv. I should (all things considered) do ϕ at t1

Using these practical arguments, two motivational cases, case 4* and case 5*, can be specified as before. They are what can occur, not cases 4 or 5, according to the provocative theory.

To this it must be replied that just as the practical arguments 4* and 5* are not the same as arguments 4 and 5, respectively, so the motivations in cases 4* and 5* are not the same as the motivations in 4 and 5, respectively. For example, the person who accepts practical argument 4 (or 5) takes the view that he still has that justifying reason even in the case his present desire to comply with past intentions (or provide for future desires) either flags or altogether ceases. His view is that in that event it is not that the justifying reason diminishes or lapses but that his motivation is defective.[7] Furthermore the provocative view misrepresents the na-

---

7 The *justificatory* view Parfit calls the 'Critical Present-aim theory' (1984, ch. 6) is neither really like practical argument 5 nor really like practical argument 5*. In one respect it is more like the latter (Humean view) in its stress on the present. However, versions of the CP theory can allow that some present desires may be excluded as reason-providers on the grounds of their 'irrationality' and furthermore that reasons may be provided by desires one does not have at all where having them is 'rationally required'. These two moves will make for a CP theory closer to the ordinary norms of prudence. However it accomplishes this by erecting a second level of justification where it is desires (rather than actions) which are assessed either as irrational or rationally required. If these second-order issues of rationality depend in the end on present aims (or desires) of the agent, the theory remains quite Humean (and probably just as far from common sense prudential norms as ever). On the other hand, if the questions of rationality and justification at this second level do not depend only on *present* aims (desires) or even only on desires, then we have a distinctly non-Humean theory and one likely to be somewhat closer to common sense prudential rationality. It does seem odd

ture of the desire one might have to live up to standing plans or provide for future desires. Usually it is not just a desire for these things for themselves (an 'unmotivated' desire, as Nagel would say) but a desire I have for reasons (a 'motivated' desire). It has that amount of structure at least. It is at least in part because I think my plans or my future desires provide some reason for acting that I now desire to so act. The reasons I accept explain the desire (rather than the desire being the justifying reason).

These are, of course, just the sort of points made in regard to the moral motivational cases. Here, however, we can examine the issue without having to contend against the 'prejudice against the moral', or at the very least the prejudice must convert itself into the 'prejudice against the normative in general'. The provocative theory of motivating reasons cannot be contained just within the confines of the moral. It breaks out into the realm of the prudential and threatens even theoretical motivations as well.

THE CHASTENED HUMEAN

The provocative Humean theory of motivating reasons is a theory posed in terms of common sense psychological notions. If we are eliminativists about such notions we also eliminate the provocative theory. On the other hand, if we do accept the conceptual framework of common sense psychology, we cannot pass off the provocative theory as just a conceptual truth, i.e., true in virtue of those common sense notions. Our ordinary concepts of motivation allow other motivational possibilities way beyond the narrow restrictions of the provocative theory. Furthermore there is rather a lot of everyday observation (laden, no doubt, with these common sense psychological concepts) which gives us reason to reject the provocative theory on empirical grounds. The counter-example

that a normative theory would be obsessive about the present at the first-order (action) level but lose that obsession at the second-order level (the evaluation of desires or aims). If all sorts of things might be thought relevant to the evaluation of a desire, why can't all sorts of things be relevant to the evaluation of an act? Parfit's CP theory might well be a hybrid view, Humean at the (first-order) level of action, non-Humean at the (second-order) level of the evaluation of aims (desires).

Of course we at this point are concerned not with theories of justification (which is what the CP theory is about) but with the issue of what sorts of theories can, when believed, motivate. Even if practical argument 5 is a bad argument, it is a separate issue whether it commonly motivates nonetheless.

cases are not only conceptually possible, we seem actually to observe many such cases. While this evidence might in principle be overturned by further evidence or empirically based theorising of the right sort, the defenders of the provocative version do not actually have this in hand, although they do have a couple of armchair ploys. These two armchair ploys, along with the ease with which the provocative version can be confused with the other, relatively innocuous, versions of the Humean theory, can make the provocative theory appear, at least, close to impregnable. This is one of those recurring conceptual illusions which, along with psychological hedonism and psychological egoism, it seems, every generation of philosophy encounters anew. Sweeping these ploys and confusions aside, we can see that the provocative version not only fails to encapsulate the deliverances of common sense, in fact those deliverances give us every reason to think it false.

There are at least three reasons why it is important that the provocative version (but perhaps not the other versions) of the Humean theory is false. The third one bears on our main reason for discussing this version, but the other two reasons should be noted as well. *First,* that this version is false is of importance for our understanding of the social sciences, such as anthropology, and our understanding of social facts and institutions. One way of trying to understand social institutions (e.g. kinship, or property, or legal institutions) is in terms of the kinds of reasons people (rightly or wrongly) think they have for acting or feeling in certain situations and the ways in which this can explain, on occasion, their so acting or feeling. Thus we may understand kinship institutions in terms of the types of 'kinship reasons' people in certain societies accept as reasons for acting. In this respect our motivational case 2, involving promise-reasons, is not unlike, in its structure, a great many other kinds of reasons for acting that are accepted in our, and other, societies. The provocative version denies that people can ever really count their own promises, or their kinship relations, or the property of others, etc., as a justifying reason for acting and be motivated somewhat by this acceptance. Instead, it claims, people really are counting the fact of their own yens for promise-keeping (or to comply with kinship obligations, etc.) as the real justifying reason.

This distorts anthropology in two respects. First it makes it seem there is less normative diversity than there really is. It makes it seem as if we are all really rather philistine Humeans about what can be a justifying reason. It tries to rationalise us all according to its own lights as to what is rational. This is on a par with turning the mythological beliefs of other cultures into proto-Enlightenment scientific theories. Even if we *should* accept only Humean-approved justifying reasons (which I doubt), let us get our matters of fact correct. In point of fact humans *do* accept a great many other kinds of reasons as well. This applies as much in prudential reasoning as in moral reasoning. Furthermore, and second, the provocative theory distorts the nature of the desires in question. It makes it seem as if the desire, say, to keep a promise or to honour a kinship obligation is invariably some sort of *sui generis* desire just for certain objects for themselves (e.g. that promises be kept). They start to look like strange yens. But what we would ordinarily count as these desires have rather more in the way of structure behind them. They involve being moved by various kinds of considerations where these considerations are not inevitably themselves the present desires of the agent. What anthropology and the study of human institutions still require is a good account of what it is to hold a normative view about what is a justifying reason. Nor can one expect to represent what it is to be motivated by the norms one holds without going into the justificatory structure of those norms.

The *second* way in which the falsehood of the provocative Humean theory is important is in regard to the Humean theory of justifying reasons. If the provocative motivational theory is false, then the Humean justificatory theory is very much harder to defend. If the motivational theory fails, it can no longer be said that the Humean theory of justifying reasons is just the one we already follow or that, in any case, it is motivationally impossible to act on any other. It seems, after all, that it is motivationally possible, indeed common, to act on non-Humean reasons. Not even in regard to prudent self-interest is it the right story. But this motivational diversity can only raise with more urgency the issue of which of the various kinds of justifying reasons which actually do motivate (whether Humean or non-Humean) have any claim to right reason. Indeed what a non-cognitivist must think on this matter is that there can be no ultimate truth or falsehood about such disputes. The Humean theory of justification is no more true or false, valid or invalid, than any of the non-Humean alternatives about. And if all that can be said in the end is that we are the way we are, in point of fact that way isn't very Humean.

Third, with the failure of the provocative theory goes the case for a strong, conceptually based first premise of any use in an influence argument capable of demonstrating non-cognitivism. With it goes that particularly confident case for non-cognitivism and, in turn, sentimentalism. There is no longer the smug argument.

BUT STILL VERY MUCH THE HUMEAN

I do claim to be a Humean, even if now a rather more circumspect one. My purpose has not been to demolish the important Humean doctrines and arguments but rather to determine where the foundations are still sound and where they are not. Hence two quite unwarranted misunderstandings of my foregoing discussion must be avoided. First, I have not argued that there is *no* good argument for non-cognitivism (and thus sentimentalism). Second, I have not argued that *no* version of the Humean theory of motivating reasons is true. I have not been trying to defeat the Humean project but only to determine on which arguments and on which versions we Humeans would best concentrate our efforts in the future.

To avoid the first misunderstanding, it should be remembered that in Chapter 2 I examined in detail only one of Hume's (and Humeans') important arguments for non-cognitivism, i.e., the influence argument. It alone, of the arguments Humeans give, is a particularly smug argument. It alone seems to make some claim to being a conclusive argument. On examination that argument actually had several importantly different versions. While versions (A), (B) and (C) require a strong, conceptually based first premise (that cognitive beliefs *cannot* 'alone' be an influence on actions or passions), version (D) needs only a relatively weak first premiss (but then requires a strong second premiss). Relying on a strong first premiss, as in (A), (B) or (C), has seemed, even to Hume, the basis of a conclusive argument for non-cognitivism.

The strong, conceptually based first premiss will just be false outright if it is construed merely as a crude claim about the causal powers of cognitive beliefs (see Chapter 4). Only as a theory about the influence provided by 'motivating reasons' can it avoid the quick counter-example. Hence the strong, conceptually based first premiss will be some version of a Humean theory of *motivating reasons*. But in taking it thus (and thereby avoiding the quick counter-example) the first premiss becomes a thesis couched in the language of common sense psychology. If it is conceptually true, as it claims, it is true in virtue of the core concepts of common sense psychology.

Even so, not every version of the Humean theory of motivating reasons will be successful as a first premiss in the influence argument (Chapter 4). One or more of the question-begging version, the defeating version or the vacuous version may be true (and in the first two cases that would be interesting in other regards). But for various reasons none of these three can be employed in an influence argument that succeeds in leading us to the truth of the conclusion, non-cognitivism. Only, it would seem, the provocative version of the Humean thesis has a chance of working in a successful and enlightening argument. It has a somewhat different defect however (Chapter 5 above). It is false. Certainly it is not true just in virtue of the concepts of common sense psychology. The versions of Hume's thesis which might be true cannot work in the argument, and the one which would work isn't true. Only the failure to distinguish between the various versions of the Humean theory of motivating reasons could make it appear there was but one thesis which always has an answer for any difficulty, which could both work in the influence argument and be true. It is from this conceptual illusion that the smug Humean suffers.

But that is not to say there are *no* arguments for non-cognitivism. I have argued, rather, that there is no smug, conclusive argument for non-cognitivism such as is promised by the influence argument. But there may be less conclusive arguments. I suppose version (D) of the influence argument has something to be said in its favour. It bases the weight of the argument on its strong second premiss, internalism. But this will not be a straightforward, uncontroversial argument. I have already mentioned some reasons for being a little suspicious of the internalism required in that argument.

I myself am very much more inclined to think we Humeans should turn away from the influence argument and put our money, instead, either on some version of the epistemological argument or else, more plausibly I think, on some eliminativist argument (cf. Chapter 2 above). I have sketched such a view elsewhere (Snare, 1984). It is not my purpose to take up these other, more promising, arguments here. An important moral of the discussion in this first half is that we Humeans should get to work on some epistemological or else eliminativist argument and no longer pretend we

142

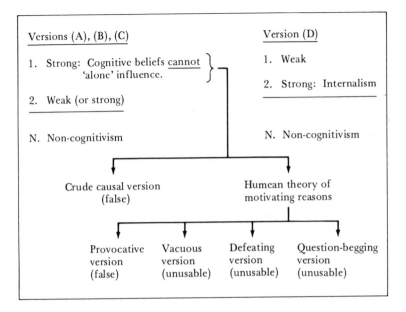

Figure 5. Hume's influence argument

have anything so conclusive (and *a priori*) as the influence argument pretended to be. We should be a little ashamed that we took the issue to be so easy that we could determine it all from the armchair, that we thought our emerging scientific accounts of society and human nature were irrelevant to the issue.

It is just as important to avoid the second misunderstanding of my discussion. I have certainly not argued that the Humean theory of motivation is false, that we must go for some non-Humean account. I have only argued that the *provocative version* is false. As a card-carrying Humean I still think *some* version of the theory is right (and something more than just the *vacuous version*). Quite obviously, no Humean can accept the *defeating version*. That version takes a cognitivist view of moral beliefs but then preserves the Humean theory of motivation by positing some quite separate 'desire to do one's duty' (or whatever). We Humean non-cognitivists hope that is not the correct version of the Humean theory of motivation. So naturally what I would like to believe is some *question-begging version* (as I called it). The label 'question-begging' is no reproach at all in the present context. That label indicates, not any circularity in the thesis itself, but only in its *employment* as a premiss in the influence argument. While we cannot use it to prove non-cognitivism, it may still be true. Indeed this version is something we have rather more reason to believe *after* we have succeeded in giving an independent case for non-cognitivism. Consequently a sensible Humean will suppose, in regard to our much-discussed cases 2 and 3, that the conative element required by the Humean theory of motivation comes in, not within the argument accepted, but in the 'accepting' of that argument (whatever its contents).

But if a plausible version of the Humean theory of motivating reasons is no part of the proof of non-cognitivism (and thus of sentimentalism), that is not to say it is irrelevant to the defence and exposition of sentimentalism. Indeed the issue of what a sensible sentimentalist must suppose is involved in 'accepting' a practical argument such as PA2 is at the very core of the main problem Hume encounters in his developing discussion of sentimentalism. It's precisely why, I shall argue, he cannot avoid talking in some detail about that particularly troublesome class of moral judgments he classifies under the heading 'justice'.

But how exactly do such cases, such 'acceptings', pose a peculiar problem for sentimentalism?

Part II

*The problems and
consequences of sentimentalism*

6

Continuity and circularity

The interesting thesis, for contemporary Humeans, in Part i of Book III of the *Treatise* is Hume's account of moral belief (broad sense), i.e., his sentimentalism, as some have called it. Hume's account has two parts. The basic, most argued for, part is a *negative* account of moral belief (III,i,1). It makes a claim about what moral judgments are *not*. They are not 'deriv'd from reason'. I have argued that this negative claim is non-cognitivism (unless it is a highly subjectivist cognitivism). The *positive* thesis (III,i,2) is an account of what moral beliefs *are*. They are, or express, or centrally involve, the having of special sentiments (unless, perhaps, they are non-inferential cognitive beliefs about one's having sentiments).

To have the sense of virtue, is nothing but to *feel* a satisfaction of a particular kind from the contemplation of a character. The very *feeling* constitutes our praise or admiration. We go no farther; nor do we enquire into the cause of the satisfaction. We do not infer a character to be virtuous, because it pleases: But in feeling that it pleases after such a particular manner, we in effect feel that it is virtuous. (471)

Sentimentalism is a meta-ethical thesis, at least in the broadest sense of 'meta-ethical', for it is a claim about the nature of moral judgments and not (obviously, at any rate) itself one of the substantive moral judgments it is about.

By contrast what Hume discusses in the rest of Book III (i.e., Parts ii and iii) seems to cover a number of substantial moral claims. His discussion seems to have consequences at the level of substantive normative ethics. Hume discusses in those Parts particular moral virtues and their main types. And his claims are often far from uncontroversial commonplaces. His basic distinction between artificial virtues and natural virtues looks like a distinctive feature of certain moral outlooks (e.g. ancient Greek ethics) but perhaps not of others (e.g. Kantian ethics). Again, his basic discussion of the artificial virtue of justice, while widely influential in contemporary moral philosophy, is not entirely without controversy. Even here, while many contemporary philosophers, e.g. John Rawls, have used the basic features of Hume's theory of justice toward a number of different political theories, Hume himself seems to develop his theory specifically toward conservative conclusions. This is no accident, as I argue in Chapter 8. The conservatism is deep-based, theory-based rather than superficial.

THE PROBLEM OF CONTINUITY

Contemporary Humeans have a problem in reading right through Book III. To them the discussion looks discontinuous. There seems to be a sudden break in the argument after Part i. It seems this way to them because most contemporary Humeans subscribe to a thesis we might call the moral neutrality of non-cognitivism. The neutrality thesis entails that non-cognitivism cannot have the practical, substantive moral consequences that are developed in Parts ii and iii. The practice of contemporary Humeans faithfully reflects their theory. Hume's views in Part i have been very influential in the contemporary discussion of meta-ethics. Again, various parts of Hume's views in Parts iii, but especially Part ii, are sometimes influential in the contemporary discussion of substantive normative ethics. But these two employments of Hume are thought to be fairly independent of each other. Contemporary philosophers essentially pick and choose from Hume. Few treat Hume's discussion as he would have wanted it to be treated, as a continuous, developing argument. In theory or in practice they subscribe to the 'discontinuity interpretation' of what Hume's best arguments achieve in Book III. In this chapter and the next I shall argue that Hume was (mostly) right in thinking his discussion continuous. I shall argue for the 'continuity interpretation' of what Hume succeeds in doing.

However the *dis*continuity interpretation has much in its favour. For one thing, there is the embarrassing 'systematic ambiguity' in Hume discussed in Chapter 1 above. Hume never quite clearly saw the difference between his meta-ethical thesis, (S) sentimentalism, and something quite different, (Vb) Humean virtue-based morality. Insofar as one sees Hume, even in Part i, arguing for (Vb), it is not at all surprising to see him continuing the discussion in Parts ii and iii on topics about the kinds of virtues and specific virtues. The systematic ambiguity would explain why Hume wrongly thought there was a continuity in his discussion. Hence the *discontinuity interpretation* can be put thus:

1) Systematic Ambiguity: Hume confuses (S), sentimentalism, with (Vb), virtue-based morality, and:
2) Contemporary Relevance: Hume gives interesting and influential arguments for (S) but no real argument for (Vb), and:
3) (Vb)-Continuity: (Vb) might reasonably be thought to be relevant to many of Hume's important and definitive claims about justice and virtue in Parts ii and iii, but:
4) (S)-Discontinuity: (S) has no real bearing on Hume's important and distinctive claims about justice and virtue in Parts ii and iii.

(1) and (3) explain why Hume might have thought his discussion continuous, i.e., he confused his sentimentalism with another thesis (Vb) which is at least of the right category to bear on his later topics of discussion. However, as per (4), in fact sentimentalism has no such bearing. Unfortunately, as per (2), the arguments of enduring interest are for sentimentalism rather than for the thesis which bears on the later discussion. Hence contemporary Humeans may go to Hume for interesting arguments for a meta-ethical thesis, (S), or else perhaps for interesting views about the virtues and justice. But, if (4) is right, they will not think the two are related in the way Hume's discussion suggests.

The *continuity interpretation* agrees with the discontinuity interpretation on propositions (1), (2) and (3). However, instead of (4), it holds:

4*) (S)-Continuity: Hume's important and distinctive claims about the virtues and justice are reasonable developments of an overall theory which begins with (S).

The continuity interpretation can agree with the discontinuity interpretation that Hume's confusion of (S) with (Vb) gives us *one* explanation of why Hume thought there was continuity in his discussion. Hume had *one* mistaken reason for thinking there was continuity. But overdetermination in explanation is quite possible. According to the continuity interpretation Hume also was right in thinking that (S) bears importantly on his later distinctive theses about virtue and justice. Even after we sweep aside the systematic confusion of (S) with (Vb) we can find an overall unity in Hume's argument which is of interest to contemporary Humeans. Hume does not just (inadvertently) change the subject after Part i, as the discontinuity interpretation contends. I shall argue that the continuity interpretation is correct.

However there is a rather influential and convincing argument apparently on the side of the discontinuity interpretation. Hume's sentimentalism, (S), is a species of non-cognitivism (or, at least, of subjectivism). By contrast his theory of the virtues and of justice seems, at least, to belong to normative moral theory. The latter seems to make the kinds of claims that non-cognitivism is about. The convincing objection here is based on what we have called the *neutrality thesis*. This is the claim that non-cognitivism (and perhaps more generally subjectivism) is in itself, and apart from quite independent values we might bring to it, perfectly neutral in regard to substantive issues of moral theory. We might, for convenience, break the neutrality claim down to two parts. Positively, no non-cognitivist meta-ethics can on its own have any positive bias, i.e., it cannot be part of the argument *for* particular substantive moral views. Negatively, no non-cognitivist meta-ethics can on its own have any real negative bias, i.e., it cannot *rule out* any real moral view. It is, by itself, consistent with any of the usual alternative moral stances.

WHAT DOESN'T FOLLOW

While I wish to reject the discontinuity interpretation there is, nevertheless, much to be said for the neutrality thesis. It is true that several important contemporary philosophers have argued that non-cognitivism involves, or at least reflects, some particular normative stance (e.g. Wiggins, 1976; MacIntyre, 1984). Even so, there would seem to be a quite decisive argument to the effect that no non-cognitivist meta-ethics can have any positive bias. Non-cognitivism cannot give us any reason (unbased in values or sentiments we already have) *for* accepting any of the moral judgments that non-cognitivism is about. We can see that a certain absurdity arises in supposing otherwise. Suppose:

H. Non-cognitivism (or some particular version thereof) entails (or, more widely, rationally supports in some way) some particular moral proposition (which we'll call *m*), where, of course, the particular judgment *m* is just the sort of thing non-cognitivism is about. Furthermore the following is just a matter of definition:

D. Non-cognitivism is the meta-ethical thesis that no moral proposition is the sort of thing which (in its entirety) can be either ('robustly') true or ('robustly') false, that is, no moral judgment is 'cognitive'.

I argued earlier (Chapter 1) that the non-cognitivist as well as his articulate critic must presuppose some sufficiently robust sense of 'true' and 'false' to make the debate worthy of interest. For example, a sense of 'true' which committed those who called a moral judgment 'true' to some form of moral realism or objectivity would be a sufficiently robust sense. At the opposite extreme, a sense of 'true' which made the word no more than a linguistic device for indicating agreement (broad sense) with a moral judgment would be much too anaemic.

Of course the non-cognitivist thinks his own meta-ethical position, his non-cognitivism, is true, and not merely in the anaemic sense. He thinks that the cognitivists have just got it wrong, have missed a philosophical truth. Thus, any kind of non-cognitivism worthy of the name holds:

C1. One example of a 'robust' use of the notion 'true' ('false') occurs in the non-cognitivist's own claim 'Non-cognitivism is true' (or the cognitivist's claim 'Non-cognitivism is false').

Furthermore, if, as is likely, neither the cognitivist nor the non-cognitivist has a completely worked out, explicit account of the robust notion of 'truth', they will nevertheless probably accept the following as one sufficient condition of a 'robust' truth:[1]

C2. One sufficient condition for a proposition's being ('robustly') true (false) is that the claim that the proposition is true (false) can be

---

1 This is perhaps an instance of the general claim that cognitivity is 'inherited' in entailment (or, more widely, in any kind of rational support). I have argued (Snare, 1977) that this may be true of entailment in a narrow sense but not of all entailments in the wider sense (where it is only true of a certain, large, class of 'interesting' entailments). Such problems may perhaps be avoided altogether if we take the moral judgment *m* in question to be a 'pure' or 'non-hybrid' moral judgment, e.g. categorical 'ought', 'reason for action', 'should' claims.

Of course the issue here is really about in what sense non-cognitivism commits one to a no-'ought'-from-'is' claim. If non-cognitivism does entail (perhaps with qualifications) that 'ought' cannot follow from 'is', it will also follow that 'ought' cannot follow, more particularly, from non-cognitivism (which must be supposed to be an 'is' claim).

demonstrated (or just rationally supported) by an argument the premisses of which are all ('robustly') true.

Together (C1) and (C2) give us:

C. One sufficient condition for a proposition's being ('robustly') true (false) is that the claim that the proposition is true (false) can be demonstrated solely by propositions which are true in that sense of 'true' which is required in 'Non-cognitivism is true' if that is to make the provocative claim both the cognitivist and the non-cognitivist think it does.

Now from (H) and (C) it would follow that if non-cognitivism is ('robustly') true then at least one moral proposition, viz. *m,* is also ('robustly') true. However, according to (D), if even one such moral proposition is ('robustly') true then non-cognitivism is refuted. Hence if (H) were the case, non-cognitivism would be self-refuting. Non-cognitivism would entail, or at least rationally support, its own counter-example. So if (H) is the case, non-cognitivism cannot be true. Conversely, if non-cognitivism is true, (H) must be abandoned. To insist on (H) is to be no friend of non-cognitivism. Nor can we be very surprised that contemporary non-cognitivists are the ones who most vehemently argue for the moral neutrality of non-cognitivism. It is not just that they want to appear fair or tolerant.

This result can be generalised in several ways. Firstly, not only does an absurdity arise in supposing that non-cognitivism by itself supports some moral position, it also arises if we suppose it can be any *part* of a rationally sound argument for such a conclusion. Let us try to suppose the contrary. Suppose there is a rationally sound argument of the following form:

1. Non-cognitivism (or some particular brand thereof)
2. p_1
3. p_2
   .
   .
   .
   _____

therefore *m*

where *m* is, as before, some particular moral stance (such as non-cognitivism is *about*) and where p_1, p_2, etc., are however many further *cognitive* propositions are required in the argument. Can such an argument be 'sound' in the sense that the premisses either entail or at least rationally support the conclusion where, furthermore, all the premisses are ('robustly') true? If that ever happens, then, according to (C), we would have as much reason for thinking the moral judgment *m* is ('robustly') true as we could ever hope for. And from that it would follow, as per (D), that we would have good reason to believe that non-cognitivism is false after all, the 'robust' truth of *m* being a clear counter-example. But this is inconsistent with our assumption that the argument was sound, for that requires that the first premiss, non-cognitivism, be ('robustly') true. Hence the supposition that non-cognitivism could be even a part of a rationally sound argument for some particular moral stance requires us to think that non-cognitivism is both true and false, true in its role as first premiss, but also false in that the conclusion it supports provides a clear counter-example to it. The only way to avoid the contradiction in this supposition is either to reject non-cognitivism or else to admit that if non-cognitivism is true, its truth cannot be even a part of the rational support for any moral judgment whatsoever. Hence accepting non-cognitivism does not, as many beginning students of philosophy suppose, give us some reason to be tolerant rather than intolerant, liberal rather than authoritarian, sexually permissive rather than Victorian, and so on. It will not even collaborate with other true propositions to any such end. It does not strike a blow for freedom, or for anything else. It will not even hand a weapon to the striker. Least of all should we expect an 'ought' to follow from the very 'is' of non-cognitivism.

This result can be generalised in a second way. It should be noticed that the usual arguments given for non-cognitivism, if they are any good at all, prove rather more than non-cognitivism. If they are any good at showing that *moral* judgments are non-cognitive they would be easily generalisable to show that most or perhaps all *normative* judgments are non-cognitive. There is nothing in the arguments non-cognitivists usually give to keep them from spilling over to apply to other normative judgments besides moral judgments. While there might be such a thing as a selective argument for non-cognitivism, i.e., an argument only for non-cognitivism in regard to *moral* judgments, the arguments actually given are not selective in this way. Hence, a clear-headed non-cognitivist cannot think non-cognitivism is any part of a successful argument for some prudential theory of justification such as what we called the 'Humean theory of justifying reasons' in Chapter 4, or (P5) in Chapter 3.

META-ETHICAL SUBJECTIVISM

This result can be generalised in a third way, with certain qualifications. It applies not only to non-cognitivism but, more generally, to any kind of subjectivist meta-ethical view (including subjectivist cognitivist views). This is worth mentioning since, although it seems more likely that the logic of Hume's best arguments leads to non-cognitivism, we cannot altogether rule out the possibility that he may have been arguing for a highly subjectivist kind of cognitivism (cf. 'Additional cognitivist versions of sentimentalism' in Chapter 1). It is more certain that Hume was some kind of subjectivist than that he was one of the particular sort we call non-cognitivist. Hence it is worth pointing out, that subjectivism of any kind seems to be in for a certain plausible 'neutrality thesis'.

First some definitions:[2]

D1. Judgment *j* is subjective *if and only if* the proposition that one person claims (or thinks) that *j* and that another 'disagrees' (as we say) with him (denying *j*) *does not entail* some party to this dispute is mistaken.

while:

D2. Judgment *j* is objective *if and only if* the proposition that one person claims (or thinks) that *j* and that another 'disagrees' (as we say) with him (denying *j*) *does entail* some party to this dispute is mistaken.

We can then distinguish two main types of meta-ethical views:

D3. Any subjectivist meta-ethical theory has the consequence that all (at least of the core, main or interesting) moral judgments are subjective (sense D1).
D4. Any objectivist meta-ethical theory holds that there are some (core, main or interesting) moral judgments which are objective (sense D2).

Naturally, all non-cognitivist theories are subjectivist in this sense, holding as they do that moral judgments are not the sort of thing to be true *or false*. Consequently we cannot automatically conclude from the fact that there is a moral dispute that someone has to be mistaken (even if sometimes parties are mistaken in regard to their reasoning or in regard to subsidiary non-moral factual matters).

However certain cognitivist views will count as subjectivist views as well on this definition. Take for example the subjectivist cognitiv-

---

2 I owe the approach in the following four definitions to Lloyd Humberstone.

ist view (S3a), discussed in Chapter 1, which takes a person's moral judgment to be a cognitive claim about the judger's own actual special sentimental reaction to the action or person the judgment is 'about'. Notice that, on such an account, if I judge or think 'act a is vicious' while you deny just that, thinking 'a isn't at all vicious' (where it is precisely the same act and circumstances, etc., which we both have in mind), there is no need that either of us be thinking anything false. For on this view we are talking about two different things, my reaction and your reaction, respectively. Neither of us need be thinking anything false. Each may understand his own psychology accurately even if there is still a 'disagreement' in the Stevensonian sense of a clash of attitudes toward a. Because in a moral dispute each is talking about his own reaction, one cannot conclude from the fact of such a disagreement that someone has to be making a mistake. Hence a view like (S3a) is a subjectivist one, even if not a non-cognitivist one. And it is at least arguable that Hume held such a view.

However no subjectivist meta-ethics can suppose that it, by itself, entails or rationally supports, some particular ethical view. For then, that ethical view would, given the truth of the subjectivist meta-ethics, have a quite objective basis. A subjectivist meta-ethics can be used in support of some particular ethical stance only at the risk of having it produce its own counter-examples. Furthermore, this result will *generally* continue to hold no matter how many further factual premises we add to the supposed argument. *Usually* there will be something distinctly paradoxical about supposing something like the following argument provides a sound rational base for believing the conclusion:

1. Meta-ethical subjectivism (or some particular brand thereof)
2. p_1
3. p_2
   .
   .
   .
   _____

therefore m

In most cases that would seem to require that at least one moral judgment, m, is quite objectively true, that anyone who disagrees with m can be shown to be making a mistake by being shown precisely the above argument and how its premises are all true.

However there might be a few cases where the paradox can be

evaded. This couldn't happen for a non-cognitivist subjectivism but it just might in the case of a cognitivist subjectivism such as we find in (S3a). Under such a subjectivist view my thought 'act *a* is vicious' is the implicitly *indexical* thought '*I* have such and such a negative sentiment toward *a*'. Just conceivably the premiss of an argument beginning with meta-ethical subjectivism might support a proposition like 'Snare has such and such a negative sentiment toward *a*' which in turn would rationally warrant *my* (but not your) thought '*a* is vicious' (according to (S3a) at least). Hence subjectivism just might be part of an argument giving rational support to my (implicitly indexical) moral thought. My thought would be demonstrably true. Even so, my thought would not be an objective moral truth. Anyone who disagreed, thinking for his part that act *a* was not at all vicious, need not be making any mistake. Nor would the argument beginning with subjectivism show *he* had made a mistake in 'disagreeing' with me.

What, of course, meta-ethical subjectivism can never do, with however much support from additional premisses, is provide a sound rational basis for an *objective* moral claim. Certainly it is quite paradoxical to suppose otherwise. There must always be the logical possibility of someone's 'disagreeing' with the conclusion *m* and making no mistake. That must be so if subjectivism is true at all. Furthermore, meta-ethical subjectivism *by itself* can have no particular bias in favour of certain moral stances over others, say in favour of liberal, permissive or tolerant moral principles. At best, under a subjectivist view like (S3a) additional contingent facts about human nature might show we share some bias and will not *actually* 'disagree' about certain things. Some would perhaps say this is the way Hume would make the study of human nature relevant to ethics. But everything waits on this empirical investigation. Perhaps our sentiments will be discovered to be illiberal, authoritarian and intolerant. Meta-ethical subjectivism does not rule *that* out. It is neutral.

WHAT ISN'T RULED OUT

Non-cognitivism (and, with qualifications, subjectivism) would seem to be morally, indeed normatively, impotent. The positive moral and value consequences of any such view are nil, and must be (unless the view is self-refuting). However, once this fact is appreciated, there is a temptation to swing over to the opposite extreme. Once one sees it is a mistake to *base* some moral claim on non-cognitivism one may then conclude too much from this, viz. that a non-cognitivist cannot *have* a moral stance. But of course it doesn't follow that there is anything *inconsistent* in holding both non-cognitivism (or subjectivism) and *also* holding a particular moral or normative view.[3] But even if it doesn't follow from our former argument, might it not be true anyway, perhaps for other reasons? In this regard we might consider two inconsistency (or, more widely, 'rules out') theses:

1. A discriminatory thesis: Non-cognitivism is inconsistent with (or at least gives some reason to rule out) *some* particular moral views (say, illiberal, intolerant ones) but not others (say, permissive, liberal ones).

2. A universal thesis: Non-cognitivism is inconsistent with (or at least gives some reason to rule out) *all* moral views.

If either of these is true, it would seem non-cognitivism is not so neutral after all.

But there is some good reason to reject both. The discriminatory thesis is especially objectionable. In ruling out some, but not all, moral views it in effect makes non-cognitivism provide an argument *for* the ethical proposition which is the disjunction of all the moral views not ruled out. That would take us back to the difficulties in supposing non-cognitivism could provide an argument for any moral proposition. But beyond that there is an objection that applies to both the universal and the discriminatory thesis. On either thesis non-cognitivism, if true, would give us reason to believe some (perhaps all) moral judgments are *false* (that rationality requires their rejection). But if even that issue is decidable by reason, non-cognitivism (and subjectivism) is refuted.

However it may not be quite that simple. Non-cognitivists typically trip over their own terminology in regard to complex, hybrid

---

3 While not really denying this, Sturgeon (1986) nevertheless holds (1) that there are certain commonly held moral principles (employing notions such as 'objective standards', 'truth', 'knowledge') which, if the non-cognitivist holds, he must *apply* in a manner quite unlike the cognitivist and, further, (2) that 'although both realists and non-cognitivists can insist on the distinction between refuting a moral opinion and showing that its acceptance would have bad consequences, only realists can offer the natural explanation for why we should do so' (p. 131).

I think, however, that where 'broad' senses of 'objective', 'true', 'know', 'refute', are employed by the non-cognitivist in the above two contexts (rather than the 'narrow' senses assumed by Sturgeon), Sturgeon's claims are less obvious.

propositions. Consider the complex proposition $c\&m$ where c is some cognitive proposition and m is some ethical proposition. Non-cognitivists may think many of the things we commonly consider moral judgments are mixed propositions in this way involving some commitment as well to factual claims such as c. Hence the non-cognitivist may insist that 'in its entirety' $c\&m$ is neither true *nor false* even when he knows c to be false. However there must still be a sense in which the falsehood of c 'rules out' the proposition $c\&m$ whether or not the latter is, in its entirety, a cognitive proposition. There might then be propositions, commonly considered moral, of the form '$c\&m$' where non-cognitivism in fact turns out to be inconsistent, not with the m-part, which has no truth value, but with the c-conjunct, which does. This might lead us to consider two further inconsistency theses:

3. Another discriminatory thesis: Non-cognitivism is inconsistent with (or rules out) certain hybrid moral propositions with a specific commitment to cognitivism but not inconsistent with any others (e.g. 'pure' moral propositions, or hybrid moral propositions with no commitment to cognitivism).

4. Another universal thesis: Non-cognitivism is inconsistent with (or rules out) every moral proposition precisely because every such proposition involves a specific commitment to cognitivism. There are no 'pure' moral propositions or even hybrid ones without this cognitive commitment.

I think the substance of (3) is to be accepted. However it also is not anything the neutrality thesis should deny. To discriminate against propositions that come loaded with a cognitivist bias is not to discriminate in a way that leads to any substantive political, moral or practical bias. Presumably the essence of illiberal, authoritarian, intolerant values can be stated and thought without adding 'And that claim is a cognitive one' just as liberal, permissive, tolerant ones can.

The thesis in (4) is a rather different matter. It depends on the quite controversial claim that every moral judgment also contains its own meta-claim, that when, for example, I think the thought 'Act a is vicious' I must, as a part of that, be thinking that what I am thinking is something cognitive. While that is an understandable thesis, it is a bit hard to imagine a non-cognitivist accepting it. It says that our thoughts, when we make moral judgments, are always cognitivist thoughts. Perhaps the idea is that, while our thoughts and conceptual framework are cognitivist, those thoughts and that framework rest on a metaphysical or factual error. They presuppose cognitivism, which is false. Perhaps Mackie's (1977, pp. 30–42, 49) 'error' (or 'projection') theory gets close to what it would be like for a non-cognitivist to hold (4). In any case this thesis is far from obvious. It is not obvious that each moral judgment comes in an inseparable package along with a meta-claim that cannot be detached (but cf. also Stroud, 1977, pp. 184–5). But even if (4) were true, it would not be discriminatory in a way that has any real political, moral or practical bias. It would treat all equally by ruling all out.

In summary the *neutrality thesis* in its most plausible form holds that non-cognitivism does not rule out any substantive moral, political or practical normative stance in favour of others. Non-cognitivism is not inconsistent with any 'purely' normative proposition, although it may be inconsistent with some hybrid complex propositions consisting partly of substantive normative claims and partly of (cognitivist) meta-ethical claims. Or, at worst, non-cognitivism is neutral because it rules out all moral stances on the specific grounds given in (4). But even in that case it takes no sides.

WHAT DOESN'T EVEN INDIRECTLY FOLLOW

While it is clearly fallacious to argue *directly* from non-cognitivism to some particular moral or normative conclusion, it nevertheless has seemed to some possible to argue to some such conclusion, but *indirectly*. It might seem that non-cognitivism can support a particular normative stance by eliminating all the normative competition leaving only one position standing. We might examine three sorts of views that might be thought to be left untouched and thus indirectly supported:

i. Certain moral principles of toleration, liberalism, liberty, rights.
ii. The Humean theory of justifying reasons (Proposition (P5) in Chapter 3).
iii. The universal permission (Proposition (P4) in Chapter 3).

Let us take up (i) first. It might seem that non-cognitivism does nevertheless discriminate in regard to practical moral stances. It might seem to undermine illiberal, intolerant, authoritarian, absolutist, Victorian, etc., views which place moral obligations or

159

assign responsibility and blame. At the same time it might seem to leave standing views which merely grant liberty, permission, rights, etc. Thus, it might seem non-cognitivism provides an indirect argument in support of at least some (i)-type views. However this is misconceived in two respects. First, there is in fact no reason to suppose non-cognitivism is inconsistent with any of the former sorts of stances. Indeed, on a sentimentalist sort of account such as Hume's, there seems to be no inconsistency at all in holding sentimentalism and also *having* illiberal, intolerant, or whatever sentiments. The only mistake would be to try to derive the latter from the fact of the former or, indeed, to suppose the latter were 'deriv'd from reason' in any way. But the having of such sentiments is not inconsistent with a philosophical belief in sentimentalism. The second mistake is even worse. Principles that grant rights and liberties thereby lay various universal obligations on all mankind, ones just as heavy and just as serious as any other moralist lays. Such principles are in practice appealed to in order to blame those who, without justification, infringe basic rights and liberties, who do not tolerate, and so on. If there really were an argument for ruling out the former sort of moral stance, there would be exactly the same argument for ruling out the liberal, tolerant ones.

For somewhat similar reasons it is sometimes wrongly thought that non-cognitivism gives some special brief to (ii) the Humean normative theory of justifying reasons or perhaps to some kinds of prudential justifications. As before this involves a quite misconceived kind of selective scepticism. It involves supposing that non-cognitivism somehow undermines the practical rationality of practical arguments such as PA2 and PA3 in Chapter 4, but not of ones like PA1 which make desires reasons. That is, it supposes that accepting non-cognitivism entails that one can no longer in consistency take on the attitude or sentiment involved in thinking a promise, or another's need, is any sort of justifying reason. But, what's more, it supposes at the same time that non-cognitivism does *not* for the same reason rule out thinking one's wants provide justifying reasons. The scepticism here is distinctly selective. But as before, this is a mistake on two counts. First, non-cognitivism is not at all inconsistent with 'holding' the normative view that a promise, or a need, is a justifying reason. Indeed, if non-cognitivism is true, holding a normative view is not easily the sort of thing to be inconsistent with non-cognitivism since the latter, but not the

160

former, is capable of being true or false. Second, if nevertheless there were grounds for the non-cognitivist's ruling out his also holding the normative views of PA2 and PA3, those grounds could hardly stop short of ruling out his even holding the normative view of PA1. All are normative views. Hume's non-cognitivism (or, indeed, sentimentalism) cannot be a reason, direct or indirect, for holding the Humean theory of justifying reasons. Nor can non-cognitivism require one's abandoning morality in favour of prudence. Non-cognitivism is quite even-handed here. It cannot discriminate against morality without doing the same in regard to prudence. In fact, it rules out neither.

However a third kind of indirect argument is somewhat more plausible than the first two. It holds that non-cognitivism rules out all moral and prudential views (e.g. on what is a justifying reason, what is right, what is wrong, what is virtuous, what is vicious, what is rational, what is irrational) leaving only:

(iii) The universal permission: Everything is permissible.

For this view not to fall to the same difficulties as arose in respect to view (i) requires that we take 'permissible' in a particularly bland sense to mean only the absence of wrongness, i.e., the absence of any obligation to do otherwise (and, of course, also the absence of any obligation to do). It cannot be that more usual sense of 'permissible' which will entail some obligation in certain others (e.g. not to interfere in certain ways). In short, this sense of 'permission' cannot entail any moral judgments; it only denies moral judgments. Thus we interpret (iii) to mean that *nothing* is ever wrong, even interfering with what others do is not wrong, indeed even making moral judgments, blaming and condemning others is not wrong. (iii) is perhaps what we must suppose applies in a Hobbesian state of nature where nothing is just or unjust. Furthermore, for this view not to fall to the same difficulties as arose with (ii), we must take (iii) to deny, not just moral, but any normative claim. It entails that nothing is even prudentially wrong, for example.

As in the cases of (i) and (ii) it would seem to be a basic mistake to suppose that non-cognitivism provides even indirect support for (iii). First, non-cognitivism does not in fact rule out or undermine the usual spread of moral views that are alternative to (iii). Second, if it did, it would rule out, on the same grounds, (iii) as well. However in an important respect this two-pronged reply is not quite as conclusive as it was in the cases of (i) and (ii). The first part of the reply might just conceivably be countered by a defence of the universality thesis in (4). That is, it might be claimed that all 'positive' moral claims (e.g. those that say acts are sometimes right, wrong, virtuous, vicious) involve an inseparable commitment to cognitivism. Hence non-cognitivism would entail a rejection of them all. The second part of the reply might be countered by the claim that (iii), the universal permission, is not a moral, or even a normative stance. Hence only (iii) survives the onslaught of non-cognitivism.

I have said already that the first part of this reply seems dubious to me. But let us grant it for the sake of argument. Does the latter part of the reply hold? It would seem not. Even the very bland sense of 'is permissible' (where '*a* is permissible' entails no 'positive' moral judgments) would seem to be taking a moral stand. To say 'Torture is wrong' is normally understood to be taking one side of a moral debate. If 'Torture is wrong' is taking a moral stand, one would think the denial of that stand would also be a moral stand, just the other side in an important moral dispute. We might put the argument more formally thus: Suppose it were the case that:

H. Non-cognitivism entails (or at least rationally supports) the proposition 'Everything is permissible'.

We could then argue as follows:

D. Non-cognitivism is the meta-ethical thesis that no moral proposition is the sort of thing which (in its entirety) can be either ('robustly') true or ('robustly') false, i.e., no moral judgment is cognitive. (Definition)
C. One sufficient condition for a proposition's being ('robustly') true (false) is that the claim that the proposition is true (false) can be demonstrated solely by propositions which are true in that sense of 'true' which is required in 'Non-cognitivism is true' if that is to make the provocative claim both the cognitivist and the non-cognitivist think it does. (Argued above)
4. 'Everything is permissible' entails 'Torture is permissible'. (Universal instantiation)
5. 'Torture is permissible' entails 'It is not the case that torture is wrong'. (Meanings of: 'permissible', 'wrong', 'not')
6. Non-cognitivism entails (or supports) 'It is not the case that torture is wrong'.
   (H, 4, 5)

162

7. Non-cognitivism entails (supports) that 'It is not the case that torture is wrong' is ('robustly') true.
   (C, 6)
8. That 'It is not the case that torture is wrong' is ('robustly') true entails that 'Torture is wrong' is ('robustly') false.
   (Excluded middle and bivalence of *robustly* true or false propositions)[4]
9. Non-cognitivism entails (supports) that 'Torture is wrong' is ('robustly') false.
   (7, 8)
10. 'Torture is wrong' is a moral proposition.
    (If it isn't, what is?)
11. Non-cognitivism entails (or supports) that at least one moral proposition is ('robustly') false.
    (9, 10)
12. Non-cognitivism entails (or supports) that non-cognitivism is false.
    (That is, non-cognitivism is self-refuting).
    (D, 11)
13. Non-cognitivism is false.
    (12)

Consequently, we have demonstrated the following hypothetical:

14. If (H) were the case, then non-cognitivism would not only be false but *self*-refuting.

Or, to put it in the contrapositive, if non-cognitivism is the case, (H) can hardly be true. It is not the friend of non-cognitivism who

---

4 It has sometimes been objected to this argument that non-cognitivism *cannot* accept bivalence. This objection seems to confuse two issues. One issue concerns which propositions (broad sense) take truth values and which do not, i.e., which are cognitive and which are not. The other issue concerns how many truth values there are available for those propositions which do take truth values. The non-cognitivist holds, in regard to the former issue, that moral judgments do not have truth values at all. They are not cognitive. In regard to the second issue a non-cognitivist may hold any view. No doubt non-cognitivists will usually take the conventional view that there are only two truth values available for cognitive propositions.
   Of course it is possible, even if not necessary, that a non-cognitivist take the unorthodox view and reject bivalence in favour of the view that cognitive propositions have more than two truth values available. However a non-cognitivist is foolish to reject bivalence simply in order to forestall my particular argument. First, that will be a quite desperate move if there is no good independent reason for rejecting bivalence. Second, at most it only counters this particular objection that the universal permission does not follow without thereby giving us any reason to suppose it does follow. Third, this view must still face the other arguments that non-cognitivism is not inconsistent with a wide range of moral viewpoints other than this one. In short, rejecting bivalence is a high price to pay for so very little.

argues for (H). To think that something is permissible is to think it false that it is wrong. But according to non-cognitivism the judgment that something is wrong is not the sort of thing to be either true *or false*. Unless perhaps one is supposing that moral judgments come in inseparable packages with a commitment to cognitivism. Under that way of thinking what is 'false' about '*a* is wrong' is the implicit and inseparable commitment to thinking '*a* is wrong' is cognitive when one thinks that *a* is wrong. But even if that were so, why not say precisely the same thing about '*a* is permissible', i.e., that it is a moral stance coming in an inseparable package with a commitment to its own cognitivism? In that event '*a* is permissible' will turn out as false as '*a* is wrong'. And non-cognitivism would warrant a quite even-handed moral nihilism that excluded one's ever thinking in moral terms at all. It would exclude thinking the thought '*a* is permissible' just as much as the thoughts '*a* is wrong' or '*a* is right'. That would leave: 'I *don't* ever think thoughts like "*a* is wrong" or "*a* is right" any more than I think "*a* is permissible". I *don't* think any of those moral thoughts. I only describe what there is'.[5] This seems more like the consequences for a non-cognitivist who also accepts the 'inseparable package' view.

---

5 The ordinary sense of 'permissible' does seem at least to presuppose a context of reasoning for and against action. Hence, even in the weakest sense of 'permissible', to say 'Everything is permissible' seems to presuppose a normative outlook, a view to reasonable choice. Sometimes it is objected that permissible judgments are 'not fully normative' because they do not 'positively' direct choice. But of course that is true of most moral judgments. Setting aside the usual examples of non-directive moral judgments (e.g. historical judgments, abstract generalisations, assessments of virtues, etc.) and setting aside merely *prima facie* moral judgments, even judgments of what acts are wrong may not direct one to what one should do in particular, for what is thereby excluded may leave a wide range of actions remaining. On the other hand in the right context the judgment that something is permissible may positively direct where the alternatives have been ruled out. Like practically all moral judgments (except categorical, overall 'ought' judgments), permission judgments *bear* on choice problems but do not by themselves determine a particular course of action. There does not seem to be an argument for excluding permission judgments from the scope of the normative which would not also eliminate just about everything but categorical, overall 'ought' judgments.

Admittedly, sentimentalism will have a special problem about giving an account of permissible judgments (and also of judgments about what is *not* a reason for acting, and judgments on what are neither virtues nor vices). To say such judgments express the sentiment that something is permissible risks the circularity this chapter is about. To say it somehow consists in the lack of a sentiment still requires that this case be distinguished from the one where one is asleep, uncon-

164

In conclusion there is much to be said for the neutrality thesis. Non-cognitivism has none of the practical consequences the newly initiated sometimes attribute to it. It entails no moral views, rules out no (substantive) moral views, takes no sides on any real moral or political debate. Contemporary philosophers are fond of saying that non-cognitivism 'leaves everything where it was' (cf. Williams, 1972, p. 42). It can, by itself, make no practical difference (except to the confused). Most certainly it is not particularly on the side of toleration, liberalism and permissivism as against more politically conservative moral stances. For those attempting to make contemporary use of Hume's discussion, that is fortunate in one respect but perhaps unfortunate in another. The relationship between Hume's sentimentalism in Part i of Book III to his rather conservative views about virtue and justice in Parts ii and iii would be very puzzling indeed if the actual consequences of a non-cognitivist meta-ethics were permissive or anything anti-conservative. So there is not the discontinuity between the parts of Hume's discussion there would be if non-cognitivism had any such anti-conservative practical consequences. So that is fortunate. But what is unfortunate is that the neutrality of non-cognitivism still makes Hume's discussion look discontinuous to modern eyes. Just as his meta-ethics can have no anti-conservative consequences, it also would seem that it cannot have the substantive, somewhat conservative, consequences that we actually find in Hume's discussion of justice and the virtues.

I do accept the *neutrality thesis* about non-cognitivism (and hence sentimentalism). Nevertheless I resist the *discontinuity interpretation* of Hume's discussion, i.e., I resist the view that Hume was mistaken in thinking his meta-ethics had anything to do with his practical ethics and political philosophy. I think Hume's overall developing discussion remains of interest to contemporary Humeans. There is more there than bits and pieces. However to solve the problem of alleged discontinuity requires first raising another problem for Hume's sentimentalism, a certain risk of circularity that any sentimentalism runs. Hume's solution to the circularity problem is also the solution to the discontinuity problem.

scious, or otherwise occupied and hence not thinking the thought that something is permissible. Perhaps it is to express a second-order sentiment in favour of one's not having a certain first-order sentiment favourable to doing the thing.

Sentimentalism (like a great many non-cognitivist accounts of what moral judgments *are*) runs the risk of circularity (Alston, 1968). In giving its positive account of what moral beliefs *are,* sentimentalism has, first of all, to find an *appropriate* particular sentiment (or moral attitude) to link with every distinct moral belief. Not any old feeling, 'pro-attitude' or sentiment will do. For exampie, aesthetic attitudes are quite often not the appropriate ones to employ in a sentimentalist account of moral beliefs. I can think that a film is morally objectionable (perhaps on account of its excessive violence) but at the same time find it aesthetically fine. On the other hand, I might find someone's mode of dress aesthetically jarring but at the same time allow, morally speaking, that he has every right to dress in that manner. It is not immoral or unjust. Presumably my negative moral judgment about the film has to be linked with some feeling of moral disapproval, not just aesthetic pleasure, and my moral judgment of the right to one's mode of dress will presumably be something other than just aesthetic disgust. Not any old sentiment existing concurrently with the moral judgment will do in a sentimentalist account of that belief. For a start it must be a *moral* sentiment, not an aesthetic one, a prudential one, etc.

Furthermore, even when the sentimentalist has narrowed the scope down to moral sentiments (or attitudes, or emotions), quite different moral attitudes will be appropriate for different moral judgments. For example the moral belief that having promised is a good reason for acting is different from the moral belief that certain needs of others are some reason for acting. This must be reflected in some difference in the sentiments in the two cases or else the sentimentalist has not given an adequate account. In summary, sentimentalism must not only give an account of how having moral values differs from having other kinds of values, it must also give an account of how having one particular kind of moral value differs from having some other kind of moral value. Indeed any 'positive' account of what moral judgments *are* must do the above two things if it is to explain the social and psychological phenomena.

The problem of circularity arises because it seems almost *too* easy for the sentimentalist to find appropriate distinguishing sentiments or attitudes. These examples illustrate: Why not just say that the judgment 'a is virtuous' expresses the sentiment (or attitude) that a is virtuous? Again, why not just say that thinking that one's having promised is a good reason for acting is just to have the sentiment that one's having promised is a good reason for acting. Again, why not explain what it is for a society to think that something is property in terms of the following sentiments: their general respect for property, their being moved by observations such as 'That's not really mine', etc.? There are several problems with defending sentimentalism with such formulae. One problem is that ordinary senses of 'attitude' or 'sentiment' (rather than technical senses) can turn such claims into platitudes rather than anything having much to do with sentimentalism. 'My attitude that p', 'my sentiment that p', like 'my opinion that p', can be just another way of speaking of my belief that p. But now it has become a quite open question whether 'sentiments' or 'attitudes' in this sense have to be a kind of feeling, emotion, or such. Even a cognitivist can speak of his 'attitude' or 'sentiments' in regard to some moral issue without conceding a thing to sentimentalism. A second way in which such formulae may seem like nothing more than platitudes has to do with what philosophers call 'pragmatic' contradictions. There is some sort of difficulty in asserting that p and then going on to deny that one believes p at all. So even a cognitivist will not be surprised if it seems odd to assert that act a is virtuous but then deny one has the sentiment (i.e., belief) that a is virtuous.

However both these points show only that sentimentalism is easily confused with innocuous platitudes, not that it risks circularity. But of course sentimentalism also risks circularity in attempting to explain the meaning of a moral judgment 'j' using the phrase 'sentiment that j' or 'attitude that j'. Likewise it risks circularity in trying to explain the difference between holding moral judgment j and holding moral judgment k by saying the former involves the sentiment that j while the latter involves the sentiment that k. I do use the word 'risk' advisedly. I only say there is a great danger, not that circularity is unavoidable. Possibly 'sentiment that j' is just a way of pointing to some psychological fact, otherwise specifiable or else of some brute nature, which in fact is the reality behind moral judgments. 'Sentiment that j' could be just a way of pointing to what in fact has to be referred to in some way or other to explain what is going on when we make the moral judgment that j. But even so, that way of referring to the fact is stunningly

167

unenlightening. Some version of sentimentalism might be true, but it will have to find a better way of pointing at its *explanans* if we are going to understand it (much less have reason to believe it).

Nor is this risk of circularity as easy to avoid as it might first seem. The problem is not just with blatantly circular specifications of sentiments (i.e., those specified in the form 'the sentiment that *j*') but just as much with specifications that hold a hidden circularity. It is a commonplace of philosophical psychology that many feelings and emotions involve or presuppose the having of certain beliefs. For example, to hope, rather than just wish or regret, involves thinking the object in question is still possible. A similar story is not implausible for moral feelings and emotions. For example, to feel moral indignation (rather than just hate or disgust) involves believing one (or someone) has been treated in a morally objectionable manner. It is plausible to suppose that the way some moral emotions differ from other moral emotions is going to be a matter of the differing moral beliefs in the two cases and that, furthermore, the way moral emotions differ from non-moral emotions will involve the presence of moral beliefs in the former cases. Hence it appears that we already need the notion of moral beliefs (and differences between particular moral beliefs) as part of the account of moral emotions (and what distinguishes them). If so, the sentimentalist who uses, say, the sentiment of moral indignation to explain, say, some judgment about injustice of treatment very much risks circularity in his account. His account will perhaps seem plausible because there is indeed a relationship between such a belief and such an emotion, but the order of priority will be just the reverse of what the sentimentalist suggests. Attributing the moral emotion (sentiment) involves already attributing the moral belief. Hence, to try to explain such a moral belief in terms of such moral emotion will only take us in circles, for that emotion, in turn, can only be explained by reference to the moral belief in question. In explaining what it is for one to hold a moral belief the sentimentalist needs a way of pointing to an appropriate sentiment (attitude, emotion, etc.) which does not already employ the notion of the judgment in question (either blatantly or covertly) in order to pick it out.

Just as emotions and feelings may come already loaded with moral beliefs, so may certain motivations. Take, for example, the motivational cases 2 and 3 much discussed in Chapters 4 and 5

Part of the specification of those cases involves being motivated by the 'acceptance' of certain moral beliefs and arguments. Even if we leave open what such a 'belief' may be (whether or not it is cognitive), this way of specifying the motivation is done by way of the moral beliefs which motivate. Being motivated in case 2 differs from the motivation in case 3 precisely because it is a different 'belief' (a different practical argument) which does the motivating. That is not to say all philosophical views agree on how these cases are to be understood or analysed. Common sense psychology insists there are such cases, but it is a matter of philosophical controversy just how we are to understand such cases. (For example the internalist may hold that we must be motivated by our moral beliefs while the externalist may think it requires an additional, distinct moral motivation.) The point that needs to made here, however, is that the sentimentalist risks circularity if he says a certain moral belief involves the having of a certain sentiment but that sentiment is in fact nothing other than the motivation of being motivated by that moral belief. If we happen not to notice the circularity in the sentimentalist's account we might just be taken in by its seeming plausibility, its triviality. Of course where we find a moral belief we will usually find some tendency in the believer to be motivated by his moral belief. But the account is circular if it cannot point to the motivation otherwise than as the 'being motivated by the moral belief in question'.

In conclusion, what is at first a source of much of the plausibility of sentimentalism is in fact actually a source of grave suspicion, i.e., the ease with which appropriate sentiments and pro-attitudes can be produced, indeed manufactured by all-purpose formulae, to suit the occasion. What we need to ask in such cases is whether the sentiment or pro-attitude could in principle be identified and distinguished from other sentiments or pro-attitudes without the prior attribution of the moral judgment they are supposed to explain. What makes sentimentalism seem plausible is the fact that there are a great many conceptual or logical relations between having certain moral views and having certain emotions (or having certain motivations). But that does not prove sentimentalism. Indeed the sentimentalist may more often than not have it precisely upside down. Rather than the sentiments (motivations, emotions) being of any use to explain the beliefs, it may be the beliefs that are needed to explain the sentiments. This sets the circularity problem for the

169

sentimentalist. The problem is to specify sufficiently many different peculiarly moral sentiments in order to account for the differences between particular moral judgments (as well as the difference between moral judgments and other normative judgments) without (even implicitly) relying on the prior attribution of the very moral beliefs and concepts in question. Of course I am not saying that all versions of sentimentalism will be circular. But there is a certain danger. And indeed many versions of sentimentalism are circular.

HUME'S METHOD

Very much to his credit Hume sees he must specify the sentiment involved in moral judgments. First, this means that moral sentiment must be distinguished somehow from other kinds of sentiments. Not just any old sentiment will do as a moral sentiment. Moral sentiments are 'of a particular kind':

An action, or sentiment, or character is virtuous or vicious; why? because its view causes a pleasure or uneasiness of a particular kind. . . . To have the sense of virtue, is nothing but to feel a satisfaction of a particular kind from the contemplation of a character. (471)

Nor is every sentiment of pleasure or pain, which arises from characters and actions, of that *peculiar* kind, which makes us praise or condemn. The good qualities of an enemy are hurtful to us; but may still command our esteem and respect. (472)

Second, Hume is clear that different moral judgments have to be distinguished by distinct sentiments (607, 617).

In fact Hume seems acutely aware of the danger of circularity. Hume seems unusually aware (unusual for a Humean) of the fact that a quick and simple reference to sentiments like 'the regard to virtue as such', or similar 'regards' to justice or honesty, or 'the sense of an act's morality' just won't do. It is not that Hume doesn't think such motivations exist. He thinks they do exist. And in that respect he is startlingly different from the Humeans we encountered in Chapters 4 and 5 who defend the provocative version of the Humean theory of motivating reasons. Such Humeans deny, for example, that motivational cases 2 and 3 ever occur (although cases 2* and 3* occur). Hume does think that motivations exist such as the motivation to act because one believes one's promise, or the need of another, morally requires the action. It is an important part of his project to give an account of such motivations. But Hume also sees that to leave the specifications at the level of 'the regard for justice as such' or, more generally, 'the regard to virtue as such' risks circularity in his sentimentalism. If he is to give an account of our moral judgments about virtue, justice or honesty, in terms of sentiments, he cannot think he has accomplished the task just by waving at the regards for virtue, justice or honesty. What his sentimentalism requires is a reduction or analysis of the regards for virtue, honesty or justice which doesn't mention virtue, honesty or justice. That is the problem. In a way 'the regard to virtue' does point to precisely the right sentiment but Hume must point at it in some other way if we are to be sure his account is not circular. Indeed no version of sentimentalism is a coherent and complete thesis until it points, in some non-circular fashion, to the sentiments which are the moral sentiments.

Hence Hume's sentimentalism really requires that he investigate and identify the sentiments peculiar to moral judgments. The 'experimental method' of the title page of the *Treatise* might then be a matter of investigating the objects of our everyday moral judgments in order to develop a theory about the kind of sentiment involved in specifically moral judgments. It is really something like an empirical search for the specifically moral sentiment. By looking at the things we regularly praise in cases where we would ordinarily count this as *moral* praise, we might get some idea as to what the sentiment involved is. It follows that the ordinary judgments of mankind are going to be Hume's starting point (cf. 546–7, 552).[6]

How then does Hume, in non-circular fashion, distinguish the moral sentiments from the other (non-moral) sentiments? In fact Hume says a number of different things in this regard and this has naturally led to a number of different interpretations of Hume, depending on which passages are emphasised. In part moral sen-

6 Mackie makes the point (1980, pp. 127–8) that Hume is not always consistent with his avowed method. Some of the things Hume calls 'virtues' he admits are not commonly believed to have *moral* worth (606). Hume dismisses this as a mere verbal dispute. But he cannot say that. His method requires discovering the nature of the peculiarly moral sentiments by looking at the things people commonly make moral judgments about. His method is to develop a theory of the sentiments they thereby express. If the sentiments his theory proposes in fact reach out to things we would not ordinarily count as moral virtues, that should be a counter-example to his theory. While there might be other ways to handle this apparent counter-example, Hume cannot dismiss the objection as just a matter of words.

timents seem to be distinguished from other kinds by their objects (what they are passions *for*) but perhaps even more importantly they are distinguished in terms of how they arise. Let us take the latter first. There are at least three (not necessarily exclusive) accounts in Hume of the distinctive nature and origin of the moral sentiment. One account is that moral sentiments arise from our 'correcting' our immediate sentiments for variation in time, distance, etc. (581–5). But, second, he also speaks of moral sentiments arising from taking 'a general view':

'Tis only when a character is considered in general, without reference to our particular interest, that it causes such a feeling or sentiment, as denominates it morally good or evil. (472, cf. also 591)

And, third, he also speaks of the special mechanism of 'sympathy' (575–6, 317, 319; Harrison, 1976, p. 104) as the source of our sentiments in regard to the natural and artificial virtues. Possibly Hume's view is that the moral sentiments are not all the sentiments arising from sympathy but only those which survive 'correcting' for spatio-temporal distances or the taking of 'a general view' (cf. D. Miller, 1981, ch. 2).

However Hume also suggests that sentiments are to be distinguished by their objects (617). In Part iii the story we get is that the objects of the moral sentiments are characteristics useful or immediately agreeable to others or the person himself (589–91; *Enquiry,* secs. 5–9). Again, in the case of our sentiments regarding natural virtues Hume sometimes suggests the object is what is normal or usual in humans, our feelings toward vice being a bit like our feelings toward deformity or monstrosity (483–4). It is not important in the present chapter to dispute how exactly Hume means to distinguish the moral sentiments. The point is rather that, whatever exactly Hume's conclusions might have been about the moral sentiments, his approach is the right one. He is out to specify the moral sentiments by their objects, their nature, their origins in a manner that does not make reference to the moral judgments these sentiments are supposed to explain in turn.

CONTINUITY AFTER ALL

Avoiding a circle in the exposition of sentimentalism requires some appropriate specification of the peculiarly moral sentiments.

Hume's method of investigation promises, at least, such a non-circular account. But whether or not it succeeds in that, Hume's method of inquiry is one which should relieve us of any remaining worries about a discontinuity in Hume's discussion. We need not worry even if we grant the thesis of the 'neutrality' of non-cognitivism (or even of subjectivism in general). We must not see the discussion Hume takes up in Parts ii and iii as addressing (except when he slips) moral questions such as 'What actions or characters really are virtuous?' Instead, following the method we now see to be an appropriate one for avoiding a non-circular exposition of sentimentalism, Hume is to be seen as investigating the origins, nature and objects of the peculiarly moral sentiments through an examination of the kinds of things we ordinarily morally praise and blame (cf. Mackie, 1980, p. 76). Something like this is precisely what the sentimentalism in Part i requires Hume to be doing in Parts ii and iii. Not only is there continuity, the former discussion would be incomplete, would leave us with qualms about possible circularity, without the latter. At the same time, granting this continuity in no way offends against the neutrality thesis, i.e., the claim that non-cognitivism can neither entail nor support any moral judgments. Hume is, officially at least, investigating what is peculiar to the sentiments we have or express in moral judgments. However the conclusions of that investigation are not themselves moral judgments. Hume is not, for the purposes of completing his account of sentimentalism, himself praising or blaming. he is only describing the nature of the sentiments behind moral praise and blame.

Nevertheless there is a way in which the conclusions of his investigations are something like moral judgments, for the right audience. Hume's claims about the sentiments we have or express in making moral judgments will not entail, or be any part of a reason for holding, particular moral views. In that the neutrality claim is correct. He only makes claims about the nature and psychological origins of these special sentiments, about what distinguishes them from others. However, given that Hume's account of human nature is true, that we really are possessed of these peculiar kinds of sentiments of approval and disapproval of certain kinds of acts and characters, we will in fact naturally go on to express these sentiments in moral judgments. It could even happen that our accepting Hume's descriptive account to be true will lead us, given we already have the sentiments Hume says we do, to approve even more of

173

such acts and characters. Hume's discussion might illuminate more clearly the special features of acts and persons which just do elicit responses from the sentiments we have. Such a discussion will not itself 'justify' either our judgments or our sentiments, but it might direct more firmly and accurately the sentiments we already have to their objects. For example, suppose Hume is correct that we approve of the acts and characters we ordinarily call 'just' out of a special sentiment arising, in part, from the mechanism of sympathy and the motivation of self-interest. (The story is rather more complicated.) Suppose also Hume is right that 'the rules of justice', as he calls them, are social conventions which have the features and arise in the way Hume says. The result of our seeing more clearly what is involved in justice may well direct more firmly our approval toward just acts and characters. Hume thinks our understanding of how we come to approve of 'just acts' as we call them, will not undermine our continuing to approve in the same way. In that respect he is quite unlike philosophers like Nietzsche, Marx or Freud whose accounts of the origins of moral belief, when understood, tend to undermine the activity they are about. Hume perhaps thought his account would, if anything, intensify the activity it is about.

Even so the conclusions of Hume's investigations of the peculiarly moral sentiments can always be represented in purely descriptive terms, as claims about human psychology and human institutions. They could be understood and accepted by a being without the human sentiments they are about (e.g. a Martian or an angel, as we might imagine) without that acceptance rationally requiring (or excluding) any particular moral or value stance. The neutrality thesis is correct. However, *for us,* for those who actually have the sentiments in question, Hume's investigation might as well be about 'what actions and persons really are virtuous'. If we really do, as Hume claims, have positive special responses to certain kinds of characters and actions, the discussion of those characters and acts will tend to elicit the response. We *will* call them 'virtuous'. This is why so many have seen Hume in Parts ii and ii to be discussing moral philosophy, to be taking moral stands. In a way it does have just that practical effect *on us.* But two things are to be noted. First, if there is that practical effect, it is not at all any of the ones canvassed earlier in this chapter. It is not anything like liberal, tolerant or permissive stances which are involved. Indeed there is perhaps a certain conservative drift to Hume's investigation. Hume does not expect his investigation will alter (unless it intensifies) the moral views we already have. It will not undermine anything. Second, Hume's investigation has these 'practical effects' only in a manner of speaking. Officially, Hume is rounding out his discussion of sentimentalism by identifying the exact sentiments involved. He is not, for that purpose, doing moral philosophy. Even so, Hume's method of investigation is (for us, at least) the closest thing to doing moral philosophy without actually doing moral philosophy.

THE PROBLEM THAT REMAINS

Hume's special method, his investigation of the peculiarly moral sentiments, derives from a concern to give an exposition of his position that avoids the circle of sentimentalism. It is a very natural development of his defence of sentimentalism in Part i. Hence there is no reason to see any discontinuity, any change of subject, when he takes up and applies this method in Parts ii and iii. Certainly Hume gives no signs that he thinks he is changing the subject. Only contemporary Humeans, with the neutrality thesis in mind, see a break in the discussion. But Hume's method of investigation does not actually offend the neutrality thesis. It does not actually derive moral consequences although for us, the subjects of his investigation, it may seem to.

Hume was quite right in presenting Book III as a continuous, developing discussion. However he was also right in another thing. Circularity is a danger. About this Hume displays more than a little concern. I shall argue that this concern provides Hume with his most interesting reason for wanting to distinguish the virtues into the natural and the artificial. It has a lot to do with why Hume spends so much of his discussion on the artificial virtue of justice.

Hume has a problem with justice.

175

7

The problem with justice

No doubt Hume had a number of reasons to be interested in justice and the judgments of justice and injustice that we make. But there is also a special theoretical reason for discussing the subject in Book III. The theory of morals developed in Part i has a special (circularity) problem in regard to what Hume calls 'justice' and that problem is what he immediately takes up in the first section of Part ii. It is in that regard that Hume is particularly concerned to distinguish the 'artificial virtues' from the 'natural virtues', arguing that the virtue of justice is artificial in an important sense. One feels things would have been so much easier for Hume if our ordinary moral judgments were only attributions of 'natural virtues', that is, if we made no justice judgments. His theory of morals, in that case, would have benefitted from a plausibility born of simplicity. It would have had no hard cases to deal with.

So the basic question we ask in this chapter is: 'What is the problem that threatens Hume's theory of morals in the case of justice and the artificial virtues but which doesn't threaten it in the case of the natural virtues?' That is, 'What is the special problem that arises in regard to justice?' But this question cannot be discussed without raising a second question at the same time: 'What exactly is this distinction between the artificial and the natural virtues and, indeed, what is the point of making that distinction?' The former question also presupposes that we know just exactly what Hume's theory of morals, developed in Part i, is. But at that point we really need to raise a third question as well: '*Which* theory of Hume's is at issue here such that it has some special problem about justice?' In Chapter 1, I discussed Hume's systematic confusion of a metaethical thesis, (S) sentimentalism, with a quite different thesis, indeed a substantive moral theory, (Vb) Hume's virtue-based moral theory. Although during Part i Hume's attention is fixed on (S) for a good portion of the time, it does seem that at the beginning of Part ii Hume blinks, just long enough for his attention to fix on (Vb) instead:

'Tis evident, that when we praise any actions, we regard only the motives that produced them, and consider the actions as signs or indications of certain principles in the mind and temper. . . . [T]he ultimate object of our praise and approbation is the motive, that produc'd them. (477)

And indeed the way Hume presents the special problem, a circularity problem, which arises in regard to justice, is as a special problem for (Vb). Once again it begins to look as if Hume's discussion of (S) is discontinuous. We were, just in Part i, discussing the meta-ethical theory (S), but now it appears the discussion has shifted, inadvertently, to the substantive moral theory (Vb), Hume's virtue-based theory of morals.

It seems to me that, just as there are two unrelated theories concerning morality which Hume confuses, (S) and (Vb), there are also two quite different circularity problems regarding justice which Hume confuses. One is a circularity problem for anyone trying to defend (S). The other is a quite unrelated circularity problem for anyone defending (Vb). What is unfortunate is that Hume in his actual exposition of the problem gives the latter, i.e., what is really only a problem for (Vb), rather than the former, i.e., what is the problem for the thesis that interests contemporary Humeans. This is especially unfortunate in my view because the problem Hume actually raises is more or less insurmountable and that is in fact a very good reason for abandoning (Vb) as an account of our conventional moral judgments. What is nevertheless fortunate, however, is that the solution Hume actually gives to the problem he claims to discuss, while no solution at all to that problem, is more like the solution to the problem we should have preferred him to discuss. Perhaps Hume blinks again, just long enough to return to (S) and the special problem about justice judgments that arises for (S). All in all, the discussion in III, ii, 1 is an improbable comedy of errors. Somehow, still juggling the systematic ambiguity between (S) and (Vb) and with several unexpected somersaults, Hume lands on his feet with the right arguments in hand and facing the right direction to continue the discussion of (S). And so Book III does, after all, provide a developing defense of sentimentalism, although, it must be said, this is sometimes in spite of Hume's efforts. Or so this chapter will argue.

177

But before we discuss the special problem that arises in regard to the artificial virtue justice but not for the natural virtues, we should first try to get clear just what this distinction is and, perhaps, why it is important for Hume. In fact Hume described the distinction between the artificial and the natural virtues in at least two (not necessarily incompatible) ways (cf. Harrison, 1981, pp. 25ff.). The two ways of marking the distinction seem to differ in their accounts of the peculiarly moral sentiment and perhaps in just where the 'artificiality' is located in the case of the artificial virtues. In one account, the 'useful and agreeable' account (587–91), the artificiality does *not* seem to be in the sentiment of the judg*er* attributing a virtue to another. Whether it be a natural or an artificial virtue which is attributed, the sentiment in the judg*er* is much the same, viz. a special sentiment arising in part from the mechanism of sympathy toward qualities (e.g. motives) in persons which are useful or agreeable to others or to the person himself. Rather, the distinction between natural and artificial virtues is a matter of just *how* the quality in question comes to be useful or agreeable in that way. In the case of the natural virtues, the quality (which attracts the approval of the judger's sentiments) is one which is *naturally* useful or agreeable to others or to the person. Hence Hume thinks the peculiarly moral sentiment will be directed toward such qualities as benevolence, compassion, prudence, industry, intelligence, good wit, etc., because such qualities just are useful and pleasing in their natural tendencies. In calling them virtues we will be expressing that peculiarly moral sentiment.

On the other hand, in the case of the artificial virtues the qualities which attract the approval of the judger's moral sentiment are not naturally useful or agreeable just by their natural effects but become so once certain conventions become established. Thus the sentiment we express toward them, in calling them virtues, is just the same as in the case of the natural virtues. We would not naturally (i.e., apart from there being an advantageous 'general scheme') approve of these acts and characters, but, given the general scheme, such acts and persons now become advantageous in a way that naturally attracts the moral sentiments. The artificial virtues are artificial only because it is under artificial (i.e., conventional) circumstances that such qualities become useful and agreeable in the way that naturally attracts the moral sentiment.

In a more specific version of the 'useful and agreeable' account, Hume says that in cases of attribution of natural virtue the single act we praise is one which, even apart form other acts of the same sort, has some tendency to be beneficial or agreeable. Individual acts of compassion or humanity are likely to be of some benefit to others. On the other hand, when we attribute an artificial virtue, we are praising, says Hume, motivations to act where the single act has no such tendency but there is some advantage to having 'a general scheme' where people act in that way. Hence we come to praise such motivations and acts but only where there is such a general scheme (cf. 497, 579–80; Mackie, 1980, pp. 91–3; Harrison, 1981, pp. 31ff., 66). In summary, by the 'useful and agreeable' account the sentiment of the judger is much the same whether the judger is attributing a natural or an artificial virtue. It is a sentiment, arising from sympathy, toward qualities useful or agreeable to others or the person himself. However where the social utility of the quality depends in a certain way on the existence of a convention, it is an artificial virtue which is attributed.

There is a second, somewhat different, account in Hume of the distinction. This is the 'natural and usual force' account of the natural virtues (483–4). Here virtue is said to be a matter of having, or acting from, passions in their natural and usual force, e.g. caring for one's children in the normal way and to the usual degree. Here the sentiment of the judger toward those exhibiting the passion in its natural and usual force seems, to me, to be rather aesthetic. Vice is something like a deformity or a monstrosity in regard to the passions:

'Tis according to their general force in human nature, that we blame or praise. In judging of the beauty of animal bodies, we always carry in our eye the economy of a certain species; and where the limbs and features observe that proportion, which is common to the species, we pronounce them handsome and beautiful. In like manner we always consider the *natural* and *usual* force of the passions, when we determine concerning vice and virtue; and if the passions depart very much from the common measure on either side, they are always disapprov'd as vicious. (483)

But it would seem that when we attribute the artificial virtues and vices nothing like this can be going on. For a start the motives we

179

praise in the case of justice and the artificial virtues are not motives which persons have naturally. Such motivations are acquired, at least in part, through parental education and 'the artifice of politicians' and require the establishment of conventions. They cannot really be said to have a natural and usual force.

This second account differs from the first, the 'useful and agreeable' account, in its description of the peculiarly moral sentiment. By the former account it is a sentiment directed toward what is socially useful and agreeable. In this second account, however, the moral sentiment, at least in the case of the natural virtues, is analogous to our aesthetic response to well-formed, as opposed to deformed, bodies. But also the 'natural and usual force' account differs in another way. The former account employs the *same* sentiment (in the judger) in explaining judgments of artificial virtue as in explaining judgments of natural virtue. But it would seem the second account cannot really explain our judgments of artificial virtue in the same way as our judgments of natural virtue. By this second account our sentiment in attributing a natural virtue seems to be some quasi-aesthetic sentiment. But this could not easily be the sentiment involved in attributing an artificial virtue.

However under both accounts of the distinction, the artificial virtues are going to be artificial in that the motives or passions praised in those to whom we attribute the virtue will not be natural. The passion Hume calls 'the regard to justice' will not be natural in the sense that it 'arises artificially, tho' necessarily from education, and human conventions' (483). This suggests a third way in which the artificial virtues might be considered artificial. It is not only that there must be conventions for them to be of any social advantage, nor is it only that their appeal must be to some sentiment other than our natural eye for what is gracefully natural. In addition, the virtues which are artificial seem to arise in a different way. The genesis of such motives as the regard to justice is, in important respects, more artificial than the genesis of the natural virtues we praise. The explanation of how people come to have the regard for justice is quite different from, say, the origins of the motivation of concern for one's offspring.

However, the best way to see what Hume's distinction between the natural virtues and the artificial virtues has to be is first to consider why it is important for him to make some such distinction.

I suggest that he has to make some such distinction because his basic theory of morals has a special problem about moral judgments about the passion or motive he calls 'the regard to justice as such', or what we might call a sense of duty or the desire to do what is right. It is no accident that the moral judgments his theory suits best are the ones which attribute 'natural virtues', while the judgments that pose rather more of a challenge to his theory are, indeed, just those which Hume would try to cover in his account of judgments attributing 'artificial virtues'. To a large extent, what is really behind the distinction between the natural and the artificial virtues is the distinction between easy cases and hard cases for Hume's theory of morals as developed immediately before in Part i of Book III. At first, it might seem odd that Hume is so concerned to discuss the distinction. It can easily seem only an idiosyncratic feature of Hume's own outlook. But in fact a special account of the artificial virtues is crucial to the defence of his theory of morals. Hume discusses justice and the artificial virtues in Part ii, not just because of the intrinsic interest for him of the subject matter, but rather more because to do so is, in effect, to discuss the hard cases for his theory. When it comes to the artificial virtues, his theory is threatened with circularity.

THE CIRCLE IN VIRTUE-BASED MORALITY

Unfortunately, Hume's own account of the circularity that threatens his account is not expressed in the way the contemporary Humean might have hoped. It is presented as a circularity that threatens Hume's virtue-based theory of morality (Vb). Hume has decidedly blinked once again and has momentarily lost his focus on his sentimentalism (S). This change of subject (from what his earlier interesting arguments seemed to be proving) not only threatens the continuity of Hume's discussion, it also would suggest that the artificial/natural virtue distinction is only an historical curiosity of no real interest to those who find (S) the theory of morals worth discussing. But our verdict on whether that is so must wait. What is the circularity problem as Hume presents it?

In III, ii, 1 Hume gives one of his clearest statements of (Vb): '... all virtuous actions derive their merit only from virtuous motives, and are consider'd merely as signs of those motives'

(478, cf. 477, 518, 532, 533). From this principle Hume concludes a certain impossibility claim, viz. 'that the first virtuous motive, which bestows a merit on any action, can never be a regard to the virtue of that action, but must be some other natural motive or principle' (478). Hume thinks the impossibility claim *follows from* (Vb) because holding both of the following pair of propositions involves, he says, a 'sophistry' (483), or is to 'reason in a circle' (478, 483):

(Vb) Virtue-based Morality: Any action which is virtuous is so only in virtue of its having a virtuous motive.

(PC) Possibility Claim: There is at least one possible case of a virtuous action where the 'first' motive 'which produc'd the action, and render'd it virtuous' was just 'the mere regard to the virtue of the action' (478).

Because Hume thinks this pair is incompatible, and because he holds (Vb), Hume concludes he must reject the possibility claim (PC), i.e., that he must hold instead the impossibility claim which is its denial:

(IC) Impossibility Claim: '... *[N]o action can be virtuous, or morally good, unless there be in human nature some motive to produce it, distinct from the sense of its morality*'. (479)

Hume argues that (Vb) entails (IC) because (Vb) and (PC) are incompatible:

For 'tis a plain fallacy to say, [Vb] that a virtuous motive is requisite to render an action honest, and at the same time [PC] that a regard to the honesty is the motive of the action. We can never have a regard to the virtue of an action, unless the action be antecedently virtuous. No action can be virtuous, but so far as it proceeds from a virtuous motive. [IC] A virtuous motive, therefore must precede the regard to the virtue; and 'tis impossible, that the virtuous motive and the regard to the virtue can be the same. (480)

Is there really a circularity or sophistry in holding both (Vb) and (PC)? Well, if there is, it will require that the former really be (Vb), Hume's theory of virtue-based morality, and not merely (V). (V), it should be remembered, is a claim that applies only to the special class of virtue (and vice) judgments but does not say anything about other kinds of moral judgments. (Vb) makes a claim about the whole of morality while (V) only makes a claim about a part, perhaps even a very small part, of morality, i.e., virtue. Admittedly,

Hume is talking about moral judgments about *actions* in his discussion of this circle or 'sophistry'. 'Virtuous action' is his phrase. However this phrase is ambiguous. We should distinguish as we did in Chapter 1 at least two kinds, or perhaps employments, of moral judgments in regard to actions:

i. Action guiding judgments (rightness judgments)
ii. Virtue assessments

Action guiding judgments (or, right and wrong action judgments) are what we use in decision making. Often they presuppose judgments of the form 'an act's having property F is some justifying reason for doing that act'. The 'practical arguments' discussed in Chapters 4 and 5 belong under this heading. For example, PA2 holds that the fact that one promised to do a certain act is (with certain qualifications) some sort of justifying reason for doing that act. That feature is claimed to be a 'right-making' feature.

However actions can be morally assessed in another way. Just as we can morally assess a person's character or traits or dispositions, we can also assess in a similar manner *his doing* particular acts. For example we can assess his degree of responsibility, his claim to merit or blame in so doing. Typically such merit and responsibility assessments rely on facts about the agent's beliefs or motives or degree of control, etc., in the particular case. His *mens rea* is, for example, a condition of his action's being blameworthy or of his being guilty of what he did. The agent's particular motivation for doing the act can often be important in assessments of type (ii).

Moral philosophers tend to agree that the facts about the agent's motivations in doing an act are usually very relevant to type (ii) assessments. Even our Clarke-like view in Chapter 1 could concede that. However it is less obvious that agent motivation is so relevant, or relevant in the same way, to type (i) judgments. It is a bit odd, in trying to decide what to do, to consider the motive one would be acting from in choosing a particular course. I think action guiding judgments in this form do occur and can be coherent. (Sometimes they strike me as a bit obsessive or narcissistic, I must say.) However even if sometimes we do count such features as relevant, it would seem many times we don't. Certainly moral philosophers have often mentioned as 'right-making' characteristics features having nothing to do with the agent's motives when he so acts but only the way it relates to its circumstances (as Clarke might have put it). So one might well sometimes think that an act is right because of its pedigree, or because of its consequences, or because of some role the agent holds. Whether or not one is always justified in so judging, there seems to be no logical incoherence in judging an act right (for type (i) purposes) on grounds having to do with features of that action not involving what the agent's motives will be in so acting.

Now (V), unlike (Vb), makes a claim restricted to (ii)-type judgments. It claims that all virtue assessments (including those of agents' doings) rely on facts about the agent's motives or passions in so acting. By contrast, (Vb) is rather more sweeping. It claims to apply to (i)-type judgments as well as to (ii)-type assessments. It claims an action cannot be *right* (for action guiding purposes) unless it proceeds from a motivation that is virtuous. It insists, as I put it in Chapter 1, that some virtue assessment of motives is prior to every (not just some) rightness judgment. A virtuous motive is requisite to render an action *right* (for action guiding purposes).

That Hume really does hold the rather more extreme (Vb), rather than the more modest (V), is clear from the fact that no circularity problem arises just in regard to (V). There is no sophistry in holding both:

(V) Virtue Morality: An agent's acting in a certain way will be virtuous (where this is a (ii) type assessment) only in virtue of his having done as he did from a virtuous motive.

(PC) Possibility Claim: It is possible for an agent's acting in a certain way to be virtuous (type (ii) assessment) where the motive that renders the act virtuous, as per (V), is just his being motivated by a type (i) rightness judgment which he 'accepts'.

The above two are compatible if we allow the possibility of motivational cases like 2 and 3 discussed in Chapters 4 and 5 where the agent's accepting a type (i) moral judgment motivates him to act, and if we also hold (in a type (ii) moral judgment) that such a motivation is virtuous and makes the act virtuous. It can still be allowed that in all cases virtue (type (ii)) is a matter of acting from virtuous motives even if sometimes the virtuous motive is just the regard to rightness (type (i)) as such (even if in other cases the

184

virtuous motive might be something else such as the natural feelings of benevolence or compassion).

There is only going to be an issue about circularity if (PC) is combined with the stronger thesis, (Vb). In that case the circularity arises because this more sweeping thesis, (Vb), is supposed to apply to judgments of right action (i.e., action guiding, type (i) judgments) as well as to all the other kinds of judgments regarding action. Hence (Vb) differs from (V) in that it entails the following claim about rightness judgments:

(Vr) The Priority of Virtue to Rightness: Any action which is right (wrong) is only so in virtue of the virtuous (vicious) motive that produced it (or perhaps: which typically produces actions of that type).

And the corresponding possibility claim to consider is:

(PCr) The Rightness Possibility Claim: It is possible that the sole (or, where several, the 'first') virtuous motive which renders an act right, as per (Vr), is just regard for the rightness of that act (or acts of that type).

If (Vr) cannot allow the motivation in (PCr) to be what alone, or even in the first instance, renders an act right, there are a number of other motivations for which there is no risk of circularity. For example, we might begin with any number of, allegedly virtuous, motives which can be specified without employing, even within opaque contexts, the notion of right action. One could begin with, say, concern for one's offspring, compassion, revulsion at suffering, etc. We might then decide to call such virtuous motives 'natural virtues' although the point of doing so would have nothing to do with how they arose or whether such motives were acquired. The point would only be that such motives make for no circularity when applied to (Vr). If we count the concern for one's own children as a virtuous motive, then, following (Vr), we might count acts right which are typically done by persons with a normal amount of concern for their children. Whether or not this is a plausible view, it is at least a coherent one. It suffers from no obvious circularity.

Another point to calling such virtuous motives 'natural' would be to make the point that they can render acts right *in the first instance*. Other virtuous motives (i.e., the artificial ones) might be incapable of rendering an act right in the first instance. Hume accepts that there might in some cases be some over-determination in right-making virtuous motives. Here is a case (cf. 479). In the first instance the virtuous motive rendering an act right might be that it is the sort of thing done by someone with a normal concern for one's children. On seeing this (and understanding why it is right) I might be motivated to do it just because it is right (perhaps I aim by practice to acquire the virtuous normal concern that I lack). Here there is a regard to rightness, but it is not what makes the act right in the first instance. In another case I might have both virtuous motives (i.e., the normal concern for children) and also the regard to the rightness of my act. In that case my act might even be right twice over for two different reasons. But the motive that makes it right *in the first instance* is still the natural concern for one's children. This makes it clear that (Vb) does not have to deny that there is such a virtuous motive as the 'sense of duty'. What (Vb) denies is that this virtuous motive could be the motive which in a given case is the 'first' virtuous motive to make an act right (478). Certainly it cannot, in any particular case be the sole right-making virtue. That is, (Vb) must deny (PCr). The implication of (Vb) must be that whenever we judge an action to be right in a type (i) judgment we must refer back eventually, in giving the ground of that rightness, to some virtuous motivation *other than* the sense of duty or the regard for right or anything like that. While these latter motives are possible and may even contribute a bit more to an act's rightness, no such motive can be what *in the first instance* makes an act right.

The plausible thesis, then, is that (Vb), not (V), entails an impossibility claim. (Vb) involves (Vr), which in turn is incompatible with (PCr). Hence Hume thinks that his holding (Vb), his theory of virtue-based morality, would seem to commit him to the impossibility claim which is just the denial of (PCr). But why exactly is (Vr), and hence (Vb), thought to be incompatible with (PCr)?

EUTHYPHRO CIRCLES

The kind of circularity that worries Hume here is well known to philosophy. It belongs to the same category as the dilemma discussed by Socrates in Plato's *Euthyphro* (9e–11b). Indeed it is a circularity problem afflicting any view which wants to make all three claims of the following form:

i.   Moral Theory: Any act *a* is morally right only because agent *P* has (does) *S* in regard to *a* where:

ii. S Explanation: In each such case where *P*'s *S*-ing in regard to *a* makes *a* right, the (motivational) explanation of *P*'s *S*-ing in regard to *a* already (in the order of explanation) involves the fact that *P* believes that *a* is morally right, where:

iii. Belief Explanation: In each such case *P*'s belief that *a* is morally right is formed solely in accordance with a correct application of the moral theory in (i).

In the theistic cases the agent *P* is God or the gods. Different theistic theories will differ in what they substitute for '*S*'. It could be an action, a feeling, an intention, a belief, etc., as long as it is something for which it is possible to have motivating reasons. Possible substitutions for '*S*' might be: 'commanding us to do *a*', 'approving of *a*', 'loving our doing *a*', 'believing *a* to be morally right', and so on. In the theistic cases it will seem unnecessary for theists to add (iii) explicitly. If (i) is the correct moral theory, then presumably God's moral beliefs are formed on that ground. Hence (iii) automatically follows on (i) where '*P*' refers to an all-*knowing* God.[1] Of course it is rather more important in the non-theistic cases to add (iii) explicitly. This could be illustrated with any number of non-theistic examples, e.g. where we substitute for '*P*': 'society' or 'the general will', or 'conscience', or 'law', but I will choose a non-theistic case that gets us a bit closer to Hume's problem. Here the God of the usual Euthyphro examples gets replaced with the individual self, and for 'have *S* toward *a*' we substitute 'do *a* out of a regard for rightness'. So we might consider whether it is possible to hold all of:

i'. Any act *a* is morally right (for me) only because of its proceeding from a regard to rightness as such, where:

1 There is nothing in this formulation of the Euthyphro problem that denies the atemporality of God. The adverb 'already' and the verb 'forms' indicate an order in the justifications God (timelessly) accepts, not a temporal order. We do not need to think of God as coming to form beliefs over time. Presumably, if God is to be said to have knowledge in moral matters, rather than just true belief, that will involve grasping (timelessly) why acts are right and never thinking acts right on any other grounds.

ii′. In each such case the explanation of my doing *a* out of a regard to its rightness involves the fact that I already (in order of explanation) believe that the act *a* is right (for me), where:

iii′. In each such case the explanation of my forming the belief that the act *a* is right is just that I correctly apply the moral theory in (i′) to the circumstances.

Moral philosophers have often maintained there is some problem in holding (i′) and (ii′) together.[2] But, technically, there is no circle or sophistry in holding both, provided (iii′) is denied. That would make for one of those soppy moralities of sincerity. On that view one *invariably* forms one's moral beliefs in the first instance on some incorrect, benighted grounds, i.e., not (i′), but nevertheless those acts one is motivated to do on the basis of these confused beliefs do become right, in virtue of (i′), but never for the reasons one 'first' thought made them right. Even so, it is scant consolation that (i′) and (ii′) may still be held if one abandons (iii′). To go this route is to concede that (i′) is not what it seems to be, a principle capable of being used as an action guide when a decision is called for. At best it gives a taint of legality, *ex post facto*. But while it might paper things over afterwards, it can never be of any use in deciding what to do at the time. It cannot be rationally employed to guide action.

This brings us squarely to the issue of the nature of the circularity involved.[3] What is the problem in holding all three of, say, (i′), (ii′) and (iii′)? One account is too easy. If we were to suppose that (i′) and (ii′) are *definitions* or analyses of 'morally right' and 'acting out of a regard to an act's rightness', respectively, the problem with holding both would be a problem of circularity in definitions. Substituting the definition of 'regard to rightness' in (ii′) for its occurrence in (i′) gives us a definition of 'morally right' that employs the term being defined in a way that is hardly eliminable. But this account of the circularity is too easy because we need not suppose that (i′) is being put forward as an analysis or a definition. The

2 Cf. Prichard (1912), pp. 5–6, Ross (1930), pp. 4–6, (1939), pp. 114–24, 130–40.
3 Socrates' account of the nature of the circularity is particularly obscure and may well lose whatever apparent plausibility it has in translation (*Euthyphro,* circa 10b,c; cf. Geach, 1972, pp. 40–1). At any rate it cannot just be the circularity in holding simultaneously propositions of the form '*x* because *y*' and '*y* because *x*'. A case for circularity that simple would require that the 'because' be of the same sort in both propositions. However in (i) the 'because' is the 'because' of justification while in (ii) the 'because' is one of explanation, i.e., of agent's accepted justifications.

obvious problem of *definitional* circularity is avoided by supposing, as seems reasonable, that (i′) makes a substantive moral claim about what feature (not identical to rightness) is the sole 'right-making' feature.

In that event a rather more subtle kind of circularity is involved. The problem is that, where (ii) is true, the agent P cannot employ (i) as an action guide. Where, as in (i′), the person P is oneself, one cannot employ (i′) in a rational manner to guide action. The formula (i′) for forming moral opinions requires that one 'already' (in the order of accepted justification) have formed a moral opinion precisely on that matter but on some ground other than what formula (i′) gives. Thus (i′) in the presence of (ii′) cannot function as a rational belief-forming device. Nor, more generally, can it be a rational belief-forming device for the person P in the versions of (i) where P is someone other than oneself. While we (non-P's) can use (i) to determine what is right by considering P's actions or reactions, the person P cannot himself be using (i). Indeed P must be making moral mistakes, if (i) is to be believed. (i) grants all the amnesties P may ever need *ex post facto*. But it is absolutely no good at giving direction to P at the time of choice.

Now given that (ii′) looks very much like an analytic truth (or at any rate true), the moral theory in (i′) seems to be *generally* defective. It is totally useless in rationally guiding action. However Hume's theory of virtue-based morality, (Vb) does not suffer from the *general* sort of incoherence that we must attribute to (i′). The reason is that, while (i′) allows only one right-making virtuous motive, viz. the regard to rightness, Hume's (Vb) quite sensibly allows a great many motivations other than 'the regard to virtue as such'. These motivations are the 'natural virtues', i.e., motivations such as compassion or concern for offspring which can be specified and explained without bringing in the agent's rightness beliefs. No Euthyphro circularity threatens in the particular cases where an act's rightness (or its 'being virtuous') arises just from its proceeding (or commonly proceeding) from a motivation such as compassion or concern for one's offspring. What (Vb) allows, and (i′) doesn't, are these quite independent grounds for rightness. Furthermore, given these independent ways in which an act might become right ('virtuous'), (Vb) can then allow the motivation 'a regard to virtue as such' (i.e., a regard to right action) to arise in a secondary sort of way. The 'first motive' making an act right

189

might just be that it proceeded (or commonly does proceed) from a certain naturally virtuous motivation such as compassion or benevolence. However, once the agent recognises this rightness (specifically on this ground), he might then be further motivated to do the act because he 'already' sees it to be right. (Vb) can allow a 'desire to do one's duty' to arise in the secondary way, i.e., to arise by way of a recursion upon other virtuous motives. But (Vb) must insist that a motivation like 'the regard to justice as such' cannot be the 'first' motive making the act right. The 'first' motive will always be a natural motive. Hence Hume's impossibility claim, the denial of (PCr), is that the 'first' virtuous motive making an act right, as per (Vb), must be some motive distinct from the regard to rightness.

So, unlike the case with (i'), (Vb) does not give us a circularity problem in *every* instance of its application. As long as the first virtuous motive making an act right is not, specifically, the regard to the rightness of the act, there can be clear, non-circular application. (Vb) presents a circularity problem only in *some* special cases. Where Hume's (Vb) might lead to a circularity is precisely where it is supposed there is a particular act A that is right ('virtuous') where:

i″. Act A is right for agent P only because P's doing A proceeds from a regard to the rightness of A as such, where:

ii″. The explanation of P's doing A out of a regard for its rightness as such involves the fact that P already (in the order of explanation) believes that A is the right thing for him to do, where:

iii″. P's belief that A is the right thing for him to do is solely based on a correct application of the moral claim in (i″) to the circumstances.

Hume says:

To suppose, that the mere regard to the virtue of the action, may be the first motive, which produc'd the action, and render'd it virtuous, is to reason in a circle. Before we can have such a regard, the action must really be virtuous; and this virtue must be deriv'd from some virtuous motive: And consequently the virtuous motive must be different from the regard to the virtue of the action. A virtuous motive is requisite to render an action virtuous. An action must be virtuous, before we can have a regard to its virtue. Some virtuous motive, therefore, must be antecedent to that regard. (478)

While (Vb) *generally* has no circularity problems, reminiscent of *Euthyphro,* it will have just such a circularity problem if it allows

190

that the above *particular* case, (i″) & (ii″) & (iii″), can occur. If it is virtuous motives that make acts right, the virtuous motive that, in the first instance, makes an act right cannot be just the regard to rightness as such.

HARD CASES

But now Hume's theory of virtue-based morality encounters a serious problem. In many of central cases of moral judgments which we make it would be difficult to see what 'natural' motive accounts for the rightness ('virtuous action') that we attribute. For example, what natural motivations would account for the obligations of property, truth-telling, promising, or (in other societies) of kinship rules. The issue here is not really at all about whether these motivations are acquired rather than ones we have naturally. Rather, the problem is one of giving a specification, account, or explanation, of such motivations which, as per (Vb), will then explain the obligations to respect property, tell the truth, etc. The most obvious candidates for such motivations, e.g. regard for the obligations of property, desire to do one's duty to tell the truth, etc., suffer from the circularity problem. They cannot be the 'first' virtuous motives making it right not to steal, to tell the truth, etc. On the other hand, the motivations which don't create any circularity problem, e.g. self-interest, a regard to the public interest (general benevolence), regard for the interests of those directly affected (private benevolence), don't actually account for (render right) our thinking these acts obligatory. In fact Hume, quite incisively, argues these, the only other candidates in the running, just don't work (480-2; cf. Mackie, 1980, pp. 77–8). Hume's problem comes from the fact that (Vb) requires that there always be a virtuous motive which accounts for why an act is right. In some important cases, i.e., the 'hard cases', no virtuous motivations are plausible candidates for the job of rendering acts right except the very regard to rightness as such (or 'the regard to justice' or the 'sense of the actions's morality' or respect for property rights, etc.). But such motivations cannot be plugged into (Vb) without making (Vb) circular in its account of what renders these acts right.

And now perhaps we understand a bit better the importance of the artificial/natural distinction. All the 'hard cases', i.e., the moral judgments about actions which we normally make but which (Vb) might well seem unable to account for without circularity, Hume lumps under the phrase 'the rules of justice'. Here he uses the word 'justice' in a rather wide sense. Any judgment of obligation or of rightness of action which threatens (Vb) with circularity gets classified here. By contrast, the 'natural' virtues are those motivations which Hume regards as virtuous and which can be employed in (Vb) to account for 'virtuous' actions without any worries of circularity. The 'artificial' virtues are those virtuous motives such as the regard to justice which are a worry to Hume.

THE WRONG SOLUTION TO
THE WRONG PROBLEM

Hume cannot just say at this point that there are no obligations of justice. Nor can he just say that there really is no such motivation as 'the regard to justice' where having the motive presupposes (in the order of explanation) that the agent believes his act right (for reasons having nothing to do with such acts proceeding from certain natural motives). While it must now appear that (Vb) really requires the elimination of such obligations and of any rational belief in obligations of that sort, Hume does not take that way out. I think the reason for this must be that Hume, with the sentimentalism (S) he confuses with (Vb) still somewhere in mind, feels he must account for the common moral beliefs people have. Moral judgments about moral obligations (say, of property, or of promises, or to obey the law) are so central that failure to give a coherent account must be a reason for eliminating Hume's theory of morals rather than for eliminating the central counter-example cases. (S) tries to give an account of all the moral beliefs there are. It is not a proposal for moral revision. By contrast, (Vb) Hume's virtue-based moral theory is more the proposal of a moral reformer. While it seems to be a coherent moral code, it is not quite the one we have now in entirety. A defender of (Vb) seems to be proposing that we abandon the notions of property, truth-telling, obligations to obey the law, and any other similar 'rules of justice' as we now conceive them. But I think this is not Hume. Hume is not proposing that we reject our present obligation morality in favour of a virtue-based morality. While others may have on occasion given reasons for such a revision, Hume has no ground for doing so.[4] His sen-

4 Possibly something this radical is suggested by some of the claims in Anscombe

timentalism must be able to account for all logically possible moral beliefs or at least for the ones which do in fact occur. (S) cannot just ignore the 'hard cases' that arise in regard to justice. And if (S) gives no ground for moral revision, neither is there any other argument in Hume for (Vb) which would give a case for the revision it implies.

In fact Hume accepts that, since self-interest, public benevolence and private benevolence fail the task, the possibility claim is correct after all. Hume admits, '[W]e have no real or universal motive for observing the laws of equity, but the very equity and merit of that observance'. But since he also holds, in accordance with (Vb), that 'no action can be equitable or meritorious, where it cannot arise from some separate motive', he concludes 'there is here an evident sophistry and reasoning in a circle' (483). The 'sophistry', as I have explained it, is that the 'laws of equity' (or 'rules of justice') cannot offer action guiding direction to the rational. But Hume nevertheless thinks there is a way out! He thinks he can, contrary to our discussion so far, hold both (Vb) and the possibility claim that the 'regard to justice as such' can be a *first* right-making motive as per (Vb). 'Unless', he says, ' . . . nature has establish'd a sophistry' (that is, as I would put it, unless what clearly does function as an action guide for those who accept it cannot be so employed), 'we must allow, that the sense of justice and injustice is not deriv'd from nature, but arises artificially, tho' necessarily from education, and human conventions' (483). Apparently Hume thinks he can get out of the circularity problem, i.e., hold both (Vb) and the possibility claim, by giving a *genetic account* of how such a motive might arise from an original situation where only natural (non-circle-producing) motivations and psychological mechanisms (e.g. self-interest, sympathy) then existed.

Yet this account, however accurate and however useful for other purposes, does not really meet the difficulty of the circularity. The

(1958). It is suggested that moral obligation talk only makes sense in a context of divine law. If so, to reject the basis of divine law would leave no place for obligation talk and might leave the field clear for a totally virtue-based morality.

An interesting question might be whether there could be a coherent 'virtue'-based theory of prudence (where the 'virtues' would not be particularly moral ones but just admirable qualities, perhaps not unlike the ones Hume discusses in III,iii,4). However the discussion of PA4 and PA5 in Chapter 5 above would suggest that our ordinary notion, at least, of prudence contains some important notions of reasons for acting which are not even prudential virtue-based.

occurrences of 'first' in Hume's circularity problem mark priorities in the order of explanation or else in the order of justification the agent accepts where that explains his acting. Nowhere in the possibility claim (PCr), for example, does a 'first' mark only a temporal priority. It might be a correct genetic thesis that 'the regard to justice as such' can only arise through education, socialisation, etc., from a pre-existing situation where no such motive existed. But even if that is so, that does not solve the difficulty (Vb) has in supposing that what (now) makes an act just is nothing but the regard to justice which the agent now has (however that motive arose). That is, it's still not at all clear how the motivation 'the regard to justice as such' whether natural or acquired, could ever be the motivation which (in the order of justification) first renders an act right as per (Vb). A genetic story does not solve the problem which logic, not nature, has established for his virtue-based morality (Vb). That theory cannot coherently allow even an acquired regard to justice to be what makes, in the first instance, an act right. That there might be natural (rather than acquired) motivations in the genetic history of the regard to justice will not help if those motives are not, either now or earlier, a part of the justificatory story.

Hume's attempt to defend (Vb) against its 'hard cases' (i.e., those central cases where no virtuous motive can ground the rightness of the act except the very regard to the act's rightness) is, in my view, a failure. He can give no account consistent with (Vb) which is both plausible and non-circular. Having put the circularity problem so nicely, Hume then fails to address that circularity problem. The genetic account does not meet the logical circularity. The conclusion Hume should have drawn is that (Vb) cannot accurately capture the structure of all of our moral beliefs.[5] Possibly this is the structure behind some of our rightness judgments but it cannot, as (Vb) asserts, be what is behind all of them. In the 'hard cases' something more like Clarke's view seems to capture the structure more accurately. Some acts, we ordinarily think, are made right in the first instance by their properties, their circumstances, or at any rate by something other than just the motive which did (or typically does) produce them. Those who have thoughts of this structure and are motivated to act in accordance with them may be said to

5 However cf. note 9 to Chapter 10 below.

have acted from the regard to rightness. A morality that is totally virtue-based cannot really pretend to have any place for 'rules of justice' or a complete account of 'the regard to justice'.

BUT THE RIGHT SOLUTION TO
THE RIGHT PROBLEM

If that were all there were to it, there wouldn't be much reason to read further in Hume. But in fact Hume's discussion gets back on the rails. The proposed solution which fails to solve the problem Hume shouldn't be discussing anyway, is perhaps more like the solution to the problem he should be discussing. Hume does have another circularity problem, a rather more interesting one, about 'the regard to justice as such'. That problem has nothing at all to do with his virtue-based moral theory (Vb). The problem is indeed a circularity problem, but it is not the Euthyphro-like circularity problem that arises in the context of (Vb). The real circularity problem for Hume arises in regard to his sentimentalism, (S), and is what I previously called 'the circle of sentimentalism'. That circularity problem is quite different from the Euthyphro-circularity problem which, admittedly, is the one Hume describes and which he also mistakenly thinks he solves.

But perhaps it is not surprising that anyone who would systematically confuse (S) with (Vb), a meta-ethical theory with a substantive moral theory, would confuse their respective circularity problems. Both circularity problems arise in regard to the same hard case, i.e., 'the rules of justice' as Hume calls them. For (Vb) the problem is one of finding a motivation in the person judg*ed* just or honest to constitute the virtue. For (S) the problem is to find an appropriate sentiment in the judg*er,* the person who thinks certain acts or persons just. Now sentimentalism requires that there be an appropriate, peculiarly moral sentiment in the judg*er* who makes such judgments. Hume's most general account, in this regard, seems to be that the peculiarly moral (positive) sentiment is some sort of approval toward objects (i.e. agents or actions) useful and/or agreeable to others and/or the agent himself where, perhaps, the mechanism of sympathy is a significant part of the story of how such a sentiment in the judg*er* can arise and be possible. On another story that Hume gives, the moral sentiment might be some *sui generis* positive sentiment of the judg*er* toward actions flowing from (or typically flowing from) natural or usual motivations in the object judged. Here the positive sentiment in the judg*er* is directed toward, as its object, the natural motives in the person judg*ed*.

Now, in a range of cases, sentimentalism can be content to specify the positive and negative sentiments (approval and disapproval) involved in making moral judgments just by the objects of the sentiments. For example, a sentimentalist can give an account of many moral judgments in terms of sentiments of approval specifically toward, say, socially beneficial acts and qualities or, again, by sentiments of approval for natural motives in their usual force (and of the acts flowing from them). In such cases, whatever other difficulties the sentimentalist account may encounter, there is no circularity problem. Here no circularity problem arises because the kind of approval or disapproval is specified by its objects which in turn are specified in non-normative terms, or at any rate not in terms of the very normative notions the specific approval or disapproval are supposed to explain. This gives us yet another, quite different, account of what is really behind the talk of 'natural' virtues: Where our moral judgments of persons, their motives, or the acts which flow from them can be accounted for by sentimentalism without any danger of circularity just by a specification of the object of the sentiments, they are to be counted as judgments attributing 'natural virtues'. Indeed it might have been much clearer to call such judgments the 'unproblematic cases' or 'easy cases' for sentimentalism.

On the other hand, there are also 'problematic' or 'hard cases' for sentimentalism, the cases where Hume talks about 'artificial virtues', 'the rules of justice', and 'justice'. These are the cases of moral judgments where the only obvious and plausible sentiments available to play the appropriate role in the sentimentalist account will be something like 'approval of just acts', 'a respect for duty', 'a regard for moral obligation', or perhaps 'appreciating that such and such is a justifying reason for doing such and such'. Now while it might be agreed on all sides that such moral judgments do express precisely these moral sentiments (if they express any at all), the sentimentalist cannot leave it at that. It is circular to explain what it means to think an action just in terms of the sentiment 'the regard to justice'. Besides explaining nothing (for it uses the notion it is trying to explain), this verbal formula perhaps plays into the hands of the opponents of sentimentalism (e.g. Samuel Clarke). The phrase 'the regard to justice' can make it sound as if there is already something existing in the world, i.e., the act's property of justice, toward which this sort of regard is directed. There is an embarrassingly cognitivist ring to this way of specifying the sentiment. Clearly the sentimentalist cannot just stop with this specification (even if the sentiment thereby specified is the right one).

It is not entirely accidental that the discussion of these 'hard cases' for sentimentalism relates to our discussion, in Chapters 4 and 5 above, of those much discussed motivational cases 2 and 3. More specifically it relates to the 'first specification' in those cases. That is, whether or not any consequent motivation occurs, there is at any rate such a thing as 'accepting', or judging, that, for example, one ought to do such and such just because one promised. Or, to put it into more Humean terms, there is such a thing as thinking one ought to do such and such because some 'rule of justice' (e.g. some rule of property, promising, or political allegiance) requires it. Of course it is not the task of sentimentalism to agree or disagree with such judgments, but only to give an account of what it is to 'hold' such a judgment, to 'accept' such a moral 'belief'. Certainly it is not the task of sentimentalism to distort the psychological phenomena in question into something else. It will not do, for example, just to pretend, as the 'provocative Humean' does, that no one ever really accepts practical arguments like PA2 or PA3. Likewise, it is just as much a distortion to pretend that what everyone (or anyone) really accepts is a totally virtue-based morality such as (Vb) so that, again, no one is thought really to accept PA2 or PA3 or indeed any practical argument that fails to mention motives as what 'first' makes an act right. But in fact, if our common sense psychology is any guide, we sometimes accept practical arguments where the ultimate justifying reasons therein cited mention neither a sentiment of the judg*er* nor a motive in the judg*ed* (nor even a motive which normally produces such acts). It could just be PA2 or PA3 which one accepts. Now sentimentalism must explain *all* the existing phenomena of moral belief. Even if one happens to think that these practical arguments are misguided and rejects the judgments which are their conclusions, one must still, as a sentimentalist, give an account of the sentiments their acceptance would express. Sentimentalism must explain the psychological phenomena, not distort them, try to change them, or mount the opposing soap box. In short, these hard cases are not to be ignored.

197

But what will the particular and peculiarly moral sentiments expressed be in these various hard cases? For example, what is the sentiment involved in 'accepting' a practical argument such as PA2, or PA3? One cannot, as some might try in regard to PA1, suppose the sentiment is to be found in the first premiss of the practical argument accepted. No sentiment at all occurs in the premisses of PA2 and PA3. So presumably a sentimentalist must say that the appropriate sentiment involved in accepting PA2, or PA3, is just the judg*er*'s 'taking the premisses of that practical argument to be good justifying reasons for acting in such and such a way'.[6] Now that may well point to the right sentiments, but the sentimentalist cannot leave it at that without risking both circularity and a formulation that rings more of cognitivism than non-cognitivism. The sentimentalist must explain further just what 'pro-attitude', 'sentiment', or 'approval state' is involved in 'accepting' that such and such a feature of an act is a justifying reason for so acting. Nor can he simply say, what all parties can admit, that to assent to some such 'hard case' moral judgment is to express a 'regard for a certain justifying reason'.

So, we might say, the real problem for the contemporary Humean about the so-called artificial virtues is really not a problem at all about Euthyphro-circles. The latter is only a doppelganger problem systematically confused with the real problem. The real circularity problem is one of finding an analysis of the sentiment 'the regard to justice as such' which can be used by the sentimentalist to explain 'hard case' moral judgments, thereby successfully avoiding the specification circle that threatens sentimentalism in just such cases. And something like analysis is indeed what we want here.

---

6 Indeed a sentimentalist should really tell the same story about PA1. 'Accepting' that one's desire is in certain circumstances a justifying reason for acting, if it involves or just is a sentiment, will not just be the desire thought to be a reason (and mentioned in the first premiss). Rather, it will be a sentiment that would more normally be described as 'thinking that the desire is a justifying reason', although that way of putting it sounds much too cognitivist and, in any case, risks a specification circle in the context of sentimentalism. It follows from this that it is as difficult for the sentimentalist to give an account of what it is to hold the Humean theory of justifying reasons (i.e., (P5) discussed in Chapters 3–5) as it is to give an account of what it is to hold any alternative view (e.g. one which accepted PA2 or PA3). Sentimentalism gives no special brief to the Humean theory of justifying reasons. It must give an account of what it is to think something a justifying reason but it does not entail the substantive claim that only one's own desires are justifying reasons.

Hume is admirably clear that the problem is one of accounting for 'the regard to justice' rather than trying to eliminate it or trying to pretend it doesn't exist. In particular, he is clear that other sentiments, such as self-interest, public benevolence, private benevolence, *are different* from the regard to justice and that the latter, rather than any of the former, is what the 'hard case' moral judgments involve. That was, in a way, the point made in Chapters 4 and 5 above.

The problem is not to eliminate but to reduce. That, I think, is how Hume sees it (cf. Harrison, 1981, pp. 50, 151). While he would have been much happier if public benevolence or some such 'natural' (i.e., non-circle-producing) motive could account for all our hard case (justice) judgments, he candidly admits the things which we praise as just are not in every case objects of these natural sentiments. Everything is what it is and not another thing. The sentiment the sentimentalist account requires is precisely the regard to justice as such. That's the right sentiment. It is not to be eliminated. But if it is not to be eliminated, the sentimentalist must be prepared to explain it, account for it further, in non-circular terms. Even if 'the regard to virtue' and no other sentiment is the one required for the hard cases, the sentimentalist cannot stop at that specification but must give an account of this sentiment that avoids the circularity problem. In Hume's case, this means analysing, or reducing, this sentiment in terms of other, more 'primitive' notions (e.g. of 'sympathy', of 'self-love', of 'convention', etc.) where these notions can be specified without using the very normative notions in question or indeed *any* normative notions. Furthermore such a reduction would not only avoid the circularity problem, it would also fit into the general task of a philosophical naturalism. To explain what it is to *accept* a moral judgment in terms of more primitive notions such as 'self-love' or 'convention' is not only to use non-normative notions, but notions that any reasonably naturalist account of reality would probably require in its account anyway. This looks very like a naturalistic account, not of the contents of moral belief, but of what it is to *have* a moral belief.

However it is important that this really be an analysis or a reduction and not merely a genetic account (even though Hume talks of 'origins'). It is not sufficient to give a genetic story about how the sentiment we call 'the regard to justice' arose from a previous situation where it did not exist. The problem, rather, is to analyse,

199

or reduce, what it is that has thereby come into existence. What is this 'regard to justice' that *now* exists in those who make justice judgments? Sentimentalism requires an analysis of this sentiment, a reduction to simpler psychological entities and mechanisms, not just a story of how the sentiment might be causally produced or brought about by things other than itself.

SUMMARY

At first glance it can seem very puzzling that Hume would jump from discussing a meta-ethical theory, sentimentalism, to discussing a distinction between the artificial and the natural virtues. Indeed, remembering the neutrality thesis of Chapter 6, we might wonder why a sentimentalist should be so particularly concerned about our judgments of virtue and vice. But in fact Hume's discussion in III, ii, 1 is rather more important for sentimentalism than it first appears. Admittedly, the discussion is systematically ambiguous and therefore almost a disaster. The original systematic confusion between sentimentalism, (S), and Hume's totally virtue-based theory of morality, (Vb), is now matched by a further systematic confusion of the specification-circularity problem for (S) with the Euthyphro-circularity problem for (Vb). With that confusion also go two different ways of looking at the point of the artificial/natural distinction. When Hume has his eye firmly fixed on (Vb), the point seems to be to distinguish between the hard cases (i.e., circle-threatening cases) and the easy cases *for* (*Vb*). But one can just as well take the point to be to distinguish between the hard cases (i.e., circle-threatening cases) and the easy cases *for* (*S*). I have argued that the Euthyphro-circularity problem specific to (Vb) is not only quite serious but probably insuperable. (Vb) cannot really handle its hard cases. But the discussion is not a disaster if we keep our eyes firmly fixed on (S), the thesis of interest to contemporary Humeans. When Hume is discussing the judgments we make attributing "artificial virtues" such as justice to actions, we may say he is in effect discussing all the hard cases for sentimentalism (S). He is discussing the cases of moral judgments people commonly make where the only plausible sentiment for a sentimentalist to propose in his account has a *prima facie* problem of circularity. The 'regard to justice as such', as he says, is precisely the sentiment required rather than others which, while they pose no circularity problem, really do not account for the judgments in question. But this sentiment has to be further analysed, or reduced, in a way that assures us no circularity is involved. This is in fact what Hume goes on to do in III, ii, 2, where an account of the problematic sentiment is given in terms of sympathy, convention, self-interest, and such.

Hume is right to think that that circle-threatening sentiment, 'the regard to justice', is *not* simply to be *eliminated*. Nor is it to be *confused* with other sentiments, which while they involve no threat of circularity, are just different sentiments. Nor will it do merely to give a *genetic account* of what brings about this sentiment, i.e., of how it can arise or emerge from a situation where it did not previously exist. The circularity problem concerns what that sentiment is that accounts for the 'hard case' judgments, not how that sentiment came about. Instead of either elimination or genesis, Hume must give something more like a *reductive account* of the 'regard to justice', reducing what it is now to more primitive, less problematic mechanisms and entities.

Consequently, what Hume goes on to discuss in his next section (III, ii, 2) is in fact more than just a little relevant to his sentimentalism (S). It is crucial to its defence. Something like a reductive account of the sentiment 'the regard to justice (or right, or obligation)' is crucial to any plausible defence of sentimentalism. It is very much to his credit that at precisely the point where so many contemporary Humeans are vague and hand-waving, Hume attempts to give what we should demand of any sentimentalist, i.e., a concrete, non-circular analysis of the sentiment involved in the 'hard cases' for sentimentalism.

Does he succeed?

8

The conservative theory of justice

Most of the core of Hume's theory of 'the rules of justice' is contained in the section 'Of the Origin of Justice and Property' (III,ii,2). Rather than a theory of 'justice' in the ordinary sense, we may think of it as a theory of those judgments of moral obligation we make which pose 'hard cases' for Humean meta-ethical sentimentalism. As a requisite preliminary, Hume gives us a description of 'the circumstances of human nature' without which rules of justice would be unnecessary and with which it is virtually a human necessity. Next, Hume gives an account of how our having 'rules of justice' can be accounted for as a socio-psychological fact, given these circumstances of human nature. Because this account employs the notion of social 'conventions', Hume must then give us some account of 'convention'. Finally, Hume gives an account of the sentiment we have which approves of compliance, and of the motive to comply, with such rules. It is an account of 'the regard to justice as such'.

TWO REDUCTIVE PROJECTS

The story Hume gives can, of course, be interpreted in ways which are an embarrassment to contemporary Humeans and which also tend to make Hume's discussion look discontinuous. It may look as if Hume has changed the subject of discussion from the defence of sentimentalism to either bad anthropology or else substantive normative ethics. For example, despite Hume's own disclaimers (493), Hume's account can look like a story about *historical origins,* as a story about a pre-history where men found it useful to 'remedy' certain problems by 'establishing' conventions. Again, Hume's account of the 'origin' of justice can look rather like a *justification,* i.e., as a story about how certain conventions are morally justified by, say, their social utility, given the circumstances of human nature. Certainly Hume's account has been used in this way by many contemporary moral philosophers.

Those of us who take Hume's discussion throughout Book III to be continuous and developing must take the above to be vulgar misinterpretations. Instead, Hume must be taken to be giving, in the first instance at least, a reductive account of the hard case notions and judgments of 'justice' which threaten his meta-ethical sentimentalism.[1] He needs to give a non-circular account of the sentiment 'the regard to justice as such' which we express, or have, in making those judgments about obligations, rights, justice which make for 'hard cases'. Hume's account of this sentiment employs notions such as 'self-interest', 'sympathy', 'convention', to mention some of the more important ones. Consequently, this is a story not about the past but about the present. It is a reductive account of what the problematic 'regard to justice', which we *now* have and express, is. Nor, again, is this reductive account, in the first instance, a justification of the rules of justice which we have. Still, if Hume is right that we do have this sentiment, his explicit account of what is really going on where there are institutions of justice will perhaps itself extract from us some approval of such rules and compliance with them. *For us,* this will be tantamount to a justification. It will engage the sentiments Hume claims we have.

There seem to be two important reductive projects in which Hume is engaged, both of which are of interest to contemporary Humeans. The first is crucial to the success of his meta-ethical sentimentalism. The issue here is whether Hume's reduction of 'the regard to justice as such' in terms of self-interest, sympathy, convention, etc., really succeeds. This seems necessary to avoid the specification circle of sentimentalism. On the success of a non-circular reduction rests the plausibility of sentimentalism. Whether it is possible to use the notion of 'convention' in the way Hume suggests to avoid the circularity problem for sentimentalism will be the topic of Chapter 10.

However there is another employment of Hume's notion of 'convention' which is of contemporary interest. Hume makes a certain

---

1 No doubt Hume is also concerned, given the systematic ambiguity in his discussion, to handle the 'hard cases' for his virtue-based morality which arise in regard to the virtue of justice. But this line of discussion in Hume is of very much less contemporary interest than is the one beginning with his sentimentalism.

important priority claim. He claims that certain important social phenomena such as property, promising and political institutions (i.e., what we now call 'institutional facts') are to be understood in terms of his account of our ideas of justice and injustice and thus, ultimately, in terms of convention (490–1, 526, 533). Hume thinks two things here. First, he thinks that institutional facts can be explained in terms of our ideas of justice and, thus, in terms of convention. Second, he thinks that convention can, in turn, be given a naturalistic explanation. Institutional facts are to be explained in terms of something like society's having certain rules or norms, but socially held rules are in turn to be accounted for in terms of naturalistic, non-institutional facts, including some psychological facts about individuals. Hume requires no queer facts which are not naturalistic (e.g. no Clarkean aFc-facts) nor does he need irreducibly social entities or facts. Hence his attempted reduction of institutional facts is in line both with naturalism and with methodological individualism. At the same time his naturalism and methodological individualism do not lead him to a crass eliminativism of the normative. There is no need to throw out the fundamental practice in history, sociology, anthropology, of employing explanations in terms of socially held norms. Hume does not deny there are institutional facts. He only denies they are irreducible facts. Hence Hume's position remains particularly attractive to many contemporary philosophers. Hume's attempted reduction of institutional facts and social phenomena will be the topic of Chapter 9.

DEEP SOURCES OF CONSERVATISM

The present chapter, while sketching Hume's theory of justice, will not be directly concerned with the above two reductive projects. Instead of bearing on the circle of sentimentalism or on naturalism and methodological individualism, it bears rather more on the issue of the neutrality of sentimentalism. Chapter 6 argued for the neutrality thesis, i.e., the claim that sentimentalism (and, more generally, non-cognitivism) can contribute in no invidious way to any particular moral or political outlook. Chapter 7 argued that we are to take Hume's theory of justice as a further elaboration, a necessary part of the defence, of sentimentalism. But, as we shall see in the present chapter, Hume's account of justice really does seem to

204

contribute to a particular moral and political outlook. Among other things it has a conservative bent to it which is not superficial or just something additional. It flows from rather deep aspects of his account. But how can the neutrality thesis allow a sentimentalist reductive account of our regard to justice to have a definite bent toward conservatism? How does Hume's account of what the sentiment of justice *is* contribute to the definite feeling that we *ought* to be conservatives?

There is no doubt that, as a matter of historical fact, Hume's discussion of justice has been a source for a variety of political views. It has not only been one source for British moderate conservatism (along with Burke) as well as a source for defenders of the liberal economic order such as Hayek, but also is the beginning point for contemporary leftish liberal egalitarian theorists such as, notably, John Rawls (1971). Again, we find a Humean starting point in contemporary 'rights-based' moral and political theories such as Mackie (1977, ch. 5). One feature of Hume's theory, his account of the 'circumstances of human nature', is something like the starting point of a wide spectrum of moral and political views ranging from conservative views (such as Hume's) on one hand, to leftish liberal-egalitarian views (such as Rawls') on the other. We will call all such views 'Hume-based' for they begin, at least, with a Hume-like account of the 'circumstances of human nature' and of the point or role of 'rules of justice'. All such 'Hume-based' views are in quite basic opposition to those who do not share this starting point (such as Marx, under certain interpretations). However within the spectrum of 'Hume-based' views those on the far right owe an additional debt to Hume. This second contribution from Hume lends a distinct conservative flavour to such views. My picture is something like figure 6. Both contributions from Hume have a moral and political bent. The element in Hume's theory which has contributed to all the views on the spectrum is still in opposition to certain radical views which reject Hume's starting point. Moreover the further element that contributes to Humean conservatism is not only anti-radical, it is anti-liberal and anti-egalitarian as well. Altogether Hume's theory of justice has a definite moral and political bent.

Where do these distinctive contributions to moral and political philosphy come from in Hume's theory? In asking this I am not raising a question of intellectual history or of the sociology of

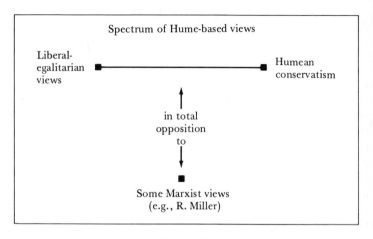

Figure 6.

knowledge. I am not interested in the various influences on Hume's political thinking and the ways in which his writings may have influenced others. Nor am I concerned to document from the various sources in Hume's writings all the passages which might count as conservative. What I am concerned with is Hume's system of thought, the developing argument still of contemporary interest, not just with every remark he let slip, every bias he may have betrayed. More precisely, my concern is with the investigation of Hume's developing defence of sentimentalism in Book III to see whether, and at what precise points, the basic line of argument veers a bit to the right. So I am looking for contributions to particular moral and political stances which are *both* (1) warranted by Hume's developing argument (as that is of interest to contemporary Humeans) *and* (2) to be found at a relatively deep level of that argument, so that the source of the contribution cannot easily be eliminated without fundamentally altering the structure of Hume's argument. Thus, as per (1), any of Hume's incidental political and social views which he betrays either in the *Treatise* or elsewhere are just irrelevant if not actually required by Hume's developing argument for sentimentalism in Book III. But also, as per (2), it is important to see whether such consequences fall out at a relatively deep level of the argument or only at a superficial level.

An example of a superficial conservative feature in Hume's ar-

206

gument would be this. We can see that some of the conservatism sometimes attributed to Hume is just a result of his ethnocentricity in the choice of his examples of 'rules of justice'. When in Part ii he considers conventions which solve certain problems of conflict, he thinks mainly in terms of rules of property, contract and somewhat Western notions of law and state. No doubt his failure to consider, say, the systems of kinship rules which we find in anthropological descriptions of other societies leads to a certain bias toward Western bourgeois ideological views. Not only marxist interpreters of Hume are quick to point out this bias. But without denying Hume's narrowness in this regard, it should be noted that it makes a difference only at a relatively superficial level. A contemporary Humean can bring to Hume's argument in Part ii a knowledge of the wider range of human social possibilities, say systems of rules where notions of private property play only a small, peripheral role. While that might rid the Humean argument of a certain part of its conservative bias, it would do so without radically affecting the *core* of Hume's account of convention, the rules of justice, or the regard to justice as such. If Hume's conservatism were just a matter of the ethnocentricity of his examples of social rules, his conservatism would not run very deep at all. A contemporary Humean could take over the interesting core of Hume's developing defence of sentimentalism without that involving any further commitment to conservative views.

The view for which I shall argue in this chapter is that the sources of conservatism run deep in Hume's theory of justice. They are not just a matter of some additional, but deletable, bias or narrowness. They are inherent in the interesting core of Hume's theory. This is important. It means that anti-conservatives need to confront Hume's argument and point out just where it goes wrong. And the fact the sources of conservatism are deep means that anti-conservatives can't resort to quick, easy dismissals of Hume's conservatism. They must go back to the very fundamentals of Hume's argument to find the flaw. It might seem tempting to do a 'C. B. Macpherson' on Hume, to take all of Hume's discussion of property, promising (i.e., contact), law, modesty, chastity as evidence for his 'possessive individualism'. A marxist might well on that basis dismiss Hume as a typical fabricator of bourgeois ideology. But if, as I shall argue, the basic conservatism comes in well before Hume gets to discussing property and contract, this standard marxist criticism becomes rather shallow and fails to confront the most interesting source of Humean conservatism. That would remain even if Hume had spoken of the kinship rules of certain primitive societies rather than of property and contract.

The core of Hume's account of justice has several parts, or really stages, each presupposing the earlier stage. Different Humean claims from different parts of Hume's core theory have made different important contributions to various kinds of contemporary Humean or Hume-based views. Thus it is useful to distinguish perhaps three stages in Hume's discussion of justice. The first is clearly independent of the two which follow. It is an account of 'the circumstances of human nature' (484–8, 493–5). According to the picture Hume paints, a source of conflict is inherent in the human situation and, while this conflict may be 'remedied' in a certain way, the source of conflict cannot just be eliminated. Hence the first stage merely gives these background circumstances. It is what all 'Hume-based' theories of justice share with Hume. The second and third stages are more to the core of Hume's distinctive theory (and are perhaps not really entirely separable from each other). The second stage supplies an account of 'convention' (489–90) and of how the existence of conventions can be explained in the context of the circumstances of human nature. Because, as I have explained, this account is of interest quite apart from its employment in Hume's theory of justice (e.g. in philosophy of the social sciences), we may for convenience consider it a distinct stage from the third. However in giving this account Hume thinks he is not merely contributing to our naturalistic understanding of institutional facts but is also thereby contributing to an account of our idea of justice. Indeed Hume thinks institutional notions like property, law, promising are not intelligible apart from his account of justice and convention (490–4). But this now takes us to the third stage. Building on his claim about the nature of 'convention' (which presupposes his account of the human circumstances) and on a story about various motivations and psychological mechanisms, Hume gives us a (reductive) account of the specific sentiment 'the regard to justice as such' (492, 495–501). If this succeeds, it is an account which is at once both naturalistic and non-circular. It is precisely what is required for a plausible defence of sentimentalism.

Hume's description of the circumstances of human nature, while presupposed by the other two stages in his account of justice, does not by itself entail them. Thus it has been adopted by many philosophers who go no further with Hume, i.e., who do not go on to accept his account of 'convention' or his particular attempt to provide an account of 'the regard to justice' adequate to the defence of sentimentalism. Of course Hume's description of the human situation is not entirely original. We find something like it very early in philosophy in Protagoras (in Plato's dialogue of that name) and, of course, in Hobbes. And after Hume we find something like his description taken up by a great many influential mainstream English-speaking moral and political philosophers (e.g. Hart, 1961; Rawls, 1971; Mackie, 1977, ch. 5; Lukes, 1985, ch. 3). I call such moral and political theories 'Hume-based' even if they lack the further features of the second and third stages of 'Hume's theory of justice' (which commit him to rather more distinctly conservative conclusions).

In Hume's explicit account there are three elements in the circumstances of human nature. One is a 'quality of mind' (494):

1) 'Selfishness' and 'limited generosity' (486–7, 494–5; cf. *Enquiry*, 185).

The claim about humans in (1) is fairly minimal. It falls very short of anything like the psychological egoism we find in Hobbes. It claims no more than the absence of sufficient (universally directed) generosity and altruism to avoid the conflicts that, given the other conditions, arise. A society of angels might have no conflicts (except of the 'No, after *you,* please' variety) and thus would lack one reason, at least, for having notions of justice. (1) is consistent with a great deal more altruism than we in fact seem to encounter, especially if the altruism in question is not universal but starts to weaken progressively, starting with family, friends, countrymen, etc.

The other two conditions concern 'the situation of external objects' (494):

2) Moderate 'scarcity' of jointly desired objects (487–8, 494; cf. *Enquiry* 183–9).

3) 'Easy change' (transferability) of jointly desired objects (487–8, 494).

The circumstance alleged in (2) is that all of us cannot satisfy our 'numberless wants and necessities' given only the 'slender means' available (484). Adding (3), the transferability of these jointly desired goods to (1) and (2) makes for a situation fraught with insecurity and instability (488, 494). Each will be motivated to deny others the objects which are insufficient to satisfy all. Hume's view seems to have been that (1), (2) and (3) together make for an ineliminable source of conflict. At the same time to weaken any of these three further would be to eliminate that source of conflict (494–6). They seem to be regarded as jointly sufficient and individually necessary for a human situation where conflict is inherent.

Hume's account of the source of instability and conflict inherent in (2) moderate scarcity with (3) easy change of desired goods and (1) limited generosity is rather too easily subject to caricature and dismissal. The account seems to assume both too much and too little. It seems to assume too much in supposing that the same sorts of objects will be desired in all forms of society and that the nature of the conflict for these desired objects will not differ significantly between societies. Thus Hume can seem rather ethnocentric in still one more way. Marxists will claim he is taking the bases of conflict specific to particular social frameworks (e.g. bourgeois society or the market) and reading these into the 'circumstances of human nature'. His 'desired goods' are really economic goods. Hume assumes they hold the same central place in every form of society as they do in ours. But as Walzer claims, it may be quite wrong to suppose that there is a 'single set of primary or basic goods conceivable across all moral and material worlds' (1983, p. 8). And even if we can find a list of bare necessities which are jointly desired, moderately scarce, and transferable in every society, that is not to say that conflict over objects in this rather limited category will be the only, or a very important part of, conflicts which arise in most societies.

Again, Hume claims rather less than he might in regard to the sources of conflict. As Harrison points out, Hume's account of basic conflict is almost entirely in terms of conflict over property (1981, p. 42), i.e., over desired objects 'easily changed'. It seems odd that Hume does not mention murder, assault, defamation, etc., in his discussion of justice. Of course there is one connection. One way to reduce a competitor's chances of getting a jointly desired object is to maim him or kill him. But that is only one sort of situation leading to murder and assault. There are a whole range of motives starting with malice, hate, revenge, etc., where what is desired is not some jointly desired object but, as often as not, precisely the injuring of another.[2] Again, even if I have no such malicious desire, it need not be that conflict arises from some object we jointly desire. It may be that we desire quite different things (not necessarily transferable) which are incompatible. My getting what I want may impede, or impose an undesired cost on, your getting what you what.

For the above two reasons contemporary Humeans replace Hume's (2) and (3) with:

2') Scarcity, but only in the sense of the impossibility of joint realisation of all individual goals within any realisable social framework (Hart, 1961, pp. 192–3; Rawls, 1971, pp. 126, 128; Lukes, 1985, p. 32).

3') 'Rough equality' or 'vulnerability' (*Enquiry* 191–2; Hart, 1961, pp. 190–1; cf. Hobbes, 1651, ch. 13).

Condition (3') is in fact very much weaker than the word 'equality' suggests. The condition is only, to put it in terms of game theory, that 'outcomes' are not determined solely by the choices of any one 'player' but depend to some extent on the choices of other 'players'. That is, no one can impose a particular distribution, say, one satisfying all his own goals, just by the powers he has in virtue of his natural characteristics (e.g. strength, ability to deceive) and apart from the workings of conventions (which may give one new forms of power). Without conventions no distributional outcome is secure against change due to enough others' altering their choices.

The scarcity condition in (2') makes a claim very much weaker than anything in Hume's (2) and (3) together. There is no longer

---

2 I think Hume would cover such cases under some appropriate 'natural' virtue or vice rather than treat it under the heading of justice or the artificial virtues. On that view the sentiments which lead us to condemn assault, murder, defamation, etc., are ones that we naturally have in regard to the motives which lead to such acts. We just naturally disapprove of excessive aggression, for example. And we would quite apart from the existence of any conventions. For Hume, our judgments of justice and injustice concern cases where, apart from the existence of conventions, there would be no approval or disapproval. Again, we naturally disapprove of single acts of murder, etc., and not simply as a matter of the act's role in an 'overall scheme'.

211

the claim that the conflict in question always finds its source in scarcity of easily transferable, jointly desired objects or that the objects of conflict must be the same ones in all societies. As Lukes points out, the notion of scarcity required in contemporary Humean versions of the circumstances of human nature is not at all as simple as Hume describes it:

Of course, scarcity is not a simple notion. Consider the following forms of it: (1) insufficiency of production inputs (e.g. raw materials) relative to production requirements; (2) insufficiency of produced goods relative to consumption requirements; (3) limits upon the possibility of the joint re-alization of individual goals, resulting from external conditions (e.g. lim-itations of space or time); and (4) limits upon the possibility of the joint realization of individual goals, resulting from the nature of those goals (e.g. 'positional goods': we cannot all enjoy high status or the quiet solitude of our neighbourhood park). (Lukes, 1985, p. 32, n. 1)

It is important to note that the contemporary Humean position in (2') and (3'), unlike Hume's position, is not undermined by the mere fact that all desires are to some extent culturally based and some are totally so based. Nor is it overthrown by the fact that certain objects are only possible under certain social frameworks. Desires for status of particular sorts can serve as an example of both these points. Hume does indeed seem to have ignored the cultural determinants of desires and their objects. Thus Hume's original formulation lends itself to easy dismissal by those who would locate the sources of his conservatism in his ethnocentricity. However the contemporary Humean version, as we find in Lukes, claims only that eliminating the sources of all important forms of conflict si-multaneously would require a state of 'co-operative abundance' that is an 'unrealizable state of affairs'. Possibly (although this should not be conceded too quickly) any *one* source of conflict that we find in a given society could be eliminated in some other social framework. There might always be other possible social frame-works and circumstances where there is no conflict of just that sort. But wherever this one sort of conflict is eliminated it will be replaced by other important kinds of conflict. The human condition is like a warped carpet. It may be possible to flatten any one bump but only to find others popping up elsewhere. Even if any *one* kind of conflict is eliminable in humanly realisable circumstances, not *all* forms of important conflict are simultaneously eliminable in any realisable form of society.

212

The contemporary Humean version would also make explicit two further conditions which we may regard as implicit in Hume:

4) People generally have a 'modicum of rationality' (as Lewis puts it).

That is, persons have some degree of understanding of their own interests and goals. One must not suppose others are much less (or much more) rational in carrying out their goals than oneself. And also:

5) Specific mutual knowledge: People generally know (or are capable of knowing) (1), (2'), (3'), and (4), or at least the application of these generalisations to their own society and circumstances, to indefinitely many levels of mutual knowledge.

That is, not only do we both individually realise these circumstances of conflict but I know that you know, and if you think about it you will realise that I know that you know, and so on indefinitely. As we shall see it is important to Hume's theory that, not only do these conflicts exist objectively in the situation, but we mutually understand that to be the situation. We make our choices based on expectations about how others will choose, knowing full well that they see the situation in much the same way, crediting us with a similar understanding, etc.

In game theoretic terms, the conditions (1), (2'), (3'), (4) and (5) would seem to provide all the features necessary for a classic 'prisoners' dilemma'.[3] This would be so even with Hume's (2) and (3) rather than the contemporary (2') and (3'). Certainly it is clear the 'game' is not one of pure coordination. It is a game of some conflict (cf. Lewis, 1969, ch. 1). However some contemporary Humeans mention another feature of the human situation which stands quite independently of (1)–(5). While having nothing to do with conflict, it provides an independent 'problem' for which the 'rules of justice' would provide some 'remedy'. This further condition is:

6) Lack of perfect information and understanding.

Thus Lukes says:

---

3 A simple exposition and further references on the prisoners' dilemma is in Mackie (1977, pp. 115–20). See Luce & Raiffa (1957, ch. 5) for a game theoretic discussion. Interesting recent discussions are in Taylor (1976); Axelrod (1984); Parfit (1984, chs. 2–4); Gauthier (1986, pp. 79–82); Pettit (1986). Cf. also Chapter 10 below.

For even under co-operative abundance, total altruism, and the unification of interests within a common conception of the good, people may get it wrong: they may fail to act as they should towards others, because they do not know how to or because they make mistakes, with resulting misallocations of burdens and benefits, and damage to individuals interests. (1985, p. 33)

Even purely cooperative games may easily give rise to difficult coordination problems. Hume's account may be faulted for failing to recognise that 'conventions' or 'rules of justice' may be required as 'remedies' in games of pure coordination as well as in games with some features of conflict.

In summary we may say that the contemporary Humean description of the 'circumstances of human nature' is something closer to (1), (2'), (3'), (4) and (5) rather than Hume's (1), (2) and (3). The contemporary version is very much less vulnerable to quick dismissal on grounds of ethnocentricity. Marxists cannot quite as plausibly persist with the claim that the contemporary account merely reflects the particular features of motivations and structures we find in bourgeois society but not in every society. Modifying Hume in the contemporary fashion allows us then to look a bit deeper for the sources of conservatism in Hume's theory of justice. If it were only to be found in Hume's employment of (2) and (3) rather than (2') and (3'), it would not run very deep. The contemporary version would have excised Hume's conservative bias without any harm and with much gain in plausibility. But in fact we shall find the deepest sources of Hume's conservatism remain intact and the overall argument is somewhat improved by the contemporary revision. Certainly the two remaining stages of Hume's argument proceed just as well, indeed better, on the basis of the contemporary revision.

CONVENTION

Hume thinks the conflicts which arise from the circumstances of human nature find a 'remedy' in 'convention' (489). We need not take Hume's claim here to depend on a genetic account or on some fantastic pre-history. It is not that pre-conventional beings notice the inconveniences of conflict and therefore 'establish' conventions for the purpose of overcoming those inconveniences. Hume himself says that the supposition of a 'state of nature' is a mere 'philosophical

214

fiction' (493). In fact Hume need only say that 'conventions' are a kind of social fact that would not long persist if, *per impossibile,* the circumstances of human nature altered in such a way as to make them 'unnecessary'. Nor, on his view, could they long persist if we did not at some level understand the circumstances of human nature. Finally, the existence of conventions involves certain behavior that must be given a very special sort of explanation. As we shall see, it is the very circumstances of human nature which require that there be a special explanation of this behavior.

For Hume a convention is a way people behave (or are somewhat motivated to behave) in circumstances that really require that a very special sort of explanation be given why they so behave. Let R be some scheme of social choice, i.e., a way of everyone's choosing. A mere scheme R is not a convention. It is merely a function assigning to each individual a way of behaving in certain circumstances. We will say an individual 'complies' with R when he does (or is motivated to do) the act R assigns to him, but we leave it quite open *why* he complies. He need not, as the word 'comply' suggests, have acted for any reason that involves reference to R. He might 'comply' by accident, mistake, or for rather idiosyncratic reasons. The scheme R itself may never have occurred to any who happen to comply with it. Clearly R-compliance by everyone does not automatically constitute a convention. It would depend rather a lot on the motivations and beliefs behind the compliance.

In certain core cases which particularly interest Hume, if R-compliance were to occur regularly, that would require some special explanation. Consider cases where both:

a) It *would* normally be to no one's benefit or interest to comply with R if all (or most) others did not also R-comply, and:

b) Everyone's (or almost everyone's) complying with R *would* be better for everyone than the likely outcome if everyone made a self-interested choice with no more information about how others would choose except what can be derived from 'the circumstances of human nature' (and perhaps also from information about the 'natural' motives of others).

Of course if we interpret 'benefit' and 'self-interest' reasonably narrowly, there will be some cases of R-compliance, where (a) and (b) hold, which can be explained in terms of what Hume calls 'natural motives'. For example some of the ways many parents regularly act in regard to their own children might be in part explicable in terms of a 'natural' concern for one's offspring, rather than some narrowly conceived benefit for oneself. The point of calling such motives 'natural' need not be to claim that these motives are inevitably innate rather than learned or culturally acquired. The point need only be that such motives operate in individuals in a way quite regardless of the features of general behavior of that sort. So perhaps, in the spirit of Hume, we should further specify the interesting core cases with this additional condition:

c) There are no 'natural' motives sufficient to explain the general R-compliance.

However situations where there is general R-compliance and where (a), (b) and (c) hold could still be either cooperative or competitive (Lewis, 1969, pp. 13–14). It would be a case of pure co-operation if, for example, both of us want to meet this afternoon. In that case we would both benefit if we both go to the museum (i.e., $R1$-comply) or if we both go to the station (i.e., $R2$-comply). But in fact the situation Hume describes in the 'circumstances of human nature' has an important element of conflict. Limited generosity, moderate scarcity and easy change combine to create an ineliminable (even if remediable) source of conflict. Thus Hume must be particularly concerned with cases of R-compliance where it is also true that:

d) For each (or some) it is true that he *would* be better off if he did not R-comply, in a certain manner, given that all (or most) others do R-comply.

This addition gives the situation the features of the prisoner's dilemma. Conditions (a) and (d) ensure that not-complying is the dominant strategy for each person even while, as per (b), general compliance is Pareto-better than the likely outcome of general non-compliance (cf. Pettit, 1986, p. 363). But, furthermore, in the core cases there will be a number of different alternative R's ($R1$, $R2$, etc.) of each of which (a), (b), (c) and (d) hold. And while $R1$ might be better for some individuals than $R2$, $R2$ will be better for others than $R1$. This is then a further source of conflict even beyond what (d) adds. So in the interesting core cases it is also true that:

e) There is at least one alternative R', of which the analogues of (a), (b), (c) and (d) hold, such that some individuals *would* be better off under

216

general R'-compliance than under general R-compliance (but others, again, would be better off under R rather than R').

If there is general R-compliance where (a), (b), (c) hold and where there are also the elements of conflict in (d) and (e), then some special explanation of the R-compliance is in order. In Hume's view, if the explanation is of just the right sort, what exists is a convention. In the core circumstances (i.e., where (a) through (e) hold) Hume requires certain features as conditions on what it is for a convention to exist. To summarise:

i. There is general 'compliance' (or at least a general motivation to comply) with a certain scheme of social choice R, where:

ii. The fact that (a) through (e) hold in regard to R means that some special sort of explanation of this general R-compliance must be given.

The trick, of course, is to say just exactly what the special explanation of such R-compliance is in the case of conventions. We can perhaps dismiss some kinds of explanation it will not be. For example, where there is a convention it is not just a matter of everyone's happening to comply by accident or mistake. Nor will the explanation be sudden mass irrationality. Again the explanation will not be in terms of some widely shared 'natural' yen to do things of just that sort. But if not these, what is the explanation distinctive of conventions?

Hume is clear that a part of the special explanation (required if the R-compliance is to be a convention) will involve the mutual recognition of the above circumstances (a) through (e), but especially circumstances (a) and (b). The 'common knowledge' (cf. Lewis, 1969, pp. 56–7) is of circumstances which not only make for conflict, but also make general R-compliance a kind of 'remedy'. Thus Hume says:

I observe, that it will be for my interest to leave another in the possession of his goods, *provided* he will act in the same manner with regard to me. He is sensible of a like interest in the regulation of his conduct. When this common sense of interest is mutually expressed, and is known to both, it produces a suitable resolution and behaviour. (490)

Thus we must add:

iii. A part of the special explanation in (ii) of the R-compliance in (i) involves the R-compliers' 'common knowledge' of the facts (a) through (e).

That is, they mutually recognise the circumstances of human nature.

217

But this common knowledge can only be a part of the explanation. Notice that the propositions which are the object of this mutual knowledge are, with the exception of (c) which is a negative, mere hypotheticals or about hypotheticals. Each knows (and knows that others know) what *would* be the consequences under various patterns of behavior. But if, as per (e), there are several different alternative R's, say $R1$ and $R2$, of which all the corresponding hypotheticals hold, our mutual knowledge of these in regard to $R1$ cannot adequately explain our actual $R1$-compliance for we also share knowledge of the corresponding hypotheticals in regard to $R2$. Moreover Hume's passage makes it clear he thinks something more is required, i.e., a mutual expression of this common sense of interest. Hume is clear he does not mean 'agreement' in the sense of a promise or a contract. His view is that institutional facts such as promising must be explained in terms of the prior notion of convention so that he cannot, without circularity, employ such institutional notions in his account of convention (cf. 490, top, and 498, top).

In this regard we need something like Lewis' (1961, pp. 56–7) notion of a 'basis' for mutual expectations of R-compliance. Examples of 'bases' which Lewis mentions are 'salience', 'precedents' and 'agreement' (cf. pp. 83–8). Salience is a special strikingness which one might expect others to notice as well. 'Precedents' are matters of what persons actually did in the past in similar situations and which we might expect all to remember. 'Agreement' is, as in Hume, not a promise or a contract, but something like an indication, perhaps a verbal one, of intentions. Using something like Lewis' notion of a 'basis' for mutual expectation of R-compliance, we might express Hume's further condition thus:

iv. A further part of the special explanation required in (ii) of the R-compliance in (i), beyond just the R-compliers' 'common knowledge' in (iii), involves there being a Lewis 'basis' for the mutual expectation of general R-compliance (rather than compliance with any of the (e)-alternatives to R).

However the conditions (i) through (iv) still leave Hume's account of convention incomplete. While these conditions say a great deal about the complex set of beliefs behind our compliance in the case of a convention, they do not tell us very much about the motivation.[4] What Hume mentions in this regard is 'the common

4 Of course this does not assume the 'provocative Humean theory of motivating

218

sense of interest'. But this expression in unfortunately ambiguous in a rather crucial way. On one hand it could merely mean every individual's self-interest. Now that motivation will be sufficient to explain R-compliance only in some cases, e.g. cases where (a) and (b) hold but (d) does not. Otherwise, where an individual can gain by not complying given that others do, each will consider it prudent not to comply. In short, mere self-interest would seem to be unable to explain compliance in situations something like the 'prisoners' dilemma'. On the other hand, the expression 'the general sense of common interest' (which Hume also uses) suggests another reading. Assuming the expression is not pleonastic, it might suggest something like an interest each individual has in the common good. Hume certainly does allow general benevolence as a motive.

Of course what Hume cannot just say, and leave it at that, is that the motivation for R-compliance is 'the regard for justice', i.e., the motivation to R-comply. Hume agrees, as per (c), that there is no 'natural' motive toward doing just the acts R requires. One is motivated, not because of the features those acts would have even if there were no convention, but precisely because of the significance such an act has, given there is a convention. That there is a convention is an important part of the reason why one complies. But since Hume is here trying to give an account of what convention is, he cannot simply appeal to motivations which presuppose the notion of convention. It does not explain what a convention is (although it is true) to say that in such a case people R-comply because there is a convention.

In summary, conditions (i) through (iv) are not jointly sufficient. They do not constitute a complete account of the sort of convention Hume needs. But they are among the important necessary conditions in Hume's, or a Humean, account. Whether the Humean can complete the task and give an adequate, non-circular account of convention usable in Hume's defence of sentimentalism is the topic of Chapter 10.

THE REGARD TO JUSTICE AS SUCH

Hume treats it as a further question why we come to '*annex the idea of virtue to justice, and of vice to injustice*' (498). What concerns

---

reasons' as discussed in Chapters 4 and 5 above. Any of the 'innocuous' versions of the Humean theory of motivation will do.

Hume is the nature of our moral disapproval of justice, the moral sentiment of approval toward *R*-compliance and the motive to *R*-comply where the fact of general *R*-compliance is to be explained in just the way that makes it a Humean convention. Here the issue seems no longer to be 'What explains our general *R*-compliance in such cases?' but rather 'Why do we also approve of such compliance (and the motive to comply)?' For Hume that is a question about the sentiment involved. He is asking 'From what sentiment do we come to approve of compliance with the rules of justice (i.e., with convention-compliance)?'

The former question ('Why do people comply?') belongs a bit more to the Humean theory of convention. The latter question ('Why do we approve of people so motivated to comply?') belongs a bit more to the Humean elaboration and defence of sentimentalism. In reply to neither question, of course, can he just say 'Out of the regard to justice as such', not because that isn't a correct answer, but because Hume must give an account, must reduce, that regard. However we will leave until Chapter 10 a discussion of whether Hume has a complete account. For the present let us just say that his account (covering the compliance, the motive to comply and the sentiment which approves of them) includes, in one way or another, the following four important elements.

First a certain role is played by:

A. Self-interest (499).

Here the story seems to be much the same as the story about why individuals, at least in small societies, are led to comply with conventions. Each sees a certain advantage for himself to general convention compliance (in comparison with a situation without convention at all). However self-interest is supplemented by the working of:

B. 'Sympathy' (499).

'Sympathy' is perhaps not a feeling itself but is a psychological mechanism which communicates passions almost 'infectiously' from one person to another via the external signs of passion (576; cf. also II,i,2, especially 317, 319). Hume says:

. . . when the injustice is so distant from us, as no way to affect our interest, it still displeases us; because we consider it as prejudicial to human society,

220

and pernicious to everyone that approaches the person guilty of it. We partake of their uneasiness by *sympathy*. (499)

Possibly what Hume thought is that self-interest explains, at least in the first instance, our *compliance* with convention, but sympathy is the mechanism which, mainly, explains our *sentiment* of approval toward compliance (especially in cases not touching our own interests). Hume says:

Thus self-interest is the original motive to the establishment *of justice: but a* sympathy *with public interest is the source of the* moral approbation, *which attends that virtue.* (499–500)

Hume also mentions two further devices that can assist in the creation of the sentiment which approves of justice (500):

C. 'Artifice of politicians', and
D. 'Private education and instruction'.

Hume seems to suggest, at least in regard to the former, that the process involved is one that begins with the 'natural' sentiments we have (e.g. feelings of disgust) and then somehow transfers or redirects these sentiments toward new objects (e.g. injustice). Here the use of words such as 'dishonourable', 'blameworthy', etc., in new contexts may be crucial. 'Politicians' use the terms which originally get their meaning from the expression of *natural* approval or disgust and associate them with convention compliance and non-compliance. Hume is suggesting that if we didn't already have the sentiments we express in praising the natural virtues and vices, politicians could not be able to bring about the approval of justice and the disapproval of injustice. Unless one already felt a natural disgust at, say, cruelty or the neglect of children, processes (C) and (D) could never redirect it toward, say, theft or breaking promises.[5]

What we may still wonder about Hume's account is whether it is at all points a reductive account. If it is merely a genetic account it might well fail to rise to the reductive task. One wonders, for example, whether the mechanisms in (B), (C) and (D) don't merely causally *produce* some new, *sui generis* sentiment, 'the regard to justice', rather than provide any account of what the sentiment so

5 The reader might be tempted to view the sentiments produced by methods (C) and (D) as 'irrational'. Of course Hume cannot put it quite that way for his official view is that no passion is 'contrary to reason' unless involving a false belief. Cf. Harrison (1981, p. 48).

produced is. Just as, say, altruistic motives can sometimes be created by a certain schedule of reward and punishment, without that present motive necessarily being reducible to the motives in the story of its production, so the sense of justice might well be inducible by exploiting psychological mechanisms which are no part of what that sentiment, when produced, is. What is required for the defence of sentimentalism is not merely a story about how the 'hard case' sentiments can be induced, but a reductive account of what such sentiments, once induced, *are*. To succeed in this respect Hume must be saying that 'the regard to justice as such' *still is* some complex psychological state which can be reduced employing such notions as 'self-interest', 'convention', 'sympathy', etc. These notions would come into the account of what this sentiment is, not merely in the story of how it might be brought about.

THE WORK OF THE IMAGINATION

There is a fifth feature in Hume's total account which Hume does not mention immediately (III,ii,2), but which soon (III,ii,3) becomes important. This involves the work of the 'imagination'. In the discussion of property it becomes clear that the particular conventions which Hume thinks 'determine property' have an important degree of arbitrariness (my word) to them.[6] As condition (e) above allows, there will usually be a number of distinct alternative schemes, $R1$, $R2$, $R3$, etc., all of which would count as 'remedies' to the conflicts which arise from easy change of jointly desired scarce objects. What explains, not that we have conventions at all, but that we have certain conventions (e.g. on Hume's view: 'occupation', 'prescription', 'accession', 'succession') rather than others? Here, self-interest, public interest, sympathy, etc., do not actually determine this particular set of rules rather than alternatives. Hume says:

6 The phrase 'rules which determine property' is somewhat ambiguous. It could mean, as Hume's actual example seem to suggest, rules which determine who gets what as property. Again, it could mean rules constitutive of the notion of property. The latter is what is assumed in the discussion in Chapter 9 below. However I have the former interpretation as much as the latter in mind in the present discussion.

Thus, in the present case, there are, no doubt, motives of public interest for most of the rules, which determine property; but still I suspect, that these rules are principally fix'd by the imagination, or the more frivolous properties of our thought and conception. (504, n. 1; cf. 515, *Enquiry,* 197–9, 309, n. 1)

Where it is only a matter of the work of the 'imagination', there is no further 'rationale' behind our preference for scheme *R1* over the alternatives: *R2, R3,* etc. Nothing in the Humean theory of justifying reasons, no appeal to the public interest, no appeal to the other moral sentiments (we have) could be a reason for preferring that convention over the others. Instead we are just naturally drawn to certain conventions rather than others because they stand out, are more striking, stimulate the imagination. They have a certain 'salience' as Lewis might say. There are no grounds (good or bad) which we have for our opting for these particular alternative conventions. There are only leaps of the imagination. No doubt it is useful and in the public interest that there are these leaps. Otherwise there might be no easy way out of the (e)-type conflicts which arise from the circumstances of human nature. There is a certain irreducible element of the arbitrary in our notion of justice. Sheer fancy helps us to alight on some particular scheme among the many importantly different alternatives, without that choice being any the less arbitrary. Here 'arbitrary' is my word. Hume, admittedly, says at one point that the rules of justice 'are not *arbitrary*' (484). I take it he does not mean that they are without any element of the arbitrary but only that they are rather less arbitrary than a sentimentalist might first suppose. Our practice of justice is not without an explanation, indeed a certain rationale, in terms of human nature. It is certainly no accident that general compliance with such rules is a (b)-type benefit to all. Nor, for that matter, is it just an accident that, of the various rules in an (e)-type conflict, some are more striking to us than others. The imagination is a part of human nature. Thus the rules it selects will never seem as arbitrary to us as, say, the results of a throw of the dice. Even so, the selection process involving the work of the imagination is arbitrary in the sense that, while the consequences are important for those whose interests are at stake in an (e)-type conflict, the selection depends on something other than the game-theoretic features of the conflict. Hume admits it is only something 'frivolous' (even if natural) in

223

our thought which fixes upon some particular rule and excludes its (e)-type alternative rules.

HUME'S VIRTUE-CONSERVATISM

The theoretically interesting conservatism of Hume's theory of justice is best seen by contrasting it with views which share elements of Hume's view but not that conservatism. Hence it is particulary useful to contrast Hume's total theory of justice with contemporary Hume-based liberal-egalitarian theories such as John Rawls' (1971). Rawls begins with a Humean account of the 'circumstances of human nature'. Furthermore, both Hume and Rawls see justice in terms of rules required to resolve the conflicts inherent in these circumstances. However there are two fundamental differences between Hume's theory of justice and Rawls-like theories. One difference accounts for the 'liberalism' we find in Rawls but not in Hume. The other difference accounts for the tendency to 'egalitarianism' in Rawls certainly not to be found in Hume. (This is discussed in the following section.) These two differences put Hume-based liberal-egalitarian theories in strong contrast to Hume's implicit conservatism.

The former difference separates Hume's theory from many contemporary Hume-based versions of liberalism. Liberals actually tend to find rather more sources of conflict in the circumstances of human nature than Hume does. They are rather less optimistic than Hume in that regard. And as a consequence, justice is supposed by them to have a much wider sphere than Hume supposed. As Lukes says:

More deeply (and this is what Rawls's account implicitly adds to Hume's and Kant's) it is the conflict of interests, resulting from different individuals' (and groups') different and conflicting conceptions of the good, that define those interests, which renders such adjudication, and the protections rights afford, necessary. (Lukes, 1985, p. 32)

Hence a contemporary version of liberalism adds to the six conditions of the circumstances of human nature yet another:

7) Conflicts of interests resulting from different individuals' (and groups') different and conflicting 'conceptions of the good' which define those interests.

'Conceptions of the good' is meant to cover various social ideals, aesthetic and environmental values, and, rather importantly, modes of assessing personal worth and merit. In this latter regard conflicts arise because one cannot, beyond a certain limit, be indifferent to the sorts of things others count as 'virtues', i.e., as admirable. We wish our own merits, as we see merit, to be counted as merits by others. Nor could anyone wish to live in a society where what one considered excellence was ridiculed or dismissed with indifference. A businessman, for example, very probably not only desires economic goods and forms of command and power, but also wishes to be seen as a success. Such a person would find, not only his basic values, but his basic interests under siege in a society, such as Homeric Greece, where mere merchants were not highly regarded. Again, for other reasons one's interests depend on the social environment. To be surrounded by persons and behaviour one considers crass and base is as blighting to one's life as a visual landscape of billboards and gutted buildings. To counsel unlimited toleration in such circumstances is not to do away with the source of conflict but simply to cater only to the interests of one party to the conflict, the one most thick-skinned and most willing to be offensive. That gives the victory to the billboard advertisers and the flat-dwellers practicing the trumpet at 3 a.m.

There are perhaps several ways to deny the necessity of conflict in regard to social ideals and conceptions of merit and virtue. Some Hellenistic philosophers advocated an attitude of *ataraxia*, of complete indifference toward the prevailing social ideals and assessments. While a certain modicum of indifference may be possible, and perhaps desirable, it does not seem to me that total indifference on the part of everyone is psychologically possible. At the very least it would require a large amount of self-deception. The Hellenistic attitude smells of sour grapes.

Hume denies any need for important conflict in precisely the opposite way. He allows that we do, indeed cannot help but, care. However he thinks we all more or less care in the same basic ways (547, n. 1). This is precisely what is behind his discussion of the 'natural virtues'. Hume thinks we basically react similarly and tend to admire and despise much the same character traits just as a matter of our human nature (even where we disagree about who has them). Indeed it is Hume's account of, and emphasis on, the natural virtues which is the source of one part of Hume's conservatism, i.e., the 'anti-liberal' element, we might put it. Hume thinks that we are in basic conflict in regard to economic goods (scarce, transferable, jointly desired objects) and so need justice. But in regard to the rest of our judgments of merit and demerit we more or less have the same sentiments, praising the same sorts of character traits. Hence no conflicts of interest arise precisely from persons' having *basically* different social ideals, conceptions of virtue and merit, etc. At any rate Hume would consider such conflicts potentially resolvable by reference to our sentiments which approve of 'natural' virtues.

The contemporary Hume-based liberal, by contrast, accepts Hume's account of justice as a 'remedy' to the basic conflicts of the circumstances of human nature but adds a great deal more to the conflict. The liberal transfers a great many of the issues which Hume wanted to discuss under the 'natural virtues' over to the realm of justice. The liberal is not nearly as optimistic as Hume. (And he is perhaps less ethnocentric.) Even if there should be some conceptions of merit we cannot help but share to some extent, there will be a number of differences about such ideals and conceptions of the good over which nothing more can be said than that we differ. But given that our interests do conflict due to our conflicting conceptions of the good, these conflicts only set further problems for justice to handle. At this point the contemporary liberal gives the notion of 'toleration' a new interpretation. Toleration is not defended in the traditional liberal way (Mill, 1859) as a way to celebrate and perpetuate a diversity of 'experiments in living' (i.e., lives centred around different conceptions of the good) perhaps as a means to 'social progress'. Instead the contemporary liberal largely sees problems of toleration in terms of justice. Yet another problem for justice arises from the basic conflicts of interest arising precisely from different individuals' and groups' holding different conceptions of virtue where there are no other rational or moral grounds (certainly no commonly held moral sentiments) for eliminating any of the conflicting conceptions.

In this regard the contemporary Hume-based liberal is opposed, first, to the cognitivist who thinks all the really contentious questions about ideals, values, assessments, admirable traits, virtues, etc., are objectively determinable. This cognitivist thinks that in some cases where there is such a conflict, at most one view will be correct. The other views are just false. But, second, the contemporary Hume-based liberal is also opposed to a Humean sentimentalism which goes on to argue that we in fact more or less agree in our sentiments regarding admirable character traits, etc., so that, even if there is no such thing as truth in such matters, there is also not sufficient disagreement to make for any real conflicts of interest in that regard.

Oddly, it is the contemporary liberal who is more sceptical about our virtue and merit judgments than Hume is. In fact, we might say it is typical of this liberal, in contrast to the Humean conservative, to feel much more intellectually secure about issues in the area of justice than issues in the area of the natural virtues. Usually sooner rather than later this liberal stops arguing for a certain table of virtues or ideals. At this point he recognises there are just competing tables. Nothing more can be said, except of course in terms of justice. It is thereafter a matter for justice to adjudicate between the conflicts of interest that arise between persons holding conflicting conceptions of the good. The most radical sort of liberal thinks that nothing at all can be said in regard to these conflicting conceptions. This view takes no stand at all on the natural virtues, but makes conflicts in that regard just another concern of justice. It does not take the virtues seriously although it takes seriously the conflicting interests depending on various conceptions of virtue. However, a more moderate liberal (e.g. Rawls) would perhaps think something can be said on the topic of which character traits, etc., are morally admirable, leaving however certain irresolvable basic conflicts which, because they involve important conflicts of interest, must be handled under the topic of justice. What makes all such views 'liberal' for purposes of this discussion is that they all recognise the interest the individual has in the furtherance of his conception of the good; fairness or justice in regard to the conflicts arising from different conceptions then becomes, at some point or other, a matter of social arrangements which allow various conceptions of what are admirable characteristics to co-exist and flourish up to a point. Some (not necessarily unlimited) toleration becomes a demand of justice. This view is like Mill's liberalism in its willingness to tolerate a range of lifestyles and conceptions of admirable characters. But if the conclusion might be similar, the argument is quite different. For the contemporary liberal the argument is put in terms of justice.

We, in fact, have a spectrum of views here (figure 7) rather than

227

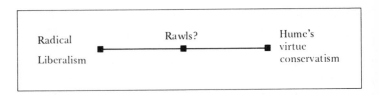

Figure 7. The liberalism spectrum of Hume-based views

any quantum jump. The views on the extreme right of this spectrum (e.g. Hume's) take our judgments of ideals and admirable characters to be treatable independently of our notions of justice. They either suppose that certain such judgments are just true (if they are cognitivists) or else that we pretty much agree in the basic sentiments which approve of such things (if they are sentimentalists like Hume). The views on the extreme left ('radical liberals'), by contrast, hold that our judgments of ideals and admirable characters are so subjective or so lacking in basic agreement and also so responsible for conflicts of interest that these conflicts can, at best, be treated only as further problems of conflict for our judgments of justice to handle. We cannot really say who is right or wrong on questions of virtues and ideals, nor do our basic moral sentiments give us a basis for agreement, so that, at best, it is for our sentiments of justice to approve of our giving room to each to pursue his ideals and conception of the good (without impeding too much on an equal pursuit by others). More moderate liberal views are to be found between these two extremes. These views think that some restrictions can be put on acceptable conceptions of the good, but not enough to determine just one conception. Enough competing conceptions remain so that the conflicts of interest arising from those holding such competing conceptions must, as before, be treated as another problem for justice. I would think Rawls' position would go someplace here, perhaps even slightly more to the right.

Any theory, like Hume's, which emphasises the virtues (either supposing there are grounds for rational agreement or that we naturally just do agree) will tend to put little emphasis on the liberalism of lifestyles. The relationship is inverse. The more room there is for the former, the less for the latter. Thus one way in which Hume's account of the moral virtues has an inherent conservative tendency is that it gives all disputes over conceptions of the good over to the theory of the natural virtues. It appeals to

228

supposedly commonly held basic sentiments. Nothing is left over for justice to adjudicate in that regard. Hume's justice is narrowly confined to conflicts of a more basic sort, e.g. over economic goods. It is in fact ironic that here the source of an important element of Hume's conservatism (i.e., his anti-'liberalism') rests on a distinct lack of scepticism on his part. He thinks we just do more or less agree in most of our basic sentiments when it comes to those sentiments we express when approving and disapproving of motives and qualities of character (in judgments of 'natural' virtue). Here the 'liberal' is more the sceptic.

HUME'S IMAGINATION-CONSERVATISM

I am, however, somewhat more concerned with another respect in which Hume's theory of justice is conservative, a way that does not at all depend on the claim that we happen to share basic sentiments when it comes to praising and blaming persons' characters. Here 'conservative' is not to be contrasted with 'liberal'. Rather the contrast is with views, like Rawls', which have rather more to say than Hume does about impartiality, fairness or even equality. Indeed what many have noticed to be striking about Hume's account of justice is its almost complete disregard of concepts many take to be the hallmark of justice, notions like 'equity' or 'impartiality' or some kind of 'equality' (cf. Harrison, 1981, pp. 28–9). This means that Hume's theory lacks at least two features which we find in Rawls' theory.

Notions like 'impartiality', 'fairness', 'equality', etc., are thought to find particularly important application where conflict of interests are of the following '(e)-type' form: Suppose a number of different alternative schemes of social choice, $R1, R2, \ldots$, are such that in 'the circumstances of human nature' conditions (a) through (c) hold (as discussed above). Notably, we would all be better off having any one of these schemes as a convention than having no convention at all. But while each R would leave us better off than having no R, the R's differ importantly in that, as per (e), for any given Ri, belonging to the above set of R's, there will be some Rj, also belonging to that set, such that, while some would be better off under Ri rather than Rj, other individuals would be better off under Rj than Ri. Particularly in cases of conflict of this sort people are inclined to ask whether certain R's might not be 'fairer', 'more impartial', 'more equitable', etc., than others. The moral and political philsophers who talk of 'impartiality' and 'fairness' tend to hold one, or both, of the following related theses (in regard to (e)-type conflicts as just described):

1. The Impartiality Thesis: Some standard of 'impartiality' or 'fairness' or 'equality' can be employed to narrow down the set of alternative R's (as described above), i.e., sometimes members of the set of such R's can be dismissed as not sufficiently 'fair' or 'impartial' between the conflicting interests of individuals in an (e)-type conflict.
2. The Non-arbitrariness Thesis: From a set of R's in an (e)-type conflict, the social choice of Ri rather than Rj cannot, without further justification, just be left to rest on something quite 'arbitrary'. That is, every (e)-type conflict gives rise to a question of justice demanding a justification in non-arbitrary terms.

Rawls, it would seem, subscribes to both. His 'veil of ignorance' approach, designed to give a procedure for selecting principles (and eventually social structures and rules, etc.), is in effect a theory of impartiality or fairness. The selected results of the 'veil of ignorance' method have, on his view, a high claim to impartiality (fairness). Fairness is central to Rawls' notion of justice. Furthermore the second thesis is in Rawls as well. Rawls is troubled that either 'social contingencies' (e.g. wealth and status of parents) or 'natural chance' (e.g. natural talents) should have an 'influence' on 'the determination of distributive shares'. He insists that 'from a moral standpoint the two seem equally arbitrary' (1971, pp. 74–5). The arbitrariness is what troubles. For example, Rawls could not, without further justification, accept Hume's rule of 'succession' (510–13), i.e., inheritance, for accidents of birth are in themselves, Rawls thinks, morally arbitrary. But Hume, while he does mention some social advantages to this rule, suggests that in the end our acceptance of it rests on something as fortuitous as mere 'association of ideas'. That does not trouble Hume in the way it does Rawls. Naturally, if one is, like Rawls, troubled by such arbitrarinesses, one must be then prepared to give an account of what would be non-arbitrary in such circumstances. At precisely this point the impartiality thesis comes into is own. The impartiality thesis offers some standard of 'fairness' as a (probably *the*) non-arbitrary ground for selecting certain rules over others. The non-arbitrariness and the impartiality theses are complementary. The non-arbitrariness thesis asserts that every (e)-type conflict gives rise to a real question of justice not to

230

be decided, without justification, on morally arbitrary grounds. The impartiality thesis offers some benchmark of fairness or impartiality as ultimately the sole non-arbitrary ground for selection in such conflicts.

With Hume it is different. Where alternative schemes of social choice present us with an (e)-type conflict, Hume has no non-arbitrary way of narrowing down the class of contenders any further. All the contenders already satisfy condition (b), so that the public interest or social utility does not help us narrow down the contenders. What Hume quite firmly does not do is appeal to some notion that certain of the R's are fairer or more impartial than others. He is not even prepared to give a sentimentalistic account of those who, like Rawls, do try to employ such a notion in regard to (e)-type conflicts. Indeed, not only does Hume not appeal to 'fairness' or 'equality' or any such thing, he in fact holds there is no non-arbitrary criterion whatsoever applicable to such conflicts. All that he offers is something blatantly arbitrary, i.e., mere 'association of ideas' or the work of the 'imagination'. Hume allows, for example, that the 'rules which determine property' are in the end more or less alighted upon by the 'imagination', i.e., by leaps of fancy, the drawing of analogies, the attraction of certain 'saliencies' (as Lewis might say), or just 'association of ideas'.

On Hume's view it is socially useful and beneficial to all that we share much the same leaps of imagination and fancy and thus tend to agree (e.g. about deceased estates and ownership of land deposited on riverbanks). If we did not, for admittedly arbitrary reasons, naturally tend to agree, workable conventions in regard to property would be much harder to achieve. However a particular scheme of social choice, R, does not in the first place attract us for being any more socially useful than any of the (e)-alternatives. In the first instance what attracts us to that R over the others is just a flight of fancy. But that is not without important practical consequence for individuals. Sons of rich men do rather better under the R which (Hume says) does strike our imagination, while others would do better under various alternative R's. While all may be better off by having some rule rather than none, a certain group does rather better under the rule that happens to strike the fancy. Other moral and political philosophers have thought there might still be questions of 'equity' or 'fairness' or 'justice' arising in (e)-type conflicts. But Hume gives us only 'the work of the imagination'.

It is in this special role of the 'imagination' in regard, specifically, to the rules of justice that I locate that source of conservatism least excisable from his distinctive theory of justice. It is this which, above all, distinguishes him sharply from other Hume-based theories, such as Rawls'. What makes Hume conservative at a theoretically deep level is not the particular rules which he discusses as the rules of justice. Admittedly, he does discuss rules of property, contract and law which are typical of bourgeois society. But that, I have argued, is not a deep feature in Hume's theory. Nor again, does this deepest source of conservatism consist in Hume's tendency to suppose that the sentiments behind the moral judgments we make involve a lot that is innate rather than acquired, that by our natures we cannot help but subscribe to certain moral judgments. In this latter regard, we should consider the claim made by David Miller:

Hume argued that important classes of judgments – including judgments about causation and the external world – could be grounded neither in reason nor in sense-experience, but derived rather from the natural workings of the imagination. These judgments could therefore be 'justified' only in the weak sense of showing that human beings could not help but make them, and equally the possibilities for correcting and improving judgment were confined within the bounds set by the imagination. (D. Miller, 1981, p. 187)

But there are several distinct strands here that need to be distinguished. First of all, we find in Hume the claim that the sentiments we express in judgments of virtue and vice are sentiments we cannot help but share if we are human. This claim is made particularly in regard to our judgments of 'natural' virtues and vice. Second, we also find in Hume some talk of 'correcting' our sentiments for spatio-temporal distance from the object of the sentiment (581–5; D. Miller, 1981, pp. 51–5). In that regard Miller finds in Hume a special role for the 'imagination'. But third, as I have just argued, Hume gives a further, quite different, role to the 'imagination' in his special account of our judgments of the artifical virtue justice (as Miller also notes, 1981, p. 188). Given (e)-type alternative conventions, the imagination, rather than some notion of fairness or impartiality, is all Hume offers to favour one rule over the others. The first strand in Hume claims that to some degree we share moral sentiments which we cannot help but have. It adds to sentimentalism the empirical claim that many such sentiments are humanly

232

unavoidable. The second strand concerns the 'correcting' Hume thinks is involved in any kind of moral judgment. But the third strand concerns that very special role Hume gives to the imagination in his theory of justice. Some rules strike the imagination more than others. After a certain point, that is all there is to say.

In certain respects the first two strands need not be particularly conservative in implication. One might attack status quo social and political organisations precisely on the ground that they inhibit individual virtue and create individual vice as judged by those very sentiments we cannot help but share (perhaps after 'correction'). There is still a wide scope here for a Rousseauean critique of society. Indeed there would actually be somewhat less room for a Rousseauean criticism of the status quo if our sentiments (contrary to Hume) merely reflected status quo social arrangements rather than something in human nature (as Hume supposes). Admittedly, this strand is conservative in a way already noted, i.e., it is anti-'liberal'. It tends to commit us all to the same list of basic individual virtues rather than just leave competing conceptions of the admirable as a further problem for justice. Indeed what is important for Hume's anti-liberalism is that we *do* agree (or would upon 'correction'), not particularly *why* we agree. It would not matter greatly if the agreement were as much due to social forces as anything innate. But in any case, the 'we-cannot-help-but-share-them' claim is fairly implausible as an empirical claim. Such anti-liberal conservatism will get excised by a contemporary Hume-based theory of justice that rejects this claim on empirical grounds.

But the role Hume gives to the work of the imagination *within his theory of justice* has a conservative force in quite a different way. Also it does not rest on any implausible empirical claims. Instead, it involves a kind of scepticism beyond the usual kinds of scepticism attributed to Hume. We might best see how Hume's view is conservative by considering a rather common type of philosophical argument given by social critics and reformers of the status quo. A particularly radical sort of criticism rests on an argument of this form: The present institutions work out in such a way that some people are worse off than if there were certain different institutions or conventions. Unless this can be justified, those who are 'worse off' under the present set of conventions are being 'disadvantaged', 'deprived', 'exploited', 'robbed', 'harmed' or some such thing. Those who do better under the status quo than under the conceivable alternative are the candidates for the membership in the class of 'deprivers' or 'exploiters'. The ground for saying such things seems to just be the assumption that such matters (i.e., the resolution of an (e)-type conflict where significantly different conventions are available) cannot be left to something as arbitrary as what our present conventions happen to be. That is the radical criticism. Such objections, it should be noted, have a tendency to degenerate into absurdity. Surely under almost any social arrangement someone or other could claim to be 'deprived' relative to some more favourable – to them – alternative. That is the nature of (e)-type conflicts. The way to avoid this absurdity is to make the comparison, not with just any tendentious alternative, but specifically with institutions or conventions claimed to be more equitable or fairer. Some non-arbitrary benchmark is required. Typically it is equality that is assumed as the benchmark for comparison.

The Humean reply to the reformer's objection contains an element of scepticism beyond anything in Hume's general sentimentalist account of our moral judgments. Hume's reply, we may imagine, is that justice *is* arbitrary after a certain point. The social reformer is raising questions of justice where talk of justice no longer has any clear sense *unless* it is appealing to the saliences that strike our imaginations. Beyond a certain point, it is no longer a question of the shared public interest. The alternatives present a kind of zero-sum game. There is an (e)-type conflict between the various possible schemes of behaviour. All that we can expect is some 'salience' in a particular rule to attract our imagination. The rule the 'imagination' thus picks out is not *in itself* more impartial or more rational than the alternatives. But because it stands out, we are more likely to agree and coordinate our choices. That is, until some social reformer opens a can of worms by actually *objecting* that the status quo rules which strike the imagination are *arbitrary*. If this ploy succeeds it only undermines the work of the imagination, leaving us (in the Humean view) with an irresolvable (e)-type conflict of alternative rules. Nor is it as if any proposed brave new society would operate any less arbitrarily. And we can be certain it will be in ways that distinctly fail to engage the human imagination.

The source of the deep conservatism (or, better, anti-rationalism)

I find in Hume does not rest essentially on the further claim he makes that the imagination involves innate, rather than socially acquired, ways of reacting to possible social schemes. The source I find lies in Hume's willingness to countenance the arbitrary in regard to (e)-type conflicts and, *a fortiori,* in his rejection of any notion of 'fairness' or 'impartiality' (where this is supposed to be something more than just what strikes the imagination). Hume's conservatism here does not rest on his *general* 'scepticism' about the role of 'reason' in all our moral judgments. It is a rather *special* kind of scepticism in regard to justice. His general scepticism consists in his view that moral judgments are not cognitive but involve, instead, the having of sentiments. This well-known Humean scepticism about morality does not, as the neutrality theses rightly insists, have much in the way of conservative import. The sentiments we have could turn out to be ones with quite radical implications rather than conservative ones. That waits on further empirical investigation. Conservatism is not intrinsic to sentimentalism itself. However, and second, Hume also has a *special* scepticism specifically in regard to justice. This consists in the view that, after a certain point, the conflicts of interest which arise are not ones that any intellectually reputable notion of 'fairness' or 'impartiality' can help resolve. Hume just leaves it to the imagination at that point. This has significant conservative force to the extent that it fends off the *criticism* that the status quo is arbitrary or that, in comparison to some conceivable (e)-type alternative, it favours the interests of certain persons or groups. The conservative response is that, at this point, it's all arbitrary. The status quo, at least, is workable, until critical philosophers try to undermine 'prejudice', 'social assumptions', 'false consciousness' and all the other work of the imagination. In short, Hume's special scepticism in regard to justice goes significantly further than his sentimentalist scepticism about morality in general. Not only is justice not derived from reason, justice also lets important conflicts of interest get resolved by nothing more than the work of the imagination.

Hume's view must raise some fundamental questions about the way many contemporary philosophers confront practical moral issues.[7] They operate on the assumption that the arbitrary is objec-

7 For a number of further references cf. Snare (1986). Striking examples are in

tionable. Here are some examples: In discussions of the issue of abortion moral philosophers typically argue that to pick some particular episode (however striking) in the development of the foetus is, without further justification, just morally arbitrary. Again, some animal liberationists and radical environmentalists claim it is morally arbitrary to draw a line between humans and non-human animals and plants. (That is 'human chauvinism'.) Indeed, they often seem to argue that *any* line drawn anywhere on this spectrum would be morally arbitrary. ('Is it not arbitrary then, to deny viruses rights, or at least moral worth? And what about rocks?') In quite another context some philosophers argue it is arbitrary to treat omissions, in general, differently from actions. ('Other things being equal, shouldn't killing Smith to save Jones be morally equivalent to letting Smith live at the cost of letting Jones die?') Again in political philosophy, philosophers like Rawls assume that if anyone is worse off under the status quo than he would be under some realisable social alternative, that raises a question of justification. Such things cannot just be left to accidents of birth or of social structure. That would be arbitrary. However rather than accept any of the above, we might regard such critiques as *reductiones ad absurdum* of the rationalising assumption that what is arbitrary (from the point of view of the universe, however striking to us) requires moral philosophy to give it some further rationale. In that regard Hume's special scepticism goes somewhat beyond Aristotle's famous deflation of the pretensions of moral philosophy. In moral matters, not only must we not expect more in the way of precision than is appropriate to the subject matter, we must also not, after a certain point, expect too much in the way of rationale. Might it not be a serious mistake to hand practical moral issues over to philosophers trained to look for a rationale in everything but, for that very reason, lacking in 'imagination'?

This gives us a second ('impartiality') spectrum, in addition to our former ('liberalism') spectrum, of Hume-based moral and political views. More to the left on this second spectrum are those views, like Rawls', which are concerned to give a major role to notions like 'fairness' or 'impartiality' in (e)-type conflicts. Intermediate on the spectrum are views which hold that some of the

Harris (1974) and (1975). Also see Sandel (1982, ch. 2) on the 'argument from arbitrariness'.

Figure 8. The impartiality spectrum of Hume-based views

(e)-type alternatives are fairer or more impartial than others, but that after a certain point such conflicts can only be left to what is arbitrary. On the far right is Hume's view which gives the resolution of all (e)-type conflicts over to the work of the, admittedly frivolous, imagination. No role in the resolution of (e)-type conflicts is played by some *further* notion of 'fairness'. In (e)-type conflicts only the imagination gives any content to whatever intuitive notion of 'fairness' we have. While all the views on this spectrum share the basic Humean description of the circumstances of human nature, they differ in what role they find for some further notion of 'impartiality' (figure 8).

On the former ('liberalism') spectrum (cf. figure 7) a slight advantage lies with the views on the left. The burden of proof lies with the views on the right, e.g. Hume's, to show empirically that there is sufficient agreement about the natural virtues so that conflicting conceptions of merit are not to be treated as just a further problem for justice. Here the views on the left hold the more 'sceptical' attitude. On the present ('impartiality') spectrum (cf. figure 8) the views on the right are the more 'sceptical' and the burden of proof rests, initially, with views on the left. The latter must actually produce some intellectually respectable, non-arbitrary notion of 'impartiality' (or whatever) to round out their claim. The Humean conservative, by contrast, gives no positive argument but simply waits for philosophical accounts of 'impartiality' and 'fairness' to be given. Of course once a philosopher, e.g. Rawls in his 'veil of ignorance' exposition, does give such a philosophically respectable account, then the burden of proof shifts and the Humean conservative must show how the attempted account fails in some important way. But clearly the Humean conservative has the easier task here. Positive accounts are usually more difficult than the criticisms of them. The advantage to the conservative lies in the nagging suspicion that an important part of our conception of justice involves the work of the 'imagination', that the philosophers who suppose there is more to it than this are taking the language of 'justice' on a holiday.

OPTIMISM AND PESSIMISM

If the role Hume gives to the 'imagination' and also his theory of the 'natural virtues' provide theoretically deep sources for conservatism, his account of the 'circumstances of human nature' provides another source, if not specifically for conservatism, at least for a moderation that is anti-radical. All the Hume-based views on the two spectra discussed above share this Humean basis. But what would it be like not to have a Hume-based view at all? What rests on the acceptance of the Humean account of the circumstances of human nature? I will consider one example of a view that rejects this starting point. In some recent literature (Lukes, 1985; R. Miller, 1984) marxism is presented as a view that rejects what is common to both the conservatism of Hume and the liberal egalitarianism of Rawls, i.e., the Humean account of the circumstances of human nature.

Sometimes marxists present the nature of their basic dispute with bourgeois philosophers such as Hume or Rawls in quite superficial terms. For example, marxists might dismiss Hume or Rawls as historically limited apologists for bourgeois society specifically because, in the case of Hume, he uses as his examples of the rules of justice, rules of property, contract (promising) and the bourgeois state. I have already argued that these features are not deep features in Hume's theory. Nor, in fact, are the analogous features in Rawls deep features of that theory. Again, marxists sometimes dismiss all moral philosophy as mere ideological superstructure dependent on the material base. Bourgeois moral philosophy is said to involve a kind of illusion or mystification hiding the true nature of economic and social relations in bourgeois society. But we have actually seen in the course of this book the argument Hume gives and the conservative tendency it has. Until that argument itself is actually countered, the above marxist objections look like no more than instances of the genetic fallacy or begging the question. If there is some 'illusion' we might beg to ask just where in Hume's argument the mistake is made. Hume's argument must be confronted, if

238

cannot just be patronisingly patted on the head in a 'sociology of knowledge' sort of way.

Sometimes it might seem marxists are doing something quite different. They might be offering alternative, non-bourgeois principles of justice. It might be a contribution principle: to each according to his average labour-time engaged in socially useful production. Or, more plausibly, it might be a needs principle: from each according to his ability, to each according to his needs. Of course such moral claims are not inconsistent with the basic account of justice we find in Hume (or Rawls). Indeed these only seem to be further alternative conventions in regard to the distribution of goods over which there is conflict. In any case such moral proposals in the absence of any deeper theoretical underpinning hardly begin to confront the issues in deeper level theories such as we find in Hume or Rawls.

But another account of the nature of the disagreement is more interesting. Lukes (1985, ch. 3) attributes to marxism a rejection of the whole Hume-Rawls model, what Lukes call the 'morality of *recht*' or the Humean account of the circumstances of human nature. On this view Marx, in a certain respect, rejects the account of the 'circumstances of human nature' which all Hume-based views claim gives rise to the need for notions of justice. The rejection arises because marxism is, in a certain respect, more optimistic than the Hume-Rawls model, but also, in another respect, less optimistic. It is *more optimistic* in regard to human possibilities. It holds that scarcity, limited altruism, etc., while true of capitalism and all past societies, is not inevitable. This more optimistic view holds that, in a *future form of society* at least, what Lukes calls 'co-operative abundance' is realisable. However this marxist view is at the same time *more pessimistic* in another regard. It is very much less optimistic about justice as a solution to conflict within *capitalist society*. Marxism holds that the conflict is much deeper than Hume and Rawls paint it. The conflicts are in fact irreconcilable class conflicts. Class interests conflict in such a way that *any* set of rules amounts to favouring one class at the expense of another. There is just a zero-sum conflict between two classes in capitalist society. It is not just that the particular prevailing rules of justice serve the interests of the ruling class. Rather, it is that any talk of justice at all rests on the illusion that there is some neutral, some impartial point of view or some notion of fairness or objectivity from which it is possible

239

in principle to bring conflicting needs and interests or conflicts of values into some fair trade-off (cf. R. Miller, 1984, p. 10, ch. 1, ch. 2). But where the conflict is as deep between classes as this, all talk of 'impartiality' or 'justice' can be nothing more than a bourgeois illusion.

In regard to the marxist optimism about a future state of 'co-operative aboundance', all Hume-based views (e.g. Rawls and Hume) will make the same reply. Both Hume and Rawls will, rightly I think, dismiss this optimism as a wildly utopian element in Marx (despite his disclaimers). The strength of the Hume-Rawls account of the human circumstances is that it fits with all the societies we know about or have any reason to project. Once Hume's own historically limited account is expanded into the contemporary Humean account of the human situation, it can no longer be dismissed as narrowly bourgeois or historically limited in some way.

In regard to the marxist pessimism about present bourgeois society, Rawls and Hume must have quite different responses. A view like Rawls' which puts much weight on notions like 'fairness' or 'impartiality' must insist that the marxist cannot just dismiss the possibility of the applicability of some such notion to the conflicts of the present society without examining the arguments put forward by Rawls. Marxists have no *a priori* grounds for dismissing Rawls' conclusion out of hand. It is not enough just to assert the conflicts are so deep that talk of 'impartiality' is of necessity illusory. Here the marxist must actually say what is wrong with Rawls argument, why it does not capture the kind of impartiality which this kind of marxist concedes justice talk rests on. By contrast Hume's (conservative) reply to the marxist pessimism will be quite different. Hume can agree well enough with the Marxist that there is no objective, i.e., non-arbitrary, method of resolving (e)-type conflicts. No set of rules is more 'impartial' (in a sense not projecting the imagination) than any other. At best, some rules are more 'salient', more striking to the 'imagination' than others. It is indeed just a zero-sum game. Here Hume agrees with the marxist and disagrees with Rawls. He shares with the marxist a certain scepticism about all this 'fairness' talk.

But Humean scepticism would seem to go even further than the marxist's. If the marxist has no moral benchmark, no set of rules of distribution claimed (at least in a certain social context) to be either more impartial or, even more salient than others, then he

240

also starts to lose his grip on any *absolute* sense to the claims that one class 'exploits', 'oppresses', or 'dominates' another. Of course such claims can make sense where the comparison is with some set of rules of distribution assumed to provide a moral benchmark. But without any such moral benchmark all that can be said is that there is a zero-sum conflict. My class might do worse (and yours better) under the status quo distribution $D0$ in comparison to some alternative distribution $D1$. But then your class might do worse (and mine better) under $D0$ than under yet some other alternative $D2$. If I can say I am exploited, dominated or oppressed under $D0$ *relative to* $D1$, you can complain about $D0$ in the same terms *relative to* $D2$. If the former was enough to say you oppress us, the latter must be enough to say we oppress you (but relative to different alternatives of course). If all notions of a moral benchmark are illusory, then notions like 'exploitation', 'oppression', 'domination' are either just as illusory or else amount to ways of speaking of a class interest in a zero-sum conflict. The use of such terms by one class, e.g. the proletariat, cannot be any less illusory or class-biased than the ideologically laden complaints of other classes. There can be nothing more behind such complaints than narrow class interest. In contrast, the Humean conservative does not deny that our sentiments would ordinarily agree, at least in paradigm cases, that certain persons or classes are exploited, dominated, etc. But the Humean thinks such judgments must involve a comparison to some benchmark distribution of economic goods and power which the *imagination* finds striking. Remove the work of the imagination in this regard, and words like 'exploit' and 'oppress' go on a holiday. They become ways of saying 'We would like even more'.

In summary, Hume's theory of justice is, at the deeper level, doubly conservative. It implies that two kinds of criticism of the status quo are dangerous nonsense. First, it rejects all criticisms based on the assumption that a state of cooperative abundance will ever be a humanly realisable alternative so that justice will no longer be necessary. Thus the Humean theory is opposed to the particular version of marxism we have been discussing above (while in agreement with all other Hume-based views such as Rawls'). Such criticisms of the status quo are also dangerous to the extent that they undermine and weaken those poor but useful conventions which we have for resolving basic conflicts. In the name of an illusory perfection, it tends to destroy what, at least, works.

Second, Humean conservatism also rejects any criticism which invokes or assumes some notion of impartiality and considers arbitrariness in distributions a vice. Here the Humean is opposed to Rawls and others like him, but, rather oddly, in partial agreement with the marxist position. It is sceptical of any philosophical notion of 'fairness' or 'impartiality'. Even more, Humean conservatism is opposed to criticism which depends on nothing more than exposing the philosophical 'arbitrariness' in our conventional moral judgments (with no clear account of the standard of non-arbitrariness). Criticisms which depend in this way on exposing the arbitrariness in our conventional social assumptions are dangerous precisely because they serve only to undermine the work of the imagination in resolving (e)-type conflicts. Just as Hobbes considered it dangerous to question and weaken the power of the sovereign, the Humean conservative must consider it dangerous to undermine the work of the imagination. The arbitrary, but striking, is all we have.

THE SCEPTICAL CONSERVATIVE

Critics of the status quo sometimes present themselves as sceptics, demythologising or deconstructing the illusions and unexamined assumptions of the status quo. They caricature conservatives as unquestioning ideologues. The Humean conservative reverses these roles, claiming the deeper scepticism. But to see this we must first locate precisely the sources of the conservatism and the relevant scepticism in Hume's theory. At first glance the conservatism and the scepticism in Hume might seem quite at odds. We might suppose the scepticism intended here is just his sentimentalism (and the role it denies to reason in moral judgments). Some might actually suppose that Hume's sentimentalism should have critical rather than conservative consequences. For example, it might seem that sentimentalism (or non-cognitivism) is part of the argument for liberalism, toleration or even universal permission. However the discussion of the neutrality thesis in Chapter 6 has made clear that it cannot be. But for precisely the same reasons, sentimentalism also can have no particular conservative consequences either.

Even so, given a rather common attitude, it might be allowed that the acceptance of sentimentalism will often have a slight conservative consequence. If we accept sentimentalism, we will probably feel there is no special reason to consider seriously any radical critique of the status quo which does not depend on sentiments we already have.[8] As long as our status quo sentiments are coherent and rest on no factual or logical errors, what intellectual reason is there to take time to listen to those who condemn those very sentiments (perhaps as 'bourgeois')? Of course for a cognitivist it is different. A cognitivist can still entertain the thought 'But even so, my present moral beliefs might be *false* and the social critic's *true*'. However the closest analogous non-cognitivist thought is not easy for a clear-headed sentimentalist to entertain. It would involve expressing a kind of standing sentiment somehow opposed to one's own deepest sentiments, a kind of self-contrasuggestibility. This is 'open-mindedness' in the silliest sense. Given the difficulty (except for some trendies) in entertaining such a sentiment, perhaps sentimentalism does, in practice, have a slight conservative bias.

However even this slight bias is far from inevitable. Sentimentalism can sometimes serve just as well the radical critic who claims to speak, not from the sentiments of the status quo, but from the sentiments of the future. 'My sentiments may not be the dominant ones now, but they will win out in the future' might be the critic's thought. Sentimentalism is, at best, a very weak ally of conservatism. Sometimes it deserts outright.

To take a quite different approach, it might seem tempting to see Hume's conservatism as resting solely on empirical claims in support of a Burkean kind of argument for conservatism. The conservatism would then rest on the claim that status quo rules or traditions embody more accumulated social wisdom than can ever be achieved by rationalising reformers who can never fully calculate the important consequences of their proposed changes. David Miller (1981, pp. 200–202) argues that Hume's claims never went as far as Burke's. Certainly no Burkean argument plays any role in the core of Hume's moral and political philosophy in Book III. The contemporary Humean who accepts Hume's sentimentalism and his theory of justice has no reason to fear he might be committed to the Burkean argument as a consequence. That is just a separate argument which stands, or falls, on its own.

However other empirical claims might seem to be more closely linked to Hume's core theory. Perhaps we should seek some con-

---

8 I first heard this point put by Lloyd Humberstone. However cf. Sturgeon (1986), particularly pp. 127–9, for further discussion and notes 7 and 8 for further references.

servative consequences from his claim that we humans more or less share the same basic sentiments. Admittedly this claim is a shaky basis at best. It is a doubtful empirical claim, but let us suppose it is true. Even so, its truth would not lead a sentimentalist automatically to conservatism; a great deal depends on the nature of the sentiments we share. Shared sentiments, e.g. regarding the natural virtues, might still form a basis for a radical criticism of status quo arrangements (in the manner of Rousseau). It thus requires some still further empirical enquiry to determine just how conservative in their implications our shared sentiments really are. However, if the claim that we share similar sentiments in our judgments of natural virtues has few conservative consequences in the context of Hume's sentimentalism, it has rather more in the context of his theory of justice. In that context it tends to anti-'liberal' consequences. It is this claim which allows Hume to avoid turning conflicts resting on different conceptions of the virtues into further conflicts for justice to resolve. However in this controversy it is not Hume, but his 'liberal' opponents, who are the more sceptical. Hume's position requires a rather strong (and doubtful) empirical claim about the extent of agreement. This is, consequently, not the most important theoretical source of conservatism in Hume.

The most formidable source of conservatism in Hume rests on two features at the very core of his theory of justice. The first is just his description of the circumstances of human nature. Suitably modified by contemporary Humeans, this empirical claim seems so overwhelmingly confirmed by history and experience that the burden falls on the utopian critic to give us some real reason (sufficient to be worth the risk) to suppose a state of cooperative adundance could ever be humanly realisable.

The second feature, however, is what goes on to make Hume's theory of justice, not merely Hume-based, but distinctly conservative. This feature rests not at all on empirical claims but consists, instead, in a certain kind of philosophical scepticism directed toward the pretensions of critics of the status quo, the nagging suspicion that, after a certain point, our judgments of justice depend on nothing more than the deliverances of the imagination. On this view, the 'critical fallacy', if I may call it that, consists in demanding a rationale, a justification, for the status quo beyond what frivolous fancy can provide. It consists in presenting the very philosophical arbitrariness of the status quo (and of the imagination) as the sole ground in the *exposé* of its 'politics', without giving us any reason to suppose all alternatives wouldn't be just as 'arbitrary' from the point of view of the universe. Humean scepticism challenges the critic to produce some standard for distinguishing the 'arbitrary' from the 'non-arbitrary' (beyond what the imagination provides). And the 'fallacy' consists in not seeing, much less trying to meet, the challenge. Admittedly, an opponent of Hume can rise to the challenge. I think we should interpret theories of justice such as Rawls' as attempts to give intellectual substance to a notion of 'fairness' applicable to (e)-type conflicts. Some such reply might succeed. Even so the burden of argument rests with those challenged. A theory of fairness is hard work. The conservative's argument is just the sceptical challenge. The challenge, not met, is the conservative's victory. Hume's conservative scepticism consists in what his theory of justice distinctly *lacks,* viz. a notion of 'fairness' or 'impartiality' (or some such standard for the non-arbitrary) beyond what frivolous fancy can provide. This Hume refuses to supply.

What Hume will supply is a theory of convention.

9

Convention and institutional facts

Hume's account of 'convention', first surveyed in Chapter 8 above and pursued in Chapter 10 below, is one which seems to employ no moral or normative notions (not even within opaque contexts such as belief contexts). Also, it seems to be an account which would satisfy most naturalists and methodological individualists (whom we would expect to have accounts of the basic psychological notions Hume employs). These two features of Hume's account are necessary for the success of Hume's 'two reductive projects' both of which employ the notion of 'convention'. The *first*, the main, project is to give an account of 'the regard to justice as such', i.e., the sentiment involved in the moral judgments which pose the 'hard cases' for Hume's sentimentalism. The notion of 'convention' employed within the account of this sentiment must be in turn explicable without recourse to the very moral notions (e.g. 'just', 'right', 'wrong') which that sentiment is used to explain. A 'norm-free', a 'value-free', account of 'convention' is necessary to avoid the circle of sentimentalism. Whether this particular employment of a suitable notion of 'convention' can avoid the specification circle of sentimentalism will be taken up in Chapter 10. The *second* reductive project, however, is the topic of this chapter.

THE REDUCTION OF INSTITUTIONAL FACTS

A plausible metaphysical naturalism requires some account of institutional facts, facts such as, in our society, contracts, property, legal institutions, etc., but in other societies such things as status or kinship rights and obligations. It must have some account of what it is to write a cheque, sell a house or vote on a bill. At issue here are not moral questions (e.g. 'Why is it right to keep promises?'), but rather the questions raised by anthropologists and sociologists (e.g. 'What are the natives doing?'). A Humean approach consists in two levels of reduction: First, institutional facts are explained in terms of certain more basic social facts, viz. 'socially held norms', as I shall call them. Second, what it is for there to be such 'socially held norms' is in turn explained in terms of the Humean notion of 'convention', a notion congenial to the programmes of naturalism and methodological individualism. Consequently disagreement with Hume can come at either, or both, of these two levels. For example to disagree with Hume at the *second level* would be to deny that there is any Humean (or suitably naturalistic) notion of 'convention' capable of adequately explaining what it is for a society to have a rule (or norm). As Chapter 8 pointed out, Hume's notion of 'convention' is incomplete as it stands, requiring some contemporary Humean to fill it out. But as far as it goes, it seems naturalistic enough. Chapter 10 will consider further whether some filled-out Humean notion can account for what it is for there to be a socially held norm.

The present chapter is mostly concerned with what it might be like to part ways with Hume at the *first level*. But even at this first level there are two importantly different ways of disagreeing with Hume. First, one might reject altogether the *general* approach. That is, one might deny that social (institutional) facts can really be explained in terms of 'socially held norms'. One might deny that 'socially held norms' exist or, more plausibly, one might claim that if they do they are not really important in explanation and understanding in the social sciences. For example, many historical materialists deny that 'norms' or 'social rules' play any part that is important in the understanding and explanation of historical and social phenomena, that they are at best mere superstructural epiphenomena. This quite fundamental way of rejecting the Humean approach (and a great many non-Humean ones as well) will be considered further near the end of this chapter.

But second, one might reject, not the general approach, but the *particular* analyses or reductions of particular institutional facts which Hume provides. That is what I do in most of this chapter. I do not reject the general project of reducing institutional facts to socially held norms, but I do question the particular reductions which Humes gives. Contemporary Humeans should consider this criticism as constructive criticism. My aim in criticising Hume's particular reductive accounts is to replace them with other accounts (in terms of 'socially held norms') which are more defensible. Hume's general approach should not suffer from too close association with his own particular attempts to understand particular social facts and institutions. When, at the end of this chapter, we confront those who reject the general project altogether, we should have in hand better particular reductions of social facts to socially held norms than Hume himself provides.

I shall choose as my example for more particular discussion the institution of property and those related social facts described in the language of ownership. And, as it becomes relevant, I will also have a few things to say about promises and contracts. (The classic account of law and legal institutions in terms of socially held norms is still Hart, 1961, chs. 5, 6.) Now the notion of 'property', or 'ownership', is of interest for a number of different reasons in moral, social and political philosophy. Hume, wrongly I think, took it to be central in understanding *any* society. Marxists, on the other hand, might emphasise the role of this notion in bourgeois societies, or at least in the ideologies which serve the interests of those dominant in such societies (Macpherson, 1962). But besides its interest in these regards I have some important further reasons for choosing the case of property to examine in more detail. The results will raise some general problems and illustrate some general points. When we have elicited a rather more adequate account of property in terms of socially held rules (than Hume's), we will see that accounting for just these sorts of rules in terms of Humean-type conventions is going to be more difficult than Hume's oversimple account of property would ever have led us to suspect. I elicit three important problems in that regard. I do not say that the problems are insurmountable (quite the contrary) but I do think the problems have to be recognised and faced. Property turns out to be particularly fruitful as a case to study.

THE RULES WHICH DETERMINE PROPERTY

The Humean project, at the first level, is to explain what it is for a society, *S*, to have an institution of property. It requires an explanation of what it is for *S* to regard a person *x* as 'owning' object *p*. And I take the point here to be to give an account adequate for sociological and anthropological purposes such as might be consonant with the larger projects of naturalism and methodological individualism. For example the account of property should be useful in contrasting different societies in regard to the kinds of things they do, or don't, regard as property and also in regard to how central a role it plays in a society. A notion of 'property' (or 'ownership') useful for understanding and explanation in the social sciences will not necessarily be exactly the same as elicited by an ordinary language investigation into the meanings of the English words 'own' or 'property' or 'mine'. Nor need it produce the same results in every respect as answers to legal questions (in our system) about ownership. I would maintain that some particular features of the English word 'own' as well as some features about what our legal system says about ownership are rather incidental, perhaps idiosyncratic, features of English or of our legal system. A notion useful in cultural anthropology will not necessarily find all the features of our system useful in comparisons. The notion we want is one which will be useful in the social sciences in making comparisons and in giving explanations.

The four rules which Hume gives in the section (III,ii,3) entitled 'Of the rules, which determine property': 'occupation' (or 'first possession') (505–7), 'prescription' (508–9), 'accession' (509), 'succession' (510–13) do nothing, in fact, to explain what property is. In the following section (III,ii,4) Hume gives what might be considered a fifth rule: 'transference by consent' which, as we shall eventually see, is somewhat more relevant. The former four rules are rules a society might (but I think needn't) have for determining what gives a particular person title to a particular thing. They are rules for determining who owns what. (Thus they are distributional rules of a certain sort.) But not only are these particular four rules not necessary for there to be an institution of property, they in any case do not explain *what* one thereby gets according to these rules. As rules which set down what shall give title to ownership, they presuppose the notion of ownership.

Hume's phrase 'the rules which determine property' is nicely ambiguous on just this point. It could mean 'rules which *define* what property is' (but cf. 310, 506) or it could mean 'rules which determine in the way of distribution who gets what property'. The latter give *title* to property, specify grounds of ownership. Hume's actual four examples of rules decidedly fall under this latter description rather than the former (e.g. Hume's rule of 'succession' which covers inheritance rules). They are distributional (really entitlement) rules which a society having an institution of property might (or might not) have.[1] But it is rules of the former sort that the reductive project requires. No doubt any institution of property must have some rules of entitlement, but it needn't be these four. (On the other hand a society which lacked completely the fifth rule 'transference by consent' would have something significantly different from property.) The actual four rules Hume gives are pretty incidental.

It would be oversimplifying only a bit to say that where a society, *S*, has and applies the notion of 'ownership' it is employing two kinds of claims in tandem. First, it must have *some* entitlement rule *or other* of the following form (for all persons, *x*, objects, *p* and for some relation *F*):

Re. xFp warrants xOp.

That is, some (perhaps natural) relation *F* between *x*'s and *p*'s recognised by *S* as giving *x* ownership, *O*, of *p*. However *what* is thereby granted is then defined by:

Do. xOp entails $N(x, \ldots, p)$.

That is, what *S* thereby recognises is a certain norm, *N*, applying to *x* and *p*, which would not otherwise normally be supposed to apply. Putting (Re) and (Do) together, what society *S* really has is a norm for applying a norm. It has a norm, (Re) and (Do) in tandem, that, whenever xFp is the case, it shall apply norm *N* to the circumstances involving *x* and *p*.

If a society is to have a notion of ownership it must have something like a pair (Re) and (Do) working in tandem. It does not matter, to its being a property institution, just what precisely the (Re) rule is. What features, F, F', F'', etc., are taken as grounds for ownership will differ from society to society (with an exception to be noted later). Indeed a single society will usually have several or many such rules, e.g. Hume's four rules. What makes it an institution of property is a matter of the exact *N* in (Do). What makes

---

1 Hume probably thought that there was some *empirical* necessity to our having these four entitlement rules. He thought they tended to strike the human 'imagination'. However I think there is no strong empirical necessity here. Societies do handle property of deceased persons in a wide variety of ways other than 'succession'. But in any case the present point is that there is no *conceptual* necessity that a system of property involve these rules.

it ownership, O, that is granted (on the basis of some F or other) is a matter of the precise normative consequences, N, society S takes to follow. The way to see that a certain word in another language is, or is not, best translated as 'own' in English is, not so much to investigate the criteria they use for applying the term in question, but rather to investigate how they think the application has implications for the normative status quo. What new norms do they take to apply once they agree application of the term is warranted? If we look only at the grounds for applying the term, it might turn out to be something quite different from ownership which is being attributed by the entitlement rule. It could be, rather, that they take x to have acquired some new obligation or responsibility or liability in regard to p, or that x only gets some conditional right of access to p, or that x has become the ritual guardian of p, and so on.

So where society S does hold the following in tandem in regard to x's and p's:

Re. xFp warrants xOp, and
Do. xOp entails N $(x, \ldots ,p)$,

the O-relation will be ownership only if the norm N that gets applied is the right sort of one.[2] What matters in making it ownership is not so much, *pace* Hume, the particular F or F's taken as entitlement grounds, but rather the nature of the norm N that is taken by S to apply as a consequence. So what norm or complex of norms, precisely, must be referred to by 'N' if 'O' is to mean 'owns'?

AN EXCLUSIVE RIGHT

A rather traditional suggestion is that, when a society recognises ownership, it is recognising a certain more or less exclusive right, an exclusive right of 'use and abuse'. Postponing until later what might be involved in a right of abuse, we might consider the claim that the following is at least a part of the story of ownership:

Do*. xOp entails x has the 'exclusive right of use of p'

2 Thus ownership statements ('xOp') are 'intermediate' between 'statements of the facts required for its truth' ('xFp') and 'the statement of the legal consequences of its being true' ('N'). Cf. Hart (1954), p. 40.

where this notion of an 'exclusive right' is not just some primitive normative notion but can be explained employing, where necessary, only the most basic of normative notions:

D1. 'x has the exclusive right of use of p'
 $=$ df
 'For a reasonably wide range of m's (manners of using p):
 a) x may m-use p (i.e., it is *prima facie* not wrong for x to m-use p), and
 b) for all y, $y \neq x$, y may m-use p if and only if x "consents" to y's m-using p (i.e., it is *prima facie* wrong for any y to m-use p without x's consent; otherwise it is *prima facie* not wrong)'

where x's and y's are persons, p's are objects, and 'to m-use p' means 'to use p in manner m'.[3]

The first condition, (a), grants a 'right' of m-use. The second condition, (b), makes that right exclusive in a special way. A case of a right of m-use that is not exclusive would be my right to sit on a public bench (provided no one else is already sitting there, etc.) or of a tribesman to use a certain well (provided no one of higher status is using it). It might seem that (a) does not grant a 'right' (*stricto sensu*) but a mere 'liberty' (Hohfeld, 1919; cf. Perry, 1977). However what (a) grants will be not inappropriately called a 'right' if we suppose certain standing or background conventions (of law or morality in society S) which generally protect individuals against such things as assault, murder, threats, etc. In that case x's m-using p will be, not merely not wrong (i.e., a 'liberty'), but also protected by the general obligation all y's have not to interfere with x in ways that, generally, are forbidden (e.g. assault). Of course these standing prohibitions do not rule out other forms of interference from others (e.g. some y's sitting on the bench first).

But it is in that respect that (b) goes on to supplement (a), protecting x's m-using p in a special way that is not just a matter of the general standing prohibitions of, say, the criminal law and tort. What (b) adds is that all others may not interfere with x's m-using p even by using p in ways otherwise lawful (unless they have x's 'consent'). Naturally this 'exclusive right' should not be exagger-

---

3 For now it might simplify things to think mainly of 'natural' objects p and their 'natural' uses m. However there is no reason why the story cannot be complicated eventually to deal with conventional objects and their conventional uses, i.e., objects and uses not possible apart from the existence of appropriate social conventions.

ated. Both (a) and (b) are merely *prima facie* norms. Even if x has the exclusive right of use of a certain knife, his wielding that knife can, in some circumstances, be, all things considered, wrong. However it won't be wrong just because he ought not to be using it in the first place but, say, because the way he wields it amounts to assault or murder or issuing a threat. So of course x's *m*-using p can in the right circumstances turn out to be wrong for other reasons. The second condition, (b), makes the right in (a), not absolute, but exclusive in a very particular way. Thus, it is an alternative to, say, the rule 'First come, first served' (as with the park bench) or 'Lower social status gives way to higher' (as in some traditional societies). Hume would be wrong, if that is what he thought, to suppose that conflicts over jointly desired scarce goods can only be resolved by rules granting exclusive rights of use. Still, that is one sort of social rule.

Setting aside for the moment the question of whether (Do*) gives the right story about ownership, let us consider what a Humean account would be like of society's regarding x to have the exclusive right of use of p. First, it would have to have an account, in terms of Humean conventions, of what it is for society S to have the (Re) rule which makes some F (e.g. birth, or whatever) the ground of an exclusive right of use. But second, it would then have to have an account of what it is for S, then, to regard a person as having an exclusive right of use of some object. The former is a problem of accounting for norms for applying norms, e.g. the norm that says a certain other norm (those involved in regarding x's as having an exclusive right over p) will apply but only conditionally upon certain circumstances holding (i.e., that x be F-related to p). Perhaps the Humean can explain norms for applying other norms in terms of suitable conditionals, i.e., norms that apply only on certain conditions.

However the core problem is the second. Is there a Humean account of what it is for a society to regard x as having the exclusive right of use of p? At least (D1) has made this task a little easier for the Humean. Insofar as it explains the notion of an 'exclusive right of use' in terms of the basic normative notions 'wrong', 'not wrong', etc., it would seem that the Humean will have an account of the former if he has an account of the latter. And surely the Humean has an account of the latter if he has an account at all. Indeed, the Humean account seems specially designed to handle norms which can be expressed in the basic language of 'wrong', 'right', 'permissible', etc. The Humean will say that whenever people in S generally 'comply' (or at least are somewhat motivated to 'comply') with a specific scheme of acting and not acting in regard to x and p and where, furthermore, there is a very special explanation of this compliance, then it will be a convention that S has. Furthermore, if that scheme of behavior is a certain special one (i.e., one readily suggested by (D1) above), then the convention which S has may be said to be, specifically, that x has the exclusive right of use of p. In general, if the content of a socially held norm can be expressed employing as normative terms only basic 'action guiding' terms such as 'wrong', 'right', etc., then the Humean will have an account of that socially held norm (if he ever has an account). Precisely because the Humean account of convention is conducted in terms of general ways of *behaving* (and the explanation of this), any socially held norm that can be expressed in terms of those norms which guide behavior will be expressible in a form the Humean account can begin to handle. Thus if ownership were just something as simple as an exclusive right of use, the way to proceed with a Humean account of ownership in terms of Humean conventions would be fairly clear. Unfortunately ownership is more complicated than that.

A NORMATIVE POWER

Having the exclusive right of use is neither a necessary nor a sufficient condition of being an owner. That it is not sufficient is clear. I have an exclusive right, at least for the while, to use my university office in the usual ways. But I do not own it. Again, a tribesman might, by birth, have exclusive right of access to certain land or objects, but not own them. In both cases the holder of the exclusive right cannot sell it or transfer it in a purely conventional manner (even if he might be able to do things which lead to the forfeiture of the right). However the fact that not all exclusive rights amount to ownership may only suggest the former needs to be supplemented with further conditions to be ownership.

Sadly, holding an exclusive right of use is not even a necessary condition of ownership. An example would be those kinds of property (e.g. real property) where 'leasing' (or some similar conditional transfer) is possible. Leasing is rather more than just permitting someone to use your property (until you withdraw your consent). Hence leasing is quite different from the 'consenting' in (b) of (D1). In a lease agreement one succeeds in transferring the exclusive right of use from the owner to another (lessee) who is not the owner and does not become the owner (cf. 529–30). Thus, while I might still be the owner of a house, I might not have right of entry or normal use if I have leased it. The lessee now has that (unless, perhaps, he has in turn sub-leased it, and so on). Even if our legal system does not regard all things owned as capable of being leased (or then sub-leased), the fact that some can be leased is enough to provide clear counter-examples to the simple identification of ownership with an exclusive right of use. Where there is a lease in force, the owner lacks the exclusive right while the actual holder of the exclusive right (the lessee) is not in fact the owner.

So perhaps the story about 'the rules which determine property' will have to be a bit more complicated. For a start we might try to get a bit clearer about this 'power of lease' which seems to complicate the story. Given that we already have the notion of 'an exclusive right of use of p', i.e., (D1), we can define:

D2. 'x has the normative power to lease to any y, $y \neq x$, part, or all, of x's exclusive right of use of p'
$=df$
'x has the "normative power" to "transfer" all, or a part, of x's exclusive right of use of p to any y, $y \neq x$, via a "mutual agreement or contract" (involving "consent acts") between x and y specifying certain (not totally unlikely) future circumstances under which the exclusive rights thus "transferred" will, or would, revert to x'.

Hereafter such mutual agreements (or contracts), $c1$, $c2$, ..., will be called 'lease contracts' and their corresponding conditions, $C1$, $C2$, ..., 'reversion circumstances'.

Now the fact that a 'normative power' (i.e., to lease, not to mention those later discussed: to sell, to bring an action, etc.) might get involved in the notion of ownership is going to complicate things greatly, not just for Humeans, but for practically everyone trying to give an account of socially held norms. A socially held norm which attributes a 'normative power' to a person does not, in the first instance, seem to be a norm that guides action. It does not prohibit, permit or require the 'exercise' of those powers (e.g. require one to lease, to sell, etc.). Rather, such norms facilitate. They make the exercise, not just permissible, but possible in the first place. Indeed a norm which confers normative powers enables the person on whom the power is conferred to alter the normative (conventional) status quo by purely conventional means provided for by the norm itself. It may be said to have one further degree of complexity than is the case with norms that merely guide action. Norms which confer powers seem to be norms which empower one to alter the prevailing norms in some respect. We can see this in the case of the normative power to lease. Suppose the normative status quo is that I have the exclusive right of use of some p. If I also have the normative power of lease in regard to that exclusive right, I can do something (itself conventional) which leaves you and not me as the current holder of the exclusive right (until some future conditions are satisfied and the exclusive right reverts again back to me).

The nature of norms which confer 'normative powers', as opposed to those which merely guide action, is much discussed in contemporary legal and moral philosophy.[4] Explaining the nature of socially held norms of this sort is a further problem that the Humean account of convention has to face. Even if there is such an account of socially held norms which guide action, that does not automatically provide an account of those norms which confer normative powers. Possibly, in this latter regard, the Humean would do best to speak of certain conditional norms. Such a conditional norm would specify some performance (otherwise of no social significance) where, on condition that the performance occurred, some special norm would be taken to apply which otherwise would not. I broached above the subject of the possibility of conditional norms. The difference here is that the change in norms is taken, conventionally, to depend specifically on an appropriate act of some individual. In any case it is clear the Humean also needs an account of a very important class of second-order conventions, i.e., conventions which provide for the altering of the prevailing first-order (or lower order) conventions. Such an account is needed to explain the nature of those social conventions which confer normative powers.

While the power of lease sometimes gets involved in the story

4 The importance of the distinction between norms which guide action and norms which confer normative powers is stressed by Hart (1961), pp. 77–9, 89–96, 238–9. Cf. Bentham (1970 ed.), ch. 9; Hohfeld (1919); Raz (1970), pp. 156–66, (1972), p. 79, (1975), pp. 98–106; Hart (1972).

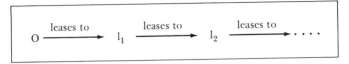

Figure 9

about ownership, the involvement is not a straighforward one. Clearly, the power of lease is not a necessary condition of ownership. That's so, not merely because many kinds of property (e.g. things that can be used only by being consumed) are not capable of being leased, but also, more importantly, because in leasing one not only transfers, for the duration, the exclusive right of use, but also gives up, for the duration, the very power of lease. Once I lease my house to you, I cannot validly lease it for the same period to another. Indeed it might be that you acquire a power to sub-lease for that period. So we must conclude that neither exclusive right of use nor power of lease necessarily picks out the current owner.

Still, these two notions are relevant in some way. Even in cases where I lease my property, I still have a kind of normative status. I am the person on whom the exclusive right of use will (or would) revert on satisfaction of all the relevant 'reversion circumstances'. In a string of leases and sub-leases (figure 9), I, the owner O, occupy the position furthest to the left.

I am furthest to the left on this diagram because the exclusive right of use I subsequently leased I did not myself acquire by lease. This illustrates what Honore (1961) calls the 'residual character' of ownership. When the 'lesser interests' lapse, then the actual rights revert to the person said to be the owner. Where the owner does not actually have the rights involved in ownership, they will (or would) nevertheless revert to him in the right circumstances. I call this status 'holding the ultimate reversionary rights'. For those concerned to see this spelled out in a way that avoids circularity while employing only notions we have thus far discussed I offer the appropriately complex:

D3. 'x holds the ultimate reversionary exclusive right of use of p at time t'

= df

a) Reversion:
Either: i) x actually has all of the 'exclusive right of use of p' (D1) at time t,

257

Or: ii) Prior to t there was a temporal series of 'valid contracts', $c1, c2, \ldots, cn$, with corresponding 'reversion circumstances', $C1, C2, \ldots, Cn$, each 'transferring' some, or all, of the 'exclusive right of use of p', such that:

In the (possible) conjunction of circumstances $C1 \& C2 \& \ldots Cn$ (after t) all the exclusive right of use of p *would* revert to x, and

b) Ultimacy:

There was *no* further lease contract, $c0$, with reversion circumstances $C0$, such that $c0$ occurred before t and any $c1, c2, \ldots cn$ that might satisfy (a, ii) above, such that:

Should x have the right of exclusive use of p at t or later (perhaps because $C1$ and $C2 \& \ldots Cn$ occur), then, if $C0$ should occur as well, x's exclusive right of use of p *would* revert from x to some y, $y \neq x$.

Thus, while the actual owner needn't in all cases have the actual exclusive right of use, he will at least have the status of being the 'holder of the ultimate reversionary exclusive right of use' (D3). Likewise, it is true that the actual owner may not always have the actual power of lease. But where this is only because he has leased the property, then he will still hold 'the ultimate reversionary power of lease':

D4. 'x holds the ultimate reversionary power of lease of the exclusive right of use of p'

= df

'If there is a power of lease at all in regard to the exclusive right of use of p, then x would have that power in the event that the actual exclusive right of use of p reverted to the holder of the "ultimate reversionary exclusive right of use of p" '

Being an owner does not always involve holding the *actual* exclusive rights of use or the *actual* normative power of lease. A more plausible thesis is that it involves *ultimate reversionary* rights and powers. But even these far from sufficient.

ANOTHER NORMATIVE POWER

One might hold the ultimate reversionary exclusive right of use as well as the ultimate reversionary power of lease in that regard and still not really be the owner. For example, the rules of a traditional society might give one these two statuses in regard to a certain piece of land. One might be assigned this status, by some (Re) rule, on the basis of birth or kinship. Hence birth would fix one's status in regard to this land. One might use it, permit others to use it, even lease it. But one could never rid oneself completely of one's ultimate reversionary ties to this land. In short, what would be lacking is a normative power of sale or gift in regard to one's ultimate reversionary statuses. Importantly different would be a society that conferred a normative power to 'alienate' one's normative statuses, i.e., to transfer the status one had to someone else. Thus for persons, x, and normative statuses, H:

D5. 'x has the normative power to alienate his present normative status H.'

= df

'x has the normative power to transfer by mutual agreement (involving "consent acts") with any y, $y \neq x$, the normative status H'.

Furthermore:

D6. The normative power to alienate one's present normative status H is recursive

iff

For all persons, u, v, w, if u has normative status H as well as the normative power to alienate H then if u alienates H by mutual agreement with v, v acquires not only H, but also the normative power to alienate H to any w.

So a rather more sophisticated account of ownership would hold, that where a society has a notion of ownership it will, first, have some entitlement rules or other of the form:

Re. $x F p$ warrants $x O p$

where the particular grounds for entitlement, F, may well differ from society to society. But, second, some such rule or rules will be put in tandem with, now more specifically:

Do**. $x O p$ entails:

1) x holds the ultimate reversionary exclusive right of use of p [cf. (D3)], and

2) x holds the ultimate reversionary power of lease of (1) above [cf. (D4)], and

3) x has the normative power to alienate his combined normative status in (1) and (2) above [cf. (D5)], and

4) the power of alienation in (3) is recursive [cf. (D6)].

Of course the notion of ownership is even more complicated than (Do**) suggests. Typically ownership involves (in a complicated manner) not merely an exclusive right of use, but also some rights to 'abuse', e.g. consume, waste, destroy, which are also exclusive in certain ways. Such rights of abuse are usually supplemented by social rules for assigning damages where some y destroys or damages x's property p without x's consent. Again there might be rules for assigning liability in cases where x's property (e.g. his ox) harms some person y or his property p' (Snare, 1972). However rules such as these seem somewhat more secondary in the sense that they apply when the more basic rules which define property are violated, or else they supplement the core rules with somewhat more peripheral sorts of rules.

No doubt the notion of 'owns' in English is rather more complicated than the notion of 'O' operating as an intermediate term relating some (Re) or other to, specifically, (Do**). At best the notion of 'O' represents the core notion or captures paradigm cases of ownership. We might well use the word 'own' or 'property' even where all the normative consequences, (1) through (4) in (Do**), are not regarded by society as holding (e.g. non-transferable theatre tickets). Even so, the degree to which a case approximates the core notion is the degree to which words like 'owns' or 'property' become more appropriate. Furthermore, even in regard to core or paradigm cases there might still be counter-examples to the analysis provided in (Do**). But counter-examples can be of two sorts: constructive or destructive. The constructive sort only call for more thought and revision leading to a perhaps even more complicated account than provided by (Do**) even if the latter provides a first approximation. By contrast, destructive counter-examples suggest that the whole approach is misconceived. I would expect that there would be many further constructive counter-examples leading to further revisions. But I put forward the present account as at least an example of the right approach. Indeed it is one fairly congenial to the Humean point of view. It tries to understand 'own' ultimately in terms of basic notions such as 'wrong', 'right', 'permissible'. It is clear that norms expressible in terms of these basic notions are the sort of socially held norm account is best in a position to explain. On the other hand, an account of 'ownership' in terms of other problematic notions (e.g. 'having an interest in') will not be the sort of thing that will be of much use to the Humean project. (What 'having an interest in p' means must be just as mysterious as 'owning p' is.)

Furthermore, this sort of account, whether or not the Humean can in turn explain its basic notions in terms of 'convention', is one that seems illuminating and useful in the comparative study of societies. Societies do differ in terms of what kinds of normative relations they take to hold between persons and objects. Many are quite different from what I have described as an ownership relation. A conventional status, for example, might well grant a person certain rights and obligations in regard to some object, but if the right is not exclusive and not transferable, it is something importantly different from a property right. Some societies are said to regulate large areas of life in terms of other sorts of rules (e.g. kinship rules) rather than property rights and what there is of property rights is relegated to a few peripheral sorts of things.

The account I have proposed is that a society has the core notion of property when it has, first, some rule or other which assigns ownership on some basis or other (differing perhaps from society to society):

Re. xFp warrants xOp

where, second, what makes it ownership that is thereby assigned is a matter of the normative consequences, N, taken to follow:

Do**. xOp entails N**

where N** is, specifically, x's holding in regard to p the normative statuses and powers in conditions (1) through (4), i.e., the ultimate reversionary rights of exclusive use and lease along with a recursive power of alienation in that regard.

An important consequence of this account is that one of the normative consequences of ownership (the recursive power of alienation) doubles back upon (Re) and provides what is really the main F-ground warranting title to ownership: the appropriate sort of 'consent' of the previous owner. While a social system with property might have other (Re) rules as well, (e.g. 'accession', 'succession', etc.) it cannot fail to have the rule which gives title to ownership via transfer from the previous owner by consent. Indeed, once a system of property in p's begins, the main way of coming to own a p will be by voluntary transfer from the previous owner. Thus Hume's four rules, not only might or might not be taken up by societies which have property institutions, they will even then only have application in peripheral cases. The most usual method of acquisition will be via Hume's 'fifth rule', i.e., transfer by consent. That, unlike the others, is no incidental (Re) rule, but an (Re) rule that is unavoidable if the object in question is property at all. Property is somewhat unusual in that the normative consequences of ownership, i.e., what (Do**) entails, actually determines the main (Re) rule for giving title to ownership.

THREE PROBLEMS

I have chosen the particular institution of property for more detailed discussion in order to illustrate certain general points. Hume's misguided account of 'the rules which determine property' prevents him from seeing the problems which a more adequate account of property poses for his conventionalist account. In this regard the exact details of my alternative account are not so important, for the main outline of that account makes clear problems which Hume fails to confront at all. Hume mostly discusses simple, but fairly peripheral or incidental, rules. But the rules and norms which are more to the core of the notion of property pose some difficult problems for an account in terms of Humean 'conventions'. Three problems stand out.

All three problems arise from the fact that normative powers (e.g. lease, sale, gift) figure so centrally in the notion of ownership. The *first problem* arises because the social norms that grant normative powers ('power-conferring rules') are not, in the first instance anyway, norms for guiding action. They are norms that facilitate, norms that make possible the exercise of normative powers. They are norms that grant the power to change the prevailing norms. I do not say that a Humean cannot give an account of these secondary norms (norms for changing norms), only that the problem has to be faced. Perhaps an account can be given in terms of suitable conditionals.[5] Such conditionals (employing only basic normative

5 But cf. Hart (1961), pp. 35–41; (1972), pp. 218–19. However Hume's account of rules in terms of 'conventions' does not commit him to the view that rules are commands or that they direct the application of sanctions or even that they must

notions such as 'wrong') might then be more amenable to a further reductive account in terms of Humean 'conventions'. But if a Humean is going to give an account of property, he will have to say something about that very important class of norms which confer normative powers.

The *second problem* concerns the role of 'consenting' in the exercising of the various normative powers which come into the notion of ownership. Indeed the notion of 'consent' seems quite central and ineliminable in the notion of property. Reference to (datable) consent acts occurred in at least three different regards. First, already in condition (b) of what it is to hold an exclusive right (D1) there was a reference to 'consenting'. In fact we can now see that this really seems to involve something like a normative power to either grant or withdraw permission. Second, consenting figures in the power of lease (D2). It is involved in exercising the power of lease via mutual agreements. Finally, consent is involved in the exercise of the power to alienate (D5). That is perhaps its most significant employment. So far we have just proceeded as if there were no problem about 'consenting', as if this were just some non-conventional performance, i.e., something which could be done even without conventions but which could, via some convention, be taken to have certain normative effects (e.g. permission, lease, sale). But a naturalist cannot just leave 'consenting' as some sort of mysterious social or psychological event. He must give a naturalistic account of it. Furthermore, it seems quite doubtful that any of these three particular kinds of consenting (in permission, lease, sale) could exist without the existence of appropriate conventions or norms. The Humean naturalist must then give some account of the very act of consenting in terms of conventions.

The clearest way to avoid supposing there are mysterious, *sui generis,* inner acts is just to suppose the relevant acts are all on the surface. In specific cases it might just be, say, making an appropriate mark on a certain paper, or nodding the head, or uttering 'I do'. Thus we might suppose that, in any society where there is property, some external 'ceremony' or other effects, by conventions pre-

---

always be backed up by sanctions. (Indeed that is among the attractions of Hume's account.) Thus, the problems that views with such commitments have in accounting for power-conferring rules in terms of *conditional commands* (or directions) are not obviously problems for a Humean account in terms of *conditional norms*. However I do mention a problem for such a Humean account in note 14 below.

vailing there, just the appropriate recognised normative effects that we have been discussing (i.e. those in permitting, lease, sale).[6] Now such an account would seem to call for some alteration in the account of property given in (Do**). It might seem that we would then have to allow that different societies sharing the notion of property might nevertheless have different rules. In one society the rule might be that wielding a pen in a certain way in certain circumstances effects the normative changes involved in sale. In another society the convention might be quite different. The same normative effects might be accomplished by nodding the head in the right circumstances or perhaps by a word-perfect verbal formula. Each occurrence of 'consent' in my account of property would have to be replaced by an exact description of the local ceremony. In different societies the ceremony would be different, and so then would the rules.

However I think this above plurality of conventions poses in itself no insuperable problem for the conventionalist view. We commonly redescribe overt external acts in ways that incorporate a reference to the normative consequences a society regards as following. Thus, nodding (in the right circumstances in society $S1$) and wielding a pen (in just such a way in society $S2$) will both be further describable as 'consenting' (in the way involved in 'selling', or 'leasing', or whatever) where the respective conventions of $S1$ and $S2$ give the respective external performances much the same normative effect. Hence our account of 'ownership' may have to replace each claim about a society's having a rule involving 'consent' acts with claims about that society's having some rule or other of

6 It is important in rules which specify an external ceremony that the performance is one that is otherwise usually 'normatively neutral'. There is no standing prohibition or requirement regarding the doing of the performance, at least not such as would explain the subsequent normative changes taken to be effected. In our legal and moral systems we usually regard the external performance as something 'arbitrary' in itself (except as regards convenience in performance or creation of evidence for later). That it is nodding rather than raising a hand will be 'purely a matter of convention' as we say.

Thus, a criminal act, even though it is taken to change the normative status quo (e.g. by giving rise to liabilities and perhaps obligations that did not exist before), is not to be thought of as a way of exercising a normative power. (We do not consider it arbitrary that, say, maiming a person rather than nodding the head is the local way of effecting those normative changes.) In the case of the exercise of normative powers we need some performance we do not otherwise consider normatively significant which we shall count as effecting some normative change.

a form which takes some external performances (this differing from society to society) to effect just the normative changes our account specifies. What will make it 'selling' (or 'leasing', or whatever) is not the particular exterior performance required by the local conventions, but the conventional role it plays in a complex conventional structure. *How* you exercise the normative power is just a matter of convention.

However this account gives rise to the *third problem*. Of course there are somewhat primitive societies for which the above account of the 'ceremonies' which count as exercising normative powers would be completely adequate. Such societies have somewhat draconian conventions which set some exterior ceremony as sufficient to effect a certain normative change. Thus, early Roman law sometimes looked only to some exterior, word-perfect ceremony to effect certain kinds of contracts and sales. Again, certain extremely serious cardplayers go by the draconian rule 'A card laid is a card played' where even a card that slips from the player's hand onto the table counts as a play. Thus there can be such conventions where only the external ceremony, the overt performance counts. The above theory can provide an account of them. Draconian second-order rules for the exercise of a normative power take certain external performances and count them as sufficient to effect certain changes in the accepted normative status quo. If the Humean has any account at all of rules conferring normative powers he certainly has an account of the draconian ones.

The problem is that we know of many conventions which not only do not take external performances as sufficient, they almost seem to make some interior performance the sole requisite. In our society we do not think that uttering 'I consent', 'I agree', nodding, etc., even if performed in the most propitious of external circumstances, will constitute 'consent' where the external performance is done under duress, or by reasonable mistake (e.g. a reasonable belief that it was only a play) or in ignorance of English or the local conventions. Even the law, which is less generous than common morality, will count some contracts as void where, although the external ceremony and circumstances were in no way defective, a 'meeting of minds' was lacking. It has often been noted that there is a certain analogy between criminal liability (which requires a certain *mens rea* condition) and the successful exercise (in our society at least) of normative powers (which also requires certain mental

265

conditions). Indeed, many of the excuses relevant in the criminal law (e.g. duress, reasonable mistake, etc.) can bear in somewhat similar ways on questions of whether a normative power was successfully exercised (e.g. whether the contract is valid).

This is perhaps the most difficult of the three problems for the Humean conventionalist account. Can the Humean give an account, not only of the draconian rules for exercising normative powers found in some primitive societies, but also of those rules, more like ours, which require certain mental conditions on the part of the performer?

MENTAL ELEMENTS

It is at this point that the 'inner act' account of consenting might seem to come back into its own again. The inner act theorist holds that consenting consists in some inner act (where perhaps the external performance or ceremony is merely evidence for, or a way of informing relevant others of, the inner state). Inner act theorists make a further claim as well, viz. that this inner act effects the normative changes, not via convention, but just by its own moral or metaphysical force.[7] Hume confronts this view, not so much in his discussion of property as in his discussion of promising. But it is the same problem. Clearly, an inadequate conventionist account of promising in our society is that we have certain (second-order) norms which count certain exterior performances (e.g. uttering 'I promise') as effecting a certain change in the normative status quo (viz. bringing about a new obligation in the performer). While there may be other societies with rules as draconian as this, it is not in fact the convention we have. We do not have the draconian rule (even if we can imagine a society which did) that uttering 'I promise' (in all the right external circumstances) gives rise to an obligation even where uttered under duress, or by reasonable mistake, or in ignorance by a foreigner. We think that where the suitable mental conditions (something analogous to *mens rea* conditions) are lacking, the performance can 'misfire' as Austin (1962) says. It is void. Now the attraction of an 'inner act' account over a conventionalist account is that it has an explanation of this. It holds that an act like promising

---

7 For a plausible, well-argued contemporary 'inner act' account (or something close to it) see Robins (1984).

(or perhaps the consenting involved in sale) is some inner act, for which 'I promise' is just external evidence, where, furthermore, that inner act itself, apart from conventions, gives rise to an obligation (or suitable complex of rights and obligations).

Hume's own view about promising and the kind of consenting it involves (III,ii,5) is almost this bizarre. Of course he thinks it false that any inner act could, apart from social conventions, bring about in the world an obligation-fact. But even so his view pays a certain tribute to the inner act view. He thinks that when we promise, we *believe* or at least *feign to believe* the inner act account is correct. Indeed Hume seems to suggest that we can succeed in promising (the social practice) only by a certain amount of deception or delusion. At best it involves 'feigning' (524), at worst it involves entertaining 'contradictions' (523). He compares it to the beliefs in transubstantiation and holy orders (524). But he thinks that, unlike with these two latter, the absurdity involved in the idea of promising is at least socially useful:

As the obligation of promises is an invention for the interest of society, 'tis warp'd into as many different forms as that interest requires, and even runs into direct contradictions, rather than lose sight of its object. (524)

But not at all surprisingly, Hume has to say much the same about the kind of 'consent' involved in the notion of property. Indeed, he speaks in that regard of a 'defect in our ideas', of making the mind fancy 'that it conceives the mysterious transition' of property, of 'a kind of superstitious practice' (515). What Hume does not rightly realise is how deeply the notion of property is infected with the notion he regards as superstitious. As we have seen, Hume wrongly thought of 'transference of property by consent' as a fifth rule, to be discussed after the basic four which 'determine' property. But in fact it is the four which are quite dispensable and, instead, various rules about various kinds of consenting which give us the notion of property. Hume seems to have thought that promising was somehow overall more superstitious than our other institutional practices. But in fact the kinds of exercises of normative powers involved in property (not to mention law and legal institutions) all have the same problem about the mental conditions typically required for the successful exercise of normative powers. It would seem that on Hume's view just about all the institutional and social facts that make up contemporary society are riddled

267

through and through with (admittedly useful) self-deception and absurdity.

While I think Hume is wrong to suppose our leading conventional practices are necessarily based on a belief in inner acts that effect metaphysical changes, he is right in some of the reasons he gives for thinking the inner act account is absurd in the case of promising. Hume argues that this inner act would have to be some distinct, *sui generis* sort of act. It could not be just identified with, say, desiring, intending, resolving or willing the thing promised, for, as Hume notes (516), we ordinarily allow that one can lack any of these and still succeed in promising. Hume concludes (516–17) that the only 'act of the mind' it could be is 'the *willing* of the *obligation*'.[8] (Philosophers sometimes speak of 'binding oneself', 'committing oneself', or 'undertaking an obligation' as the inner act.) But even willing the *obligation* is not a *sine qua non* of promising. As Hume later notes:

> [N]or will a man be less bound by his word, tho' he secretly give a different direction to his intention, and with-hold himself both from a resolution, and from willing an obligation. (523)

Nor will we say he hasn't succeeded in promising. At most the condition is that he represent himself as resolving or willing some such thing. Insincerity in that regard is an 'abuse' but not a 'misfire'. He still promises. But, in response, perhaps the inner act view is, not that the inner act is always necessary, but that it is sufficient (or part-sufficient). Promising requires either willing an obligation or, in deviant ('abuse') cases, representing oneself as doing so (Hume's 'feigning'?).

But then the non-deviant cases must be somewhat strange. How does one will an obligation? Furthermore whatever precisely this inner act is supposed to be, it would have to carry with it the realisation of what one is thereby doing. If I could perform this act of mental gymnastics not realising the significance of what I was thereby doing, there would be just as much reason to say I had not really promised as if I had accidentally performed the external ceremony not realising its social significance. An inner ceremony is

---

8 Here Hume perhaps means 'act of the mind' in a broad sense. His own theory of the will in Book II makes it an 'internal impression we feel' (399) rather than a performance. Of course inner act theorists, by contrast, typically do mean an act rather than a modification of mind.

no better than an outer one in that regard. The mysterious inner act must, then, not only be one that one cannot perform without realising it, it must be one that one cannot perform without believing it to give rise to an obligation. While perhaps not logically impossible, this inner act is mysterious in more than just one respect. Are we necessarily pretending to believe in such things when we promise? When we sell? When we lease?

A BETTER CONVENTIONALIST ACCOUNT

I think there must be a conventionist account better than Hume's. It may be true that *sometimes* social conventions get intertwined with superstitious beliefs (but even they are more likely to involve beliefs in external word magic than in inner act magic). But Hume's account really supposes that the norms of sophisticated (nondraconian) societies in regard to the exercise of normative powers *necessarily* involve the belief in some superstition. To avoid being draconian, it would seem, we must become superstitious. We can get a start at what an alternative conventionalist account might look like by considering again the analogy between the mental conditions commonly required in successful exercises of normative powers and the mental conditions commonly required for one to be criminally liable for an act forbidden by the criminal law. The sensible approach in the latter regard is not to look for some distinct inner act or state (for which the external act is mere evidence) but instead look at the manner in which the act was performed (e.g. by accident, by mistake, not deliberately, inadvertently, unintentionally, etc.). Similarly, we might think of 'consenting', not as some purely internal performance but as a manner of doing external acts. On this view some otherwise indifferent performance (external or internal) is always involved in the exercise of a normative power but where the conventions making the performance significant are of the less draconian sort, the manner of the performance (voluntarily, knowingly, etc.) is also relevant.

And for a start we should not exaggerate, even in regard to our moral and legal conventions, the nature of this act modification. Philosophers, litigious children, and even some writers on jurisprudence tend to exaggerate the mental elements our legal and moral systems require for successful consenting and promising. No 'willing' or 'internal binding' is a requisite. It is not even right to

269

say, what we read in some books on jurisprudence, that the parties must *intend* to effect legal relations of (roughly) the appropriate sort. That is too strong. The actual requirement is fairly minimal, i.e., that each party realise (or reasonably should have realised) that his performance would, conventionally, be taken to have (roughly at least) certain normative effects. One could be quite uninterested in bringing about those legal effects (either as means or end). One might only be aiming to make a certain impression on a third party at the time of the performance, or perhaps just to indulge a whim for dramatic ceremony. Certainly one's intentions could be quite devious or perverse. Only in that sense of 'intend' whereby one is said to 'intend' the foreseen consequences of one's act will 'intending' to effect certain normative changes be something like the usual requirement for succeeding. And I'm not even too sure that is always necessary either. A person who thoughtlessly and negligently performs what he should have known (if he'd thought just a moment) is commonly counted as effecting certain normative changes might well be reasonably taken to have succeeded. As in criminal law, neither 'I didn't intend to' nor 'I didn't realise' will always be a sufficient excuse where one failed to take sufficient care.

Still, even in this latter case, the performer must have realised (or been capable of realising) the convention applying generally to performances of that type, even if he failed to apply that knowledge to the particular instance. So some, rather minimal, 'realisation condition' seems to be a requirement even here. Thus, where the rules for exercising normative powers are of the *non-draconian* sort, there is at least some condition about realising (or being able to realise) the significance of what one is doing, i.e., that a certain prevailing convention applies to it. And it is precisely this mental element in non-draconian conventions which gives rise to the main difficulty for any conventionalist account.[9] The problem is whether the non-draconian conventions incorporating even the most minimal 'realisation condition' can be formulated without vicious self-reference (cf. Anscombe, 1969). It would seem, to the contrary,

---

9 Stronger mental element conditions (e.g. intending, willing, etc.) give rise to the same problem precisely because such states of mind involve the realisation element here discussed. In discussing the 'realisation' condition for non-draconian exercises of normative powers we thereby discuss the difficulty these stronger conditions involve.

that any non-draconian power-conferring rule will involve a 'realisation condition' making reference to itself:[10]

Rn. External performance P in circumstances C shall effect normative consequences N provided (perhaps among other mental conditions) that the performer *realise* that convention (Rn) applies to his performance of P in C.

where, of course, different societies (and usually the same society) will have different external ceremonies (doing P and C) for effecting the same N. Now the problem with non-draconian conventions of form (Rn) is that they refer to themselves. And to substitute for the references to (Rn) the provisions of (Rn) leads to an infinite regress. For the same reason there is no finite, spelled-out way of expressing just what belief the performer must have to succeed in effecting the normative change. It is perhaps this difficulty, more than anything else, that has led some philosophers to suppose that what is required of the agent beyond the external performance is some bootstrap, self-referring, inner act (or at least a 'feigning' thereof).[11]

10 Actually (R1) puts the 'realisation condition' rather too narrowly. A person who got the convention *roughly* right might satisfy all the belief condition necessary and his performance might be considered to effect the normative change. A rather simple person who wrongly believed in word magic, or who wrongly thought the utterance 'I promise' (whatever the mental state) would give rise to the obligation, might, by courtesy, be counted as having satisfied the belief condition. His belief would be close enough at least for the purpose of promising. So a convention with a more generous 'belief condition' might be:

Rn'. External performance P in circumstances C shall effect normative change N provided *either:*
   a) the performer has some appropriate mistaken belief about how his performance effects N, *or:*
   b) he realises it is (Rn') which applies to his performance.

But any such more generous version will still have a self-reference problem arising in disjunct (b), unless, as Hume might suggest, everyone who succeeds in exercising a normative power has some mistaken belief such as we find in (a), the belief in (b) being impossible even if we delude ourselves into thinking we entertain it.

11 The inner act (willing the obligation) account of promising does not really escape the problem of self-reference. Notice that there are many ways a person might will that an obligation arise depending on *how* he thought the obligation might be then brought about. For example, he might make up his mind to bring about an obligation to certain others by encouraging certain expectations in others, getting them to depend on certain expectations about how he will act or, more

I think there must be a better conventionalist account of non-draconian power-conferring rules than Hume's 'feigning' account. It would be easier to settle for Hume's account if it were only needed to explain one particular institution of our society, i.e., promising. But as we have seen the problem infects the greater part of our institutions of property and law as well. On Hume's account what really follows is that a society cannot advance to less draconian rules for conferring powers from having more primitive draconian ones (e.g. from ancient Roman law to contemporary Western law) except with the superstition or pious fraud of norm-altering mental acts. But in fact a conventionalist has many alternatives to the Humean 'feigning' account.

The *first* account is the 'defeasibility account', suggested by a solution offered to the analogous problem in regard to the mental conditions required in non-draconian systems for assigning liability and responsibility (cf. Hart, 1948–9). We might observe that in applying a power-conferring rule to determine whether a performer of P in C has succeeded in effecting normative change N, we commonly place the burden of proof in a quite specific manner. We presume that if the external ceremony, doing P in C, has occurred, then the normative change has been effected. However that presumption is 'defeasible', i.e., it can be rebutted by *positive* evidence of the right sort, e.g. that the person doing P in C doesn't understand English, or was drugged, or was acting under duress, or was acting in a play, etc. We commonly do not require positive evidence for the existence of some mental element additional to the external performance but, instead, rely on the *absence* of positive

crudely, by harming them so as to give rise to duties of recompense. Such obligations' arising depends on quite general obligations (e.g. not to frustrate reasonable expectations, to compensate for harm one has done, etc.). Of course the inner act view (unlike some other accounts of promising) does not think those are the ways in which the obligation arises in the case of promising (even if sometimes these other obligations arise as well). Nor is that the inner act account of what the promiser standardly believes. Instead the inner act account would seem to be:

IA. The obligation of a promise arises (in the non-deviant cases at least) from *willing* that the obligation arise while *supposing,* specifically, that it will arise, not just in any old way, but via (IA).

The inner act account 'solves' the problem of self-reference by concealing it in the mystery of the inner act. One can appreciate why Hume would have thought this account not merely false but absurd.

272

evidence of the sort which defeats the presumption that the ceremony produced the normative changes.

While this observation about burdens of proof is not without significance, I do not think it entirely solves the self-reference problem in the case of non-draconian power-conferring rules. Of course where we already know a power-conferring rule is accepted in a society, the best explanation for a person's performing the otherwise arcane P in C will involve the performer's realising that the rule is so accepted. Given that explanation, the burden of proof is then placed on anyone who maintains that, nonetheless, the relevant mental element was lacking. However I think this first approach is not sufficient. The fact that this is the usual order in which we place burdens of proof does not prove that the required mental element is itself an *absence* rather than some positive fact about the performer's state of mind.[12]

The *second* alternative account takes seriously, i.e., treats as something more than an absence, the mental condition required by non-draconian conventions. It takes such conventions to require an *indefinite* belief:

Rn*. External performance P in circumstances C shall effect normative consequences N provided (perhaps among other mental conditions) that the following indefinite belief can be attributed to the performer:

The belief that there is *some* prevailing power-conferring convention, Ri, under which his doing P in C satisfies, not necessarily *all* the conditions, but at least all of the *external* conditions from those conditions jointly sufficient to effect N.

At least (Rn*) does not refer to itself. But I am not entirely sure the difficulty of self-reference is avoided. Of course in some instances there will be no danger of self-reference because the agent has a false (but close enough) belief about the relevant prevailing convention. For example, someone who wrongly (where (Rn*) is the actual rule), believes that word magic or the metaphysical force of some inner act is a necessary part of the story will still be counted *by (Rn*)* as having a belief such that we can attribute the appropriate indefinite belief to him. Up to a certain point we don't count as

12 Of course in cases of negligent performance the mental element might consist in a lack (the agent's failing to take steps to consider). But in the more usual case where the agent does realise the conventional significance of his performance (and thus satisfies the mental element condition) the realisation will involve some positive fact about the agent rather than a lack.

void the performances of those with silly beliefs. But setting these deviant cases aside, what of the more usual and central case where the performer does not have some superstitious or absurd belief but the right belief about the prevailing convention? It would seem that we can attribute to that more normal sort of person the 'indefinite' belief required in (Rn*) only on the basis of knowing that he has a more definite one, i.e., the belief that (Rn*) is the relevant prevailing rule. But, as before, we can't even state what this more definite belief is without falling into the problem of self-reference.

It seems to me the *third* alternative account to Hume's is the most promising. This is the *two levels of rules* account of non-draconian power-conferring rules. At the first level are rules addressed to those wishing to effect certain normative changes. At this level there is no distinction between draconian and non-draconian rules. Rules at the first level just present a recipe, an external ceremony, for effecting the normative changes:

R1. Doing P in C is how to effect a certain normative change N.

No further 'taking thought', or 'inner act', or 'mental gymnastic' is a requirement. Furthermore, (R1) is a rule addressed to those who act in good faith. It is not directed, or particularly concerned with, those who wish to abuse the rules, e.g. those who wish to deceive others into thinking the change has been effected where in fact the performance will later be counted by society as void. There may be other social rules directing us how to deal with such people (as the *objects* of further measures), but (R1)-type rules are not addressed to such people nor aim to facilitate their machinations.

However first-level power-conferring rules of type (R1) will be supplemented with second-level rules.[13] Second-level rules are not addressed to those who want to know how to effect normative changes, but merely to those who want to know what changes have been effected so that they can guide their behavior by whatever the resulting rules are. In the case of non-draconian institutions the second-level rules have more this form:

13 In the case of *non*-draconian power-conferring rules, that is. Where the power-conferring rules are draconian the rule at the second level will be no different in form from the rule at the first level, no mental element being a further condition. The level difference will only be a difference in persons addressed, those seeking to change the normative status quo as opposed to those seeking to guide their actions by the most current norms.

R2. Someone's doing P in C effects N, provided the performer was not acting under duress, etc. . . . , and realised, or was capable of realising, that his doing P and C fell under (R1), or something roughly like (R1).

Here rule (R2) makes reference to (R1) but not to itself.

Where what one wants is, not a recipe for changing the normative status quo, but only to guide one's actions by the current norms, then (R2) is what one needs. On the other hand, if one wants the recipe, then (R1) is the rule one needs. Mental elements in the performer's mind are relevant to those applying (R2) to find the current norms by which to guide their behavior, but not to those who wish to change the status quo norms. For example, to make a will, or sell a car, or lease a flat, all I need to know is an external ceremony. However, to know what obligations and rights now prevail in regard to a given estate, car or flat may depend in some cases on knowing something about the states of mind of those performing certain relevant external ceremonies in the past. The person who consults (R1) already satisfies the main 'realisation' condition in (R2). However that condition is not something required by the (R1) rule itself. Certainly that is not among the steps the recipe specifies ('Step three: reflect on the fact that you are following this recipe'). Some, the corrupt, may wish to know how to perform the external ceremony now so as to make it look later that the mental conditions were not satisfied so that society will not in the end count the normative changes as effected. Even those acting in good faith might be concerned that it not (wrongly) *appear* later that one of the mental conditions was lacking so as to invalidate the exercise of the normative power. For example, if I have reason to think it is going to be an issue, I should perhaps take steps to establish my sanity at the time of my making out a will. But while this is prudent, it is not among the steps of the recipe in (R1). Even if in some unusual circumstances it would be prudent of me to create what will later count as evidence that I did understand (R1) at the time of doing P in C, that will not be a matter of taking some special thought or doing some extra mental gymnastics. Whatever (R1) requires and whatever a prudent eye to (R2) might advise, it is not that. No lessons in inner acts, or feigning inner acts, are necessary.

I conclude that power-conferring social norms of the non-draconian sort can be understood in terms of conventions which involve no vicious self-reference.[14] A conventionalist is not forced to Hume's, or to anything like Hume's, view that our main institutional practices initially rest on absurd beliefs in metaphysical transactions or else the 'feigning' of such beliefs.

HUME'S GENERAL APPROACH

I have argued against Hume's *particular* account of institutions such as property, promising and law. In the case of property, the rules he gives ('accession', 'succession', etc.) are the wrong ones. Furthermore, his failure to get property right is related to his failure to see how important and prevalent are social rules making possible the exercise of normative powers. And had he seen how really prevalent such power-conferring norms are, he might have seen how implausible it is to continue on a global scale to account for them in terms of endless varieties of feignings and self-deceptions.

Still, I am in sympathy with his *general* attempt to account for institutional or social facts in terms of complexes of socially held norms and then to explain the latter naturalistically in terms of Humean 'conventions'. Actually I have argued against the details of Hume's particular accounts of institutions in order to make his general account more plausible. But now we might consider what it would be like to disagree with Hume at the level of his general account. That has been done. I will consider only one alternative view here, one that rejects even Hume's general account. That alternative is one version of historical materialism. According to this view socially held rules and norms either do not exist (but are illusion) or else exist only as mere epiphenomena. In either case socially held norms are not to be given the importance in understanding and explaining social phenomena which Hume attributes to them.

14 This third way out of the self-reference difficulty may provide some further problems for an account of power-conferring rules in terms of Hume's notion of 'convention'. The Humean account of convention is tailored to account for socially held norms which guide action (prohibit, require, permit) but does not obviously account for those, like (R1), which only provide 'recipes' for changing norms. The third way out depends on giving a meaning to recipe rules like (R1) which is something other than a conditional about what norms would be affected in various circumstances (performances). That is what we get in (R2). So if, as the third way out insists, (R1) is something other than (R2), it would seem (R1) is something other than a conditional norm. If so, it is less clear there can be an account of (R1) in terms of Humean 'conventions'.

The useful comparison between Hume and Marx comes in regard to the role marxists give to 'relations of production'. Historical materialism distinguishes between (a) 'material base' and (b) 'superstructure'. Any historical materialism worthy of the name must claim that superstructure, (b), is largely dependent on, and/or explicable in terms of, the material or economic base, (a). Superstructure includes, among other things, 'ideology', morality, law. (Certainly it would include Hume's philosophical views in Book III of his *Treatise*.) On the other hand the base is said to consist of (i) 'productive forces' (e.g. tools, techniques, knowledge used in production) and (ii) 'relations of production'. Typically, marxists employ the notion of 'relations of production' in at least two important ways. First, this notion seems to be an important part of what distinguishes one kind of socio-economic structure ('mode of production') from another. For example, feudal societies differ from capitalist societies, both of which, in turn, differ from the later stages of communist society in terms of their different 'relations of production'. Second, marxists typically employ the notion of 'relations of production' in defining a marxist notion of 'class'. One's objective class membership has a lot to do with one's actual position in the 'relations of production' (rather than, say, with one's conscious attitudes or beliefs).

It is this notion of 'relations of production', so central in historical materialism, which provokes a direct comparison with Hume's views. We might naturally ask a marxist whether the relations of production of a given society are to be understood in terms of, or are to be explained in terms of, or depend upon any of the socially held norms of that society. To this question there are two kinds of marxist response.

Some writers (e.g. H. Collins, 1984, pp. 85–90) reply 'Yes'. This version of marxism has no particular disagreement with Hume's general approach. It employs some notion of 'socially held norms' in explaining the basic marxist notion of 'relations of production'. However, unlike Hume it does little to go on to explain what this important sort of social fact amounts to. Such a version of marxism need not be 'materialist' in any deep philosophical sense (only in the sense that it gives 'economic' explanations of social change, etc.) It certainly does not seem to start with anything so basic as human needs confronting nature. It employs the notions of socially held rules (in regard to production at any rate) without giving us any account of what that sort of thing is. Hume at least goes deeper. Furthermore, this version of historical materialism actually puts into the 'base' (specifically in to the 'relations of production') what many other marxists naturally suppose is only superstructure, viz. socially held norms.

Other writers (notably Cohen, 1978) reply with a resounding 'No'. While socially held rules may be said to exist (at the level of 'superstructure'), no social norms are required to define or explain the relations of production which, in turn, are so central to marxist understanding and explanation of society and social change. But of course there is a certain embarrassment for this view.[15] Almost inevitably plausible attempts to *specify* relations that can perform the marxist task employ moral or legal terms. For example the most plausible accounts of the 'relations of production' specific to capitalist society (our example from now on) typically involve terms like 'own', 'lease', 'sell', 'contract', 'right', 'obligation', and so on.

Cohen (1978, ch. 8, sec. 2; cf. ch.2, sec.1, ch. 3) tries to eliminate such embarrassing normative notions by employing a 'transforming' (p. 219) or 'matching' (pp. 220–1) operation. For example, each embarrassing normative expression in the list to the left gets 'transformed' or 'matched' with the phrase immediately to its right (Cohen, 1978, p. 220):

1. right to use means of production (or labour power) — power to use means of production (or labour power)
2. right to withold means of production (or labour power) — power to withold means of production (or labour power)
3. right to prevent others using means of production (or labour power) — power to prevent others using means of production (or labour power)
4. right to alienate means of production (or labour power) — power to alienate means of production (or labour power)

A marxist such as Cohen wants to describe the 'relations of production' of, say, capitalism solely in terms of something like re-

15 Sometimes this is called 'the problem of legality' (cf. Plamenatz, 1954; Acton, 1970; Cohen, 1970, and 1978, ch. 8, sec.2). That title is either misleading or construes the problem much too narrowly for it is a problem about norms in general, not just legal ones. It would better be called 'the problem of normativity'. Also, the problem is usually construed too narrowly, as in Cohen, as a problem of definition or of just avoiding certain embarrassing words. I argue in the text that the problem needs to be construed more widely as a problem of order of understanding, explanation and dependence.

lations of power or control, but not in terms making reference to normative relations such as rights and obligations. The list on the right is supposedly more the vocabulary the marxist wants to use in describing the particular relations of production prevailing in a given mode of production. Hence, the word 'power' which occurs repeatedly in that list must mean a physical power, or at least not a 'normative power' in the special sense we employed in the previous sections. (Of course some of the 'rights' on the left list are really normative powers.) It must indicate something more like a control relationship.

Of course Cohen does not think a phrase on the left list *means* the same as the one to its right. Nor does he think that the paired phrases are *co-extensive* in their applications. For example a thief has effective control over what he doesn't have the right of use, while the owner may have that right but has lost the control. To take another case, a person may have the right to do what he lacks the resources to do (e.g. build another story on a house). Finally, Cohen denies there is even a *rough correlation* between what a phrase of the left list ascribes and what the 'matching' right phrase ascribes. Instead 'transforming' is said by Cohen to be a mere 'syntactical' relationship between the paired phrases (not a relationship between the things the phrases stand for). 'Transforming' is an operation that replaces one phrase (the left) with another (the right). Cohen's basic claim then seems to be that whenever historical materialist explanation seems to require the use of embarrassing phrases referring to social norms, in fact it only requires phrases produced by 'transforming' embarrassing phrases. Whenever it seems to need the language of social norms, it is really only the language of power and control that the historical materialist needs.

Cohen's view challenges the general Humean account of social institutions. Cohen's view would conduct basic social and historical explanation in terms of a 'base' which involves no socially held norms but only power and control relationships. It should be noted that the appeal to some brute notion of power or control has not been unusual in the history of social and political philosophy. Philosophers as far from Marx as Hobbes or John Austin have thought they could explain political and legal institutions in terms of a sovereign who has somehow managed, quite apart from the existence of socially held norms, to get some brute power or control. However, to return to the case of Cohen, merely to produce a vocabulary that doesn't involve embarrassing normative notions (although we may wonder what 'alienate' is still doing around) doesn't solve the issue. The question remains whether the power and control relations required for historical materialist explanations really never require in their own *explanation* (not just definition) facts about prevailing socially held norms. Some power relationships (e.g. just superior physical strength) can indeed be explained otherwise. But the more interesting ones (e.g. how it can ever be that the stroke of a pen by an invalid could make a difference to how goods and labour power get distributed) seem mysterious unless facts about behavior based on the social acceptance of norms somehow get in. Naturally the rights and powers granted by socially held norms typically are not coextensive with the actual configurations of power to dispose. The issue is only whether the existence of the former is not often an important part of the explanation (along with other factors) of the actual configuration of power and control relationships.

What is still required of Cohen beyond a purified vocabulary is an account of how all the relevant power relationships in, say, capitalist society can be *explained* without recourse to the existence of prevailing social norms. It is not enough simply to *describe* the power relationships. Furthermore it would need to be explained how so complicated and specific *de facto* powers (as say the power to 'alienate') could arise or be explained without recourse to social norms of the complexity we have discussed in regard to the notion of 'ownership'. Marxists may be right that a great many socially held norms belong to the 'superstructure', that most norms do not explain but are to be explained by the economic 'base'. This seems plausible in regard to rules of sexual morality or of petty manners. But the issue here of course is whether an adequate notion of the economic base (of say capitalism) can be explained without recourse to *certain* socially held rules (e.g. those that determine property, contract, legal institutions) specifically in regard to *certain* matters (e.g. means of production, labour power, etc.).

I myself doubt whether we could make the sense we usually do of the marxist distinctions between different 'modes of production' (e.g. feudal, capitalist, etc.) without recourse to the different socially held norms that prevail in each (in regard to means of production, labour power, etc.). If we merely looked at the actual configuration of power and control (e.g. at who did what labour, where the

280

product of that labouring went, whose will got complied with and whose was ignored in these matters) we would find no real basis for distinguishing societies into 'feudal', 'capitalist', etc. The power of a given capitalist employer might well seem more similar to a certain feudal lord (in terms of what he can get done and how things actually get distributed) than the power of another capitalist in a somewhat different situation or different time. (Would this then be a different 'mode of production'?) The usual distinctions between feudalism, capitalism, etc., depend on *how* these things get accomplished, *why* one person's command is followed and another's is not, and so on. For example in capitalism the actual configurations of power and control are to be explained in some part (not that there is always a co-extension between might and right) by wage labour contracts, ownership of means of productions, the existence of a class with only their labour power to sell, etc. In a feudal society the (in some cases not all that different) actual configurations of power and control are more to be explained in terms of socially held norms granting certain normative statuses based on birth or some such qualification and all the rights and obligations that go with that status (especially those in regard to disposal of means of production, labour power, distribution of product, etc.).

There is, to sum up, a kind of dilemma for historical materialists. On one hand this view might simply expropriate the basic, unanalysed notion of 'a socially held norm' in its account of relations of production. This has the advantage of making historical materialism a plausible and perhaps defensible account of society and social change. But it has the disadvantage of leaving open, for all that has been said, any account of what a socially held norm may be. This leaves a dangerous opening for something 'superstructural' to creep in at a quite crucial point. Of course this is not to let everything superstructural in. A marxist can still distinguish between ideology, mores, petty manners, etc., on the one hand and socially held norms regarding the disposal of such things as means of production and labour power on the other. Only the latter is in danger of creeping into the account of the base. The problem is more that this alternative leaves historical materialism as a fairly incomplete philosophical theory. Even Hume has much more to say about socially held norms than this view. It does not go very deep even into the basic questions of philosophy of society. Hume is deeper.

On the other hand the historical materialist might try to eliminate socially held norms, not only definitionally, but in any account or explanation of the 'base'. This makes historical materialism seem rather more 'materialist'. But I think this version will either involve cheating (supposing configurations of power and control that seem inexplicable without reference to some prevailing rules) or else will be crudely implausible (as in the more technological versions of historical materialism). It does seem to me that in any case Hume is by far the deeper philosopher than Marx on this matter (contrary to first appearances). He both sees the importance of socially held norms and is concerned to give a naturalistic account of what they are.

CONCLUSION

I think Hume is right to employ the notion of a socially held norm (or a convention) in the explanation of social institutions and facts. But on the particular details he is mistaken. And these mistakes of detail, for example in his account of 'the rules which determine property', keep him from seeing some of the serious problems (e.g. about power-conferring rules) which a theory such as his needs to confront. But I think a contemporary Humean might well rise to this task and do it better. And so Hume's general approach does not seem to me misconceived. The important Humean project is to reduce social facts to complexes of socially held norms (even if not the particular norms Hume suggests).

Of course that (the subject of this chapter) is only half of Hume's task. After social facts and institutions are reduced to appropriate socially held norms, these latter must in turn be explained. What is it for a society to have a norm (convention)? And so the second part of Hume's task is to give a reductive account of socially held norms ('conventions') in terms acceptable to a naturalistic methodological individualism. But Hume needs to give an account of 'convention' for another reason as well. Giving a suitable account is crucial if Hume is to avoid the circle of sentimentalism. Hume must give a naturalist account of 'convention' in order to explain, non-circularly, the sentiment which approves of just acts and just persons.

Does the Humean account of 'convention' really avoid that circularity?

10

Convention and the regard to justice

Hume requires a theory of convention for two reasons. One is somewhat incidental to his defence of sentimentalism, but is relevant to the broader project of a naturalistic methodological individualism. Hume's approach, in this latter regard, is to explain social institutions (such as legal institutions or the marketplace) and social practices (such as promising or buying) in terms of social norms or rules (i.e., 'convention') which, in turn, he wants to explain in terms of acts and properties of individuals themselves plausibly susceptible of a naturalistic account. The second reason Hume needs a theory of convention is in order to give a naturalistic account of the special sort of sentiment which approves of just acts and persons. Hume needs, specifically, an account that can be used non-circularly in a sentimentalist account of our judgments of justice and injustice, i.e., for the judgments which are 'hard cases' for his theory.

Many philosophers have been concerned, in the context of philosophy of the social sciences or philosophy of language (that is, rather than in the context of moral philosophy) to propose theories of convention (or rules, or norms) within a general naturalist and methodologically individualist framework (e.g. Grice, 1957; Shwayder, 1965; Lewis, 1969; Blackburn, 1984, ch. 4). However, Hume attempts to produce a satisfactory theory of convention falling under a further constraint beyond what these philosophers require. His theory must also, must most of all, be adequate to meet Hume's second project as well, i.e., to defend his sentimentalism against the charge of circularity. Consequently Hume sets himself a much harder task than most theorists concerned to propose a theory of convention. The latter are content with succeeding in the methodological individualist task of explaining (i.e., reducing) social facts in terms of conventions (or social rules) which, in turn are explained in terms of facts about individuals (i.e., their actions, properties, relations). Typically these facts about individuals will involve facts about their 'desires', 'preferences', 'motives' and 'motivating reasons' in the broadest sense. Such 'desires' and 'preferences' will include such things as an individual's desire to do his duty, his respect for certain moral value, his 'regard for justice as such', and so on. Thus the explanation of social facts and social rules will, on some accounts, be reducible to facts about individuals, although among those facts will be such things as, for example, a person's being motivated somewhat by his belief that he ought to keep his promise (motivational case 2 discussed in Chapters 4 and 5 above).

Of course Hume would not consider that sort of reduction a sufficient reduction where the project is a credible defence of sentimentalism. Indeed I have some doubts whether such should really be counted as a successful reduction even for the purposes of a naturalistic account of social facts and institutions. While it may satisfy some methodological individualists to see social facts reduced to facts about individuals (including, notably, their desires to follow the norms they have), the naturalist in metaphysics cannot be completely satisfied until some account of norm-based desires can be given in naturalistic terms. In fact this does a lot to explain the persistence with which naturalistic philosophers attempt to conflate, say, being motivated by one's belief that one ought to keep one's promise (motivational case 2) with just some yen for promise-keeping. That makes it seem as if there is not much of a problem about giving a naturalistic account of cases ordinarily described in the former way. In my view a more plausible naturalism will face up to 'reason-based' (or 'norm-based') desires and preferences by accounting for them in naturalistic terms, terms which give due recognition to their complexity and special explanatory power in common sense psychology. Hence I would think a philosophical naturalism, no less than a meta-ethical sentimentalism, will require that something more be said about 'the regard to justice' and such. Neither will really be content simply to leave that as an unanalysed, presupposed 'desire' or 'preference' in its account of society and human nature. In any case Hume, in his theory of convention, sets himself this much harder task. I think he is right not to make it any easier.

The defence of Hume's sentimentalism requires that a non-circular account be given of the specific sentiment we have, or express, in 'hard case' moral judgments, i.e., in judgments that a person or his act is just. Here it would seem Hume must give a (non-circular) account of two apparently separate psychological phenomena:

i) The *motive* involved when, as Hume says, a person acts out of 'a regard for justice' or out of 'a sense of duty or morality'.

ii) The *sentiment* one expresses in judging the motive (or act) in (a) above to be a virtuous one.

(i) is the motive from which the person, whom we judge just, acts. (ii) is the sentiment we have or express in approving of those who act from the motive in (i). It is the sentiment we have in judging someone or something just.

Hume's account of 'convention' is also, and inseparably, an account of the motive in (i). On Hume's account, there can be a convention where, given the circumstances of human nature, the fact that persons generally (tend to) comply with a certain scheme of behavior is, apart from some special explanation, rather remarkable; where the explanation of this social regularity (or tendency) is *of just the right sort,* Hume will say both that there is a convention and also that 'the regard to justice' figures in the explanation of the behavior. Of course the actual explanation does not employ the term 'regard for justice', but instead involves features of the social choice situation as well as the standard psychological notions which Hume uses: 'self-interest', 'sympathy', and certain other workings of the mind (e.g. 'imagination'). But once the total explanation is given, Hume can point to what in the explanation corresponds to 'the regard to justice'. That is, Hume's reductive account of 'convention' is at the same time, and inseparably, a reductive account of the motive in (i).

Having explained the motive in (i) in the very giving of his account of convention, Hume can then regard the sentiment in (ii) as the sentiment which approves of the motive in (i) (and also, it would seem, of certain acts). The sentiment in (ii) has, perhaps among other things, such acts and motives *as its object.* Thus Hume also needs to explain how such a sentiment with just such objects should arise or else how sentiments we already have can be directed toward such objects. Perhaps we should not expect the motive in (i) to be unrelated to the sentiment approving of such motives in (ii). Those who have the motive to comply will be likely to approve of such motives (and vice versa). The point is not that the sentiment is always distinct from the motive but that Hume has two tasks, not just one. He must explain what motive is the object of the sentiment and then make it plausible that we do have a sentiment that approves of just such motives.

The way to see how Hume hopes simultaneously to give an account of 'convention' and of 'the regard to justice' is to look at *the sort of case* of social regularity where he thinks a special explanation of that regularity is required and where, if it is the right sort of explanation, what we have will be a convention. It will simplify exposition to consider a particular, vivid, instance of the sort of case Hume has in mind where there is need of a special explanation. This particular case is chosen so as to embody the main problems Hume's account must be able to handle if his defence of sentimentalism is to succeed.

To oversimplify just for the moment, let us suppose a society of two persons (or classes). We will consider later what differences the multi-party case makes. Let us suppose that the two persons, 'Column-chooser' and 'Row-chooser', are each presented with three choices: R^*-comply, R-comply, or 'defect'. R and R^* are two different 'schemes of social choice', as we called them in Chapter 8, each calling for specific (but not necessarily similar) behavior from Column-chooser and Row-chooser. 'Defecting' is some third way of behaving which is contrary to both what R and R^* require for the occasion. The matrix in figure 10 represents the 'payoffs', for the individual choosers, for each of their joint choices (a box), Row-chooser's in the lower left, Column chooser's in the upper right of each box.[1]

---

1 At this point in the discussion the payoff numbers are to be taken to indicate no more than an *ordering* of the outcomes for each of the two individuals. (Cf. for example Taylor, 1976, ch. 1.) Thus intervals and zero points are entirely arbitrary. Nor are any points or intervals of interpersonal comparison assumed.

Even so, it might be appropriate to make the interpretation slightly stronger by taking the '0' payoffs to indicate an outcome near the borderline between 'acceptable' and 'unacceptable' for each player (but still without assuming any interpersonal comparison). More weakly, the '0' payoffs of general defection

Row-chooser \ Column-chooser	R^*-comply	R-comply	Defect
R^*-comply	2 General R^*-compliance 3	0 Mismatch 0	5 Exploitation −2
R-comply	0 Mismatch 0	3 General R-compliance 2	5 Exploitation −2
Defect	−2 Exploitation 5	−2 Exploitation 5	0 General defection 0

Figure 10

Two details about the matrix in figure 10 should be kept in mind. First, while the configuration of 'payoffs' is to be taken to reflect 'self-interested' preferences in a broad sense of 'self-interest' (e.g. to cover concerns for one's family, team, club, nation), it cannot be taken to cover moral desirability or moral preferences (or at least not those involving justice or duty). Since Hume's project is to give an account of the (artificial virtue) moral sentiments and motives, such cannot be assumed in the background to his account of convention. Specifically, none of the preferences reflected in the payoffs involve anything like 'the regard to justice' or some equally question-begging moral motive. Second, the problem is not just the usual game-theoretic one of determining rational strategies for

might be considered by both parties as a kind of benchmark, a 'state of nature' base, as it were.

our two players or predicting the likely outcomes of those strategies. We are given something more, viz. that the actual behavior (or at least tendency) is 'general R-compliance'. Hence the centre square is cross-hatched to indicate that this is the observed outcome. That's what the parties do. Now at first glance, this is a bit remarkable. Merely given the features of the matrix in figure 10 and the usual assumptions about rationality, self-interest, and common knowledge of each other's self-interest and rationality, this result is not readily explicable.[2] It requires some further explanation involving perhaps further details. Indeed this general R-compliance is in need of further explanation for not just one but two reasons. The choice matrix embodies, and was designed to embody, two different elements of conflict of interest. The general R-compliance is in need of explanation twice over. Or, to put it another way, this particular choice matrix involves the two parties in two kinds of conflict of interest such that their convergence on general R-compliance requires an explanation in both those regards.

TWO SORTS OF CONFLICT

The matrix in figure 10 exemplifies all the five features, discussed in Chapter 8's section on 'convention', that make R-compliance in need of some special explanation where, if that explanation is of the right sort, will make for a convention. To begin:

a) It is not to anyone's interest to R-comply if all others do not,
b) General R-compliance is in everyone's interest in comparison with 'general defection',

where 'general defection' is the outcome we might expect where everyone chooses purely in terms of (broad) self-interest in total absence of any information as to how the other will choose. This matrix has the usual 'prisoners' dilemma' feature that defecting is a dominant strategy in such circumstances. Whatever the other party chooses, one will do better by defecting. Where both parties choose this dominant strategy, the expected outcome is that general defection sometimes called a 'state of nature'.

2 In fact more than the three choices indicated are available to each player. There are also the infinitely many *lotteries* over the three actions, sometimes called 'mixed strategies' (cf. Gauthier, 1986, ch. 3). But I take it that even a wider analysis in terms of mixed strategies is not sufficient to explain general R-compliance, or for that matter even fairly frequent general R-compliance.

Now of course there could be explanations of this general R-compliance which would make it not the sort of thing Hume is interested in. For example there might be some natural, perhaps wired-in, motivation to do R-type acts quite regardless of whether one expects general R-compliance. Of course we could just build such motives into a wider notion of 'self-interest'. But where this might seem to stretch that notion too much we can just add the further stipulation to isolate the case at hand:

c) There are no 'natural motives' which explain the general R-compliance.

Furthermore, our choice matrix also exemplifies the following 'prisoners' dilemma' feature:

d) For each it is to his interest to defect if all others are going to R-comply.

(a) and (d) together make defecting a dominant strategy. (b) makes general R-compliance Pareto-superior to general defection. Those two features are sufficient to make for a prisoners' dilemma sort of conflict. That is one ingredient of conflict in the matrix in figure 10. Consequently one thing that needs explaining is how the parties manage to overcome the prisoners' dilemma elements of conflict in the situation and somehow converge on general R-compliance.

But of course that is only a part of what has to be explained about their behavior. Even if there is some explanation as to why the parties do not choose the dominant 'defect' strategy, it would still have to be explained why it is there is general R-compliance rather than, say, general R^*-compliance. For our matrix also exemplifies nicely the fifth feature:

e) The R^* analogues of (a) through (d) above hold of R^*-complying.

We may think of the R^* scheme of social choice as an alternative to the R scheme of social choice. General R^*-compliance is also Pareto-superior to general defection. Similarly, whether or not the other party is going to R^*-comply, one does better to defect. However, the formal features of the matrix provide us with no explanation of why it is R-compliance, rather than R^*-compliance that the parties have converged upon. Of course there is one slight difference. The actual general R-compliance is more favourable to Column-chooser than the general R^*-compliance would have been, whereas just the reverse is true for Row-chooser who would have done better in the latter case. But this element of conflict does not explain why there is actual general R-compliance. That is the nature of the second sort of conflict of interest. Even those not tempted to ask 'Why not defect?' might still ask 'Why just *this* scheme of social choice rather than some other?' Those who would do better under some envisaged alternative scheme might feel their interests in conflict with those who do better under the status quo.

In the particular case I am using as an example, Hume will regard general R-compliance as a convention *provided* the explanation of that R-compliance is just the right sort. We have a start on some of the features required for the explanation to be of the right sort (see Chapter 8 above). A part of the explanation of the R-compliance will involve the parties' 'common knowledge' of all the features of the case discussed so far (i.e., common knowledge of features (a) through (e), common knowledge of the 'limited generosity', rationality, etc., of the players). Furthermore, another part of the explanation will involve something about R that is somehow the basis for the players' mutual expectation of general R-compliance rather than, specifically, general R^*-compliance. The special sort of explanation Hume thinks is involved where there is a convention will involve the above two elements. But clearly something more than these beliefs must be involved. What we remain to be told is the sort of motive or desire that leads the parties to R-comply in the special case that there is a convention. It won't do just to say it is the desire to follow a certain convention or that it is the regard to justice or the desire to do one's duty. What Hume requires is a motive (specifiable in a non-question-begging way) which figures in those special explanations of general R-compliance where being susceptible to just that sort of explanation is what makes it a convention (as well as what makes possible the motive 'the regard to justice'). What is that explanation?

WHY JUST THESE RULES?

It might be easier to explain R-compliance in the face of the second sort of conflict than it is to explain it in the face of the first sort. That is, it might be easier to explain why people R-comply rather than R^*-comply than it is to explain why they R-comply rather than 'defect'. To see this let us delete, for the moment, the latter kind of conflict (i.e., the prisoners' dilemma aspects of the problem).

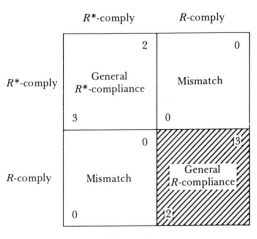

Figure 11

We can do this by simply eliminating the right hand column and the bottom row from figure 10 to get figure 11.

Here both general R-compliance and general R^*-compliance are coordination equilibria. There are no prisoners' dilemma features to the matrix in figure 11 for when a party thinks the other will R-comply (R^*-comply), he will prefer to R-comply (R^*-comply) as well. The 'mismatch' outcomes leave both players with payoffs worse than if either (but not both) had chosen otherwise.

To explain how actual R-compliance comes about (in just the case that makes it a convention) the contemporary Humean can rely on the account in Lewis (1969). A simple version of the Lewis account is (p. 58, but cf. p. 78):

A regularity R in the behavior of members of a population P when they are agents in a recurrent situation S is a *convention* if and only if it is true and it is common knowledge in P that, in any instance of S among members of P,

(1) everyone conforms to R;
(2) everyone expects everyone else to conform to R;
(3) everyone prefers to conform to R on condition that the others do, since S is a coordination problem and uniform conformity to R is a coordination equilibrium in S.

We may take it that what explains that there is this general conformity (i.e., compliance) in (1) is, in each case, the belief in (2)

291

and the preference in (3), which in turn have to be explained in terms of the 'common knowledge' of (1), (2) and (3). On the Lewis account of 'common knowledge' (p. 56) this means there must 'be some state of affairs A (such that A holds, everyone in P has reason to believe that A holds, and A indicates to everyone in P that everyone in P has reason to believe that A holds) which indicates to everyone in P'' that (1), (2) and (3) above hold (p. 58). The state of affairs A in such a case is the 'basis' for common knowledge, e.g. something like salience, precedent or agreement.

Thus in Lewis we have a contemporary Humean account of what would explain the general R-compliance in figure 11 in a way that would make it a convention. However in the specific context of Hume's discussion some important further specifications would have to be made. Lewis leaves it quite open what kinds of (conditional) preferences might play the role in (3) of his definition (the preferences to comply with R on condition that others do). Of course the fact that they are preferences conditional on what others are expected to do automatically means they cannot be what Hume would call 'natural' motives to R-comply. Such motives are unmindful of what others may do in that regard. However, more importantly, there is one important class of preferences which will not do for Hume's purposes. They cannot be justice-based preferences, i.e., preferences based on the regard to morality or duty. Such preferences are precisely those Hume needs to explain in the process of giving *his* account of convention and so that very account cannot just presuppose those motives in explaining what makes general R-compliance a convention.

But the fact that Hume sets himself a much harder task by eschewing all reference to certain sorts of preferences is no bar to his use of the Lewis account when explaining why the parties R-comply rather than R^*-comply. In setting the case in figures 10 and 11 it was stipulated that the payoffs were to reflect only the parties' 'self-interested' (in a quite broad sense) preferences. Thus, while the preferences might reflect such things as concerns for one's family, friends or country, they do not include justice-based preferences, e.g. the preferences that promises be kept, property not violated, authority respected, the legal system obeyed, etc. In short, the preferences pointedly do not include the very regard to justice itself. But since the Lewis account can explain why there is general R-compliance *rather than* general R^*-compliance just in terms of the self-interested preferences reflected in figure 11, it provides an account that can be used in the context of Hume's project as well.

For both Hume and Lewis what is further required to explain the actual R-compliance in figure 11, beyond the given features in the matrix, is that there is something that singles out R-compliance over R^*-compliance which gives the parties reason to think the others will so comply. For Lewis this is some state of affairs A which serves as the 'basis' for the appropriate 'common knowledge'. For Hume it is some feature of R-complying which, unlike R^*-complying, strikes the imagination. To the human imagination the former seems less arbitrary, less artificial even though in itself R is no less 'arbitrary' than R^*. However it would be wrong to suppose that it makes no difference to the interests of the parties that it is general R-compliance, rather than general R^*-compliance, that results. On that issue the interests of the parties are at odds. It is not 'just a matter of convention', in the sense that it makes no difference at all. While in many of the cases which the Lewis account handles it may make no difference which coordination equilibrium is achieved as long as one is, in the problem in figure 11 it does make a difference. General R-compliance is better for Column-chooser (but worse for Row-chooser) than general R^*-compliance. Hence even parties with no motive or temptation to 'defect' can still have their interests in conflict in a different way. 'Why just these rules of justice rather than some alternative one where I (but not all others) would be better off?' It is precisely about conflicts of interest of this sort (what in Chapter 8 were called (e)-type conflicts) that Hume's theory of justice has nothing further to say. Justice (e.g. R-compliance rather than R^*-compliance) is just a matter of what strikes the imagination. On Hume's view to find some quality of justice in R but not in R^* is rather like supposing causation is some necessary connection in the world. That, in both cases, is the mistake of projecting the operation of the imagination onto the world.

In summary, a part of Hume's account of convention can, following Lewis, be accomplished purely in terms of (broad) self-interest without recourse to any other working of the mind (beyond the imagination). With the help of Lewis Hume can explain why there is general R-compliance *rather than* general R^*-compliance employing no motivations beyond (broadly) self-interested ones. Even where Row-chooser would do better under general R^*-

compliance than general R-compliance, if he thinks Column-chooser will R-comply, so will he (in order to avoid the even worse 'mismatch' outcome).[3]

Of course it may seem hardly clear that this has yet given us an account of the motive 'the regard to justice' since we assume the parties are acting only self-interestedly. But it does seem to capture Hume's notion of the just *act* (in this case R-compliance). Perhaps that is why Hume says *'self-interest is the original motive to the* establishment *of justice'* (499). In the case of the matrix in figure 11 Hume can give an account, employing only (broadly) self-interested motives, of the rudimentary idea of a just act ('the rules of justice').

---

3 Indeed it would even seem possible that some conceivable (even if artificial-looking) schemes of social choice might be better *for everyone* than general R-compliance even though it is the latter that actually occurs (see figure 12).

Of course the clear Pareto-superiority of general R^*-compliance over general R-compliance is a striking fact about the former which, in some circumstances, might lead to general R^*-compliance. However if the *status quo* is R-compliance, few will be willing to risk choosing to R^*-comply. For, where others can be expected to continue to R-comply, the individual choice to R^*-comply is likely to lead to a "mismatch" worse for everyone than even the status quo general R-compliance. 'These people are trapped', says Lewis (1969, p. 92). Thus, on Hume's view it might turn out that R-compliance, being what strikes the 'imagination', is what social choice converges upon despite the fact that there is a Pareto-superior alternative. Even a reformer proposing a scheme Pareto-superior to the status quo might be making a proposal too artificial-seeming to be a realistic proposal.

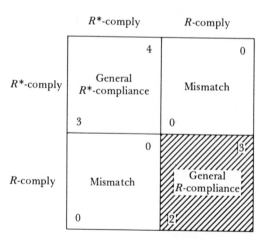

Figure 12

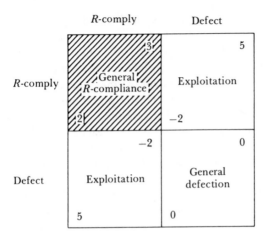

Figure 13

WHY NOT 'DEFECT'?

Let us assume that Hume, perhaps with help from Lewis, has an explanation, of the sort he wants, of why people R-comply *rather than* R^*-comply. That is, there is such an explanation in regard to the matrix in figure 11. What remains for Hume is to provide an account of why they R-comply *rather than* 'defect'. Thus we might, for the moment, consider only the prisoners' dilemma features of the problem by deleting from figure 10 the upper row and the leftmost column.[4] This gives us an instance of the prisoners' dilemma (figure 13).

Naturally, general R-compliance is in need of an explanation since 'defecting' would seem to be a dominant strategy for both players. Now in fact Lewis (1969) also gives an account of general R-compliance in such circumstances (pp. 93–4). It is explained *not* as a (Lewis) 'convention' (as quoted above) but as a (Lewis) 'social contract' (cf. pp. 88–9). However this account, in terms of a (Lewis) 'social contract' which is not a 'convention', is not one that Hume

---

4 This is misleading oversimplification. The two conflicts in figure 10 make for a game which is rather more than the sum of the two games in figures 11 and 13. For example the availability of the threat to defect must sometimes (i.e., when it is credible) complicate the conflict between the party favoured by general R-compliance and the party favoured by general R^*-compliance.

can employ. Lewis' account explicitly employs the notion of 'acting from a sense of duty'. The Lewis account, as applied to the general R-compliance in figure 13, can be given in two ways. First, Lewis says, we might take the 'payoffs' (and the preferences they reflect) in a *narrow sense* as 'the resultant of choice-determining forces *other than* a sense of duty' (p. 93). This is indeed what we have assumed in regard to figure 13. In that case the Lewis account explains the actual general R-compliance in terms of each person's acting 'against his own ['narrow'] preferences because he considers himself to be under a moral obligation to do so' (p. 93). Alternatively, Lewis allows us a *wider sense* of 'preference' such that 'accepted obligations will count as a component of preferences' (p. 94). But in that event the payoffs we have given in figure 13 must be redescribed to reflect these additional moral preferences. That, of course, will make for a different matrix, one lacking the prisoners' dilemma features of figure 13. No longer will 'defecting' be a dominant strategy for an individual, *all* his preferences considered.

In short, on this Lewis account either we keep moral preferences out of the computation of the payoffs (giving the problem an initial look of a prisoners' dilemma) but then later allow moral preferences to operate as 'an independent choice-determining force' *or else* we build those moral preferences into the calculations of the payoffs from the very beginning (and abandon any pretence of a prisoners' dilemma). In either case the Lewis account of the general R-compliance involves recourse to preferences based on 'an accepted obligation', on a 'sense of duty'. While that explanation of general R-compliance may be suitable for Lewis' purposes, it renders such an account unavailable to Hume. Hume's harder project is to explain the motive the 'sense of duty' in the process of explaining what a 'convention' (in Hume's, not Lewis' sense) is. Hence that explanation cannot just assume the notion of acting from a sense of duty. The Lewis account of R-compliance in a prisoners' dilemma situation (in terms of a Lewis 'social contract' which is not a Lewis 'convention') would render Hume's sentimentalism circular.

It is important to continue to distinguish two quite radically different approaches to giving a philosophical account of 'convention', 'social rules', 'institutions', etc. One approach simply begins with the unanalysed (although perhaps further analysable) notion of a moral motivation, e.g. motivations such as those in motivational case 2 in Chapters 4 and 5 above. This approach accounts for social rules in terms of moral preferences along with such things as common knowledge of the moral preferences, etc. This approach might well be counted as methodologically individualist since it tries to account for social facts in terms of facts about individuals (including their moral preferences). It will be naturalistic as well if these latter (including moral preferences) can be given a naturalist account.

Hume's approach is just the reverse. He intends first to give an account of 'convention' and then with that notion give an account of 'the regard to justice as such'. In the end he hopes to have an account of motivational case 2 and, more generally, of the sense of duty. But that comes after, or perhaps with, his account of convention. Hume's account is just as individualist as the former approach, but it is rather more obviously naturalistic in that it does not assume, but indeed tries to explain, moral preferences.

SELF-INTEREST

While Hume cannot just assume the regard to justice already, it does not follow that he must be restricted to self-interested motives (even in our very broad sense of 'self-interest'). I will consider what else might be available to Hume in the way of other (non-question-begging) motivational explanations in the following sections. But in this section I consider just how far self-interest might do the job for Hume. It is still possible that self-interest might go a great way to explain why (in the first instance) there is general R-compliance in the cases that interest Hume. The temptation to think that self-interest can provide no such explanation no doubt comes from thinking of Hume's problem in the terms of the classic prisoners' dilemma (as in figure 13). But the sort of case that concerns Hume is more complicated in at least two important respects. First, Hume's case is not a once-off interaction as in the prisoners' dilemma. Rather, it is what the literature calls an (indefinitely) *iterated* prisoners' dilemma, a game with, in fact, importantly different features from the classic prisoners' dilemma. Second, Hume's case is not just a two-party game (not even many simultaneous two-party games), but a *many-party* game. Both of these features make important, indeed crucial, differences.

First, let us consider the two-party (indefinitely) *iterated* prisoners' dilemma (leaving until later the 'many-party' complication).[5] In this game the choice is between 'strategies', i.e., ways of choosing and responding to the choices of another in an indefinitely repeated game with that other. (Of course one could exercise the strategy in any number of such simultaneous two-party games with others.) Unlike the single, once-off case, a strategy may bring into consideration the past choices of the other player, speculation as to his strategy and, most importantly, speculation as to the effects of one's present choices on the other player's choices in future interactions.

Some rather striking work on the indefinitely iterated prisoners' dilemma has been done recently by Axelrod (1984) and others (notably Taylor, 1976).[6] The results of such work is to make cooperation (i.e., R-compliance) rather less surprising. Under certain

5 A rather more ambitious, but I think also rather less plausible, approach is taken by Gauthier (1986, pp. 158–74). Gauthier's relatively uncontroversial claim is that under certain circumstances those having a certain disposition (something like the disposition to cooperate with those one can reasonably expect to be similarly disposed) can expect to do better than those who are 'straighforward maximizers'. Hence one would be rational to choose to have the former disposition where this is possible. However Gauthier is concerned to argue for two rather more controversial claims as well: First, Gauthier thinks not only that it is rational to choose to be so disposed, but that it follows from this that the acts following from such a disposition are also rational (Gauthier, 1986, pp. 182–4; for contrast cf. Parfit, 1984, pp. 19–23). But second, Gauthier thinks his argument also shows how it is sometimes rational to choose to cooperate rather than to defect in the classic (i.e., once-off) prisoners' dilemma (cf. Gauthier, 1986, n. 19 on p. 169). This is a remarkably strong claim indeed.

Now for Hume's project to succeed nothing as strong as Gauthier's two controversial claims is required. What Hume requires is not *justification,* but merely explanation of cooperative behavior. For this Gauthier's 'relatively uncontroversial' claim above will perhaps almost do. If those with Gauthier's conditionally cooperative disposition tend to do better than those with other dispositions, there might then be the basis of some 'natural selection' type argument which would *explain* how such dispositions tend to flourish and how cooperative behavior becomes more likely. This would still be an explanation in terms that brought in self-interest whether or not in the (once-off) prisoners' dilemma it is *ever* rational to choose to cooperate rather than defect.

6 Such approaches typically require only slightly stronger assumptions about the meanings of the 'payoff' numbers than those mentioned in note 1 of this chapter. Typically they include: a) That the payoff numbers assigned to an individual player reflect intervals (unique up to any positive linear transformation) (Taylor, 1976, p. 30); b) That each player has his own discount parameter (or discount rate) in regard to the payoffs of future games (Axelrod, 1984, p. 13; Taylor, 1976, pp. 8–9). However there still need be no assumption of an interpersonal comparison of any sort.

Cf. also Dawkins (1989), ch. 12, on the iterated prisoners' dilemma.

plausible assumptions (e.g. that individual 'discount parameters' – i.e., the regard for future possible payoffs – are sufficiently high, that the chance of repeated interaction with the same individual is sufficiently high, that the payoffs for defection are not too high in comparison to the payoffs for cooperations) the so-called tit-for-tat strategy does best in its overall response to a wide range of 'environments' of counter-strategies. It is a particularly 'robust' strategy, resisting 'invasion' from other strategies while able to 'invade' other strategies even from remarkably small beginnings. Over time it tends to flourish even more in a process that 'simulates survival of the fittest' (Axelrod, 1984, p. 50). Furthermore, as 'tit-for-tat' gains ground in this manner, the actual behavioral outcome (from those using this strategy as well as, very often, many responding from other strategies) will be cooperation (i.e., general R-compliance). Thus, in many circumstances of a not unusual sort we may expect there will be rather strong self-interested forces leading to cooperative behavior. It should be noted that this is the sort of account that Hume requires in his account of convention. He does not require a self-interested *justification* of cooperative behavior. Rather he requires an *explanation* in terms of self-interest of how such patterns of behavior might come about and then be maintained. Taylor provides an (equilibrium) account of how such cooperation might be maintained when brought about (in some way or other) while Axelrod actually gives arguments to show that there are also forces tending to bring it about in the first instance.

While impressive, there are still two respects in which the Axelrod sort of approach does not quite complete the explanatory task for Hume. First, it assumes there is only one way to cooperate rather than several importantly different ways. That is, it is concerned with (iterated) dilemmas like that in figure 13. Hume's case must be rather more complicated for it is concerned with (iterated) games like that in figure 10. But the Axelrod-Taylor sort of approach ignores the further sort of conflict that arises when alternative modes of cooperation are available (i.e., not just R-compliance but also $R*$-compliance). Hence the possibility arises that defection will sometimes be used as a threat, not merely to get the other to comply, but to get the other to comply in one way rather than another (i.e., in the way more favourable to oneself). This complication, I am inclined to think, may dilute the self-interested forces tending to cooperation.[7]

The second respect in which the Axelrod-Taylor approach may not quite complete Hume's task is that it concerns only two-party cases (even if any number of simultaneous ones) rather than the *many-party* case. In the many-party case the outcomes for each depend on the choices of all the parties. Now the problem of the many-party extension has been nicely brought out by Pettit (1986). Admittedly in *a certain kind* of many-party (indefinitely) iterated prisoners' dilemma, we can still expect rational (self-interested) parties to employ the 'tit-for-tat' strategy with the result tending toward general R-compliance. Specifically, in what Pettit called 'foul dealing' prisoners' dilemmas, the 'tit-for-tat' strategy is sufficiently credible to lead to general R-compliance. Nevertheless in certain *other cases* (what Pettit calls 'free riding' prisoners' dilemmas) the 'tit-for-tat' strategy lacks credibility so that something else is still required to explain general R-compliance in such cases.

But in the context of Hume's discussion, even Pettit's qualified result is some progress at least. *Some* cases of general R-compliance in prisoners' dilemma situations can be adequately explained in terms of rational strategies adapted by self-interested individuals. Furthermore even these cases of general R-compliance of the other sort (free riding cases) might admit of an *indirect* explanation in terms of self-interest. To give only one example, law and legal institutions might attach sanctions to those who defect rather than R-comply making it prudent for parties to do so (i.e., changing the 'payoffs'). Naturally law and legal institutions are themselves social facts for which a Humean account in terms of convention must ultimately be given. But *if* the relevant general compliance in that regard arises in the context of prisoners' dilemmas of the foul dealing sort (where 'tit-for-tat' is credible), there will not only be

7 It seems to me a particular inadequacy of Taylor's account (1976, cf. p. 6) that he does not consider such conflicts. Such conflicts – what in earlier chapters I called (e)-type conflicts – may be as much a barrier to cooperation as prisoners' dilemma type fears of defection by the other. Hence an anarchist argument against the need for government, such as we find in Taylor, needs to confront not only the argument that government is sometimes needed to solve prisoners' dilemma type conflicts but also the argument that it has a role in solving conflicts of the other sort as well. (Indeed, as figure 10 suggests, it may be that the two conflicts cannot be considered separately.)

a direct explanation of sanctioning institutions but an indirect explanation of other general behavior not explicable just in terms of 'tit-for-tat' strategies employed directly.[8] Well, at least a Humean might try to see just how far such an approach in terms of self-interest might plausibly be pushed.

In short, there is some hope of an explanation of general R-compliance employing something like self-interest in a significant fashion. But that is not to say even Hume thinks self-interest *is* the same as the motive which we regard as virtuous. The regard to justice as such is not the same as self-interest even when the latter is engaged in complicated coordination strategies which tend to the same acts as the former. At most self-interest provides the 'original motive', as Hume says, to do those acts which *are just*. Self-interest, in the right circumstances, provides some motive to do what is also the object of the virtuous motive. Thus Hume's account in terms of self-interest doesn't tell us as much about the virtuous motive as it does about the kinds of actions which are the *object* of that motive.[9] What the account of convention employing only (broad)

8 This suggests another, quite different, reply to Taylor's anarchism. Government is also typically defended as a way of solving 'free riding' prisoners' dilemmas even if not all types of prisoners' dilemmas.

9 It has been suggested to me that if sentimentalism, (S), can avoid circularity in the manner I suggest, then virtue-based morality, (Vb), might also, in an analogous fashion avoid circularity (even if this makes for a view that does not fit with everything in the text of the *Treatise*). Thus we might distinguish three things: a) Acts of R-complying in the context of an appropriate Humean convention (i.e., 'just' acts in some morally neutral sense), b) The motivation to R-comply (i.e., 'the regard to justice' in some morally neutral sense) and c) The moral sentiment which then approves of the motive in (b) and the acts flowing from it (perhaps because such a motive is useful and pleasing to the person and others). Consequently those of us with the sentiment in (c) will account acts flowing from the motive in (b) as 'virtues' (where that now *is* a moral notion). In short, acts are made *virtuous* because they flow from the motive in (b), but they are made *just* because of their appropriate role in a Humean convention.

Such a version of (Vb) does avoid the circularity problem but only at certain costs. One naturally wonders what it has to say about 'moral rightness' judgments in the context, not of assessment, but of *decision making*. There are perhaps two possibilities: 1) In decision-making situations the thought 'This would be R-complying' can sometimes count as some (morally) justifying reason just in itself and apart from considerations about the motives which will produce the act. But this then is to abandon the central claim of (Vb) that every moral quality of an act depends in some way on the motives which produce it. 2) We might think of morality mainly in terms of virtue and vice assessments and not at all in terms of the usual decision-making problems. This approach gives us much in the way of a 'moral aesthetic' but very little in the way of moral decision procedures. I self-interest as a motive supplies is a way of picking out the objects of the regard to justice, i.e., 'the rules of justice'. In the case described with the matrix in figure 10 that would be R-compliance. However what the motive to R-comply has to be for us to praise it and why we could approve of such a motive are further questions.

SYMPATHY AND 'CORRECTING'

Sympathy comes into Hume's account of why we praise the regard to justice. I have suggested it might be reasonable to bring it into the story of the motive itself. Sympathy, in Hume's sense, is not a feeling but a psychological mechanism whereby one feels what one supposes others feel (576, cf. 317, 319). Furthermore, the sentiments involved, in Hume's view, in the making of moral judgments involve more than just the results of the workings of sympathy. They involve 'correcting' (582) such sentiments and they are, more properly, the sentiments which result from such 'correcting'. Hume supposes this further mechanism of 'correcting' somehow adjusts our sentiments for spatio-temporal distance (581–2):

Our servant, if diligent and faithful, may excite stronger sentiments of love and kindness than *Marcus Brutus,* as represented in history; but we say not upon that account, that the former character is more laudable than the latter. (582)

I do suppose here that Hume thinks that what results from 'correcting' the sentiments we already have is a new sentiment rather than merely a belief about what one's sentiments would be at some other spatio-temporal distance. The former keeps Hume a sentimentalist while the latter turns him back into some kind of cognitivist (cf. Stroud, 1977, pp. 190–2).

The story Hume gives about the sentiments which arise via the correcting of sentiments arising in turn via sympathy seems to come very close to a *general* account of the peculiarly moral sentiment. The working of 'sympathy' keeps the result from being just self-

think this has to be a proposal for a new moral outlook rather than an account of the moral judgments we now make. But admittedly such an 'aesthetic' approach is very close to what we very often do find in Hume.

interest in the narrow sense and the 'correcting' keeps it from being merely 'private benevolence'. As Hume says:

> ... every thing, which give uneasiness in human actions, upon the general survey, is call'd Vice, and whatever produces satisfaction, in the same manner, is denominated Virtue; this is the reason why the sense of moral good and evil follows upon justice and injustice. (499)

Thus, while self-interest may be the original motive to the establishment of justice, it is a 'sympathy with public interest' which is behind our praise of justice (499–500). If there is a sentiment such as this, we might well imagine that, with reference to figure 10 again and the Pareto-superiority of general R-compliance over general defection (and also the unworkability of general R^*-compliance), such a sentiment would approve of acts and motives tending toward general R-compliances. Self-interest may set, and perhaps even solve to some extent, problems of coordination. But a sympathy with the public interest approves of convergence upon coordination. In looking at figure 10 it takes 'a general view', sympathising (in a 'corrected' way) with the 'payoffs' to others.

Now the account of this sentiment, whatever other difficulties it may have, is at least not circular in the context of Hume's sentimentalism. Perhaps there are problems about the mechanisms of 'sympathy' and 'correcting'. (A contemporary Humean might have different proposals.) But at least Hume tries to explain the moral sentiments in a naturalistic manner not employing reference to the moral judgments it must in turn account for. Also Hume has, to some extent, specified the *object* of the sentiment (in justice judgments). It approves of acting in accordance with 'the rules of justice', a way of acting that can be explained employing the notion of 'convention' with only self-interest as the (original) motive. Of course what Hume still fails to provide is an account of the motive (for acting in just this way) which we praise. He has an account of 'the rules of justice' and even why we might approve of general compliance, but not yet of 'the regard to justice' which we praise as a virtuous motive.

It seems to me that the obvious thing for Hume to say is that the sentiment (arising from correcting the results sympathy) which approves of there being such rules is not unrelated to the motive which can sometimes produce such acts. It, in turn, is what we praise as the virtue of justice. While Hume may require only talk

303

about self-interest to isolate the sort of R-complying behavior he has in mind, when that sort of behavior is motivated specifically by something like 'sympathy with the public interest' (rather than by accident, mistake or narrow self-interest), it is the motive we praise as virtuous.[10] Furthermore in regarding this motive as virtuous we perhaps thereby express that same 'sympathy with the public interest'. Both the person acting from 'the regard to justice' and the person who judges his motive virtuous are acting on, or judging from, respectively, sentiments produced by (perhaps 'corrected') sympathy. In the case of justice judgments, the sentiment which praises and the motive it praises cannot help but be closely related. This would allow Hume's account of 'the regard to justice as such' to be something more than (even broad) self-interest without that account being circular for his purposes.

A MIXED ACCOUNT

An account of the motive 'the regard to justice' purely in terms of self-interest (in the context of certain social coordination problems) would fall short of an account of the motivational case 2 (in Part I above), to take just one example. Even if there can sometimes be a self-interested motive to keep promises, that is not the same as being motivated by the thought that having promised is a justifying reason. A better account might be in terms of motives resulting from a person's 'correctings' of his sentiments arising from sympathy. A person having a sympathy with the public interest would consider the problem in figure 10 from more than just the perspective of a single player. He would be concerned with more than just the (even the long-term expected) 'payoffs' for himself, or even

---

10 Of course Hume is quite clear (480) that the regard to justice is not the same as the regard to the public interest. Justice may require that we act contrary to the public interest in particular cases. But we should notice his exact words: '[P]ublic interest *is* not naturally attach'd to the observation of the rules of justice; but is only connected with it, after an artificial convention for the establishment of these rules' (480). So the public interest *is* connected to the observation of these rules, only not 'naturally'.

There are three points to be made here: a) Apart from an appropriate convention there would be no particular social advantage to R-complying. b) The social advantage may in some cases come, not from a single act of R-compliance, but from there being a convention which is repeatedly respected. c) It may be one's having the motive to R-comply which is to the public interest rather than any given act following from that motive.

for those about whom he is naturally concerned. He takes a general view.

Even so, this account may seem not to go far enough in accounting for all cases or all aspects of the regard to justice. There is at least one sort of person, motivated by the regard for justice, who thinks it right to keep his promises even if all others do not. There would seem to be a certain element of this even in more standard cases of the motivation. To some extent the motive would seem to be *not* conditional on how others are expected to act. Sympathy for the public interest might explain why we praise such motives, but it would not explain this additional element. Even that sympathy with the public interest which rates general *R*-compliance over all other outcomes does not praise single *R*-compliance where no others will comply.

But Hume has available an account even of this. Here he speaks of two further mechanisms: the artifice of politicians who use public praise and blame and, again, private education and instruction. The former, at least, involves transferring ('association of ideas') the sentiments we naturally have (and express) in judgments of the '*natural* virtues' but now toward new objects. Analogously, 'disgusting' which might have been used of certain smells or sights might be applied to failing to *R*-comply. The second mechanism (education and instruction) might put rather more emphasis on sheer 'custom', i.e., developing habits. Now while Hume does not actually say it, the reader must feel that the states of mind arising in such a manner are not unlike those Hume, in another regard, calls 'superstitious'. This manner of acquiring motives is authoritarian and blind, and involves a certain element of deception (the 'transferring'). Perhaps the difference is that in the present case the mechanisms merely reinforce motives having other bases. Hume, unlike Mandeville, does not think the regard to justice can be entirely explained in terms of such mechanisms.

The motives such mechanisms produce must be somewhat inflexible. They would tend to produce, for example, a preference to *R*-comply *not* conditional on the general *R*-compliance of others. (In that respect it would be rather like natural motives such as the concern for offspring, except that it would have been acquired rather than innate.) And Hume is perhaps right that a somewhat inflexible motivation is at least an element in (even if not the whole of) the regard to justice. Indeed a certain degree of inflexibility might even be necessary for making general R-compliance as stable as it is. Even the person who acts from corrected sentiments arising from sympathy cannot always be too sure how many others actually will R-comply. The effects of a general regime of public praise and blame and private habituation may, not only give one extra reason to believe others will comply, but will also make one less concerned to calculate whether they will.

Whether or not Hume's account of the regard to justice is adequate in detail or in the various psychological mechanisms it employs, it seems to strike something like the right balance in including ingredients of three quite different sorts. First, there is self-interest (broadly conceived to cover perhaps even 'private benevolence'). In some cases at least a 'tit-for-tat' strategy might be rational and credible enough to lead to a convergence on general R-compliance. Second, there is 'sympathy with the public interest', a motive that takes 'a general view'. Such a motive might lead one to prefer to R-comply (rather than defect or comply with some R^*) where it is clear that others R-comply. But, third, there are somewhat more inflexible motives arising in a manner that, were that all involved, would perhaps have led Hume to regard justice as a mere superstition (cf. *Enquiry*, 198–9).

The combination of elements of these three different sorts may work to give the common impression of a *sui generis* motivation, 'the regard to justice as such', incapable of further reduction. But in Hume's view, it is capable of reduction even if there is not just one simple reductive story. Furthermore, what would be a counter-example or a difficulty for any one single reductive account may be less of a difficulty for a mixed account. Nor should we expect, under a mixed account, that the ratios of the three ingredients will be the same in each case the motive occurs or for all persons. Hence a particular case that involves some of the elements in Hume's account but not the other is not necessarily a counter-example to the mixed account.

THREE RESULTS

Hume's mixed account of the motive 'the regard to justice' and his (related) account of the sentiment which approves of such motives bear on three important issues discussed in this book.

First, the account of 'the regard to justice' bears on the problem of what account is to be given of one's being motivated by one's acceptance of a justifying reason. I argued (Chapters 4 and 5 above) that the *provocative version* of the *Humean theory of motivating reasons* gets it wrong. But that is not to say Hume does not have available an interesting proposed solution to this problem. In the case of justice, Hume can explain the features such a person takes as justifying reasons (e.g. that one promised, or that it is someone else's property) as features relevant to achieving social coordination in a situation where interests are in certain sorts of conflict. Corrected sympathy may move one to choose acts with the relevant feature (i.e., on account of that feature). In addition the motive to choose acts with that feature in that context can be strengthened and rendered rather less flexible as a result of the right sorts of training. But what is crucial to the success of such an account, I take it, is that the person with such a motive does not merely count his motive (or desire) as the justifying reason. He does not think that, had he less motivation, there would be less justification. The motive involved in 'the regard to justice', however strong or weak it may be, must take its *object* not to depend on the degree of the strength of that motive. The object will be something like general *R*-compliance or one's own *R*-complying. Hume's account of 'the regard to justice' is capable of avoiding the vulgar and crass theories of motivation which, to this day, bear his name.

Second, Hume's account of the sentiment which approves of this motive bears on his success in avoiding the *circle of sentimentalism* (Chapters 6 and 7). Insofar as Hume has a plausible (and noncircular for his purposes) account of 'the regard to justice', it would seem that he also will have such an account of the sentiment that approves of that motive. Hume's project is to account for 'the rules of justice', 'the regard to justice', and the sentiment which approves of such without referring to the justice judgments it is the task of Hume's sentimentalism to explain. Whatever difficulties there may be in the details of Hume's account, it does not seem to me that circularity is among them. Hume, at least, is trying for a reductive account which, if successful, would avoid that circularity. Hume stands out among Humeans in that regard.

Third, Hume's account of the sentiment which approves of justice seems to come very close to being, not just description, but something like a justification (cf. Chapter 8 above). This is odd. It is not what the *neutrality thesis* (Chapter 6) would lead one to expect

307

as a consequence of a sentimentalist theory. However, in part, the consequences are of a negative sort. Hume thinks some alternative stances are based on misunderstandings about 'the rules of justice', 'the regard to justice' and the sentiment which approves of them. Of course Hume is opposed to all rationalist accounts of justice, i.e., views, perhaps Clarke's, that the 'sense' of justice is, as the word might suggest, a kind of perception of properties or relations in the world. But while Hume wants to give an account in terms of sentiments, he is, even so, just as opposed to those accounts (perhaps Mandeville's or, after Hume, Nietzsche's, Freud's, or Marx's) which, when understood by us, tend to 'undermine' that very sentiment. Hume, by contrast, is concerned to show that our moral sentiments are not just 'superstitious' ones, that they do *not* involve processes the understanding of which would tend to diminish those very sentiments or else prompt sentiments against our having those sentiments. Of course Hume, in giving a role to 'politicians' and 'parents', allows an element of this sort in his own account, but he thinks there is much more to the 'regard to justice' than that.

At the core of his account are sentiments arising from 'sympathy' and 'correctings' in regard, specifically, to social coordination problems involving certain kinds of conflict. Furthermore, when we understand how these sentiments arise, that understanding does not, given the sentiments we have, 'undermine' the sentiment so produced. That is, philosophical understanding of it increases our approval of 'the regard to justice', at least, if Hume is right about the kinds of sentiments Hume says we have. While the debunkers of morality think their accounts of how our moral sentiments arise will undermine those sentiments, Hume thinks his account will have precisely the opposite effect. Or it does if we really do have the sentiments Hume says we have. And that is all in the way of 'justification' one could ever expect of a sentimentalist, i.e., some sort of appeal to the sentiments it is believed we already have.

However Hume's account can also allow that our ordinary notion of justice is subject to certain exaggerations and distortions, especially at the hands of philosophers and social critics. More specifically, the work of the 'imagination', which makes certain schemes of social choice stand out as more striking (and which is useful in solving coordination problems), can give rise to the illusion that there is some quality of justice or impartiality in the scheme itself.

When this leads philosophers and social critics consciously to *discount* the working of the imagination and to look for some standard of justice beyond what it can provide, they are simply being confused (at our peril) by the concept of justice. Taking justice too seriously may be regarded as a rationalising excess, an 'enthusiasm'. Hume's account of justice is as opposed to the enthusiasts who take justice much too seriously as it is to the debunkers who dismiss it as mere 'superstition'. We can indeed expect something of our notion of justice.

But not too much.

Bibliography

Acton, H.B. (1970) 'On Some Criticisms of Historical Materialism, II', *Proceedings of the Aristotelian Society, Supp. Vol.* 44, 143–56.

Alston, W. (1968) 'Moral Attitudes and Moral Judgments', *Nous* 2, 1–23.

Altham, J.E.J. (forthcoming) *Desire for Morality*, Oxford: Blackwell.

Anscombe, G.E.M. (1958) 'Modern Moral Philosophy', reprinted in Anscombe (1981), 26–42.

(1963) *Intention*, 2nd ed., Oxford: Blackwell.

(1969) 'On Promising and its Justice, and Whether it Need be Respected *in Foro Interno*', reprinted in Anscombe (1981), 10–21.

(1978a) 'On the Source of the Authority of the State', sec. ii, reprinted in Anscombe (1981), 138–46.

(1978b) 'Rules, Rights and Promises', reprinted in Anscombe (1981), 97–103.

(1981) *'Ethics, Religion and Politics:* The Collected Philosophical Papers of G.E.M. Anscombe, vol. III, Oxford: Blackwell.

Ardal, P.S. (1966) *Passion and Value in Hume's Treatise*, Edinburgh: Edinburgh University Press.

Armstrong, D.M. (1983) 'Recent Work on the Relation of Mind and Brain', *Contemporary Philosophy. A New Survey* 4, 45–79, The Hague: Nijhoff.

Aune, B. (1977) *Reason and Action*, Dordrecht, Holland: Reidel.

Austin, J. (1832) *The Province of Jurisprudence Determined*

Austin, J.L. (1962) *How to Do Things with Words*, Oxford: Clarendon Press.

Axelrod, R. (1984) *The Evolution of Cooperation*, New York: Basic Books.

Ayer, A.J. (1936) *Language, Truth and Logic*, London: Gollancz.

Bedford, E. (1956–7) 'Emotions', *Proceedings of the Aristotelian Society* 57, 281–304.

Bentham, J. (1970 ed.) *Of Laws in General*, ed. H.L.A. Hart, London: Athlone.

Blackburn, S. (1981) 'Reply: Rule-Following and Moral Realism', in S.H. Holzman & C.M. Leich, eds., *Wittgenstein: To Follow a Rule*, London: Routledge & Kegan Paul, 163–87.

(1984) *Spreading the Word: Groundings in the Philosophy of Language*, Oxford: Clarendon Press

Bond, E.J. (1983) *Reason and Value*, Cambridge: Cambridge University Press.

Brandt, R.B. (1979) *A Theory of the Good and the Right,* Oxford: Clarendon Press.

Bratman, M. (1981) 'Intention and Means-End Reasoning', *Philosophical Review* 90, 252–65.

(1987) *Intention, Plans, and Practical Reason,* Cambridge, MA: Harvard University Press.

Brink, D.O. (1984) 'Moral Realism and the Sceptical Arguments', *Australasian Journal of Philosophy,* 62.

Broad, C.D. (1930) *Five Types of Ethical Theory,* London: Routledge & Kegan Paul.

(1949–50) 'Egoism as a Theory of Human Motives', reprinted in *Ethics and the History of Philosophy,* London: Routledge & Kegan Paul, 1952.

Broiles, R.D. (1964) *The Moral Philosophy of David Hume,* 2nd ed., The Hague: Nijhoff.

Butler, J. (1726) *Fifteen Sermons Preached at the Rolls Chapel,* London.

Churchland, P.M. (1985) *Matter and Consciousness,* Cambridge, MA: MIT Press.

Clarke, S. (1706) *Discourse upon Natural Religion.*

Cohen, G.A. (1970) 'On Some Criticisms of Historical Materialism, I', *Proceedings of the Aristotelian Society, Supp. Vol.* 44, 121–42.

(1978) *Karl Marx's Theory of History: A Defence,* Oxford: Clarendon Press.

Collins, H. (1984) *Marxism and Law,* Oxford: Oxford University Press.

Collins, J. (1988) 'Belief, Desire, and Revision', *Mind* 97, 333–42.

Curley, E.M. (1976) 'Excusing Rape', *Philosophy and Public Affairs,* 5, 325–60.

Davidson, D. (1963) 'Actions, Reasons and Causes', reprinted in Davidson (1980), 3–19.

(1970) 'How is Weakness of the Will Possible?' reprinted in Davidson (1980), 21–42.

(1980) *Essays on Actions and Events,* Oxford: Clarendon Press.

Dawkins, R. (1989) *The Selfish Gene,* new ed., Oxford: Oxford University Press.

Edgley, R. (1969) *Reason in Theory and Practice,* London: Hutchinson.

Elster, J. (1983) *Sour Grapes: Studies in the Subversion of Rationality,* Cambridge: Cambridge University Press.

(1984) *Ulysses and the Sirens: Studies in Rationality and Irrationality,* rev. ed., Cambridge: Cambridge University Press.

(1989) *The Cement of Society,* Cambridge: Cambridge University Press.

Falk, W.D. (1947–8) ' "Ought" and Motivation', *Proceedings of the Aristotelian Society* 48.

Feinberg, J. (1975) 'Psychological Egoism', in *Reason and Responsibility,* 3rd ed., Belmont, CA: Dickinson.

Finnis, J. (1980) *Natural Law and Natural Rights,* Oxford: Clarendon Press.

Fitzgerald, P., ed. (1966) *Salmond on Jurisprudence,* 12th ed., London: Sweet & Maxwell.

Foot, P. (1958–9) 'Moral Beliefs', reprinted in Foot (1978), 110–31.

(1963) 'Hume on Moral Judgement', reprinted in Foot (1978), 74–80.

(1972a) 'Morality as a System of Hypothetical Imperatives', reprinted in Foot (1978), 157–73.

(1972b) 'Reasons for Action and Desires', reprinted in Foot (1978), 148–56.

(1978) *Virtues and Vices and Other Essays in Moral Philosophy*, Oxford: Blackwell.

Frankena, W. (1939) 'The Naturalistic Fallacy', *Mind* 48, 464–77.

(1958) 'Obligation and Motivation in Recent Moral Philosophy', in A.I. Melden, ed., *Essays in Moral Philosophy*, Seattle: University of Washington Press, 40–81.

Gauthier, D.P. (1963) *Practical Reasoning*, Oxford: Clarendon Press.

(1979) 'David Hume, Contractarian', *Philosophical Review* 88, 5–8.

(1986) *Morals by Agreement*, Oxford: Clarendon Press.

Geach, P.T. (1972) 'Plato's *Euthyphro*' in *Logic Matters*, Oxford: Blackwell, 31–44.

Grice, G.R. (1967) *The Grounds of Moral Judgement*, Cambridge: Cambridge University Press.

Grice, H.P. (1957) 'Meaning', *Philosophical Review*, 66, 377–88.

Haakonssen, K. (1981) *The Science of a Legislator: The Natural Jurisprudence of David Hume and Adam Smith*, Cambridge: Cambridge University Press.

Hare, R.M. (1952) *The Language of Morals*, Oxford: Clarendon Press.

(1963) *Freedom and Reason*, Oxford: Clarendon Press.

Harman, G. (1976) 'Practical Reasoning', *Review of Metaphysics* 29, 431–63.

(1977) *The Nature of Morality*, Oxford: Oxford University Press.

Harris, J. (1974) 'The Marxist Conception of Violence', *Philosophy and Public Affairs* 3, 192–220.

(1975) 'The Survival Lottery', *Philosophy* 50, 81–2.

Harrison, J. (1976) *Hume's Moral Epistemology*, Oxford: Clarendon Press.

(1981) *Hume's Theory of Justice*, Oxford: Clarendon Press.

Hart, H.L.A. (1948–9) 'The Ascription of Responsibility and Rights', *Proceedings of the Aristotelian Society* 49, 171–94.

(1954) 'Definition and Theory in Jurisprudence', reprinted in *Essays in Jurisprudence and Philosophy*, Oxford: Clarendon Press, 1983, 21–48.

(1961) *The Concept of Law*, Oxford: Clarendon Press.

(1968) *Punishment and Responsibility*, Oxford: Clarendon Press.

(1972) 'Bentham on Legal Powers', reprinted as 'Legal Powers' in *Essays on Bentham*, Oxford: Clarendon Press, 1982, 194–219.

Hobbes, T. (1651) *Leviathan*.

Hohfeld, W.N. (1919) *Fundamental Legal Conceptions*, New Haven, CT: Yale University Press. Reprinted in 1923, 1964.

Honore, A.M. (1961) 'Ownership', Essay 5 in A.G. Guest, ed., *Oxford Essays in Jurisprudence*, London: Oxford University Press.

Hughes, G.E. & M.J. Cresswell (1972) *An Introduction to Modal Logic*, London: Methuen.

312

Jackson, F. (1974) 'Defining the Autonomy of Ethics', *Philosophical Review* 83, 88–96.

Kemp, J. (1964) *Reason, Action and Morality*, London: Routledge & Kegan Paul.

Kovesi, J. (1967) *Moral Notions*, London: Routledge & Kegan Paul.

Kydd, R. (1946) *Reason and Conduct in Hume's Treatise*, London: Oxford University Press.

Laird, J. (1932) *Hume's Philosophy of Human Nature*, London: Methuen.

Lewis, D. (1969) *Convention*, Cambridge, MA: Harvard University Press.

(1988) 'Desire as Belief', *Mind* 97, 323–32.

Louden, R.B. (1984) 'On Some Vices of Virtue Ethics', *American Philosophical Quarterly* 21, 227–36.

Luce, R.D. & H. Raiffa (1957) *Games and Decisions*, New York: Wiley.

Lukes, S. (1985) *Marxism and Morality*, Oxford: Clarendon Press.

McDowell, J. (1978) 'Are Moral Requirements Hypothetical Imperatives?' *Proceedings of the Aristotelian Society, Supp. Vol.* 52 (1978), 13–29.

(1981) 'Non-Cognitivism and Rule-Following', in S.H. Holzman & C.M. Leich, eds., *Wittgenstein: To Follow a Rule*, London: Routledge & Kegan Paul, 141–62.

MacIntyre, A. (1984) *After Virtue*, 2nd ed., Notre Dame, IN: University of Notre Dame Press.

Mackie, J.L. (1977) *Ethics: Inventing Right and Wrong*, Harmondsworth: Penguin Books.

(1980) *Hume's Moral Theory*, London: Routledge & Kegan Paul.

Macpherson, C.B. (1962) *The Political Theory of Possessive Individualism*, Oxford: Oxford University Press.

Mandeville, B. (1723) *Fable of the Bees*.

Mill, J.S. (1859) *On Liberty*.

Miller, D. (1981) *Hume's Political Thought*, Oxford: Clarendon Press.

Miller, R.W. (1984) *Analyzing Marx*, Princeton, NJ: Princeton University Press.

Moore, G.E. (1903) *Principia Ethica*, Cambridge: Cambridge University Press, chs. 1, 2.

Nagel, T. (1970) *The Possibility of Altruism*, Oxford: Clarendon Press.

(1979) 'Moral Luck', in *Mortal Questions*, Cambridge: Cambridge University Press.

Norman, R. (1971) *Reasons for Actions*, Oxford: Blackwell.

Parfit, D. (1984) *Reasons and Persons*, Oxford: Oxford University Press. Reprinted with corrections.

Perry, T.D. (1977) 'A Paradigm of Philosophy: Hohfeld on Legal Rights', *American Philosophical Quarterly* 14, 41–50.

Pettit, P. (1986) 'Free Riding and Foul Dealing', *Journal of Philosophy* 83, 361–79.

(1987) 'Humeans, Anti-Humeans, and Motivation', *Mind* 96, 530–3.

Plamenatz, J. (1954) *German Marxism and Russian Communism*, London: Longmans.

Plantinga, A. (1974) *The Nature of Necessity*, Oxford: Clarendon Press.

Plato. *Euthyphro.*

Platts, M. (1979) 'Moral Reality', ch. 10, *Ways of Meaning: An Introduction to a Philosophy of Language,* London: Routledge & Kegan Paul, 243–63.

(1980) 'Moral Reality and the End of Desire', ch. 4 in *Reference, Truth and Reality,* London: Routledge & Kegan Paul, 69–82.

(1988) 'Hume and Morality as a Matter of Fact', *Mind* 97, 189–204.

Price, H. (1989) 'Defending Desire-as-Belief', *Mind* 98, 119–27.

Prichard, H.A. (1912) 'Does Moral Philosophy Rest on a Mistake', reprinted in *Moral Obligation,* Oxford: Oxford University Press, 1968, pp. 1–17.

Prior, A.N. (1960) 'The Autonomy of Ethics', *Australasian Journal of Philosophy* 38, 199–206.

Putnam, H. (1981) *Reason, Truth and History,* Cambridge: Cambridge University Press.

Raphael, D.D., ed. (1969) *British Moralists 1650–1800,* Oxford: Clarendon Press.

Rawls, J. (1971) *A Theory of Justice,* Cambridge, MA: Harvard University Press.

Raz, J. (1970) *The Concept of a Legal System,* Oxford: Clarendon Press, 2nd ed. 1980.

(1972) 'Voluntary Obligations and Normative Powers', *Proceedings of the Aristotelian Society Supp. Vol.* 46.

(1975) *Practical Reason and Norms,* London: Hutchinson.

Raz, J., ed. (1978) *Practical Reasoning,* Oxford: Oxford University Press.

Richards, D.A.J. (1971) *A Theory of Reasons for Action,* Oxford: Clarendon Press.

Robins, M.H. (1984) *Promising, Intending and Moral Autonomy,* Cambridge: Cambridge University Press.

Ross, W.D. (1930) *The Right and the Good,* Oxford: Clarendon Press.

(1939) *Foundations of Ethics,* Oxford: Clarendon Press.

Sandel, M.J. (1982) *Liberalism and the Limits of Justice,* Cambridge: Cambridge University Press.

Selby-Bigge, ed. (1897) *British Moralists,* 2 vols., Oxford: Clarendon Press.

Shelling, T. (1960) *The Strategy of Conflict,* Cambridge, MA: Harvard University Press.

Shwayder, D. (1965) *The Stratification of Behavior,* New York: Humanities Press.

Slote, M.A. (1964) 'An Empirical Basis for Psychological Egoism', *Journal of Philosophy* 61, 530–37.

Smith, M. (1987) 'The Humean Theory of Motivation', *Mind* 96, No. 381, 36–61.

Snare, F. (1972) 'The Concept of Property', *American Philosophical Quarterly* 9, 200–6.

(1975) 'The Argument from Motivation', *Mind* 84, No. 333, 1–9.

(1977) 'Three Sceptical Theses in Ethics', *American Philosophical Quarterly* 14, No. 2, 129–36.

(1984) 'The Empirical Bases of Moral Scepticism', *American Philosophical Quarterly* 21, No. 3, 215–25.

(1986) 'Misfortune and Injustice: On Being Disadvantaged', *Canadian Journal of Philosophy* 16, No. 1, 39–61.

Stevenson, C.L. (1944) *Ethics and Language,* Hew Haven, CT: Yale University Press.

Stich, S. (1983) *From Folk Psychology to Cognitive Science: The Case Against Belief,* Cambridge, MA: MIT Press.

Stroud, B. (1977) *Hume,* London: Routledge & Kegan Paul.

Sturgeon, N. (1986) 'What Difference Does It Make Whether Moral Realism Is True?', *The Southern Journal of Philosophy* 24, Supplement, 115–41.

Taylor, M. (1976) *Anarchy and Cooperation,* London: Wiley.

Urmson, J.O. (1968) *The Emotive Theory of Ethics,* London: Hutchinson.

Walzer, M. (1983) *Spheres of Justice,* Oxford: Blackwell.

Werner, R. (1983) 'Ethical Realism', *Ethics* 93, 653–79.

White, A.R. (1985) *Grounds of Liability: An Introduction to Philosophy of Law,* Oxford: Clarendon Press.

Wiggins, D. (1976) 'Truth, Invention, and the Meaning of Life', *Proceedings of the British Academy* 62, 331–76.

Williams, B. (1972) *Morality: An Introduction to Ethics,* Cambridge: Cambridge University Press.

(1976) 'Moral Luck', reprinted in Williams (1981), 20–39.

(1980) 'Internal and External Reasons', reprinted in Williams (1981), 101–113.

(1981) *Moral Luck,* Cambridge: Cambridge University Press.

(1985) *Ethics and the Limits of Philosophy,* London: Collins.

Wollaston, W. (1724) *Religion of Nature Delineated.*

Woods, M. (1972) 'Reasons for Actions and Desires', *Proceedings of the Aristotelian Society Supp. Vol.* 46, 189–201.

Index

316

319

320